JOURNAL FOR THE STUDY OF THE OLD TESTAMENT
SUPPLEMENT SERIES
71

Editors
David J A Clines
Philip R Davies

BIBLE AND LITERATURE SERIES
18

General Editor
David M. Gunn

Assistant General Editor
Danna Nolan Fewell

Consultant Editors
Elizabeth Struthers Malbon
James G. Williams

Almond Press
Sheffield

QOHELET AND HIS CONTRADICTIONS

Michael V. Fox

The Almond Press · 1989

Bible and Literature Series, 18

General Editor: David M. Gunn
(Columbia Theological Seminary, Decatur, Georgia)
Assistant General Editor: Danna Nolan Fewell
(Perkins School of Theology, Dallas, Texas)
Consultant Editors: Elizabeth Struthers Malbon
(Virginia Polytechnic Institute & State University, Blacksburg, Virginia)
James G. Williams
(Syracuse University, Syracuse, New York)

Published by Almond Press
Editorial direction: David M. Gunn
Columbia Theological Seminary
P.O. Box 520, Decatur
GA 30031, U.S.A.
Almond Press is an imprint of
Sheffield Academic Press Ltd
The University of Sheffield
343 Fulwood Road
Sheffield S10 3BP
England

Typeset by Sheffield Academic Press
and
printed in Great Britain
by Billing & Sons Ltd
Worcester

British Library Cataloguing in Publication Data available

ISSN 0260-4493
ISSN 0309-0787
ISBN 1-85075-148-X

CONTENTS

ACKNOWLEDGEMENTS

Parts of the present book have appeared in different forms in scholarly journals. My study of *hebel* was published in the *Journal of Biblical Literature* 105 (1986). Part of ch. 3, a study of Qohelet's epistemology, appeared in *Hebrew Union College Annual* 58 (1987). My interpretation of Qoh 12:1-7 (Excursus ii) was first presented in the *Journal for the Study of the Old Testament* 42 (1988). I should note that while my main conclusions are unchanged, my interpretations of specific passages and meanings have occasionally departed from those published in the above articles.

My study of Qohelet began in earnest at the Hebrew University of Jerusalem, where I wrote a dissertation on "The Book of Qohelet and its Relation to the Wisdom School" (Hebrew, 1972). The present book is independent of the dissertation and differs considerably in its approach and conclusions, but it too owes a debt of gratitude to my advisor, Professor Menahem Haran. His guidance and criticism of the earlier work influenced the present one as well.

I am indebted to Paul Manuel, John Hobbins, Lowell Ferris, and Prof. James Crenshaw for reading and criticizing manuscripts of this book. Along with his penetrating critique, Mr. Hobbins suggested a number of original and interesting interpretations of his own. I did not incorporate most of them, but I hope he will soon publish them for scholarly consideration. Rev. Ferris worked with me on the translation and paraphrase and contributed greatly to improving their literary value. Kelvin Friebel prepared the index.

I had the pleasure of reading a manuscript of Professor Crenshaw's Qohelet commentary (Old Testament Library), but this came at too late a stage to enable me to give it the consideration it deserves. While my own approach and interpretation differs considerably, I recommend it for its clarity and erudition. Other works that appeared too late for me to use (except for a couple of remarks I have added in footnotes) are Ogden's commentary and the linguistic studies by Fredericks and Isaksson (on the latter see my review, to appear in *JBL*).

Grants from the University of Wisconsin Graduate School and the Wisconsin Society for Jewish Learning enabled me to carry out the research for this book, and the latter aided in its publication as well. I am especially grateful to the latter for its ongoing financial and moral support for the research and educational activities of the Hebrew Department at the University of Wisconsin.

Madison, Wisconsin
June 1988

INTRODUCTION

§0.1 *On reading Qohelet*

A quick reading of the book of Qohelet in its canonical form presents to commentators a reasonably clear message along the following lines:

> Everything in life is vanity. There is no point in striving too hard for anything, whether wealth or wisdom. It is best simply to enjoy what you have when you have it and to fear God.

This message emerges with fair consistency despite the tangle of contradictions that scholars as early as the Tannaim have observed and attempted to unravel. Many of these contradictions are real and striking, but they do not submerge the message that rises to the surface over all the philosophical inconsistencies and structural disarray. All substantial variations from the above interpretation entail the attribution of parts of the book to someone other than the original author.

The interpretation summarized above may seem obvious, as indeed it should. For Qohelet's position, described by the epilogue as teacher of wisdom to "the people" (12:9), required him to formulate and reiterate clear, sharply etched teachings. Qohelet's message is not a mystery waiting for its solution until the twentieth century, or rather, always waiting for the next scholarly study to solve it. If it were that, the book would be either esoteric or a failure, especially in its role as a work of popular instruction, which the epilogist, at least, thinks it is suited to play.

The book is by no means esoteric. Qohelet does not seem aware that his teachings are unorthodox: he neither flaunts his audacity nor screens his unconventionality from his audience, "the people". Nor does the book fail to communicate broadly, for its fundamental teachings and many of its secondary ones have been understood in essentially the same way by most commentators. This consensus emerges from C. D. Ginsburg's lengthy survey in the introduction to his commentary, together with the more recent surveys by Blank (prolegomena to Ginsburg) and the various commentators. What Sternberg says about the "foolproof composition" of biblical narrative applies to the book of Qohelet as well: the essentials are transparent to all readers (1985:50f.).[1]

The message that a quick reading takes from a text belongs to its meaning no less than do the ideas extracted by closer readings. An author creates the surface as well as the depths of the work and knows that the surface will be seen first. But there are meanings beneath the surface: obscure teachings that can be clarified, unspoken assumptions that can be made explicit, unsystematic ideas that can be organized, and concepts, even clear ones, whose interpretation can be fine-tuned. And behind the meaning there is the reasoning (the sequence of thoughts and sets of assumptions that govern and justify the author's ideas), and around the meaning there is the rhetoric (the means of persuasion). It is the meaning beneath and beyond the surface that the following essays examine. The resulting interpretations will shift emphases, reevaluate attitudes, and describe thought with greater precision. They will not overturn the basic lines of interpretation common to most interpreters.

The following essays offer a rethinking of some of the main issues facing Qohelet's interpreters and an attempt to elucidate his meanings, the reasoning behind them, and the ways in which he expresses them. Without seeking to provide a survey of Qohelet's vocabulary or ideas or to reduce Qohelet's statements to a systematic philosophy, the essays combine to reinforce three main conclusions about Qohelet's thought:

(1) Qohelet is not primarily concerned with the value of possessions or the worth of human striving, but rather with the *rationality of existence*. This rationality he denies by calling everything *hebel*. But even in failure, rationality remains an irreducible value, one by which life must be judged.

1. This is so, Sternberg says, because the biblical narrator is completely reliable and does not deal in the esoteric. In the case of this text, the speaker (Qohelet) is almost entirely reliable, notwithstanding the slight distance that the epilogist, who is probably the author of the book, sets between himself and Qohelet, his persona (see Excursus III).

(2) Qohelet does not attack wisdom, the wise, or the doctrines of Wisdom Literature, but expresses his esteem for the value of wisdom and his disappointment that its excellences are not properly compensated.
(3) Having confronted the failure of meaning, Qohelet affirms the grasping of *inner experience*, emotional and intellectual, as the one domain of human freedom. This does not provide the desired meaning either; nevertheless, experience, both emotional and intellectual, is (like reason) an irreducible value, to be embraced for its own sake.

I approach Qohelet's ideas by taking as my starting point the most severe of the contradictions that have vexed the commentators and *interpreting* them rather than trying to eliminate them. While the severity of some of the contradictions can be reduced by closer definition of the terms, there are major contradictions that cannot be eliminated without recourse to massive excisions or to harmonizations too ingenious to be persuasive. As I see it, Qohelet's contradictions state the problems rather than resolving them, and the interpreter likewise must leave many of the observations in tension.

Qohelet does not, however, embrace the contradictions as paradoxes that, like Zen koans, can give enlightenment in the inexpressible. He sees paradoxes in the truths he discovers, but they are a dead-end road. He observes them, insists on them, then moves on. Never does he suggest that meditation on them gives new types of insight into God's nature.

Nor do I take the book's contradictions and tensions as symptoms of disturbances in Qohelet's soul (contrary to Galling, 1932:281). A psychologistic explanation explains nothing, because a disturbed soul could very well be extremely consistent in expressing its discomforts. I maintain that Qohelet is not merely caught up in contradictions (though this does happen occasionally). Rather, he recognizes and even sharpens them as evidence for his claim that "everything is absurd". In fact, they are more than evidence. Qohelet uses contradictions as the lens through which to view life; it is appropriate, then, that we use his contradictions as the angle of approach to his thought. Exegesis has usually sought to push Qohelet to one side or the other, to show him consistently pious or consistently skeptical and pessimistic. I have tried to be faithful to the uneasy tensions that I see as characterizing Qohelet's attitudes and world view.

To interpret these contradictions we must clarify their terms and context and determine as precisely as possible what conclusions Qohelet draws from them. This task requires us to describe abstractly and systematically ideas expressed in unsystematic utterances, thereby retelling the text in a form that can more readily be discussed analytically and compared with other texts. Such a redescription is not identical with the thought it describes; in fact, it inevitably entails some distortion. No systematic discussion can (or should) replicate Qohelet's thought, with its episodic, discontinuous, staccato character. Qohelet "goes about" the world observing and reacting to events, actions, qualities, and values as he encounters them. His response to something in one place need not be the same as his response elsewhere. And even a single response may be compounded of various attitudes and remain resolutely unstable. The interpreter can describe a pattern in the various pronouncements on an issue without denying tensions in the ideas and attitudes from which the pattern is woven. On the contrary, these tensions belong to the substance of Qohelet's thought.

The topics of each chapter are as follows:

0. Introduction
   Excursus
      I. The treatment of contradictions in Qohelet
1. The Meaning of *hebel* for Qohelet (with a consideration of *r*^e*'ut ruaḥ*).
   Hebel means "absurd". It is the word Qohelet uses in reacting to contradictions.
2. Toil and Pleasure
   The contradiction: toil (*'amal*) is absurd and without advantage, yet it provides wealth, the source of pleasure (*śimḥah*). Then why is it absurd, and in what way is it good?
3. Wisdom: Qohelet's Epistemology
   The contradiction: Qohelet seems both to affirm and to deny the possibility and the value of wisdom and knowledge. What precisely is affirmed and what denied? What can we know and why should we know it?
4. Justice and Theodicy
   The contradiction: Life is unjust, but God is just. What, then, is the moral quality of the world?

5. Commentary
This chapter examines various interrelated issues that are best considered together in the context of the passages in which they appear. The commentary should be consulted for explanations and justifications of the exegetical positions presupposed in the other chapters. The commentary considers:
   a. Philological and textual difficulties
   b. Rhetorical structures: the literary-rhetorical units and the forms of argumentation
   c. Key words in Qohelet (in addition to those discussed in the earlier chapters); in particular, derivatives of the roots HYH, ʻNH, and ʻŚH (surveyed in the introduction to the chapter [§5.1] and examined in context as they occur)
   d. Exegetical problems in various passages. I sometimes suggest new solutions to old problems, but I consider it equally important to offer new arguments for old solutions.
   e. The central teaching of each passage
   f. Excursuses:
      II. Aging and death in Qohelet 12 (at 12:1)
      III. Author and speaker; the epilogue (at 12:8)
      IV. *Ḥakam* as "sage" (at 12:14)
   g. A paraphrase of Qohelet

These studies, though largely independent, are united by a focus on Qohelet's *values*—qualities, actions, and principles he considers worthwhile and important, whether or not he finds them realized in the world about him. Certain values are best seen in Qohelet's negations, such as his judgments of things and situations as *hebel*, the negation of meaningfulness. Chapters 1, 2, and 3 approach concepts through the words used to express them. Chapters 4 and 5 discuss themes, with less concentration on the terminology that communicates them, since that terminology is less problematic, and understanding the ideas does not depend on the precise sense of certain words.

SOME PRELIMINARIES

§0.2 *Qohelet and Camus*

Throughout my study of Qohelet I have been impressed by the affinities between his thought and that of Albert Camus, especially in *The Myth of Sisyphus* (in *The Rebel* he takes a divergent path and seeks to transcend the absurd in a politically oriented ethic).[2] The epigraphs to the following essays and some additional quotations from Camus are suggestive of some of these similarities. I make most active use of Camus in discussing the meaning of *hebel*, which I understand as meaning "absurd" in a sense close to that in which Camus uses it. There is a fundamental congruity between the two thinkers in their insistence on life's irrationality, in their sense of the world's opaqueness, in their exaltation of the value of lucidity, and in the zest with which they invoke the power of unaided reason to undermine its own foundations. For both, a dogged pursuit of the consequences of their beliefs and observations produces contradictions, some accidental, some the deliberate products of honest observation, most of them well-recognized by their respective interpreters. Both thinkers insist on the value of knowledge, understanding, and experience in a world whose irrationality seems to confound all values, and the result is the most intractable of contradictions:

> L'absurde en lui-même est contradiction. Il l'est dans son contenu puisqu'il exclut les jugements de valeur en voulant maintenir la vie, alors que vivre est en soi un jugement de valeur (*L'Homme révolté*, p. 19).

This contradiction, recognized in *The Rebel*, infuses *The Myth of Sisyphus*, the earlier work, as well. This same contradiction, more severe than any of the inconsistencies that commentators have focused on, pervades Qohelet. It should not be smoothed over in art or in life (as Camus accuses various philosophers of trying to do), because it is an expression of a contradiction perceived in reality. Both thinkers show the resiliency of the human spirit in living with this contradiction and in affirming values despite it, and this

2. I do not speak of similarities between Qohelet and existentialist thought in general (a concept I would not attempt to define, and which Camus refused to apply to himself). For a brief sketch of some lines of resemblance see K. James (1984). Worth noting is James's understanding of the significance of joy for Qohelet: "If the security of 'conceptual knowledge' is taken away from us, we still have a center that feels strongly about life, and it is to this emotional center that Qoheleth turns as a possible source of meaning in life" (p. 89). This insight, which James does not develop, is close to my understanding of the function of pleasure in Qohelet's value system; see §2.22.

resiliency makes them both far less negativistic than is commonly thought.

That is not to say that Camus's ideas can be transferred whole to the book of Qohelet. The differences are significant. The two works respond with different forms of expression to radically different intellectual contexts. As for their philosophical divergences, the most profound is that Qohelet does not believe the world is masterless, though his universe with an incomprehensible master has little more to say to man than the void Camus sees. Nor does Qohelet advocate "rebellion", Camus's (not quite appropriate) catchword for man's unflinching awareness of his hopeless fate. For Qohelet, to recognize and embrace life's limited possibilities accords with God's will. Another profound difference is Camus's lack of interest in injustice (in the *Myth*; not so in the *Rebel*, hence the epigraph for my chapter on justice must come from the latter work). Devoid of an expectation of justice, the *Myth* does not bother to address the absurdity of injustice; it does not even use injustice as evidence of absurdity.

But for all their differences, the kinship between Qohelet and Camus runs deeper than the gap that must be reckoned with in the heuristic use of modern thought to interpret ancient literature. By invoking Camus it is not my purpose to prove similarity, but only to use as part of my interpretative language the similarities that, according to my reading of both works, do exist.

When Camus himself mentions Qohelet, he sets Qohelet at a certain distance, because he sees Qohelet as representing an extreme of pessimism. In describing Don Juan, whose illusionless choice of the quantitative ethic makes him a hero of the absurd, Camus says that it is a great mistake to see in this character "un homme nourri de l'Ecclésiaste. Car plus rien pour lui n'est vanité sinon l'espoir d'une autre vie" (*Mythe*, p. 98). Camus implies that to regard everything as vanity is a more profound negation of life's value than to regard everything as absurd, and he does not demand such negativism of "l'homme absurd". For within the realm of the absurd it is possible to find values and truths; not everything is "vanity". Camus's attitude toward Qohelet arises from a sensitivity to the implications of calling everything "vanity", as *hebel* has traditionally been translated. But, I will argue, Qohelet does not say that everything is vanity, i.e., worthless or trivial. He asserts the irrationality and impenetrability of life; but within this setting he seeks to discover values and truths. In this dual affirmation the two thinkers are in accord.

§0.3 *Greek parallels*

Qohelet's affirmation of individual experience, in particular the experience of pleasure, seems to me to bear a fundamental similarity to Hellenistic popular philosophy, whose central concern was to find a way to individual happiness—whether through pleasure and freedom from fear (Epicureans), through the attainment of self-realization by shedding desire, or through virtue and duty, whose goals and expectations, like Qohelet's, did not include social change. Qohelet's purely anthropological question about the profitability of human experience is likewise the problem of philosophical anthropology in Greek thought (Braun, 1973:168).

This is not to say that Qohelet's thoughts and attitudes had a specific "source" in Greek philosophy, but only that Qohelet shared the concerns and attitudes of various philosophies known in the Hellenistic period, that focused on the achievement of happiness by the individual in an indifferent, if not inimical, universe. Particularly significant are Qohelet's affinities with Epicureanism, which regarded sensory experience as the ultimate source and arbiter of knowledge (see §3.211), and which affirmed pleasure (intellectual as well as physical) as the only good for man (see §2.22). I note these Greek parallels without pursuing the broader issue of Greek influence further. The concern of this study is with describing Qohelet's thought in and of itself, not with determining external sources and parallels. Braun (1973) has reopened the issue of Hellenistic-Greek influences in Qohelet. Although many of the parallels Braun adduces are not persuasive, he has undoubtedly made the case that Qohelet was not isolated from his contemporary intellectual context. Henceforth, *comparative* studies of Qohelet will have to give serious attention to Hellenistic thought. The most significant parallels will, I believe, be the least provable—similarities of attitude, epistemology, fields of inquiry, underlying questions addressed, and the types of answers offered (though not necessarily the specific answers).

§0.4 *Some terms*

§0.41 *Wisdom and the wise*

The meaning of "wisdom" and "wise" is discussed in §3.1. Here I will merely point out a terminological distinction I draw between "wisdom" and "Wisdom" and a parallel distinction between "wise man" and "sage".

wisdom: an attribute, praised by Wisdom Literature. This attribute is not identical with the literary genre that teaches it.

Wisdom (and *Wisdom Literature*): the literary genres that comprise what modern scholars call Wisdom Literature, as well as the ideas, assumptions, goals, and attitudes characteristic of such works. This technical term will be marked typographically by capitalization (at the beginning of sentences it should be unambiguous, referring to the attribute rather than to the genre).

wise man/woman: the general usage, referring to anyone blessed with wisdom.

sage: one of the creators and teachers of Wisdom.

§0.5 *Abbreviations*

AEL	*Ancient Egyptian Literature*. Lichtheim, 1973ff.
Aq	Aquila
AV	Authorized Version (King James translation)
BDB	Brown, Driver, and Briggs, *Hebrew and English Lexicon of the Old Testament*
BH	Biblical Hebrew
BHS	*Biblia Hebraica Stuttgartensia*
ET	English translation
GKC	*Gesenius' Hebrew Grammar* (ed. Kautzsch-Cowley)
HAL	Baumgartner, *Hebräisches und aramäisches Lexikon*
HB	Hebrew Bible
K-R	Kennicott-Rossi
LXX	Septuagint
MH	Mishnaic Hebrew
MT	Massoretic Text
NJV	The new Jewish Publication Society translation of the Bible
RSV	Revised Standard Version
SPOA	*Les Sagesses du Proche-Orient Ancien*. Paris, 1963.
Syh	Syrohexapla
Sym	Symmachus
Syr	Syriac (Peshiṭta)

TDOT	*Theological Dictionary of the Old Testament* (ed. G. J. Botterweck and H. Ringgren; 1977ff.).
Theod	Theodotion
UT	C. H. Gordon, *Ugaritic Textbook*
Vul	Vulgate

Commentaries are referred to by author's name only, other works by author:date. Information on ancient Wisdom texts (Ptahhotep, Merikare, etc.) is likewise given in the bibliography.

§0.6 *Transliteration*

I use a relatively broad transliteration, distinguishing vowel length only where necessary for comprehensibility (as when proposing emendations). Compound shewas: ĕ ŏ ă. Shewa: ^{e}. The so-called *shewa medium*, being actually zero, is not marked. *y* generally marks the *mater lectionis yod* after *ṣere*, though not after *ḥiriq*. The *mater lectionis heh* is represented by *h*. The purpose of this transliteration is to call to mind the orthography rather than to represent the MT vocalization with exactitude.

Roots are written in upper case and are not italicized since they are abstractions, not words in another language.

EXCURSUS I
APPROACHES TO THE CONTRADICTIONS IN QOHELET

The first reported discussion of Qohelet dealt with the book's internal contradictions. These are said to have troubled the Tannaim and brought the book's sacred status into dispute.

> R. Judah b. R. Samuel b. Shilath said in Rav's name: The sages sought to withdraw the book of Qohelet because its words are mutually contradictory. Why then did they not withdraw it? Because it begins with words of Torah and it ends with words of Torah (*b. Shab.* 30b).

According to this tradition, the Tannaim considered the presence of internal contradictions serious enough to raise the possibility that a book was not inspired (the same issue arose for Proverbs; *b. Shab.* 30b). But, as this discussion is reported, they did not try to resolve the contradictions as their first step (this seems to have been left to the Amoraim). Rather, the observation of an orthodox framework in the book—provided by Qoh 1:3[3] and 12:13—was sufficient to neutralize the book's internal contradictoriness, which, it seems from the solution they chose, they did not deny.

(1) *Harmonization*

Subsequent scholars, however, have commonly tried to eliminate the contradictions. The traditional approach is harmonization, which reconciles apparently conflicting statements by showing that they use words differently or deal with different matters. In the discussion in *b. Shab.* 30b, the Amoraim (at the turn of the 3rd-4th cent.) reconcile some contradictions to explain the acceptance of Qohelet.

3. The school of R. Yannai interpreted Qoh 1:3 as asserting the futility of activities "under the sun" (i.e., mundane activities) while affirming the value of matters "before the sun" (i.e., the study of Torah, for the Torah was created before the sun) (*b. Shab.* 30b).

For example: "I praised *śimḥah*" (8:15) is said to pertain to the happiness that comes from fulfilling commandments, whereas "and *śimḥah*—what does this accomplish?" (2:2) speaks of pleasure that does not proceed from the commandments. Most systematic of the harmonizers is Ibn Ezra. Believing that "even the least of the wise would not write a book and contradict his own words in his book" (in his comment on 7:3), he uses four principles in attempting to eliminate all the apparent contradictions in Qohelet (see Zer-Kavod, pp. 28-31). For example, "irritation rests in the breast of fools" (7:9) means that irritability remains with fools at all times. When so interpreted, this verse does not contradict Qohelet's commendation of irritation or anger in 7:3, for the wise man's anger is not permanent but timely and temporary. Likewise, "It is good... to eat and drink, etc." (5:17) is valid only with respect to the fool, who toils to grow rich without enjoying it, whereas "Better to go to a house of mourning than to go to a house of feasting" (7:2) is the truth, i.e., not restricted to certain persons or situations. Zer-Kavod adds two principles to the list and proceeds to save Qohelet from inconsistency by applying whichever one works most easily.

Loader (1979) develops a harmonization of a different sort. He points to numerous sets of contradictions (many of which, in my view, are not actual) and distinguishes in each a "pole" and a "contra-pole". These, he feels, are balanced in what he calls a "tension". Loader's analysis is harmonistic insofar as it gives Qohelet consistency by ascribing one side of each of the contradictions to someone else (i.e., to advocates of Wisdom, which Loader calls the "general *ḥokmā*"). Like the theory that the book is a disputation or diatribe (below, section 3 and n. 11), Loader's approach has Qohelet raising "chokhmatic" ideas in order to override them.

But apart from this type of harmonization, Loader offers the significant insight that Qohelet leaves the "poles" in "tension" (p. 123). He says that the patterns of polarity share a basic similarity: "*Their contents are structured as pole A::pole B—where God always works in such a way that a negative, unfavourable tension results (hebel)*" (p. 105; italics in original). I agree with this conclusion in principle, except that I would not try to impose it on the entire book (as I believe Loader does), and I do not always find both "poles" of a contradiction in a single passage. Moreover, even if Loader's conclusion is right, I do not think his analysis of specific passages leads to it. For example, he schematizes 7:23-8:1 thus:

> Pole: General *ḥokmā* (A). Contra-pole: God's work (= eventualities) (B). Tension: Powerlessness of general *ḥokmā* (C).
> But this is the chokmatic view of Qohelet. Thus: Pole: Qohelet's chokmatic view (C). Contra-pole: General *ḥokmā* (A).
> Tension: Relative advantage of Qohelet-wisdom (D) (p. 52).

Loader's analysis of this passage (and many others) is puzzling, for if the "powerlessness of general *ḥokmā*" is Qohelet's view, then the "tension" (which affirms the "relative advantage of Qohelet-wisdom") is in fact a *resolution*; the "general *ḥokmā*" has been refuted and laid aside, or at least been assigned to a more restricted range of validity than it claimed for itself. On Loader's interpretive method see further §3, n. 38. See also the review by Wilson (1987), who observes that the oppositions Loader isolates are often not truly polar, and that Loader's positive-negative schema often results in forced interpretations.

Hertzberg's use of the "Zwar-Aber Tatsache" as an interpretive principle is likewise harmonistic insofar as it resolves contradictory propositions by relating them to different objects or different points of view, in spite of an absence of linguistic indicators of such shifts (i.e., the Hebrew lacks equivalents for the "zwar" and "aber"). In a "Zwar-Aber Tatsache", one statement expresses the commonly held idea, and a second declares the first to be true only in relation to a limited perspective.[4] According to this interpretation, Qohelet is saying in 2:13-16: "Granted that wisdom has (as they say) a practical advantage over folly, nevertheless the wise man and fool die alike, so wisdom has no real advantage" (my paraphrase; cf. Hertzberg, pp. 91f.); or in 8:11-14: "Granted that as a rule the righteous live long and the wicked die young, nevertheless there are cases where the opposite happens" (my paraphrase).[5]

It is true that many passages in Qohelet can indeed be formulated as a "zwar-aber" relation, but that formulation generally heightens the contradiction rather than eliminating it. The "zwar-aber"

4. This fits Ibn Ezra's resolution of the tension he felt between 5:17 and 7:2; see above.

5. Hertzberg (p. 30) mentions the following as examples of the "Zwar[Z]-Aber[A] Tatsache": 1:16 (Z) 17f. (A); 2:3-10 (Z) 11 (A); 2:13-14a (Z) 14b ff. (A); 3:11a (Z) 11b (A); 3:17 (Z) 18ff. (A); 4:13-16a (Z) 16b (A); 7:11f. (Z) 7:7 (A) [note transposition]; 8:12b-13 (Z) 14-15 (A); 9:4b (Z) 5 (A); 9:16a (Z) 16b (A); 9:17-18a (Z) 18b, 10:1 (A); 10:2-3 (Z) 5-7 (A).

relation would resolve a contradiction only if Qohelet did not fully accept both of the contradictory propositions. As Hertzberg defines the "Zwar-Aber Tatsache" (though not always as he uses it in the course of the commentary), this is indeed the case. Qohelet quotes a notion held by others and accepts it as partly valid, but then declares its inadequacy by presenting his own opinion (pp. 30f.). The "Zwar-Tatsache" proves too superficial; the "Aber-Tatsache" is "die rechte" (p. 91). Now to show an idea's inadequacy is to argue against it, thus to distance oneself from it. The "Zwar-Aber Tatsache" implies a philosophical adjudication between rival ideas that affirms the second, the "aber", and pushes the first, the "zwar", to the periphery (Hertzberg, p. 175). In fact, however, neither proposition is subordinated to the other; neither is disputed. Qohelet does not argue against the "zwar" on behalf of the "aber". He does not begrudgingly grant a "zwar" or merely make concessions to a commonly held viewpoint. The opinion Hertzberg calls the "zwar" is as much Qohelet's belief as anyone else's. The "aber"—the recognition of anomalies—*imposes* itself on Qohelet, who would prefer to retain the rule. He observes the superiority of wisdom, then bewails its treatment; he insists on divine judgment, then complains of the existence of injustices. The relation between the two propositions is "this is true *and* that is true", and it is this conjunction that constitutes and reveals the world's absurdity.

The "zwar-aber" interpretation implies that Qohelet is solving a problem by effectively, if not completely, undermining a belief he does not really share (the "zwar"). This interpretation, like the assumption of quotations, requires us to assign one of the propositions expressed to someone other than Qohelet and is similarly flawed by a certain arbitrariness in deciding which view to assign to someone else. As I see it, in the passages representing the major contradictions in the book, Qohelet is stating the problem, not solving it. Rather than adjudicating between rival propositions, Qohelet makes them clash, then despairs of rational resolution. Hertzberg is right in contending that in certain passages (but not in all those he lists), two viewpoints confront without invalidating each other. Yet he subtly distorts the relation between the two statements by weakening the tension between them.

A certain measure of harmonization is a proper and necessary part of the reading process, for a reader must attempt to construct a coherent picture of an author's thought by interpreting one statement in light of another. The goal of a coherent reading makes the reader strive to discover coherency in the text. But appeal to extraneous factors (such as divine commandments in the discussion of *śimḥah*) and ad hoc definitions makes for a forced and unpersuasive harmonization. Harmonistic interpretations become objectionable especially when they do injustice to specific passages[6] or when they use makeshift and arbitrary explanations (such as Zer-Kavod's grab-bag of six principles) to achieve consistency. Excessive exegetical ingenuity may make an author consistent at the price of making him incoherent.

(2) *Additions*

When harmonization begins to collapse of its own weight, one may try to ease the tension by identifying some of the opposed statements as additions by a second party. Of the major commentators, Barton, McNeile, and Podechard most notably take this course. Currently it is followed (more moderately) by James Crenshaw in his commentary. The hypothesis of additions too is a reasonable procedure.

Yet this procedure presents us with a dilemma: where do we find Qohelet's thought? The passages most often considered secondary are not mere explanatory glosses or theological elaborations, but statements of ideas that both bear directly on the central issues of the book and contradict the material considered authentic. The text with these passages is a very different book from the text without them. To a scholar who excludes certain passages as containing unauthentic ideas, any interpretation that uses them in reconstructing Qohelet's thought is, at best, addressing a later stage in the book's development, one in which the author's thought had been superseded if not entirely undermined. Conversely, to an interpreter who maintains the authenticity of the disputed passages, any reading that excludes key passages has large gaps that leave the reconstruction not only incomplete but irreparably distorted. The two interpreters are talking about different books.

In my view, the attempt to bring consistency into Qohelet by excisions does not succeed for several reasons.

6. Perhaps we should say *too many* passages, for in text criticism we must sometimes go so far as to override the text of certain passages in favor of a larger coherence.

(a) First of all, the sentences commonly eliminated are often linked syntactically to material that is almost certainly original, this originality being shown mainly by its unorthodox thought and secondarily by style (the latter argument is less weighty because style can be imitated, whereas ideas would not be imitated by someone who is trying to defuse them by orthodox additions). For example, the praise of wisdom in 2:13-14a (assigned by Siegfried to an annotator) is introduced by a phrase of perception typical of Qohelet, *wĕra'iti 'ani še-*. More important, 2:12a looks forward to a statement about wisdom, and this is lacking if vv. 13-14a are excised. The bitter remark about the universality of death—certainly original to Qohelet—could not follow directly upon v. 12, because without v. 14a there is no antecedent for *kullam*, "both of them" (v. 14b). And if even one emphatic expression of praise for wisdom must be left to Qohelet (as even Podechard and Barton concede must be done here), there is no reason to assign (as they do) other such statements to a "Chakam". In the same way, the affirmation of divine judgment in 3:17aβ (assigned to a "Chasid" by Siegfried, McNeile, Barton, and Podechard) is introduced by a typical phrase of perception in v. 17aα and followed by a motivation typical of Qohelet's thought and cast in his characteristic vocabulary (v. 17b). The orthodox sentiments of 8:12bβ (*yihyeh*. . .)-13 are linked to the complaint of 8:11-12a by the phrase *ki gam yodea' 'ani 'ăšer*. Furthermore, the putative annotator would have left the severe complaint of 8:14 untouched, though he could have softened that as well by placing his addition after the verse.

(b) The glosses do not fulfill the purposes ascribed to their authors. A scribe reading 8:11-12a + 14 alone would face a sharp repudiation of God's absolute justice. If he wanted to make the text assert God's justice unequivocally but was unable to eliminate the offending words, he might add—after v. 14—an assertion that the day of reckoning will eventually come, when the punishment of the wicked will outweigh their prosperity and the reward of the righteous will outweigh their suffering. As it is, however, the hypothetical scribe, though motivated by pious goals, has let Qohelet's painful doubts have the last word and has merely produced an uneasy tension between observations of injustice and assertions of justice. Such a tension might serve the purposes of a bold thinker who wishes to portray the world's absurdities. It in no way promotes a pious belief in God's invariant justice.

In general, a corrective gloss can be expected to follow the statement it is supposed to correct; otherwise the glossator's views are themselves neutralized. In the passages at the center of this discussion—2:12-16; 3:17; 8:5-7; 8:10-14—it is the "skeptic" who is allowed the last word.

(c) Even with all the additions that Podechard, McNeile, and Barton claim to have discovered, the skeptical and pessimistic character of the book remains blatant. If the book was considered so offensive as to require extensive glossing, why (as Gordis asks [p. 71]) did the glossators not take the simpler and more effective step of suppressing it? That is to say, why did they choose to copy it? Glossators such as those presumed to have worked on Qohelet must have been copyists, not marginal annotators, for the presumed glosses do not explicate, but rather counteract, the ideas of the text proper. Such additions would have been useless in the margin, for they had to be ascribed to Qohelet-Solomon if they were to counterbalance his ideas. The addition-hypothesis requires us to assume that a scribe (or several) who fundamentally disagreed with Qohelet undertook to copy the work, then inserted additions that were supposed to counterbalance Qohelet's skepticism and yet manifestly fail to do so.

(d) Most fundamentally, excising passages as later additions does not result in consistency. For example, McNeile, Barton, and Podechard (among others) attribute 3:17; 8:5-7; 8:11-13; 11:9b to a *ḥasid*-glossator. Galling attributes 3:17aβγ; 8:5; 8:12b-13; and 11:9b to a redactor. (Almost all modern interpreters attribute 12:13f. to a later redactor.) Nevertheless these four commentators leave 5:5b and 7:17 to Qohelet, though both these verses affirm retribution no less clearly than the verses they believe Qohelet could not have spoken. (These concessions are not merely lapses in thoroughness, for both sentences are necessary to the passages to which they belong, and neither has the tone of pious moralizing.) If we leave the book with any significant inconsistencies in central matters such as wisdom and justice, we are undercutting the criteria whereby the putative additions were discovered.

(3) *Quotations*

Gordis advocates an approach to the contradictions that has much the same effect as the hypothesis of additions (earlier, Levy had taken this tack). Gordis understands Qohelet (and other biblical writers) to frequently quote other sources for various purposes (he notes four types with various sub-types), quite often without a *verbum dicendi*. In many cases Qohelet quotes traditional Wisdom in order to refute it. Whybray (1981) too accepts the presence of unmarked quotations and tries to develop a typology of quotations in Qohelet in order to determine which come from traditional Wisdom.

The quotation hypothesis, as it has been used throughout the history of Qohelet-exegesis, too quickly becomes a magic wand for the easy—and illusive—elimination of difficulties, making significant complexities disappear in the process. In "The Identification of Quotations in Biblical Literature" (Fox, 1980a), I point out ways in which quotations are marked. If a quotation expresses the speaker's view, the quotation need not be marked as such, since its identification is not decisive for interpretation. On the other hand, we can expect quotations expressing an opinion contrary to the author's to be marked in some way as coming from another source. The more important for interpretation it is for the reader to dissociate certain words from the primary speaker, the more clearly the writer must mark them as belonging to someone else. Marking may be explicit, by means of a verb of speaking or thinking, or it may be virtual. Three forms of virtual marking are (a) the mention of another person besides the primary speaker in the immediate context, to allow the reader to easily associate the words with another voice; (b) a virtual *verbum dicendi* (e.g., a reference to "mouth" or "words"—anything that implies speech); and (c) a shift in grammatical number and person.

There is no marking, explicit or virtual, in Qoh 8:12b-13, or in the other verses that Gordis identifies as quotations of views not Qohelet's (2:13-14a; 4:5, 8bα[7]; 9:16aβ, 18a). Nevertheless, Gordis supplies a transition phrase in translating 8:12: "though I know the answer that" (in 2:13 he supplies, "I have heard it said" where the Hebrew has "I saw"). Although he probably does not intend these phrases as literal translations, they are not even implicit in the Hebrew. *Yodea' 'ani 'ăšer* means "I know that", not (even as

7. This, according to Gordis, is a quotation of something the toiler never said, in fact, never even *thought* of saying. Gordis supplies, "*He never asks himself.*" (Can we call this a "quotation"?) With such license, there are few difficulties a commentator cannot easily explain away.

paraphrase) "I know the answer that". To "know that" something is so is to accept it as a fact.[8]

In the absence of quotation markers, we could just as well attribute 8:11-12a + 14 (the "skeptical" remark) to someone else—to a pupil, for example—and say that Qohelet rejects this idea. In fact, Podechard does reverse the identification of quotations by taking all of 8:11-13 as a later addition of a "Chasid", who is supposedly echoing Qohelet's sentiments in vv. 11f. and expressing his own in v. 13. Levy regards all of vv. 11 + 12aβ-13 as a quotation of the pious explanation for the delay of retribution. The traditional commentators often used a similar tactic. The Targum, for example, makes the *skeptical* remark of 2:16 into a quotation: "And as people say, the end of the righteous is like the end of the guilty". Ibn Ezra says that 9:4b, "a living dog is better off than a dead lion", is "the thought of people", but not Qohelet's. Similarly, he ascribes 9:10, the denial of activity in Sheol, to the people whose hearts are full of madness (mentioned in 9:3b), while the affirmation of judgment in 3:17a he considers Qohelet's own thought, "the truth".[9]

The quotation theory is a variation of an earlier approach that viewed the book as a dialogue. These commentators associated the skeptical opinions with someone less wise than Qohelet, such as an "inquirer" or "student".[10] One could reverse the roles and have a skeptical Qohelet quoting conventional wisdom in order to refute it. Thus A. Miller (1934) describes the book as a condensed literary rendering of a school-disputation in which the master raises and dismisses the opinions of "friends and students" who include representatives of the "Weisheitsideal" and "Lebensfreude und hohe

8. Qohelet's use of the *perfect* of *yada'* to introduce his own ideas in other passages does not (contrary to Hertzberg) indicate that the participle in this one marks the knowledge as someone else's. On the contrary, the participle emphasizes the *presentness* of this knowledge more than the perfect would, for the perfect might be understood as introducing an idea held in the past.

9. Ibn Ezra's discussion of contradictions comes in his comment on 7:3. See further Zer-Kavod, pp. 30f.

10. For commentators that take this approach see Ginsburg's summaries of Heinemann (84), du Hamel (165), Herder (184), Eichhorn (185), and Nachtigal (192). The understanding of "Qohelet" as referring to an "assembly" (q^e*hillah*) of individuals with different views is mentioned (and rejected) by Ibn Ezra (on 7:3); see Ginsburg, p. 57.

Lebensführung" (p. 109).[11] The uses to which quotation-identifying can be put are limitless. A recent one is Lohfink's attempt (1979) to save Qohelet from the charge of misogyny by making 7:26 a quotation from traditional Wisdom of an idea that Qohelet rejects.

Even if we accept Gordis's or Whybray's identification of quotations from traditional wisdom, we do not know *a priori* Qohelet's relation to the views they express. As Gordis recognizes, one may bring a quotation to strengthen or express one's own position. Thus, unless we also assume that Qohelet rejects the ideas he is quoting, the quotation hypothesis in itself takes us nowhere. We have yet to determine which view is Qohelet's, just as if we never assumed the presence of quotations at all.

I try to read Qohelet without "solving" the problems raised by the contradictions in his perceptions of toil, wisdom, and justice. I am not sure I entirely succeed, because there is a tremendous interpretive pressure to raise the valleys and lower the hills, to make the way straight and level before the reader. But a reading faithful to this book, at least, should try to describe the territory with all its bumps and clefts, for they are not mere flaws, but the essence of the landscape.

11. Allgeier, Ausejo (1948), and Lohfink (10) have classified Qohelet as a diatribe and used this assumption in similar ways.

Chapter 1

THE MEANING OF *HEBEL* AND *R^e^'UT-RUAḤ* IN QOHELET

> Mais ce qui est absurde, c'est la confrontation de cet irrationnel et de ce désir éperdu de clarté dont l'appel résonne au plus profond de l'homme.
>
> Camus, *Le Mythe de Sisyphe*, p. 37

§1.1 *The problem*

Qohelet begins and ends his teaching with the declaration that all is *hebel*; this seems to constitute his primary insight into life. But what exactly does he mean when he calls something *hebel*? And what does he mean when he calls everything *hebel*? This chapter is not a "word study", an attempt to define the meanings of *hebel* in the HB, but an examination of the particular use Qohelet makes of a common word whose meanings elsewhere in the Bible are fairly clear.[1]

The literal, and probably original, meaning of *hebel* is "breath" or "breeze", a sense apparent only in Isa 57:13, but verified by MH, Jewish Aramaic, and Syriac. The word is almost always used in a transferred sense. It sometimes means "ephemeral", the sense most directly derivable from its literal meaning; for example: Prov 21:6; Job 7:16; Pss 39:6, 12; 144:4. It is commonly used to indicate inefficacy (thus Isa 30:7; 49:4; Job 9:29). It is also used to mean "deceitful", a sense not metaphorically derivable from "breeze", but rather transferred from the notion of inefficacy, since something that does not fulfill what it is supposed to do is deceitful. Thus *hebel* can be used as a synonym of *kazab*, *šeqer*, *'awen*, and *ma'al* and mean "deceit", "lie" (e.g., Zech 10:2; Ps 62:10; Job 21:34; etc.). The implication of both inefficacy and deceit makes *hebel* a fitting epithet for false gods, "who have no efficacy (*mo'il*) in them" (Jer 16:19); for

1. For a review of the etymological background and the distribution of the term in the Bible, see Loretz, 1964:218-25, as well as the commentaries and Seybold, '*hebhel*', *TDOT*, III, 313-20.

example: 2 Kgs 17:15; Jer 2:5; 8:19; 14:22; Jon 2:9. After examining Qohelet's usage, we can consider how it relates to the uses present elsewhere in the language.

§1.11 *Some suggested solutions*

Let us begin by considering some of the words that have been suggested as the meaning of *hebel* in Qohelet. Although *hebel* may still carry some connotations of "vapor", most of the *hebel*-predications in Qohelet are not live metaphors, because they do not demand a two-level interpretation: a literal interpretation overridden by a new, metaphorical one.[2] In any case, the image of vapor does not provide much guidance in ascertaining the meaning of this word in Qohelet, because a vapor can represent many things. While the ephemerality of vapor is relevant to the way Qohelet applies *hebel* in some verses (e.g., 3:19 and 11:10), no quality of a vapor can be applied to the situations that he calls *hebel* (e.g., 2:23). It cannot be said that a vapor "is done" or "occurs" (*naʿăśah*, 8:14), nor can it be said that "everything" is vaporous or ephemeral (1:2; 12:8).

We may try out a few of the common glosses for *hebel* in connection with 8:14:

> There is a *hebel* that occurs on the earth: there are righteous people who receive what is appropriate to the deeds of the wicked and there are wicked people who receive what is appropriate to the deeds of the righteous. I said that this too is a *hebel*.

The situation described is clear, and, more important (as we shall see), the grammar is clear: the *hebel*-judgments, "There is a *hebel*" and "this is a *hebel*", frame a situation (cf. 6:1-2). The description provides no antecedent for "this (*zeh*)" other than the whole situation. To call this situation "vaporous" gives no information about it; none of the qualities usually associated with vapors seem to apply. It is not "transitory" or "fleeting"—if it were, that would be all to the good. Nor is it a "Nichtiges", a zero, an absence; it is quite substantive, very much a reality. Nor is it "vain", if by that traditional but ambiguous rendering we mean "trivial", for the injustice described is certainly not that. Nor is it "vain" in the sense of futile. It is true that the deeds of the righteous may prove futile,

2. On metaphor as a move between two levels of interpretation see, i.a., Ricoeur, 1976:46-54.

but the passage also describes what happens to the wicked, and that cannot be said to show the futility of *their* actions.[3] Nor does "incomprehensible" adequately denote the quality that troubles Qohelet in observing this situation. While the injustice described in 8:11-14 is indeed incomprehensible, it is not the mysteriousness of the situation that pains Qohelet, but its inequity.

No single English word corresponds exactly to the semantic shape of *hebel* as Qohelet uses it, but it is possible to render the word by an equivalent that comes close to doing so and that bears similar connotations. The best translation-equivalent for *hebel* in Qohelet's usage is "absurdity",[4] understood in a sense and with connotations close to those given the concept in Albert Camus's classic description of the absurd, *The Myth of Sisyphus*.[5] The essence of the absurd is a disparity between two phenomena that are supposed to be joined by a link of harmony or causality but are actually disjunct or even conflicting. The absurd is irrational, an affront to reason, in the broad sense of the human faculty that seeks and discovers order in the world about us. The quality of absurdity does not inhere in a being, act, or event in and of itself (though these may, by extension, be called absurd), but rather in the tension between a certain reality and a framework of expectations. In Camus's words:

> Je suis donc fondé à dire que le sentiment de l'absurdité ne naît pas du simple examen d'un fait ou d'une impression mais qu'il jaillit de la comparaison entre un état de fait et une certaine réalité, entre une action et le monde qui la dépasse. L'absurde est essentiellement un divorce. Il n'est ni dans l'un ni dans l'autre des éléments comparés. Il naît de leur confrontation (*Mythe*, p. 48).

Absurdity arises from a logical contradiction between two undeniable realities: "'C'est absurde' veut dire: 'C'est impossible', mais aussi: 'c'est contradictoire'" (*Mythe*, p. 47). Life is filled with specific

3. "Futile" is properly predicated of an intentional action and refers to its failure to achieve its goal. "Absurd" can be applied at a higher level of abstraction. In other words, "toil" may be futile, but *the fact that* toil is futile is absurd.

4. Although a noun, *hebel* usually has a descriptive function and is often best translated "absurd".

5. English "absurd", we may note, is the same as French "absurde" because the contemporary sense of the term in English has been shaped largely by Camus's use.

absurdities. Absurdity is humanity's condition of existence.[6] The connotations with which Camus imbues the concept of the absurd, particularly in the *Myth of Sisyphus*, are highly congruent with those Qohelet gives to the concept of *hebel*: alienation from the world, a distancing of the "I" from the event with which it seems to be bound,[7] along with frustration of the longing for coherence and a stale taste of repeated and meaningless events, even resentment at the "gods".

Basic to Qohelet's thinking are certain assumptions about the way reality *should* operate. His primary assumption is that an action and a fitting recompense for that action are cause and effect; one who creates the cause can justly expect the effect. Qohelet identifies this expectation with the reasonableness he looks for in the working of the universe. At the same time that he cleaves to this expectation, he sees that there is in reality no such reasonableness, and his expectations are constantly frustrated.

The sense of the absurd is much older than Camus. As one scholar of Camus observes, "Whatever the special character of Camus's conclusions, the absurd itself remains a contemporary manifestation of a skepticism as old at least as the Book of Ecclesiastes" (Cruickshank, 1959:44). The sense of the absurd is, in fact, much older than Qohelet. Absurdities are a favorite theme of the Egyptian "Prophetic Lament" genre; for example: "The weak-armed is strong-armed, / One salutes him who saluted. / I show you the undermost uppermost, / What was turned on the back turns the belly" (Neferti; *AEL* I, 143); "He who gave orders takes orders, / And the hearts of both submit" (Khakheperre-Sonb; *AEL* I, 148). In these works, however, the absurdities currently dominant will be overcome by a "messianic" restoration of order. The unrelieved absurdity of life is the message of the Babylonian "Dialogue of Pessimism" (Lambert, 1960:139-49), in which the slave shows that values are stripped of meaning because a clever mind can rationalize every action and its

6. *Mythe*, p. 7. Lazere (1973:52f.) distinguishes between metaphysical and epistemological absurdity; both are included in Camus's use of "absurd" and in Qohelet's use of *hebel*.

7. Gese has well described this sense of alienation as a "... Distanzierung der Person, Distanzierung des Ich von dem Geschehen, mit dem das Ich verknüpft zu sein scheint, der als Absonderung und Herauslösung des betrachtenden Subjekts beschrieben werden kann" (1963:141).

opposite equally well. Absurdity is by no means a modern concept, one that might be considered *a priori* unlikely to appear in an ancient text. I am not aware, however, of any single word in Hebrew, Egyptian, or Akkadian that expresses the concept as well as does *hebel* in Qohelet's usage.

There are other terms in the semantic field of "counter-rational" that have been suggested as equivalents of *hebel*. E. Good has argued that *hebel* means "incongruous", a sense close to "irony" or "ironic", (1965:176-83), and indeed most of the phenomena that are called *hebel* do involve incongruities. Incongruity is a broader concept than the absurd, not identical to it. But incongruities and ironies may be merely puzzling or amusing; the absurd (as understood by Qohelet and Camus) is never that. Some incongruities or ironies may satisfy a sense of justice, as when a man is caught in the trap he set; the absurd never does. Incongruities and ironies may lie within the grasp of human intellect and evoke a variety of reactions. *Hebel* for Qohelet, like "absurd" for Camus, is not merely incongruous or ironic; it is oppressive, even tragic. The divorce between act and result is the reality upon which human reason founders; it robs human actions of significance and undermines morality. For Qohelet *hebel* is an injustice, partly synonymous with *ra'ah*, "inequity, injustice" (see 6:1-2; 9:3; cf. 2:21; 4:8).

B. Pennacchini, in an illuminating essay surveying Qohelet's themes, defines *hebel* by saying that it is used of a series of situations that are "... absurd, realities incomprehensible because of lack of sense; realities contrary to the contemporaneous logic and not homogeneous with the cultural climate of the moment; realities of situations which constantly show themselves to be a trick" (1977:496). Pennacchini is right in defining *hebel* in the context of logic ("logic" in a broad, not a technical, sense), but he errs in blunting the severity of Qohelet's judgments by making the *hebel*-judgments relative to a cultural setting. To be sure, the presuppositions by which reality is judged absurd are largely social in origin, but that is not what *Qohelet* means by the term. He is not saying that life is irrational only in the context of the logic of his contemporaries or the current cultural attitudes, as if complaining that his society's perspectives were limited while implying that his own was broader. Nor can I agree with Pennacchini (p. 508) that Qohelet's assertions of absurdity merely state limitations on human reason, an interpretation offered also by A. Barucq, who translates *hebel* by "absurd", "absurdité"—

"dans la ligne de certaines philosophies modernes" (1968:55). Barucq says that the Hebrew word "signifie quelque chose d'inconsistant, comme le souffle, le néant", and further notes that "il est bien entendu que Dieu en dirige le sens mais l'homme ne perce pas le mystère de cette action. C'est la faillite de la sagesse" (pp. 55f.). While Qohelet would agree with this statement, it is not what he means by the word *hebel*. As I see it, *hebel* designates not the mysterious but rather (and this is a fundamental difference) *the manifestly irrational or meaningless*. To call something *hebel* is an evaluation of its nature. Whether or not there is meaning beyond the visible surface of events, that surface, which is the world as it presents itself to humans, *is* warped. Similarly, while *hebel* is a near-synonym of "meaningless", the terms differ insofar as "absurd" is not merely the absence of meaning, but an active violation of meaningfulness.

For this reason, *hebel* is not equivalent to "incomprehensible", "mysterious", or the like (thus Staples, 1943).[8] To be sure, the sense of "incomprehensible" does approach the meaning of "absurd", for the absurd is, by definition, incomprehensible.[9] And comparison of

8. Staples (1943) contends that *hebel* means "unknowable, incomprehensible". He argues that in many of its uses outside Qohelet, *hebel* has a "distinctly cultic flavor" and originally referred to Canaanite rites. "The word *hebhel*, therefore, originally carried some such idea as cult mystery, and so something unfathomable, something unknown or unknowable to man. It may even signify something which it would be impossible to discover" (pp. 65f.). Hence, according to Staples, Qohelet, like Zophar and the author of Job, is calling everything under the sun mysterious and unknowable to the finite mind—an attitude common to the rest of the HB. Staples's reasoning is clearly a string of false analogies based on mistaken assumptions. For further discussion, see Seybold, *TDOT*, III, 315-18.

9. Rashbam, who understands *hebel* to mean "futile" in most contexts, in 8:10 and 8:14 defines it as that at which people wonder (*tohim*) and are amazed (*mištomᵉmim*). In his comment on 8:10 he explains: "that which is hidden from men, which men cannot understand clearly and do not know why the Holy One is so long-suffering with them, is called *hebel* because men wonder and are amazed at it" (Japhet and Salters, 1985:174).

With regard to the authorship of the commentary in Hamburg Codex Heb. 32 (catalogue no. 37; first published by Jellinek), Japhet (pp. 19-33) argues persuasively that it indeed is the work of Rabbi Samuel ben Meir. I will refer to the author of this commentary as "Rashbam", though the identification is still disputed.

8:17 with 1:14 suggests that the phrase "man cannot apprehend (*lo' yimṣa'*) anything that God brings to pass" is roughly equivalent to saying that everything that happens under the sun is *hebel*. But there are important differences between the two terms. To call something "absurd" is to claim a certain knowledge of its quality: that it *is* contrary to reason—perhaps only to human reason, but that is the only reason accessible to humans without appeal to revelation. "Incomprehensible" indicates that the meaning of a phenomenon is opaque to human intellect but allows for, and may even suggest, that it is meaningful. "Absurd" denies meaning, "incomprehensible" denies only its knowability. To call something "incomprehensible" may be a way of avoiding a judgment of absurdity. Zophar says that God's acts are incomprehensible; Job—before the revelation—believes they are also absurd. Moreover, absurdity is "infectious" in a way that incomprehensibility is not. Entities locked into an absurd situation become absurd, whereas the factors of an incomprehensible situation are not themselves necessarily incomprehensible. Thus the fact that Qohelet's wealth must be passed on to someone who did not work for it (2:21)—an absurdity—does not make his toil "unknowable" or "incomprehensible", but it does make it absurd. Growing wise produces no permanent distinction between wise man and fool; the cause for this, though not the rationale, is quite knowable. Qohelet does not explicitly deny that beyond the sphere of events "under the sun" or within the divine intellect there might be a resolution of absurdities, but he (unlike the author of Job) does not affirm or even suggest that there is one. Such a resolution is simply of no use to Qohelet, any more than the unknowable possibility of an afterlife can solve the problem of mortality for the living. Absurdity is defined in terms of human reason, and any resolution inaccessible to it does not eliminate the absurdity. A mouse caught in a trap for nibbling a piece of cheese would be right to judge his fate absurd, however explicable his pain and death may be in the "broader picture".

Qohelet's thematic statement, "Everything is *hebel*" implies that there is some meaning common to the various occurrences of the term. To define the word, as commentators commonly do, by offering a list of translation equivalents such as "vapor", "futile", "empty", "nothing", "ridiculous", "incongruous", "transitory", "illusory", "insignificant", "vain", "incomprehensible", and more, is inadequate.[10] Most of these renderings seem to fit some contexts; in fact, in some contexts several quite different renderings seem to work. On the other hand, we cannot say that the word *hebel* is a bundle of all the qualities denoted by these renderings. *Hebel* does not include all of these senses in every application. The renderings suggested by the various translations and commentaries are, it should be stressed, distinct qualities, not merely different nuances or colorations of one concept: what is fleeting may be precious, what is frustrating may be no illusion, what is futile may endure forever.

Since several qualities—ephemerality, ineffectuality, futility, and inequity—evoke the *hebel*-judgment, why not translate *hebel* variously, as "ephemeral" or "futile" or "ineffectual" or "inequitable", in accordance with context? NJV, alone of the major translations, takes this approach, using eight different words to render *hebel*. Ordinarily this context-sensitive approach would be acceptable; a word can, of course, be used in different ways in one text.[11] Such an approach, however, does not work for this word in this book. The thematic declaration that everything is *hebel* and the formulaic character of the *hebel*-judgments show that for Qohelet there is a single quality that is an attribute of the world, and further, that this very quality is manifest in the particular *hăbalim* that Qohelet identifies by the formula, "This too is a *hebel*". The *hebel* leitmotif disintegrates if the word is assigned several different meanings. The approach taken by NJV gives us no hint that the generalization of 1:2 and 12:8 is derived from specific conclusions reached in the course of the book. Furthermore, if Qohelet were saying, "X is transitory; Y is futile; Z is trivial", the summary,

10. Loretz, for example, concludes that according to the use of *hebel* elsewhere in the Bible, "... ist *hebel* mit 'Windhauch, Hauch' zu übersetzen und ein ansprechender Ausdruck zur Bezeichnung des Vorübergehenden, Gewichtlos-Leichten, des Wertlosen, Leeren, Macht- und Hilflosen, kurz, ein Wort für Nichtiges, Hinfälliges" (1964:223).

11. Nevertheless, too many shifts of meaning in a single word would block communication. As a rule we should try to minimize the number of senses a word, especially a theme word, has in a given text. When the "context-sensitive" approach becomes a fill-in-the-blank operation, it degenerates into a guessing game whose results are far more arbitrary than the traditional approach, which requires of itself the discipline of attempting to discover the locus of a word's meaning and rendering "the" meaning of a word by a corresponding word in the target language.

"Everything is *hebel*" would be meaningless. It would, in fact, be specious reasoning or, at best, a rhetorical trick, to generalize from disparate categories just because they can have the same label applied to them. To do Qohelet justice, we must look for a concept that applies to all, or, failing that, to the great majority, of the specific *hebel*-judgments.

We should distinguish the *qualities* that evoke the particular *hebel*-judgments (ephemerality, inequity, inefficacy, futility, nonsense) from the *meaning* of *hebel*. If we render *hebel* by terms designating the qualities that evoke the *hebel*-judgments, not only does the leitmotif disintegrate but the judgments become banal. Obviously it is inequitable for the wicked to enjoy the fate the righteous deserve and for the righteous to suffer the fate the wicked deserve; it is tautological to say that toil which fails to achieve its goal or which benefits no one is futile. It is not, however, a truism to declare that these examples of inequity and futility are *absurd*, for the predicate then adds new information to the subject. The best evidence that the *hebel*-judgments are not truisms if *hebel* means "absurd" is that some of them—particularly those directed against pleasure and labor—are open to dispute.

§1.12 *The uses of* hebel

Qohelet applies the term *hebel* to various types of phenomena: beings, life or a part thereof, acts, and events. The last two categories must be distinguished from each other. An act is something done *by* people; it is distinguished by human *agency*. Experiences, in particular pleasure, can be included in this category, since Qohelet speaks of it as a type of behavior that can be an object of intention. In contrast, events are circumstances that happen *to* people (an ongoing event is a "situation"). This distinction might be contested on a philosophical level, but it is adequate in describing the phenomena of which Qohelet speaks.[12] An

12. More precisely, actions are a subset of events; an event that has an agent is an action. For purposes of simplicity, I will use "event" to refer to occurrences that are not (human) actions, though they may comprehend them. D. Davidson defines "agency" in accordance with a semantic criterion: "A person is the agent of an event if and only if there is a description of what he did that makes true a sentence that says he did it intentionally" (1980:46, and see ch. 3, *passim*). Making agency a semantic category allows us to circumvent the problem of determinism in discussing act and event. While it may be the case that God gives a man the task of toiling (2:26), that toil may be spoken of as intentional. To say a man toils implies that he intends to toil—whatever the cause of that intention.

action is called *hebel* by virtue of the distortion between expectation and outcome; in a situation or event it is the *relationship* between action and outcome that is called absurd. In other words, "toiling" is an action, while "one man toiling and another enjoying the wealth" is an event. *Hebel* is most often applied to events or situations in Qohelet.

The best way to decide upon the meaning of *hebel* is to review the 38 occurrences of the word in Qohelet. These may be organized in terms of the referent of *hebel*. The most instructive passages, to which we shall pay the closest attention, are those which present a *hebel*-judgment—*gam zeh hebel* or the like.

The attempt to determine the meaning of *hebel* in Qohelet runs up against a special grammatical problem: it is frequently difficult, sometimes virtually impossible, to identify the antecedents of the pronouns in the *hebel*-judgments. Thus in particular cases it is uncertain what exactly is being judged—a certain thing or action mentioned in the context, or the entire event or situation described. It is, however, usually possible to discuss Qohelet's underlying reasoning even in passages where this ambiguity cannot be resolved, since an act or thing is judged to be *hebel* because it is part of an absurd event: the act or thing derives its absurdity from what *happens* to the actor or to the product of the action.

Hebel is used of the following classes of referents:

(1) Human behavior
 (a) Toil and its products: homo faber
 (b) Pleasure: homo ludens
 (c) Wisdom: homo sapiens
 (d) Speech: homo loquens
(2) Living beings and times in their lives
(3) Death
(4) Divine behavior—events of this world
 (a) Divine justice
 (b) "Everything"

Categories 1a and 4b are the most important, involving together over half the occurrences of *hebel*.

The above categorization is intended for greater ease of description; the categories are not discrete or exclusive. Several occurrences apply to situations which embrace factors of more than one class. After reviewing the contexts, we shall consider some of the implications of the understanding of *hebel* as "absurd" for the meaning of the book. Many of the verses with this term are difficult, and a different interpretation of these passages might place some occurrences in different categories (for exegetical details see §5). This would not, however, fundamentally affect the understanding of the meaning of *hebel*, nor should it be allowed to do so, for the definition of a word should be derived from passages whose meaning is relatively clear.

(1a) Toil and its products (2:11, 19, 21, 23, 26; 6:2; 4:7, 8; 4:4; 5:9)
In 2:11, Qohelet calls his "labors and toil" (i.e., toilsome labors) *hebel*, but he does not at this point say why. We have to go back to 2:1-2 for the reason for this evaluation. Inasmuch as pleasure, the best possible product of toil, is "inane", and "does nothing", toil is not worth the strain. "Futile" could serve as a translation-equivalent here (thus NJV), but so can "absurd", because the significance as well as the value of the effort resides in its productivity, and this is not commensurate with the unpleasantness of toil. In fact, "absurd" is preferable, because toil is not truly futile, since it does produce wealth, the means of pleasure, though this product is not adequate to save the act from absurdity. (It may be absurd to sweat and strain for three dollars an hour when someone else receives much more for less work done with less skill, but the underpaid labor is not truly futile.) This judgment receives further justification in 2:18-26, where Qohelet complains that his wealth will pass on to someone else after his death, someone who did not work for it (the same complaint may also be present in the obscure v. 12).

Qoh 2:18-26 describes a single situation: One man toils and someone else receives what was earned. Qohelet broods on this event, formulating it in various ways and calling it *hebel* four times (2:19, 21, 23, 26), as well as *ra'ah rabbah*, a "severe evil", and *r^e'ut ruaḥ*, a "pursuit of wind". In 2:21-22 it is a complex of events that Qohelet is calling *hebel*, since nothing in these sentences presents itself as the antecedent of "this" in v. 23 besides the situation in its entirety. It is not wealth that is *hebel* and a "severe evil"; if it were, Qohelet would not be embittered at the thought of its going to the undeserving. Nor can we isolate Qohelet's toil, mentioned in v. 20b, as the antecedent, ignoring the rest of the complex situation.

Why does Qohelet care what happens to his wealth after his death? Why does he not take pleasure in the thought that someone will benefit from it? It is not the ephemerality of wealth or its triviality that galls Qohelet but rather the inequity of its distribution: one person did the work; another gains possession of the product. (The possibility that the recipient may be a fool exacerbates the absurdity but is not the heart of the problem. Verse 19aα is parenthetical; the possibility of the recipient being a fool is not mentioned again.)

It is self-evidently absurd for a wise man to toil industriously only to pass his wealth on to a fool. But in 2:26 Qohelet realizes that in a sense this does not happen, for the situation defines the character of the people involved in it. The man who drives himself to amass wealth must be offensive to God, while the beneficiary, as the benefit he receives shows, must enjoy divine favor and he, as his avoidance of toil shows, must be the wise one. But neither God's favor nor the fortunate man's "wisdom" makes the situation reasonable or just. The crisscrossing of effort and result is still unfair and absurd. Qohelet is pained not by the thought of losing his wealth so much as by the affront to his sense of justice.

In 6:2 Qohelet complains about the case where God gives a man wealth but lets a stranger consume it. This is essentially the situation called *hebel* in 2:19, 21, and 26. There is no labor mentioned that might be reckoned futile or ephemeral, and the wealth itself can hardly be isolated as the thing that Qohelet calls *ra'ah*, *hebel*, and *ḥŏli ra'*; if it were, the toiler's loss would not be an "evil sickness". *Zeh* refers to the whole situation described: God gives a man wealth but instead of permitting him to enjoy it, takes it away (by a misfortune or by death) and gives it to another who did not toil for it.

Further *hebel*-judgments upon toil: In 4:7-8 Qohelet speaks of the self-depriving toil of a lone man (again Qohelet indicates he has himself in mind, as he slips into the first person). Neither he nor a close relative receives benefit from the lone man's toil (this is the sense of the rhetorical question). The introductory *hebel* in 4:7 is most naturally taken as characterizing the particular form of behavior Qohelet is about to describe, namely, that of the lonely man who continues toiling and depriving himself of pleasure although he has no one else to benefit from his earnings. The *hebel*-judgment in 4:8 reiterates the statement of v. 7 and has the same object. In 4:4, the *hebel* is either skilled work or the fact that skilled work is motivated by envy. No further reason is given for the statement, but one may be implicit in the association of work with envy, a passion that destroys the person afflicted by it (cf. Prov 14:30). In 5:9, the subject of the *hebel*-judgment is a situation: the person who loves wealth is always dissatisfied with what he has.

(1b) Pleasure (2:1; 6:9)

Pleasure (*śimḥah*), Qohelet says in 2:1, is *hebel*, because amusement (*ś^e^ḥoq*) is "inane", and pleasure (*śimḥah*) "does" nothing. He is not judging trivial amusements alone, not saying merely that trivial merrymaking is *hebel*—a banality by any definition of *hebel*—but is declaring that all pleasures, even legitimate and reasonable ones such as described in 2:4-9, fail to prove meaningful and thus are "inane" (*m^e^holal*) and irrational. At this stage of his investigation, at least, Qohelet had hopes of finding something productive, but he did not find it in pleasure, his portion in life.

Qoh 6:9 makes a similar statement: the immediate experience of pleasure (even without satisfaction) is better than mere yearning but is nevertheless absurd. Qohelet does not give a reason for this judgment.

(1c) Wisdom (2:15; 7:6 [?]; 4:16)

Although growing wise is possible, and although wisdom has great advantages (2:13-14a; 7:11-12, 19; etc.), amassing wisdom is absurd, for the wise and the fool end up the same (2:14b-15). One who grows very wise becomes aware of life's injustices (7:16) without being adequately compensated for the discomfort this causes. This is no condemnation of wisdom in itself but a complaint against an injustice. It is unjust, incongruous, absurd, for such different causes (ways of life) to have the same effect (death).

In 7:6 it is unclear whether *hebel* is said of the merry noise of fools—in which case the observation is rather trite—or of the rebuke of the wise, judged absurd because their wisdom is vulnerable to lust for gain (v. 7).

Qoh 4:13-16 is obscure, largely because of unclarity in the antecedents of the pronouns. In 4:16, what is called *hebel* is probably the entire situation described: a poor youth rising by virtue of his wisdom to the heights of power only to pass his office on to another and be forgotten by the masses. This anecdote shows that the wisdom that gains political power is subject to an absurd fate just like the wisdom that gains wealth (2:21).

(1d) Speech (6:11; 5:6)

Many words increase *hebel* (6:11). What is it that they increase? Surely not transitoriness; not even futility, for while a lot of words may be futile, there is no more futility after than before they are spoken. What increases with such talk is the quantity of irrationality in the world. The context of 6:11 concerns disputes with "one [God] who is stronger than he [man]" (6:10). In such a dispute, words are only meaningless, ridiculous sounds.

Qoh 5:6, where the plural is used, is obscure, but since the verse warns against excessive words (again in the context of speaking to God; cf. v. 1), *hăbalim* probably bears a sense close to that of *hebel* in 6:11.

(2) Living beings and times in their lives (3:19; 11:10; 6:12; 7:15; 9:9)

If *hakkol* in 3:19 means "both" man and beast, then "ephemeral", rather than "absurd", could be the best translation of *hebel* here. Nevertheless, the overtones of absurdity are carried over to this usage too. For Qohelet, ephemerality usually entails absurdity, for it obliterates distinctions that are essential if human effort is to be rationally rewarded. If, however, *hakkol* in 3:19 means "everything", as in 1:2 and 12:8, Qohelet is saying that the reason man has no advantage over beast is that both live in an irrational world that overrides meaningful distinctions.

In 11:10 the time of youth is called *hebel*. Here alone something is called *hebel* in order to emphasize its preciousness. While youth may be absurd in various ways, that quality is not the point of this statement, for Qoh 12:1 shows that it is the brevity of youth that increases the urgency of seizing the opportunities it offers. "Ephemeral" is therefore the word's primary meaning in this verse. The absurdity of youth (or its futility, triviality, or any other negative quality besides ephemerality) would not be a reason for enjoying it. Nevertheless, the connotations of absurdity the word bears elsewhere are not absent from this occurrence. Though youth is precious, it is rendered absurd, as is life itself, by its brevity. Like toil, its significance is inevitably undone. Like pleasure and growing wise, it is at once absurd and good.

In 6:12, 7:15, and 9:9, *hebel* refers to human life in general, and it is impossible to determine just what Qohelet has in mind; "ephemeral" or "absurd" (or a number of other adjectives) could apply equally well.

It may be that all five occurrences under this rubric resist the understanding of *hebel* as absurdity. I would, however, maintain that the connotation of absurdity, established in the great majority of occurrences, carries over even to cases where the primary denotation is "ephemeral".

(3) Death (11:8)

Death, being *sui generis*, is a category by itself. In 11:8, *kol šebba'*, "all that comes" (sc., after life) refers to all that comes after death. We should enjoy ourselves now, Qohelet emphasizes, because we can expect nothing better after death. None of the meanings usually ascribed to *hebel* is appropriate here. Death (not the process of dying, but the eternity spent in death) is not futile (it is not an effort with goals that can be frustrated); it is not vain or trivial (it is of ultimate existential significance and overwhelmingly powerful); it certainly is not transient. And *hebel* never means literal nothingness. Qohelet is probably warning us not to expect greater meaning or rationality after death than we face before it. In 3:19-20 Qohelet implies that if different beings had a different fate in death, death might be other than absurd. But he brushes this possibility aside, and death retains its absurdity for him.

(4a) Divine justice (8:10, 14 [twice])

Some of the passages discussed in other categories (especially 2:15, 26; 6:1-2; 9:1-2) could go here as well, for they speak of inequities whose source is in God's rule. One passage, however, focuses directly on divine behavior, no human action being concomitantly judged absurd. Unlike the uses in the following category, this verse describes a particular type of divine action, rather than the entire scope of God's activity in this world.

In 8:11-13 Qohelet describes a single absurdity: a sinner may live a long life. In v. 14 Qohelet generalizes: some people receive a fate contrary to the one they deserve. Not only do the wicked and righteous both die (in itself an absurdity), but the righteous sometimes die younger than the wicked. This radical disjunction between moral deserts and fate is the epitome of absurdity.

"This too is *hebel*" in 8:10b probably introduces 8:11-14 and refers to the same inequity described in 8:11-14 (see commentary). If, however, this phrase concludes the preceding observation (8:10a), the antecedent of "this" is still an inequitable situation: the wicked receiving a fine burial while the corpses of the righteous lie unattended.

(4b) "Everything" (1:2; 12:8; 9:1; 6:4)
Hebel in 1:2 and 12:8 must be used in the sense predominant in the book, for those verses summarize Qohelet's thought and encapsulate his *hebel*-judgments. Qohelet is calling everything absurd.

> *Hăbel hăbalim, 'amar qohelet, hăbel hăbalim, hakkol habel* (1:2 [12:8])

The statement, "Everything (that happens in life) is absurd", unlike the statements produced by the other renderings of *hebel*, comprehends most of what Qohelet describes, even in passages where he does not use the formulaic *hebel*-judgment. That is to say, Qohelet describes many situations, such as the fool being given high status (10:5-7—a *ra'a*) or the wise man being forgotten by the city he saved (9:13-15), which, though not called *hebel*, are indeed absurd. Understanding *hebel* in the sense of "absurd" thus brings out the book's unity in a way that a less generally applicable translation (such as "vain", "insignificant", or "fleeting") does not. See further the discussion in the commentary.

Hakkol, "everything", itself requires further specification. In 1:2 it refers not only to the human life span or to worldly goods (understandings implicit in traditional interpretations), for Qohelet is disturbed not by the brevity of life so much as by what happens within it, and the triviality of worldly goods is not one of his concerns at all. On the other hand, Qohelet does not speak of realms of reality beyond this world, but leaves them aside as irrelevant.

The scope of "everything" can be restricted further, for Qohelet is actually concerned only with what happens in human life. (Natural phenomena are described in 1:4-8 only because they are perceived as illustrating in large the futility of human efforts, and animals are mentioned in 3:19 only by way of human fate.) Other realms of existence may not be characterized by the qualities he sees in human life. *Hakkol* in 1:2 and 12:8 is therefore synonymous with *kol 'ăšer na'ăśah taḥat haššemeš* (and variants), "all that happens under the sun", in 1:9, 13, 14; 2:17; 8:17; 9:3, 6.

Hakkol hebel, understood as speaking of the *events* of human life, encompasses likewise the *hebel*-judgments describing actions (toiling, speaking, getting wisdom) and experiences (pleasure), for these prove absurd in the context of absurd events.

"Everything" is not truly universal, even within the range of the events of human life. It is not, after all, absurd (or, if one prefers, "vain" or "futile" or "nothing", etc.) that wisdom proves more beneficial than an inheritance (7:11) or that one's property may be damaged if he fails to pay his vows (5:5). It is not absurd (or "futile" or "vain" or "nothing") that wisdom saved a city (9:13-15)—only the subsequent treatment of the wise man was absurd. It is not absurd that "God will judge the righteous and the wicked" (3:17); the absurdity lies in the delay in the execution of the sentence. *Hakkol* refers not to every event but to events in general, to life's occurrences taken as a whole. A bad day is made so by a few things—sometimes even one—going wrong, though most of what happens that day may be satisfactory. Similarly, within the totality of events many things are not absurd—some important values stand, some fundamental rules are valid—but the absurdities spoil everything.

In 9:1-3 Qohelet applies *hebel* to "everything" in different words. Qoh 9:1 continues and reformulates the idea of 8:16-17, according to which no one, however wise and diligent, can apprehend *ma'ăśeh ha'ĕlohim*, that which God brings to pass, reformulated as *hamma'ăśeh 'ăšer na'ăśah taḥat haššemeš*, the events that occur under the sun (8:17). What God makes happen in an individual life is an expression of divine "love" and "hate". But because events are not coordinated with deeds, God's "love" and "hate", his favor and disfavor, are opaque.

"Everything one sees is *hebel*" (9:1bβ; see commentary) takes up the notion that "man has no knowledge of [God's] love or hate" (9:1bα) and goes beyond it. God's will is not only mysterious; it is in some regards a manifest violation of reason. God imposes the same fate on all people, regardless of their individual behavior. Even when a person does receive an appropriate fate during his lifetime, death sets the seal on life's absurdity.

In 6:4 *hebel* is an epithet of life—not the individual lifetime (for which see above, category 2), but the whole sphere of human existence. (In this verse *hebel* is not predicated of the events of life, but serves as a trope for them.) *Hebel* does not mean "ephemerality" here, because life's brevity would not be a reason for the claim that one who experienced life was worse off than the stillbirth, whose existence was, after all, less than brief. *Hebel* is rather a quality worse than nothingness, worse, in fact, than pointlessness, for the existence of the man who loses his wealth is no more pointless than the stillbirth's. But his existence is more *absurd*, for he has seen and suffered life's irrationality.

§1.2 *"Everything is absurd": assumptions and implications*

Qohelet's application of the word *hebel* is rooted in the meanings it commonly has elsewhere in the HB (see above, §1.11). "Absurd" would seem to be an appropriate translation of *hebel* in many of the word's occurrences outside Qohelet too, because ephemerality, inefficacy, and deceitfulness are indeed absurd if permanence, efficacy, or reliability are expected of the phenomena that have these failings. Nevertheless, the use of *hebel* in Qohelet is distinctive; nowhere else is *hebel* predicated of an event. Moreover, whereas *hebel* is elsewhere applied to the irrationality of some persons and actions, it does not elsewhere imply a violation of the rationality of the world. Qohelet extends the application of this word because he is probing not so much the reasonableness of human actions as the reasonableness of the system in which they occur.

An action may be called absurd in condemnation either of its performance or of its outcome. When the intention is to condemn the performance, the performer is blamed, for he could have avoided the absurdity simply by desisting from the action. This is the way in which one might call idolatry or drunkenness absurd. When, however, we believe that an action is in principle ethically good, or at least neutral, and yet find that it does not yield what we consider proper results, then it is not essentially the action that is absurd but rather the *fact* that there is a disparity between rational expectations and the actual consequences. When Qohelet calls laboring for wealth and growing wise absurd he is in fact bemoaning the irrational treatment of these actions by events. This treatment renders the human condition absurd, whether one chooses a life of laziness and folly or of industry and wisdom.

Qohelet's evaluation of human effort is thus not (contrary to a common understanding of the purpose of the book) meant as advice to take it easy, to enjoy life's gifts as they come. Taking it easy is not really something one can choose. Qohelet feels that some people—he has himself in mind—are driven by an insatiable ambition into an incessant striving for more and more, whether of wisdom or wealth (6:7). Qohelet knows he is laboring for no one's benefit (4:8), yet finds himself unable to stop. Since this constant, fruitless striving is forced on the "offender" by God himself (2:26), there is little hope of escape. Likewise, whether one is allowed the prerequisites of pleasure is dependent on God's will (2:26; 3:13; 6:2; etc.).

Qohelet speaks of futile activities not in order to warn against them so much as to muster the fact of that futility as evidence for the absurdity of life. The book of Qohelet, taken as a whole, is not primarily lamenting the brevity of life or exposing the vanity of worldly wealth and pleasures. Qohelet is not at root saying that everything is insubstantial, or transitory, or useless, or trivial. He does indeed observe these qualities in many beings and actions, but he mentions them mainly to reinforce and exemplify his main complaint, the irrationality of life as a whole.

Underlying Qohelet's *hebel*-judgments is an assumption that the system *should* be rational, which, for Qohelet, means that actions should invariably produce appropriate consequences. In fact, Qohelet stubbornly expects them to do so; see 3:17; 5:5; 7:17; 8:12b-13. Qohelet believes in the rule of divine justice. That is why he does not merely resign himself to injustice. He is shocked by it: it clashes with his belief that the world *must* work equitably. Injustices are offensive to reason. And the individual absurdities are not mere anomalies. Their absurdity infects the entire system, making "everything" absurd.

"Everything is absurd" is finally a complaint against God, one put more directly in 7:13, *rᵉ'eh 'et ma'ăśeh ha'ĕlohim, ki mi yukal lᵉtaqqen 'et 'ăšer 'iwwᵉto*, "Observe what God has brought to pass: no one can straighten what (God) has twisted". That "twisting" or distortion is the severance of deed from consequence, which severance strips human deeds of their significance.

For Qohelet the reliability of the causal nexus fails, leaving only fragmented sequences of events, which, though divinely determined, must be judged random, and thus meaningless from the human perspective—and any other perspective does us no good. The vision of the absurd is, quite literally, de-moralizing; it fills the heart with "evil" and "inanity" (9:3). When the belief in a reliable causal order fails, human reason and self-confidence fails with it. But this failure is what God intends, for after it comes fear, and fear is what God desires (3:14).

§1.3 *R^e'ut ruaḥ*

Since in all but two of its nine occurrences the phrase *ra'yon/r^e'ut ruaḥ*[13] is appended to a *hebel*-judgment and thus has precisely the same context, it is extremely difficult to distinguish *r^e'ut ruaḥ* from *hebel*; it may be a synonym or a distinct concept. There are no occurrences of the phrase outside Qohelet that might give us an independent bearing on its meaning. We can, however, attempt to infer the special meaning of *r^e'ut ruaḥ* by considering the reasons given for the judgment in passages where this phrase is added to *hebel* and in passages where *r^e'ut ruaḥ* is used alone. (Because it is used alone only twice, it is not possible to grasp its precise nuance there.) While "pursuit of the wind" is probably its literal meaning, the term is a metaphor referring to the emotional effect on the "pursuer", i.e., his "vexation". If *hebel* is primarily an intellectual judgment ("absurd", "contrary to reason"), *r^e'ut ruaḥ* is primarily an emotional one.

The etymology of *r^e'ut ruaḥ* is uncertain and of limited value in ascertaining its meaning.

(1) LXX's προαίρεσις πνεύματος, "choice/will of wind/spirit", equates *r^e'ut/ra'yon* with the same words in Aramaic.[14] But "a desire of the spirit" is a neutral phrase that would add nothing to the *hebel*-judgment, which, in any case, is not usually used in the context of desire.

(2) Three independent ancient translations agree in giving the phrase a psychological application. Syr (*ṭurapa' druḥa'*), Targum (*t^ebirut ruḥa'*), and Vul (*afflictio spiritus*[15]) all seem to associate the

13. There is no discernible semantic difference between *r^e'ut ruaḥ* (1:14; 2:11, 17, 26; 4:4, 6; 6:9) and *ra'yon ruaḥ* (1:17; 4:16). They appear in the same constructions and contexts and are handled the same in the Versions. I will use *r^e'ut ruaḥ*, the more common form, to refer to both.

14. Thus BDB, p. 946b. *Ra'yon* appears in MH as well (Jastrow, *Dict.*).

15. Thus in 1:14, 17; 2:17; 4:16. The phrase is rendered *afflictionem animi* in 2:11, *cassa solicitudo mentis* in 2:26, *cura superflua* in 4:4, and *praesumptio spiritus* in 6:9.

phrase with Aramaic Rʿʿ, "break". The resulting sense works well in all contexts, but the implied derivation is dubious, since RʿH/RʿY (from which the forms *reʿut* and *raʿyon* are derived) does not appear as a by-form of the Rʿʿ that means "break".

(3) Most modern commentators translate *reʿut ruaḥ* as "pursuit of the wind", comparing Hos 12:2, where *roʿeh ruaḥ* is parallel to *rodep qadim*, "pursues the east wind", deriving *reʿut* from RʿH, "busy oneself with, pursue". (A derivation from Aramaic RʿY, "desire", gives a similar meaning.) Compare also *roʿeh zonot*, "one who busies himself with [or 'pursues'] prostitutes (Prov 29:3). Another problem is whether *ruaḥ* is an objective genitive (thus, "pursuit of the wind") or a subjective genitive ("the spirit's pursuit"). Staples (1943:96) argues for the latter, comparing *raʿyon libbo* in 2:22. But *libbo* has a possessive suffix and would not be an exact syntactic analogy. In any case, *reʿut ruaḥ* in the sense of "the spirit's pursuit" would be a neutral phrase, not a negative evaluator that would strengthen a *hebel*-judgment.

The parallel to Hos 12:2 makes the translation "pursuit of wind" the most likely, but we cannot move directly from it to the meaning of the phrase in Qohelet. First of all, we must decide what is implied by having the "wind" as the object of a pursuit. "Pursuit of the wind" may convey the notion of chasing after something that cannot be caught. But in Qohelet the activities called *reʿut ruaḥ* do attain their immediate goals; the problem is that the activity of pursuit (when this is present in the context) and the objects of desire turn out to be unpleasant. Thus the phrase, as Qohelet uses it, points to the psychological experience of the pursuer rather than to a characteristic (such as elusiveness) of that which is being pursued. Furthermore, some of the phenomena called *reʿut ruaḥ* are not efforts or strivings that can literally be called pursuits, but are instead events or situations. "Vexation" (or, where appropriate, "vexatious"), which can be predicated of both activities and events, is a suitable translation of the metaphor, whether we derive *reʿut* from *RʿH (Rʿʿ), "break", or from RʿH, "busy oneself with", "pursue".

Reʿut ruaḥ is used in the following contexts (numbered as above):

(1a) Toil and its products
—skilled work (4:4), because it is actually self-destructive envy.

—all Qohelet's work and toil (2:11); on the reason for this judgment, see above, §1.12.

—one man toiling and another receiving the product (2:26). Understanding *r^e'ut ruaḥ* as pointless pursuit here would require taking the antecedent of "this" to be the toil of the disfavored man, and it would be banal to call such toil merely "pointless". In 2:21 Qohelet calls the same situation (and there it is undoubtedly the *situation* that is being judged) "a *hebel* and a great evil". Similarly, in the closely parallel passage, 6:1-2, *ḥoli ra'*, "an evil sickness", replaces *r^e'ut ruaḥ*. These interchanges suggest that "pursuit of wind" is a type of affliction.

—a concomitant of toil. Only in 4:6 is *r^e'ut ruaḥ* not in the predicate of an evaluative sentence: "Yet better one handful earned calmly than two fistfuls of wealth with vexation [*'amal ur^e'ut ruaḥ*]". *R^e'ut ruaḥ* does not refer to a completely fruitless effort—for toil with *r^e'ut ruaḥ* can gain two handfuls. Rather, *r^e'ut ruaḥ* is a concomitant of toil and an antonym of *naḥat*. *Naḥat* does not mean merely inactivity, but relaxation, ease, security (see commentary). This verse, one of the two in which *r^e'ut ruaḥ* is not conjoined to *hebel*, helps distinguish the two terms. *Hebel* could not be substituted for *r^e'ut ruaḥ*, since the sentence does not describe an absurdity (or a "futility", or a "vanity", or an "ephemerality", if one prefers those translations of *hebel*).

(1b) Pleasure

—the experience of pleasure (6:9). We should note that "the sight of the eyes" is a psychological experience, and while it might be called an activity in the broadest sense, it is not in itself a laborious occupation.

(1c) Wisdom and growing wise

—attaining wisdom and knowledge (1:17; *hebel* is not used here).[16] The next verse explains this judgment: increasing wisdom increases one's anger and pain. The reasoning in these verses shows that to call an activity a *ra'yon ruaḥ* does not mean that it is entirely futile (since wisdom can be obtained and increased; v. 16) or useless (since Qohelet often speaks of wisdom's benefits; e.g., 2:13-14a; 8:1b).

16. The object of this judgment is only wisdom, not wisdom and folly; see comment ad loc.

—an inequity: a poor youth rising by wisdom only to pass his power and popularity on to another (4:16). *Rᵉʿut ruaḥ* is not predicated of an activity—there is none in the immediate context—but of a situation, one of whose components is a pursuit.

(4b) "Everything"

—all the events (*ma'ăśim*) that occur under the sun (1:14), and—"everything", sc., "the events that occur under the sun" (2:17). Again, events comprise more than activities. Here "vexatious" is an especially appropriate interpretation of the metaphor because Qohelet says that these things distressed him (lit., were "bad upon" him) and made him "disgusted with life".

While *rᵉʿut ruaḥ* may be translated "pursuit of the wind", this metaphor should be understood as indicating the psychological state of the pursuer, in other words, his vexation. This brings us close to Vulgate's *afflictio spiritus*, though the sense is derived differently. "Vexation" is close enough to "absurdity" in range of applicability to be easily collocated with it for emphasis, yet sufficiently distinct to make it more than a mere repetition. The connotation of vexatiousness I take from the occurrences that focus on the irritation that the phenomenon in question causes the human spirit, an irritation elsewhere expressed by such terms as *ka'as*, *mak'ob*, and *ra' 'elay*, and defined by contrast with *naḥat*.

Chapter 2

TOIL AND PLEASURE

> On ne découvre pas l'absurde sans être tenté d'écrire quelque manuel du bonheur.
>
> Camus, *Le Mythe de Sisyphe*, p. 167

§2.0 *The problem*

Qohelet's experiment with pleasure produced results that pull in two directions. He begins:

> (2:1) I said in my heart, "Come, let me make you experience pleasure [*śimḥah*] and have enjoyment [*r*^{e}*'eh b*^{e}*ṭob*]. But I realized that it too is an absurdity. (2) Of amusement [*śeḥoq*] I said, "Inane!" and of pleasure, "What does this accomplish?"

After trying out various pleasures, he concludes:

> (10) Whatever my eyes saw I did not withhold from them. I did not restrain my heart from any type of pleasure, so my heart got pleasure through all my toil, and this was my portion [*ḥeleq*] from all my toil.

Then he seems to change his mind:

> (11) But when I turned to consider all the things my hands had done and the toil I had laboriously performed, I realized that it was all an absurdity and a vexation, and that there is no adequate gain [*yitron*] to be had under the sun.

If pleasure is inane and absurd and not a *yitron*, in what way is it a good portion? This chapter considers how toil fails and pleasure succeeds. We begin by looking at the vocabulary for toil and its desired products, and for pleasure and related concepts.

§2.1 *Terminology*
§2.11 *Toil and its products*
§2.111 *'amal* (noun and verb) and *ma'ăśeh*

Throughout the HB, *'amal*[1] carries heavily negative connotations. It commonly connotes burdensomeness without necessarily denoting labor. Thus Job 16:2, *m^enaḥămey 'amal kull^ekem*, "you are all burdensome comforters", or Ps 73:16, *'amal hi' b^e'eynay*, "it was a burdensome/futile task in my eyes". *'amal*, when referring to effort, always implies arduous, strained effort, "overdoing" rather than "doing". Outside Qohelet, it is usually not applied to a type of effort (toil, strenuous labor) at all. The noun could mean "toil" (arduous labor) only in Pss 73:16; 107:12; Deut 26:7; Isa 53:11 (though in these verses too "misery" is an equally likely interpretation). The verb means "to toil" in Jon 4:10; Ps 127:1; Prov 16:26. The noun *'amal* often means "trouble" or "iniquity", and is frequently collocated with or parallel to words meaning "iniquity", "deceit", "futility"; for example: Isa 10:1 (//*'awen*); Ps 94:20 (//*hawwot*); Prov 24:2 (//*šod*); Ps 7:15 (with *'awen* and *šeqer*); and Hab 1:13 (//*ra'*). It may also mean "misery" (or "miserable person" *'amel*), as in Job 3:10, 20 (//*marey napeš*); 5:7; 7:3 (//*šaw'*); 11:16; Jer 20:18 (with *yagon*); Ps 10:14 (with *ka'as*).

'amal in Qohelet sometimes refers to life's strains in general, not only to occupational labors directed at gaining wealth. The word can be applied to any activity requiring special effort. It would not be used of activity that adjusts itself to reality, such as the sort Qohelet recommends in 9:10a (see commentary); 11:6; and (implicitly) 11:4. In Qoh 3:9,*'amal* clearly refers to efforts generally, since it follows a listing of a wide range of activities, most of them not remunerative. In 8:17, the verb *'amal* is applied to the search for understanding. In some other verses too it seems that *'amal* refers to "life's toil", or "life's drudgery"; see in particular 2:22; 2:24; 3:9; 4:9; 8:15; 10:15. Note further that 3:12 expresses the same idea as 3:13 and 2:24 (the latter employing similar language, but substituting *ḥayyayw*,"his life", for *'ămalo*, with no apparent change of meaning).[2] This usage

1. The writing *'amal* will be used to indicate both the noun *'āmāl* and the verb *'āmal* unless one or the other is indicated.

2. Qoh 3:13, in accordance with one of Qohelet's characteristic literary techniques, restates the preceding verse and expands on it, thus reinforcing the partial synonymity of *ḥayyim* and *'amal*.

does not represent a different meaning of *'amal* so much as a way of showing life's activities in a special perspective, speaking of them as if they were all part of a great, wearying task. This broad application of *'amal* has precedents in Job 3:10, 20, and 5:7.

A troublesome ambiguity encumbers the understanding of the terms for "toil" and "work": sometimes they refer to the activity of toiling, sometimes to the material fruits of that activity, namely earnings or wealth. Ginsberg states (rather apodictically) that *'amal* "almost always" means "acquire/possess" (*qnh wrḥš*) or "possessions" in Qohelet (p. 14).[3] *'amal* in this sense is unusual in BH. It is found elsewhere only in Ps 105:44 (and arguably in Prov 16:26), but Qohelet's vocabulary may be idiosyncratic in this regard as in others. Even if "earnings" were not one of the lexicalized senses of the word, "toil" could easily be used metonymically for the product of toil. Because of the uncertainty as to which sense is applicable in specific occurrences, I translate *'amal*, whenever possible, as "toil"/"to toil" (or "labor at") with the understanding that this might be a metonym for "earnings"/"to earn by toil". (In the paraphrastic translation I try to resolve the ambiguity, but do so without certainty.) By translating the verb as "to toil/labor at/for", we can preserve the nuance of toiling, regardless which of the two senses the noun has in a particular context.

In several occurrences of *'amal*, it is nearly impossible to decide which sense is most appropriate. In 2:10, for example, Qohelet can equally well be saying that he got pleasure (directly) from his earnings or (indirectly) from his labor. In 2:11 he may be calling his toil or his wealth absurd. And there are passages where he seems to vacillate rapidly between the two senses; see the commentary on 2:18-26, and consider especially v. 21. One may try to identify the most appropriate sense in any particular occurrence, and I do so in the commentary and paraphrase. But the grounds for decision are often extremely slight.

A similar problem arises with derivatives of 'ŚH. Ginsberg (p. 14) says that *'aśah* and *ma'ăśeh* sometimes mean "acquire" and "acquisitions" (as well as "do" and "make happen"; see §5.13). This is not a well-attested usage outside Qohelet, but *'aśah* clearly means "acquire" in Gen 12:5. *Ma'ăśim* can refer to material objects,

3. Rashbam assigned that sense to the word in 2:18, 19, 24. Ginsburg translates the noun as "gain" in 2:18, 19, 20.

especially in the phrase *ma'ăśeh yad* (Cant 7:2; Deut 4:28; Ps 102:26). But *ma'ăśim* alone does not seem to mean "property" or "wealth". Still, the semantic shift from deed to product is easy and attested for many words, and the term could well be used metonymically in Qohelet. In Qohelet, words derived from 'ŚH are often collocated with *'amal* (2:10, 11; etc.) or appear in equivalent contexts (3:22//3:11; etc.), so our decision on their meaning depends on our interpretation of *'amal*, the term with the more restricted range. There is, however, no ambiguity in 5:5, where *ma'ăśeh yad* undoubtedly means "property". In translation, the similar ambiguity of English "work" allows us to leave the question open, though occasionally synonyms must be used. Unlike *'amal*, words from 'ŚH do not in themselves connote unpleasantness or arduousness, although in a particular application they can receive this connotation by collocation with *'amal* (e.g., 2:11).

One may also ask whether there is any point in attempting to draw a distinction that the author seems indifferent to marking. In this case the answer is yes—in principle. The distinction between "toil" and "wealth" is the difference between cause and effect, and this is not merely a matter of nuance. After all, one might toil without earning anything, and someone else might receive another's earnings without having toiled for them. Even if Qohelet is vague or vacillant in his use of the word, he is quite aware of the actual distinction.

In passages where Qohelet affirms the value of *'amal* as a source of pleasure, the thematic (as opposed to the lexical) problem is less severe (2:10; 2:24; 3:13; 5:17; 8:15; 9:9; similarly 3:22 with *ma'ăśim*). Whether *'amal* means "toil" or "wealth" in those verses, it is clear that what is actually being praised is toil's product. Qohelet nowhere commends arduous labor for any intrinsic value such as, say, being a means of disciplining the spirit or occupying the mind. Toil is a source of pleasure only insofar as it provides the means of pleasure. Thus if *'amal* means "toil", the phrase *liśmoaḥ ba'ămalo* (and variants) does not mean "to take pleasure in his toil", for Qohelet does not preach the "joy of labor" (though he does urge simple activity for its own sake in 9:10). It may mean "to enjoy pleasure[4] during one's [life of] toil", or "to get pleasures by means of toil". The latter sense is more likely, because Qoh 8:15 seems to show that

4. *Śamaḥ* is undoubtedly used absolutely in 8:15 and 11:9 (in the latter it governs a temporal *bet*).

'amal means "toil" in the series of passages that speak of pleasure *b^e'amal*. There the usual phrase *liśmoaḥ ba'ămalo* is expanded into *w^eliśmoaḥ, w^ehu' yilwennu ba'ămalo*. Pleasure is more appropriately said to "accompany" a person in an *activity* than in a material possession. This ambiguity can be replicated by English "through his toil".

More is at stake when Qohelet *deprecates 'amal* for not creating its own compensation (1:3; 3:9) or for being absurd and vexatious (2:11). Is he calling wealth or toil an absurdity? In other words, is he warning against materialism or excessive effort? No syntactic features resolve the question.

In two key-verses, 1:3 and 3:9, Qohelet clearly speaks of toil not wealth. Since nothing in the poems preceding 3:9 and following 1:3 deals with remunerative work, the value of wealth is not at issue. The issue is undoubtedly the efficacy of arduous efforts. The similarity of 2:11 to 1:3 and 3:9 (all three deny that there can be any *yitron* in *'amal* "under the sun") suggests that *'amal* means "toil" in 2:11 as well.

The toil/earnings ambiguity faces us in several other verses, in particular 4:6, 8; 5:14, 15; 6:7. I will attempt to resolve the ambiguity of these verses in the commentary. In these verses too the solution is uncertain, but the problem may be partly circumvented by identifying the actual target of Qohelet's anger (see below, §2.21). However *'amal* is understood in a particular verse, the essential point is that Qohelet derives pleasure from his wealth, which was gained through toil, while he finds his toil inadequately compensated.

§2.112 *Ḥeleq*

Scholars have sought to differentiate *ḥeleq* from *yitron* in a way that would explain how a person can have the former (2:10) while lacking the latter (2:11).

The terms are commonly contrasted as antonyms opposed on an axis of time, with *ḥeleq* taken to mean "temporary gain".[5] To be sure, all possession is temporary, since it must end when life does. But the word *ḥeleq* does not in itself imply temporariness. In 9:6 it would be trivial to say that the dead have no more *temporary* portion among the living. Likewise, temporariness is not a component of the meaning of *ḥeleq* in 2:21, because we would not translate "but to one

5. See below, n. 7.

who has not toiled for it he will give it as his *temporary* portion", since Qohelet's point here is that a later man, if God-favored, may receive unearned benefits, not that these benefits are transitory. On the contrary, the complaint would be weakened if the word *ḥeleq* denoted the ephemerality of the unearned gain, for we would be reminded that the fortunate recipient is getting a merely temporary benefit. Furthermore, the portions that man can possess, according to Qohelet, may last as long as life itself (9:9).

Nor does *ḥeleq* mean a benefit received passively from God. One may, of course, gain a *ḥeleq* by good fortune (in Qohelet's formulation: God's favor—2:21, cf. v. 26), but also "from" (*min*) one's labor (2:10). In any case, Qoh 2:10-11 would lack meaning if Qohelet were complaining that as a result of his labors he passively received a benefit from God (a "*ḥeleq*"), but then saw that this was not an earned gain.

Galling's frequently quoted statement, that *ḥeleq* is "geradezu *terminus technicus* für den der menschlichen Existenz zugewiesenen Raum" (1969:89), is deficient as a definition, for instead of specifying what is distinctive about this word it encompasses the context common to *everything* in life. In any case, Galling's definition is awkward in context. Thus in 2:21 we cannot say that the toiler must turn over his wealth as the "space allotted to human existence" to "a man who has not worked for it". The fortunate successor already possesses the "space allotted to his existence"; he will receive something to enjoy within that "space". Galling's definition is likewise unsatisfactory in 5:18, where Qohelet declares that it is good for one to "take [NŚ'] his *ḥeleq*". This *ḥeleq* is not a man's allotted "space", since he fully possesses that independently of any volition on his part. It is something existing within the "space" allotted to a man, who can choose to take his *ḥeleq* or to ignore it.

The usual translation of *ḥeleq*, namely "portion", is adequate, so long as this is not understood to imply a part as opposed to the whole, contrary, for example, to W. Zimmerli (1963:135), who says: "Das Wort 'Teil' (*ḥeleq*) enthält bei Kohelet den Akzent der Begrenzung. Gott 'teilt' zu—das 'Ganze' behält er in seiner Hand". What could the "whole" be, on such an understanding, other than the whole world? But surely Qohelet is not complaining that he can have only a *part* of the world—a meaningless complaint, for how could one conceivably possess everything, and what would he do with it if he did?

In two verses the portion consists in material possessions (2:21; 11:2). More often the portion is the pleasure derived from possessions (2:10; 3:22; 5:17, 18; 9:9). More precisely, since Qohelet speaks of the possibility of having a portion without utilizing it, we may infer that one's portion consists in the potential for experiencing pleasure, rather than in the experience of pleasure in and of itself. A portion is, so to speak, a claim-chit, which God may give or take away. Even 2:21 allows for this understanding. To be sure, it is absurd that God may give a toiler's property to someone who did not earn it; but once it is transferred, the lucky recipient has the potential and the right to enjoy his new possessions. After all, this possession is a sign of God's special favor (2:26).

Having a portion does not necessarily entail being allowed to "take" (*naśa'*) it, to derive benefit from it:

> Furthermore, if God gives anyone wealth and property and enables him to partake of it and to take his portion and to have pleasure through his toil—that is a gift of God (5:18).

This verse shows that one might have a portion, i.e., have the right to pleasure—it is, in any case, "*his* portion"—yet fail to "take" it, if God so wills. For one to enjoy his portion, God must, of course, first grant the requisite wealth; but his special gift is to allow one to enjoy his portion (5:18b; 2:24; 3:13).

One's *ḥeleq* is something from which one properly *should* benefit, not only something that one possesses or might possess. Thus Qohelet can argue for his advice to take pleasure in one's wealth by reminding the reader that this is man's portion:

> And I saw that there is nothing better than that a man get pleasure through his activities, for that is his portion.
> . . . (3:22)

Similarly in 9:9. Refusing to take one's portion is a refusal to accept God's will.

Ḥeleq is applied to other types of experiences in 9:6:

> Even their love, their hatred, and their jealousy have already perished, and they no longer have any portion in all that happens under the sun.

One's portion in life here includes the potential to have emotions such as love, hatred, and jealousy.

§2.113 *Yitron* (*motar*, *yoter*)

Yitron means "advantage" (when two things are being compared) or "adequate gain" (when used absolutely).[6] *Yitron* (together with its synonyms *motar* and *yoter*) is commonly translated "profit". But this translation is problematic because Qohelet, who denies that *yitronot* derive from toil (see especially 1:3; 2:11; 3:9), nevertheless does find profit in that activity and others. The portion he received from toil—pleasure, which he will praise as "good" (2:24; 3:12, 22; 5:17; 9:7-9)—was surely a profit by any reasonable understanding of that word. Pleasure was the answer to the question, "What is good for man to do. . . ?" (2:4). One's *ḥeleq* may indeed be profitable.

The most common understanding of *yitron* is that it signifies an enduring gain (whereas *ḥeleq* is supposed to mean "temporary benefit"; see above).[7] But how long, by this understanding, must something endure to be a *yitron*? Wealth may endure until the end of one's life—Qohelet expects his own to do so (2:20-23)—and yet fail to be a *yitron*. And if *yitron* meant a gain that endures *beyond* life, the existence of a *yitron* would be precluded by definition for one who, like Qohelet, does not believe in a life beyond death. In any case, nowhere is ephemerality in and of itself given as the reason something falls short of being a *yitron*.

6. By this I do not mean "absolute profit", an unclear notion sometimes ascribed to *yitron*. I refer rather to the use of this word apart from comparisons, explicit or implied. In the section on wisdom's value (§3.32), I discuss the concepts of "absolute" and "relative" value as commentators have used them (misleadingly, in my view).

Yoter is an adverb meaning "very", "exceedingly", in 2:15 and 7:16. In 12:9 and 12 it is a conjunction meaning "furthermore", "at the same time".

7. Many commentators follow Plumptre in taking *yitron* as a commercial term meaning a surplus, a positive bottom-line on a balance sheet—in other words, a profit. The concept of profitability is then thought to extend metaphorically to temporal terms. Wölfel, for example, distinguishes the terms as follows: "Der erste [*yitron*] geht aufs Dauernde, der letztere [*ḥeleq*] bleibt im Zeitlich-vorläufigen. Er bleibt dabei im Bereich des materiellen Gütergenusses" (p.75; followed by Hertzberg, p. 89). This interpretation is found in Rashbam: "*mah yitron*: what reward or gain [*rewaḥ*] has a man in return for all the labour in which he engages under the sun, since at his end he passes out of the world and it will not be well with him?" (Japhet and Salters, 1985:92; the last clause should probably be translated "and he will have no more enjoyment").

When not comparative ("advantage"), *yitron* should be translated "adequate gain" or "return", rather than "profit". The difference between the two is significant: $10,000 a year realized from a business that demands twelve-hour days may be a profit, but it is not adequate compensation for the toil. It is not clear if the notion of adequacy is lexicalized in *yitron* or peculiar to Qohelet's application. If the latter, Qohelet might be using a word equivalent to English "profit" but in a heightened sense: "a *real* profit", "*significant* profit".

The senses of *yitron* are as follows:

(1) "Advantage" (comparative) (2:13 [twice]; 3:19; 5:8; 6:8, 11; 7:11, 12; 10:10)

Yitron in this sense takes its meaning from a comparison between two phenomena: one thing is, or possesses, or offers, something superior to something else. The object of comparison (that with which the subject is compared) is sometimes vague, especially when Qohelet is denying the existence of a certain advantage.

In four occurrences of *yitron*, the comparison is explicit, marked by *min* ("over"): 2:13 (twice; *yitron* is used); 6:8 (*yoter*); and 3:19 (*motar*). In other verses, the comparison is implicit, and the second term of the comparison is to be supplied from context: 10:10 (the advantage of the skilled man over others who must use brute force [*ḥăyalim*]); 7:11, 12 (the advantage of wisdom over wealth); 6:11 (the lack of advantage of much speech over silence, which is implicitly advised in vv. 10 and 12); and perhaps 5:8 (obscure, but there seems to be an implicit comparison between the land in this verse and the unfortunate state mentioned in the preceding one).

(2) "Adequate gain (1:3; 2:11; 3:9; 5:15; 10:11)

1:3 is fundamental to the consideration of Qohelet's views on compensation and profit. It should not be read as a categorical denial of the existence of either advantages or gains. Rather it asserts that *'amal*—strained, drudging labor, such as that of the natural forces in 1:4-8—offers no sufficient net gain.

2:11. For Qohelet, pleasure is certainly a positive value and *is* a profit (2:10). But since it is not, in Qohelet's view, meaningful or truly productive (2:1f.), it is hardly a reasonable return for the strain invested in earning it.

3:9. "What *yitron* does one who does something get from toiling?" (3:9). Here "toiling" ('ML) is distinct from "doing" ('ŚH), but the point of the verse is not the praise of the one over the other. Rather it teaches that strained labor is not adequately compensated, because man's efforts cannot significantly affect the divinely determined course of events. If you "do" something, there is no point in going further and straining at it.

5:15. The phrase, "for the wind" is tautological, emphasizing the negation of *yitron*. Nothing can be adequate repayment for a struggle whose rewards must be left behind.

10:11. The possessor of knowledge—in this case, knowledge of snake charming—receives no sufficient compensation for his knowledge if he does not use it soon enough.

§2.12 *Happiness and its synonyms*

The terms for happiness in Qohelet have been translated variously as "pleasure", "happiness", and "joy", but these imply quite distinct experiences. For practical purposes we may distinguish among them as follows.

Pleasure (as I will use the term) is not an independent, isolated emotion or sensation, but an experience or, more precisely, a concomitant of a more comprehensive experience. We may further distinguish between "a pleasure" (plural: "pleasures"), which is a thing or an action expected to produce (the feeling-tone of) pleasure,[8] and "pleasure" (no plural), which is the quality of experience defined above. "Pleasure" in the latter sense is synonymous with "enjoyment". "A pleasure" is an object of desire and a *means* to pleasure. One may indulge in "pleasures"—parties, movies, eating rich desserts—yet not get even momentary pleasure from them, let alone happiness.

Happiness sums up a state of consciousness, of which pleasure is only one factor. A person may be experiencing pleasure in one act (e.g., dining) while at the same time be feeling unhappy with life. The individual sets the criteria by which to make the reckoning: what aspects of life will be weighted (sexual pleasures, love, business success, and the like), and what period is taken into account (we may speak of a happy life, a happy year, etc.).

Joy refers to an intense form of happiness directed at a specific object ("joy" *in* one's children, etc.).

8. Duncker (1940:400) explains that pleasure is a "feeling-tone" inasmuch as it is not a feature of the external object, but a way in which it *affects me*, i.e., a way I 'feel'.

§2.121 *Śimḥah, śamaḥ*[9]

Śimḥah in Qohelet means pleasure, not happiness. Qohelet uses the word in one of the many senses available in BH, where the word is applied to the entire range of pleasant experiences, from deep joy to trivial diversions. Sometimes it means "happiness" or "joy" of the deepest sort (e.g., Isa 30:29; Pss 21:7; 122:1; 126:3). But it often, perhaps usually, means "pleasure", without necessarily implying happiness. It frequently refers to the activities of merrymaking, e.g., Esth 9:17f., 22 (*yom mišteh w^{e}śimḥah*); 1 Sam 18:6 (*śimḥah* refers to the sounds of merrymaking; it is coordinated with "tambourines" and "triangles"; cf. Gen 31:27). *Śimḥah* may be purely external, unaccompanied by any happiness. The doomed revelers in Isa 22:13 are certainly not happy. *Śimḥah* may even be pleasureless, as in Ps 137:4: "And our tormenters [demanded of us] *śimḥah*", i.e., merry song. It may refer to trivial and even self-destructive amusements, as in Prov 21:17: "One who loves *śimḥah* is an impoverished man. He who loves wine and oil will not grow rich".

Qohelet uses *śimḥah* in two ways: (1) "enjoyment", the sense of pleasure (the experience or feeling-tone) (= *śimḥah*-1), and (2) "a pleasure" (a thing or action expected to produce pleasure; e.g., wine and music) (= *śimḥah*-2). It is sometimes impossible to know which sense applies in a particular occurrence of *śimḥah*. In the repeated praise of pleasure (3:12;5:18; and 8:15 [twice]), ŚMḤ is ambiguous, as in 11:8. But both senses are clearly attested in the book.

> Examples of *śimḥah*-1 (the internal experience of pleasure): In 2:10 *libbi śameaḥ* is the outcome of his pleasurable activities, i.e., the result of "not withholding" his heart from any *śimḥah*. In 2:26 *śimḥah* is an internal state, like wisdom; likewise in 5:19; 9:7 (*//leb ṭob*); 10:19; and probably 4:16.

> Examples of *śimḥah*-2 (pleasurable things and actions, merrymaking): In 2:1, 2 and 10b (*mikkol śimḥah*), Qohelet refers to the pleasurable activities he tried, those listed in vv. 4-8. This is the meaning of *śimḥah* in the phrase *beyt śimḥah* (7:4; = *beyt mišteh* in 7:2). A verbal usage corresponding to *śimḥah*-2 is "to do pleasurable things", as in the sentence, *ś^{e}maḥ baḥur b^{e}yalduteyka* (11:9), which

9. For convenience I will use the word *śimḥah* as a concept that includes the ideas of the verbal and the adjectival derivatives of the root ŚMḤ. The different forms do not carry any special connotations besides those obvious from the morphosyntactic transformations.

advises the young man to *do* something, not to *feel* something (thus the parallel "follow your heart").

Śimḥah in Qohelet never means "happiness" (or "joy"), as the following considerations show.

(1) Qohelet lists some of the things that constituted his *śimḥah*—food, wine, gardens, singers, concubines, and so on. These are all pleasurable but do not yet constitute happiness.[10]

(2) Qohelet himself had a great deal of *śimḥah*, as he testifies, but little happiness, as he shows.

(3) Qohelet could not reasonably call *happiness* inane, absurd, and unproductive (2:1-2). Happiness is inherently a valuable state, whereas pleasure (in both senses) can be brittle and hollow, even while being "good" and, of course, pleasurable.

(4) There is no need to urge people to be happy; everyone wants happiness. All the more so is there no need to recommend "joy". On the other hand, it is not a truism to declare that pleasure—i.e., pleasurable activity—is the best thing to "do". On the contrary, it is a disputable proposition, one that can be affirmed only by insisting on the worthlessness of much else that is commonly thought valuable and conducive to happiness.

(5) It is pointless to *advise* happiness, because people cannot impose happiness upon themselves. They can choose to indulge in pleasures and to be aware of and sensitive to an experience, but they cannot directly induce happiness at will. On the other hand, the advice to undertake pleasurable activities and to enjoy them *can* be carried out; one can steep himself in pleasure even when his heart is heavy.

§2.122 *Ṭob* (noun, verb, and adjective)

Ṭob (= *ṭobah*) is the word of positive evaluation Qohelet uses most frequently. It means "beneficial", "efficacious",[11] "virtuous",[12] and

10. Nor does living with a woman one loves, though a more significant type of pleasure, in itself constitute happiness. Qohelet classes women—at best—with other means of pleasure.

11. Qoh 2:3, 24; 3:12, 22; 4:6, 9; 5:4, 17a; 6:9, 12; 7:1, 2, 3, 5, 8a, 8b, 11, 18; 8:15; 9:16 (or "virtuous"?), 18a (or "virtuous"?); 11:6. The verbal equivalent of *ṭob* in this sense is *yiyṭab*, "to benefit" (intran.), "be improved"; cf. 7:3b.

12. Virtuous person: 9:2 (twice); virtuous (behavior): 7:2; 12:14.

"good fortune", "fortunate".[13] I will here consider those uses that overlap the semantic field of *śimḥah*.

(1) Noun: *Ṭobah* = the experience of pleasure (equivalent to *śimḥah*-1): 4:8.[14] *Ṭob(ah)* in this sense usually occurs in the phrase *ra'ah (b^e)ṭob/ah)*, lit., "see good" = experience enjoyment: 2:1, 3:13, 5:17, 6:6, 2:24 (*her'ah 'et napšo ṭob*). *Ra'ah b-* in 2:1 may perhaps mean "scrutinize" or the like, but the evidence for this is slight.[15] Ginsberg (p. 92) explains R'H in this phrase as a variant of RWH, "drink one's fill, "be saturated". But "experience" is well attested as a meaning of R'H (BDB p. 907a), and furthermore Ginsberg's understanding of the phrase implies that Qohelet calls for nothing less than complete hedonistic satiation, and not simply enjoyment of what one possesses. Such satiation is an impossibility (6:7), whereas "seeing good" is possible and advisable.

(2) "Doing good" (*'aśah ṭob*) in the sense of doing pleasant things (= *śimḥah*-2): 3:12.

(3) Adjective:

(a) "Pleasing": 2:26 (twice); 7:26 (of divine pleasure); 11:7.

(b) "Pleased": 9:7.

(4) Verb:

y^eṭib^eka libb^eka = "let your heart give you pleasure": 11:9.

The sense of *ṭob(ah)* is determined by the same contextual factors that define *śimḥah*, and there seems to be no difference between the two words in their area of overlap. Outside Qohelet *ṭob* occasionally means "pleasurable", "pleasant" (sc., to the senses), e.g., Gen 41:5; Prov 24:13; Cant 1:3; see BDB p. 373b); in Esth 9:19, *yom ṭob* is synonymous with *śimḥah umišteh* (similarly v. 22). Elsewhere the connotation of pleasure usually derives from collocation with words

13. Noun: 7:14; 8:12, 13; 9:18b; adjective: 4:3, 9, 13; 6:3b; 7:10; 9:4.

14. *M^eḥasser 'et napši miṭṭobah* is equivalent to *mana'ti 'et libbi mikkol śimḥah* (2:10).

This might be the sense in 6:3 as well. But since *ṭobah* does not elsewhere have the article when it means pleasure, it is likely that here it means "goods", as in 5:10.

15. Podechard says that *b-* with verbs of perception, especially *ra'ah*, "indique un intérêt spécial pris à un objet" (p. 258); similarly BDB, pp. 907b-908a. Some occurrences definitely contradict Podechard's observation; e.g., 1 Sam 6:19 (even a glimpse, let alone scrutiny, of the ark would prove fatal); Esth 8:6 (it was not only scrutiny of the Jews' destruction that Esther could not bear; any perception of it would be too much).

that restrict the reference to sensual pleasantness, for example: *ṭub lebab* ("goodness of heart", "cheer") = *śimḥah* in Deut 28:47, similarly *ṭob leb* in Judg 16:25 (the merriment of feasting and intoxication); 1 Sam 25:36 (again, the merriment of drunkenness); *ṭob . . . lᵉma'ăkal*, "good to eat" (Gen 3:6). Outside Qohelet, *ṭob(ah)* by itself never unambiguously refers to pleasure of the sort that Qohelet speaks about; in some sentences, however, the nature of the "goodness" is equivocal. Outside Qohelet, the idiom *ra'ah ṭob* appears in Job 7:7 and 9:25; with *her'ah* in Ps 4:7. In these verses, *ṭob* seems to refer to happiness or good fortune (the usual sense of the word), rather than to pleasure.

§2.123 *Śᵉḥoq*

Śᵉḥoq, usually translated "laughter", may also mean "amusement", "merriment". "Laughter" is too restricted a translation for the word in 10:19, where it is a metonym for feasting. In 7:3 it seems to mean "laughter", or perhaps a favorable smile, the contrary of rebuke. Likewise in 2:2, *śᵉḥoq* (along with *śimḥah*) refers to pleasures such as described in 2:4-8. In 7:6 *śᵉḥoq* does refer to the sound of laughter, for it is compared to the noise of crackling thorns, but it also represents, pars pro toto, the noise of merrymaking, parallel to the "song" of fools (v. 5).

In none of these verses does Qohelet condemn *śᵉḥoq*, whether as "laughter" or as "merriment", in and of itself. The *śᵉḥoq* of the fool is, of course, irritating and meaningless (7:6), but that is because it is the fool's. When the noblemen prepare food and wine for *śᵉḥoq* (10:19), it is neither their food and wine *nor* their merriment that is contemptible, but their excess—they start in the morning and drink to drunkenness. Observe that in this verse, *śᵉḥoq* is what *food* produces, while wine makes for *śimḥah* (*yᵉśammaḥ*). This is the opposite of what we would expect if *śᵉḥoq* denoted frivolous or immoderate pleasure.

Thus *śᵉḥoq* does not denote trivial or contemptible amusement, although specific instances may refer to that sort of activity.[16] Nor is

16. Contrary to Glasser, among others, who gets all this out of the word *śᵉḥoq*: "Le rire est à entendre au sens péjoratif qu'il a en 7,3.6; c'est la vie dissipée, étourdissante et toute superficielle de l'insensé, lequel n'a jamais réfléchi à l'énigme de la condition humaine ou tout simplement manifeste son inconscience du sérieux de la vie" (1970:46).

that the word's necessary connotation elsewhere in BH. The most common meaning of the word in the HB is "mockery", but that connotation is not bound to the word. The *śᵉḥoq* of the returning exiles, for example, is quite different (Ps 126:2; cf. Job 8:21).

§2.124 *Śaba‘* (verb and noun)

In Qohelet, as elsewhere in the HB, *śaba‘* means both (1) "derive satisfaction from, enjoy" and (2) "be satisfied, sated", i.e., to the degree that one does not want more. Recognition of this dual meaning resolves an apparent contradiction as to whether Qohelet considers satisfaction possible (6:3) or impossible (4:8; 5:9; cf. 6:7). Deriving satisfaction from something (1) is, in Qohelet's opinion, possible, while being truly satisfied (2) is not. This distinction corresponds to the one between *ḥeleq*, a possible benefit of toil, and *yitron*, a truly sufficient—and unobtainable—profit.

Śaba‘ means (1) "derive satisfaction" when it governs *min*, "from"; and (2) "be sated with" when it governs a direct object. There are too few occurrences of *śaba‘ min* to determine whether the distinction is systematic.[17]

(1) "Derive satisfaction from": Qohelet says that a toiler has wasted his life if "his appetite does not receive satisfaction from [*lo’ tiśba‘ min*] his property" (6:3), implying that this result is both desirable and possible. It is equivalent to "experiencing pleasure [R’H *ṭobah*]" (6:6).

(2) "Be satisfied, sated": *Śaba‘* in this sense is synonymous with "be full", as in 6:7, "although the appetite is never filled". This is the sense in 1:8b, *lo’ tiśba‘ ‘ayin lir’ot* ("The eye is not sated with seeing"), where *tiśba‘* governs the infinitive as a direct object. Likewise in 4:8, the toiler works endlessly *gam ‘eyno lo’ tiśba‘ ‘ošer*, "and his eye is never sated with wealth"; thus he is driven always to strive for more. Further, one who loves money—seeking it as an end

17. *Śaba‘* used absolutely or with a direct object means "be sated, have one's fill"; e.g., Isa 1:11; 2 Chron 31:10; Mic 6:14. Possible exceptions are Ps 17:15 and Prov 5:10, where *śaba‘* + dir. obj. may mean "derive satisfaction from". *Śaba‘ min* usually means "derive satisfaction from"; e.g., Isa 66:11; Ps 104:13 (Job 19:22 is exceptional). *Śaba‘ min* means "be sated, "have one's fill" when the prepositional phrase specifies the kind of satisfaction rather than the agent, e.g., *middᵉrakayw yiśba‘ sug leb*, "a twisted-minded man shall be sated of his own ways" (Prov 14:14), that is to say, he will get his fill of what he does rather than of what he desires.

rather than as a means—*lo' yiśba' kesep*, "will not be sated with silver" (5:9). (A wise person would, we might say, *yiśba' min hakkesep*, "get satisfaction from money".) A similar nominal use is *haśśaba'* = i.e., a surfeit of property, "wealth" (5:11).

§2.2 *The evaluation of toil and pleasure*

§2.21 *The negative evaluation*

Why does Qohelet judge toil to be without adequate profit (1:3; 2:11; 3:9) and thus absurd (2:11)? After all, it produces wealth, and that makes pleasure, Qohelet's summum bonum, possible. (Wealth is not disparaged, but only its loss and the failure to make use of it.)

Qohelet's essential complaint in 2:1-11 is directed at the effort he invested in acquiring his wealth, not the wealth itself. He is not complaining of a failure intrinsic to property. He values wealth for providing the means of pleasure and is grieved at the thought of its loss. Although he is not fully satisfied with the pleasures wealth allows, they are still the best that life has to offer. Wealth, especially unearned wealth, is God's reward to his favorite (2:26). Earnings *gained through toil* may, to be sure, be infected by the absurdity of toil. But wealth, especially windfall wealth such as the fortunate man receives (2:18-26), is not intrinsically absurd or vexatious. It is not even "worthless" (if one prefers that translation of *hebel*), for if it were, it would not be a sign of God's favor to receive it or a sign of his disfavor to lose it. Thus whatever the meaning of *'amal* (and *ma'ăśim*) in 2:11, the true target of Qohelet's anger there is not his wealth. It is his toil, for that is both unpleasant and insufficiently rewarded. The fundamental question is one of justice, which for Qohelet translates into a question of rationality. Toil, for all its unpleasantness, does not yield the proper and expected benefits. In other words, Qohelet feels that the pay-off for his work was not big enough. Why, exactly, does toil fail to provide this?

(1) It fails by reason of its very nature. It is—almost by definition—oppressive (2:22f.). By choosing a term with such negative connotations to designate the type of effort he warns against, Qohelet is predetermining the issue. It is almost a tautology to say that *'amal* is absurd and vexatious. Whereas Qohelet advises "doing", as in 9:10a, "All that you are able to do, do in accordance with your strength [*k*^{e}*koḥăka*, see commentary]", he consistently warns against *'amal*, which could be translated "overdoing". His advice does not go contrary to conventional Wisdom. Qohelet's

attitude is similar to that of Prov 10:22: "The Lord's blessing is what makes one rich, and strain (*'eṣeb*) will add nothing to it". God's favor is not gained through passivity, but one cannot push beyond the blessing He grants. To attempt to do so is hybris.

And yet Qohelet is not content with realizing moderate, if uncertain, benefits from moderate toil. Qohelet recommends such contentment, but he himself is not satisfied. For Qohelet, if greater investment of effort does not produce a corresponding rise in rewards, the significance of human powers fails. Qohelet requires an *exclusive and proportionate causal relationship* between an effort and the outcome for that behavior to be adequately profitable, and of course he finds no such relationship.

(2) It is not efficacious. In 1:3-8, Qohelet draws an analogy to the prodigious labors of nature. Since their enormous efforts accomplish nothing new, human toil, however protracted or intense, certainly cannot do so.

In 3:9, Qohelet concludes that the cyclical actualization of event-types makes it impossible for an individual to effect something truly new. Every building up will be followed by a tearing down, every tearing down will be displaced by a building up. And God determines when this will occur. Human labor is truly Sisyphean: it can get its rock to the top of the mountain, but the rock will, sooner or later, roll down again, for rolling down has a time. And apart from the fact that the effects of an action will be obliterated by the occurrence of its opposite, the cyclical pattern of events overwhelms the *significance* of human actions even before their effects are wiped out. Deeds become as meaningless as words uttered into the wind.

(3) Even what toil can produce it cannot secure, for God interposes his inexplicable will between effort and outcome. Qohelet does not go so far as to conclude that man can effect nothing whatsoever. He often speaks of the wealth and pleasure that can be earned (he himself being a case in point), and he even gives advice on how to approach work (9:10; 11:6). There is, to be sure, a logical contradiction here, but there is a widespread tension between assertions of divine determination and the assumption of some degree of human freedom. This tension, which is perhaps inevitable in theism, is not usually felt to constitute a major problem.[18]

18. Compare the moderate determinism in Egyptian thought, which resembles that of Qohelet (and other Wisdom Literature); see Morenz and Müller, 1960.

(4) Toil's best product, pleasure, is hollow and ineffectual. Qohelet is by no means a "preacher of joy", as Whybray (1982) has designated him. Qohelet recommends "pleasure" not "joy" or "happiness".[19] He does not speak of *'ošer* or *gil*, terms that unequivocally do mean that. But even his praise of *śimḥah* is not wholehearted. The negative judgment in 2:1-2 is not overridden. It is sealed by 2:11 and reinforced by 7:2-4, where he declares it better to be in a house of mourning than in a house of feasting (*beyt mišteh* [7:2] = *beyt śimḥah* [7:4]).[20] Qohelet is ambivalent about what he recommends and vague in his reasons for recommending it.

Qohelet does not explain in what way he found pleasure inane and absurd, except insofar as his rhetorical question, "what does this accomplish [or "do"—*'ośah*]?" (2:2) means that pleasure has no significance beyond itself. Pleasures at best give pleasure; they are not productive deeds. It is not only the amusements of the fool that crackle with emptiness (7:6), but amusements of all sorts, however legitimate. For that reason they are "inane", like the gesticulations of a lunatic, and like them, they are absurd.

In attempting to eliminate the tension between the deprecation of pleasure and its commendation, commentators commonly distinguish two types of *śimḥah*, one recommended, the other condemned. The distinction usually drawn is between foolish, trivial, or degenerate forms of amusement (supposedly the objects of the investigation and repudiation in 2:1-11), and pleasures of a deeper, quieter sort, such as are more conducive to happiness. C. D. Ginsburg, for example, expresses the traditional understanding in speaking of Qohelet as denouncing "pleasure and mirth" while allowing "innocent cheerfulness and pleasure" (p. 276).

But the pleasures Qohelet disparages in 2:1-2, describes in vv. 4-9, calls his portion in v. 10, and indirectly judges absurd in v. 11, do not

19. Strictly speaking, he makes recommendations or gives counsel only in 9:7-10 and 11:8–12:1. Elsewhere he speaks *about* the value of pleasure. But such praise is tantamount to a recommendation, and we may speak of these statements as advice.

20. The point of this passage is not to condemn feasting as such, but to praise an open-eyed awareness of human mortality. Those who use merrymaking to avoid facing this fact are, Qohelet says, fools. It seems that the sort of amusement Qohelet commends is a private activity, not public feasting, but he does not draw this distinction clearly.

differ from those he lauds elsewhere. There is, first of all, no distinction in terminology; the same words are used in reference to pleasure in 2:1-2 as elsewhere in the book: *śimḥah*, *ṭob*, *ra'ah b^eṭob*, *ḥeleq b^e'amal* (2:1, 2, 10). *Ś^eḥoq* (v. 2), while not used in the positive passages, does not in itself denote trivial or vapid mirth (§2.123). Moreover, there is certainly no indication that the portion he calls *śimḥah* in 2:10 differs qualitatively from the portion he calls *śimḥah* elsewhere.

The diversions described in 2:4-9 are neither trifling nor improper. They are all reasonable forms of enjoyment, indisputably legitimate for a king who gained his wealth through wisdom. The enjoyment of wine too is permissible and recommended. Its anesthetic value is appreciated by Proverbs (31:6f.), and Qohelet himself commends it several times (9:7; etc.; "drinking" [2:24; 3:13; etc.] refers, of course, to the drinking of wine). The sages would, of course, condemn excess in eating and drinking, as Qohelet does in 10:17, 19, but nothing suggests that Qohelet got drunk. To be sure, MT of 2:3 says that he decided to "seize folly" until he could discover what is good for man to do. But this cannot mean that the *śimḥah* described in vv. 4-8 was a special type of pleasure, namely foolish pleasure, for if these deeds were foolish, then 2:10, Qohelet's summary of this experiment, would mean that man's portion and best activity is *foolish* pleasure, inasmuch as the pleasures he calls his portion in v. 10 are none other than those described in vv. 4-10. If MT *le'ěḥoz b^esiklut* (2:3) is to be maintained, "to seize folly" might be construed as another negative judgment on pleasure in general. But we should probably read *w^elo' 'oḥez b^esiklut*; see the commentary.

Hertzberg (followed by Lauha) distinguishes two types of pleasures according to the way they are obtained. Foolish pleasures, "der Weg der Torheit" (p. 86), are those that are reflective, i.e., deliberately sought after, while wise pleasures are unreflective, i.e., they are not a goal, not pursued, but rather are given by God to a passive recipient. Yet Hertzberg's distinction does not hold either, because the passages that recommend *śimḥah* also speak of the pleasure that comes from one's toil, that is to say, from the wealth toil may bring. Although it is true, of course, that excessive striving can prevent enjoyment of pleasures, that is because the toiler forgets to make enjoyment an immediate goal, not because he aimed at attaining it. Zimmerli, we may note, describes the rejected pleasures as "das blinde Sich-

Hingeben an die Freude" (p. 157), nearly the opposite of Hertzberg's description. But neither description is to the point, because Qohelet does not distinguish two types of pleasure. The wise course is to enjoy pleasures—deliberately, but without excessive strain. Although one should not strain or toil for pleasure, because toil is itself painful and restricts the time one might devote to pleasure, the pursuit of pleasures need not prevent their enjoyment, if one pauses to enjoy them.

Gordis seeks to resolve the problem differently. He recognizes that it is physical pleasure that Qohelet describes and recommends in 2:1-10. But, in Gordis's view, Qohelet "denies that pleasure is an adequate goal in life, in the "*absolute* or philosophical sense—but it remains the only *practical* program for human existence" (p. 216). Pleasure falls short because it is not an 'enduring good' (p. 139). Barton too regards pleasure's ephemerality as its true failing (p. 47, and see his remarks on 2:1-11, 24). But, contrary to this harmonization, Qohelet is not holding out for a permanent good and rejecting whatever is transient. He is not *that* demanding. He is looking for what is good for man in this life--"under the sun". Qohelet never condemns pleasure for its ephemerality. It is arbitrary to allocate his positive judgments to permanent benefits (of which there can be none) and his negative judgments to transitory ones. Furthermore, Qohelet is looking for anything good (2:3), not just an "absolute" or "philosophical" good (whatever that may mean). To say that something is "inane" and "absurd" and "achieves nothing" does not merely mean that it falls short of absolute value.[21] Qohelet may indeed be recommending pleasure as a "practical good", as Gordis says, but this label does not ease the tension between the two judgments. The pleasures called inane in 2:1-2 are, after all, the product of a practical program; they are not "absolute" or "philosophical" values.

Qohelet's ambivalence toward pleasure is psychologically plausible. A person may be having fun at a party while deep down being depressed and feeling that the pleasure is meaningless, even ridiculous—"Even in merriment the heart may hurt" (Prov 14:13).

21. Gordis paraphrases Qohelet's negative judgment on pleasure as a limp demurral: "He then discovers that pleasure is no more satisfactory than wisdom as an attainable goal" (p. 139). But pleasure surely *is* an attainable goal—as is wisdom (see 2:16f.).

But then, out of the very melancholy that darkened the fun, he may conclude that since everything else is so dreary, pleasure is, all in all, the best available option. Qohelet's duality is of this sort: he recognizes that something may be *hebel* and yet have good aspects; this is true of pleasure, of toil, of growing wise, and of life as a whole.

§2.22 *The positive evaluation*
More often and more emphatically Qohelet *praises* pleasure. He says it is "good", i.e., beneficial (2:24; 3:12, 22; 5:17; 8:15), man's "portion" (2:10; 5:17; 9:9), favored by God (9:7), and a gift of God (2:24, 26; 3:13; 5:18).

Pleasure, he says, is the best thing in life (3:22). In fact, he says (though probably in hyperbole) that it is the *only* good thing:

> So I praised pleasure, because there is nothing good [*'eyn ṭob*] for man under the sun except [*ki . . . 'im*] to eat, drink, and experience enjoyment [*ṭob*] . . . (8:15a; cf. 3:12).

However long one lives, if he has not experienced pleasure, he is no better off than the stillbirth, because both have the same end (6:6). This implies the converse, that the life of one who does experience pleasure is at least a little better than non-existence. Therefore Qohelet recommends the enjoyment of pleasures throughout life (11:7), but especially in youth, for the ability to enjoy oneself dissipates with age (11:9-12:1).

Qohelet's endorsement of pleasure is especially expansive in 9:7-9: eat and drink in pleasure, wear white garments, anoint yourself with oil, and enjoy life with a beloved woman, for this is what God wants you to do (v. 7b). In other words, it is the portion allotted you. But we must still ask, why does Qohelet consider this portion good?

The one specific benefit of pleasure that Qohelet mentions is oblivion: one who is permitted to enjoy the fruits of his labor "will not much call to mind the days of his life, since God is keeping him occupied with his heart's pleasures" (5:19). Pleasure is an anodyne to the pain of consciousness. To be sure, this did not work in Qohelet's case, at least not for long. Nevertheless, the pain of lucidity (1:18) is not for everybody, and Qohelet can recommend for others an escape that he denies to himself. But Qohelet does not return to this line of reasoning except to counter it in 7:2, and it does not have an important role in his thought.

Qohelet most frequently argues for his advice by testimonial, telling that he "realized" or "found" pleasure to be good (3:12, 22; 5:17; 8:15). Pleasure is good because it feels good, even if it confers no benefits outside the experience itself. There is a certain circularity inherent in his choice of words. In Qohelet's vocabulary, "good" is a term for pleasure (2:1; 3:13; 5:17; etc.). His frequent use of *ṭob* to designate pleasure, a usage not common elsewhere, thus has a rhetorical function; it makes the commendation of pleasure seem self-evident: experiencing *ṭob* is *ṭob*. Of course, this tactic may be Qohelet's way of convincing himself as well as others.

Qohelet most often motivates his counsel to enjoy life's pleasures by stating that this is man's portion.

> [Enjoy yourself throughout your life] because that is your portion in your life and in your toil. . . (9:9).

The fact that an experience is one's portion is, for Qohelet, a reason it *should* be embraced. To understand the force of this reasoning we should examine what contexts lead into the advice to enjoy life:

(1) Unjust distribution of rewards
- (a) One man toils and another gets the wealth the first man earned (2:20-26).
- (b) A man toils and earns wealth, then loses it suddenly (5:12-19).
- (c) The righteous and the wicked do not always get the fate they deserve; deeds do not determine destiny (8:14-15).

(2) Human ignorance
- (a) Man is unable to apprehend what God brings to pass (3:10-13).
- (b) Man cannot know what comes after death (3:21).

(3) Death
- (a) Death wipes out distinctions between man and beast (3:19-20).
- (b) All trace of the dead disappears (9:5-10).
- (c) Death goes on for a long time (forever?) (11:7-10).

The common denominator in all these passages is the theme of *ineffectuality*. Humans cannot affect what happens to them. They cannot secure wealth by hard work or assure long life by righteousness. They are ignorant of the future and thus cannot plan for it. They cannot hold on to existence or even traces of existence, such as a remembrance. Secure possession of wealth, knowledge, and life are thus not man's portions; pleasure is. Qohelet observes that this is what God gives humans—some of them. When Qohelet's frustration at human helplessness peaks, he advises pleasure. It is almost a counsel of despair. We cannot do much, but this at least we can choose—if God allows us the means to do so. If we are given the means of pleasure, it is within our power to enjoy it. Qohelet teaches a true carpe diem: seize the moment, experience what you have while you have it. The best of what you have is pleasure, and you are free to choose it or reject it.

To be sure, pleasure is a gift of God. This repeated statement is joined to passages that advise pleasure in 2:25; 3:13; 5:18; 9:7. It means that God determines who will obtain and keep the means of pleasure, not that God infuses a person with the experience of pleasure or makes him psychologically capable of enjoying it. Thus, according to 2:24, eating and drinking and "giving [oneself] enjoyment [*ṭob*] in his toil" is "from the hand of God", i.e., given by God. Just how God gives these things is exemplified in v. 26: he makes one man toil and turns over his earnings to a fortunate recipient. The nature of "God's gift" is also defined in 5:18, which describes the same situation as 2:26: God gives a man wealth and enables him [*hišliṭo*] "to partake of it and to take his portion and to get pleasure [*liśmoaḥ*] through his toil". The last phrase, "to get pleasure though his toil", is consequent upon the preceding infinitives: God enables a man to get pleasure out of his toil by enabling him to consume his property. Qoh 6:2, in describing the opposite of this fortunate situation, shows that God's "enabling" [*hišliṭ*] a man to consume his wealth means simply that God does not take it away from him. God neither forces nor prevents the experience of pleasure in one's possessions as long as they are held. Divine determination of events does not extend to the inner experience of pleasure.[22]

Qoh 7:14 reinforces the concept of inner freedom: *b^{e}yom ṭobah hĕyeh b^{e}ṭob*, "in a day of good fortune, enjoy the good" (7:14). The gender distinction between *ṭob* and *ṭobah* (though not usually significant for this word) here alerts us to the switch in meaning. When in an (externally) good situation, Qohelet teaches, we should seize the opportunity to experience enjoyment, lit., to "be in good".

22. Qoh 3:14b does not show otherwise, for it is to be translated, "And God has done this so that people will fear him".

This word-play helps convey two ideas: (1) in a situation of good fortune it is only reasonable to enjoy oneself—the hidden "logic" of the paronomasia links the two phenomena called *ṭob*; and (2) good fortune does not guarantee pleasure. The imperative reminds us that in a good time we will be "in good" only if we put ourselves "in good". The first "good" in the sentence is not in our control; the second is.

The reasoning behind Qohelet's recommendation of pleasure has implications that go beyond that particular experience. In 9:7-10, he first advises pleasure as man's portion, then expands the range of his advice to all activities, including intellectual ones. He urges the reader to perform—in accordance with his ability—whatever he undertakes, on the grounds that there is no activity in Sheol (v. 10). He recommends these activities not because they are necessarily rewarding or pleasing, but because they are what we have now. Whatever their drawbacks, they will soon be gone. He recommends "doing" not for the sake of what it accomplishes (it may be ineffective), nor *because* it is pleasant (the contrary is often true), but because it is man's portion, something he truly and rightfully possesses.

Although pleasure is the only portion that Qohelet recommends, it is not man's only portion. Love, hate, and jealousy are also "portions" of the living (9:6). Love is commendable (4:9-12; 9:9), but the other two emotions are not. Nevertheless, 9:4-6 does imply that even *their* cessation at death is regrettable. Even such destructive or disagreeable experiences as hate, jealousy, and knowledge of one's mortality in some way constitute an advantage of the living over the dead. The potential for having such emotions is in itself the substance of living.

Qohelet's affirmation of the intrinsic value of free experience is at odds with his preference for oblivion in 4:3 and distraction in 5:19. Just as he is ambiguous about pleasure, so he is ambiguous about the intrinsic value of life's experience—whether it is better to live and taste life's bitterness or to be dead and rest in oblivion. For himself he chooses the first course and pursues wisdom in full awareness of the pain it brings (1:16-18), but he is sometimes tempted by the second. Nevertheless, he ends up affirming experience as the substance of consciousness and the arena of human freedom.

Pleasure, like the gesticulations of a lunatic, may be senseless, but for the lunatic it makes sense to gesticulate. These actions have some sort of meaning in his private, circumscribed world, and he seems somehow compelled to make them. And one might well encourage a lunatic to do what he desires to do. In similar fashion Qohelet encourages normal people, whose actions are, he believes, no less meaningless, who are in fact themselves mad (9:3), to do what pleases them.

This explanation does not eliminate the illogic of the contradiction, because if something is beneficial, it does make sense; it does "do" something. Still, what remains with the reader is less the impression left by Qohelet's negative evaluations than his repeated and intense commendations of pleasure.

Although Qohelet does not preach happiness, does not even have a word for it, the book is, for all its gloom, "quelque manuel du bonheur" (as *Le Mythe de Sisyphe* describes itself [p. 167]), for it teaches us ways to be closer to happiness, if not yet quite happy. It tells us how to make the best of a bad situation, where to find "portions" and "good things". Qohelet hardly knows the way to happiness, but he does point to some things, including pleasure, that can take us a bit further away from unhappiness. And his recommendation of pleasure suggests a broader affirmation, implicit in his words but not yet formulated: the advocacy of the intrinsic value of experience. In the darkness of death we will have inactivity, ignorance, and cessation of sensation, so we might as well have activity, knowledge, and sensation now. By exploiting our limited possibilities we become most fully human. That is the sum and meaning of human happiness.

> . . . la mort et l'absurde sont ici, on le sent bien, les principes de la seule liberté raisonnable: celle qu'un cœur humain peut éprouver et vivre.
>
> Camus *Le Mythe de Sisyphe*, p. 83

Chapter 3

THE WAY TO WISDOM: QOHELET'S EPISTEMOLOGY

Commencer à penser, c'est commencer d'être miné.

Camus, *Le Mythe de Sisyphe*, p. 17

§3.0 *The problem*

Qohelet praises wisdom, spells out its benefits, and calls it as superior to folly as light is to darkness. Yet he also teaches that human wisdom is strictly limited and cannot achieve its goals, that it might fail to provide the promised benefits, is vulnerable to folly, and in the face of death is as helpless as folly. Qohelet's ideas on wisdom seem to be pulling in all directions. To sort them out we must ask first about the way he views wisdom's validity—in other words, about his epistemology—and second, about the way he views wisdom's power and value.

Epistemology asks: what can we know and how do we know it? Everyone who claims to know something has at least a latent epistemology answering these inseparable questions. Qohelet has more than that, for he speaks explicitly about the possibility of knowledge and how he gained it. Indeed, the problem of knowledge—its possibility, its powers, and its limitations—is one of the central concerns of his book. Thus his epistemology must be in part accessible from his statements about knowledge as well as from his description of his procedure and the way he argues for and presents his conclusions.

Qohelet's epistemology is, it must be stressed, inchoate and unsystematic, and it lacks the refinements in vocabulary necessary to make unambiguous certain distinctions important for clarity in this matter.[1] Yet his thought is not chaotic. He reflects on the ways and

1. Thus he uses *ḥokmah* both of the faculty of reason and of the knowledge to which reason can lead. *Ra'ah* is applied both to the perception of data and to the inference of conclusions on the basis of that data. *Yada'* is used both of awareness of facts and of understanding them. These distinctions are not drawn lexically or in fuller statement.

possibilities of gaining knowledge and on the scope of the knowledge to be gained. His ideas on these matters, though marked by some inconsistencies, form a coherent whole and allow for systematic exposition.

After a consideration of the terms for wisdom and knowledge (§3.1), I will argue that Qohelet has an essentially empirical methodology: he seeks both to derive knowledge from experience and to validate ideas experientially (§3.21). He often reports his findings introspectively, communicating his discoveries as perceptions (§3.22). He conceives of knowledge as the product of human thought (§3.23). He emphasizes the limitations of wisdom, but in some ways he also extends wisdom's field of activity beyond those approved by conventional wisdom (§3.24). Qohelet teaches the great utility of wisdom (§3.31), but recognizes its vulnerabilities and failings as well (§3.32). Finally, he believes that there is an imperative to pursue wisdom, regardless of its utility (§3.4).

§3.1 *The terminology of knowledge: what wisdom is*

First, a few words about a vast topic: the words for wisdom and knowledge in the HB. *Ḥokmah* is the primary but not the only word used to designate wisdom and associated concepts. Intellectual qualities and activities encompassed by the term *ḥokmah* are designated also by derivatives of YD', BYN,[2] and MṢ'. In describing the concepts designated by *ḥokmah* (and its synonyms), we are defining a notion that was probably shifting and vague, by means of terms (such as "intelligence", "reason", "knowledge") whose meanings are certainly shifting, vague, and variously understood in English. The best we can do is to gloss the Hebrew terms with words we can define, albeit loosely, in ways that conform to the common English usage.

Ḥokmah has two fundamental aspects: (1) Reason, the faculty and mode of thought by which one may rationally seek and

2. *Binah* and *t^{e}bunah* are denotatively indistinguishable from *ḥokmah*. (The distinctions the lexicons draw are derived from etymology.) All three may refer to wisdom in its various forms: practical sagacity, technical expertise, common sense, social adeptness, ethical-religious awareness, personified wisdom, and more. *Binah* and *t^{e}bunah* are most commonly "B"-words, following *ḥokmah* in parallelism (e.g., Prov 3:13) or sequence (e.g., 1 Kgs 7:14). Qohelet does not use *binah* or *t^{e}bunah* (or the verb *hebin*).

comprehend truth.[3] This is the instrumental aspect of wisdom, the ability to discern knowledge and to act successfully. It is partly inborn (and thus close to the modern concept of intelligence)[4] and partly acquired. This aspect is in focus in, for example, Qoh 1:13; 2:3; Isa 44:19. It is *ḥokmah* as reason that enables Solomon to judge the prostitutes (1 Kgs 3:28). The faculty of reason is predominant when *ḥokmah* is used in reference to skills, such as those of an artisan, although these consist in knowledge as well as in ability (English would not usually use either "reason" or "wisdom" of manual skills, but Hebrew applies its terms for wisdom to various mental powers that English keeps distinct). (2) Knowledge, that which is known (knowledge of causes or motives may be called "understanding"). This is wisdom that is transmitted from father to son and is often parallel to "words", "doctrine", or the like; e.g., Prov 1:2; 2:2; 4:5; 5:1. An unambiguous example of *hokmah* as knowledge is Dan 1:4, where the Jewish youths are said to be "learned in all *ḥokmah*".

In biblical literature, wisdom is perceived as a single mental faculty with different aspects or components—knowledge and reason—and many different applications. These applications should not be viewed as different meanings of *ḥokmah*, as if *ḥokmah* in one

3. This is not an attempt to define "reason", a word used in various and incompatible ways in philosophy, but to find a word in English whose common use generally accords with a particular aspect of the biblical concept of *ḥokmah*. In this discussion, "reason" should not be understood in one of its technical senses, such as the faculty of deductive, as opposed to experiential, reasoning, as the Kantian "Vernunft", or as an antonym of "faith". "Reason", when used with respect to the biblical concept of wisdom, will refer generally to the faculty of ordered, self-governing thought that may infer ideas from observed facts or draw conclusions logically from principles, and that applies such knowledge to behavior.

4. Whybray (1974:6-14) identifies the fundamental meaning of *ḥokmah* in the HB as "superior intellectual ability whether innate or acquired, in God, men, or animals" (p. 11).

Ḥokmah (//*binah*) refers to native intelligence in Job 39:17, where it is said of the ostrich that "God has deprived her of wisdom, and has not allotted her understanding". Among the verses that speak of wisdom (or folly) as an innate quality are Prov 14:6 and 17:16 (the ability to acquire wisdom requires the right predisposition); and Sir 15:9. The last verse refers to the faculties God created in mankind; these include "knowledge of understanding" (Greek; Syriac: "wisdom and understanding").

place meant artistic skill, in another, knowledge of divination, in another, knowledge of ethical behavior, and so on (the lexicons take this approach). Rather, wisdom, with its dual nature, may be used in whatever people undertake to do, with the relative importance of the two aspects varying according to the task, the person undertaking it, and the circumstances of its performance. The sages of Wisdom Literature in particular speak of wisdom as a single, known attribute that can be praised, described, and personified without further definition. This unitary conception of wisdom is conveyed dramatically in the personification of wisdom in Proverbs 8, where she introduces herself and describes her origins, her relations with God and humanity, and her various powers, uses, and effects. Both aspects may be present in any one occurrence of the word, and full wisdom comprises knowledge together with the reasoning ability to apply it. But usually one aspect is more prominent in any single occurrence. Qohelet too intends a unitary mental quality throughout, designated both *ḥokmah* and *da'at*, though this quality may manifest itself differently in different persons and situations. (In the paraphrastic translation [§5.8] I represent *ḥokmah* by various terms in an attempt to suggest which aspect of this mental quality is most significant in context.)

In denotation, the noun *da'at* is scarcely distinguishable from *ḥokmah*. The distinction English makes between "wisdom", which implies sound judgment and sagacity, and "knowledge", a non-evaluative term for reasoned awareness of facts, does not apply to the Hebrew terms commonly translated by these words. Both terms in themselves are ethically neutral and can imply either sagacity or simple knowledge of facts. In Wisdom Literature, both are almost always ethically positive, and *da'at* as well as *ḥokmah* implies more than mere storage of information.[5] Prov 1:7 shows this conclusively,

5. Partial exceptions are Prov 3:5, which implicitly distinguishes "your understanding" (or "reason"—*binah*) from God-given wisdom, and Prov 21:30, which denies that any wisdom, understanding, or planning can stand "against" the Lord. *Ḥokmah* and synonyms here encompass a type of wisdom whose efficacy is denied. Ben Sira too (19:24) speaks of the "(God)-fearing man who lacks understanding (σύνεσις)", preferring him to the one "who has much intelligence (φρόνησις) but transgresses the law". Both σύνεσις and φρόνησις almost always denote genuine, ethical wisdom (they commonly render *da'at*, *binah*, *t^{e}bunah*, and *śekel*), not mere cleverness.

for it says that the beginning of *da'at* is the fear of the Lord (in 9:10 this is said of *ḥokmah*).[6]

It is not clear whether *ḥokmah* (= *binah*, *t^ebunah*) and *da'at* in general BH usage could refer to all types of knowledge and reason (including skills). *Da'at*, judging from the range of the verb *yada'*, probably could be so used. Outside Wisdom Literature, the various terms for wisdom can refer to types of knowledge as diverse as seamanship (Ps 107:27), divination (Gen 41:8), business acumen (Ezek 28:3), and statecraft (whether used for better [2 Chr 1:10] or worse [Isa 29:14]). Wisdom Literature usually applies the terms only to knowledge of God's will, the causal relation between deed and consequence, and the principles of proper behavior, as well as to the reasoning ability to apply such knowledge. When I speak of "knowledge" in the epistemology of Qohelet and other Wisdom Literature, I am referring to knowledge of the sort *they* speak about. My observations might not apply to knowledge of other, ethically neutral, types (whether called *ḥokmah* or *da'at*) such as craftsmanship, arithmetic, or literature.

In view of the near-synonymity of these terms, we may refer to Qohelet's search for "knowledge" as a search for "wisdom". He himself calls the knowledge he acquired, including the sort that causes discomfort, both *ḥokmah* and *da'at* (1:16, 18).

Ḥokmah in BH differs from English "wisdom" in never referring to the literary genres modern scholars have grouped under the designation "Wisdom Literature", or to the ideas, assumptions, goals, and attitudes characteristic of those genres.[7] This distinction is

6. The difference between *ḥokmah* and *da'at* is that the latter can be used of knowing a specific fact (e.g., Job 10:7), while *ḥokmah* refers to a broader complex of knowledge. (This seems probable particularly on the basis of the corresponding verbal usages). The difference is more a matter of deep syntax than of choice of referents, with *da'at* remaining a verbal notion that can take a semantic direct object in bound form (e.g., *da'at m^ezimmot* = "knowing plans" [Prov 8:12]; *da'at d^erakeyka* = "knowing your ways" [Job 21:14]).

7. Thus Whybray (1974:6-14), with whose understanding of the concepts "wisdom" and "wise" the following description essentially agrees.

Von Rad too draws a sharp distinction between "wisdom" as an intellectual quality and wisdom as a "geistige Bewegung". "Die Bezeichnung eines Textes als 'weisheitlich', überhaupt dieser ganze Begriff von 'Weisheit', als eines Gesamtphänomens ist ja in den Quellen keineswegs unmittelbar verankert" (1970:18f.).

important for defining *ḥokmah* and synonyms. Without it, one may confuse the description of the entire Wisdom enterprise with the meaning of one word, albeit a very important one, used in Wisdom Literature.[8] Definitions of "wisdom" often are unclear on what they seek to do. Gordis, for example, says that "Ḥokmah may be defined as a realistic approach to the problems of life, including all the practical skills and technical arts of civilization" (1965:31). This might be an adequate description of the Wisdom enterprise—what the sages were trying to accomplish—as well as the activity of anyone else whose work required intellectual or manual skills (though a description of an enterprise in terms of its self-image may go beyond what the enterprise actually *was*). But it is certainly not a definition of *ḥokmah*, as an attempt to substitute the definition for the word defined makes clear. Likewise Crenshaw's discussion of "wisdom" (1981a:11-25) pertains to the activities and attitudes to which we might apply the term "wisdom". It does not define *ḥokmah*:

> ... wisdom is the reasoned search for specific ways to assure well-being and the implementation of those discoveries in daily existence. Wisdom addresses natural, human, and theological dimensions of reality, and constitutes an attitude toward life, a living tradition, and a literary corpus (1981a:25).

This is an apt description of the intellectual and cultural phenomenon I will call "Wisdom". It is not what any of the sages meant by the term *ḥokmah*.

In BH *ḥakam* refers to a wise man, an individual possessing wisdom, and only rarely to a member of the class of sages, the Wisdom teachers or the authors of Wisdom writings.[9] I do not think there is any evidence for a "Wisdom School". It is more appropriate to speak of Wisdom Literature as a group of literary genres.[10] To

8. Not nearly so important, however, in Egyptian Wisdom Literature as in Israelite, and not so important in Prov 10-31 as in Prov 1-9. As significant as the word *ḥokmah* (along with its synonyms and Egyptian equivalents) was in Wisdom Literature, it was not indispensable in teaching and describing wisdom.

9. In this too I concur for the most part with Whybray (1974:15-54). I do not, however, agree that *ḥakam* is *always* a personal attribute rather than a group identification. See Excursus IV.

10. These minimally include didactic, speculative [Job], and psalmodic Wisdom. More refined taxonomies can easily be produced (see Murphy, 1981, *passim*), but since these do not seem to correspond to differences in epistemology, they are not important to the task at hand.

describe the intellectual framework in which this literature was molded and transmitted, we may, however, speak of a Wisdom *tradition*, a term implying the assumption that certain texts or oral compositions were transmitted in a way that preserved their special formal and ideological characteristics, and these characteristics expressed a coherent group of attitudes, assumptions, methods, and beliefs. There is no justification for assuming that different genres were produced by different "schools",[11] or that an intellectual tradition is the exclusive possession of certain individuals who were ignorant of if not hostile to other traditions. The possibility that the same people can participate in more than one intellectual tradition is shown by the fact that the teachers whose proverbial wisdom is quoted in *Avot* (who also were called *ḥăkamim*) participated as well in the development of Halakhah and Midrash. Just as we may speak of midrashic traditions without implying the existence of a special school of midrashists who knew and were influenced only by midrash, so we can speak of the sages of Wisdom Literature without imagining them bound to Wisdom Literature.

§3.2 *Qohelet's epistemology: method and theory*

Qohelet's epistemology is essentially empirical. I apply this term to Qohelet's thought by analogy to the Western philosophical theories known as empirical, although Qohelet does not offer a philosophical theory or pursue a consistent methodology.[12] Much that he says comes from traditional learning, impulse, or vague deduction. Many of his ideas he formulates *a priori* (e.g., 3:17; 8:12b) or derives from assumptions that lack experiential grounding (e.g., 7:11-12). Nevertheless, the "empirical" label is justified, first, by Qohelet's conception of his investigative procedure, which looks to experience as the source of knowledge and the means of validation, and second, by his concept of knowledge, according to which knowledge is created by thought and dependent on perception.

11. See Whybray, 1974. As to the existence of an Egyptian "Wisdom School", see my remarks in Fox, 1980b:128f.

12. Using the concepts of Western philosophical empiricism, we can say that he holds a primitive form of the type of empiricism (the "weak form") that maintains that all knowledge comes from experience because every proposition is either a direct report on experience or a report whose truth is inferred from experience; see the *Encyclopedia of Philosophy*, II, p. 499.

Qohelet is unusual in his emphasis on validation, especially validation by empirical evidence. He is only vaguely paralleled in his introspective description of the experience of search and discovery. And he is alone among the sages in claiming to have pushed beyond tradition and to have discovered new knowledge on his own (1:12-16).

§3.21 *How knowledge is gained*

The attainment of new knowledge has two inseparable components: the procedure of discovery and the form of argumentation—inseparable because argumentation may turn a belief into knowledge (and so become part of the discovery process) and may also replicate the process of discovery. These components may, however, be distinguished for purposes of discussion.

§3.211 *Procedure of discovery*

Qohelet has a deliberate procedure of discovery, which he explains when he introduces himself (1:12-18 + 2:1-3). He will investigate the world with the aid of *ḥokmah*; this means that he will use his powers of reason rather than his prior knowledge in his inquiry. He never invokes prior knowledge, anything he "heard", as an argument for his convictions. He will proceed by seeking experience, observing it, and judging it, then reporting his perceptions or reactions. He will also (though he does not mention this in the introductory passage) use experience in *arguing* for his propositions. He does not follow this procedure at every step, but he does speak of it as pertaining to his entire investigation. He mentions the investigation again in 7:23, 25, 27; 8:16, and he maintains its continuity by referring back repeatedly to his explorations, telling how he "turned" (PNH, ŠWB, SBB) from one thing to another or urged his heart to observe something new. All his teachings are encompassed by the framework of this report, and thus, it is implied, came to be known during the investigation described in 1:12-18 and exemplified in 2:1-26. The procedure described in these passages is, in Qohelet's view, the method underlying his teachings as a whole.

Qohelet seeks out experience as a source of knowledge. After a preliminary meditation, he introduces himself and reports his decision "to investigate and explore with wisdom all that occurs under the heavens" (1:13; see commentary). He then proceeds to relate how he investigated various activities, facts, and situations. In his first experiment (2:1-11) he chose an object of study, namely pleasure, then directed his heart to experience it and to observe its effects. He tried pleasures not in order to enjoy them, but as a means of answering a philosophical question: "what is good for people to do?" (2:3). So Qohelet did not merely go through life commenting on what he noticed. He chose a heuristic procedure deliberately and pursued it with determination, if not with consistency. This, I believe, is revolutionary: a sage chooses to seek out experience as a path to insight.

Before experience becomes knowledge, it must be interpreted by reason. Qohelet uses *ḥokmah*, reason, as an instrument of guiding, organizing, and interpreting experiences (1:13). He says that he "spoke to" [or "in"] his heart (1:16; 2:14, 15; etc.), "set" (*natan*) his heart (1:12; 1:17; 8:9, 16), "set" something "upon" (*'el*) his heart (8:9; 9:1), "explored" in his heart (2:3), "turned with" his heart (7:25), said to his heart that he will make it experience pleasure (2:1). He reports that he did not withhold pleasure from his heart (2:10) and that he rid his heart of illusions (2:20). His heart, for its part, "sees" wisdom (1:16), conducts itself in wisdom (2:3), and receives pleasure.

Qohelet does not consistently distinguish his heart from *himself*—the "I" or ego that speaks to the heart. Yet the prominent role he gives his heart in the passages where he discusses his investigation (1:12–2:26) suggests that he does ascribe distinctive functions to it. Qohelet mentions his heart twelve times in 1:12–2:26,[13] a frequency 13.8 times greater than elsewhere in the body of the book (he mentions his heart elsewhere only in 7:25; 8:9, 16; 9:1 [twice, emending to *wlby r'h*]).[14] This uneven distribution indicates that Qohelet's interest in his heart is not merely a habit of style. He mentions his heart so frequently in 1:12–2:26 because he is reflecting on the process of perception and discovery, and the heart has a central role in this process. He is not only exploring but also observing himself explore. He is his own field of investigation.

We may schematize the heart's role thus: (1) The person (Qohelet,

13. He also twice refers to the heart of the toiler in this unit (2:22, 23), where he is generalizing from his own situation.

14. Qohelet refers to a "man's" heart (in the third person) in 2:22-23, where he sees himself an example of such a man.

the "I") desires knowledge and (2) directs his heart to attaining it (1:13; 2:1a; 8:9). It seems that Qohelet must persuade his heart to take part in the investigation (we might say: he must persuade himself). (3) The person does something so that his heart may "see" or "observe" (usually R'H) the sensation it causes (2:1a, 10bα). (4) Since the heart is the seat of wisdom/reason (1:13, 16, 17; 2:3), it can assimilate and evaluate the sensations it perceives, in order to produce knowledge and report this knowledge to the person. Thereupon the person realizes (YD') a fact. We see the heart's experience ("e") enabling the person to attain knowledge ("k") in several places: 1:16 (e)—1:17 (k); 2:1a (e)—2:1b (k); 2:3abα (e)—2:3bβ (k); 7:25 (e)—7:26 (k); and 8:16 (e)—8:17 (k).[15]

§3.212 *Argumentation*

Empirical argumentation too proceeds from sensory experience. Qohelet does not always present arguments on behalf of his ideas, but when he does, he generally uses experiential ones.

Qohelet's argumentation is often in the form of *testimony*. In testimony one claims to have observed the fact that is being asserted or a fact from which conclusions are drawn. Qohelet uses testimony most prominently in 2:1-10, where he infers the value of pleasure from his experience with it. In 4:1, Qohelet observes oppressions; this is a conclusion as well as a basis for a further inference about the value of life (4:2). He argues for the proposition, "Better a wise youth than an old king who no longer knows to take care" (4:13), not by declaring the rewards of wisdom, but by recounting an incident he claims to have seen (4:13-16). In 7:15-16 he makes an observation and derives advice from it. In 8:9 he testifies in a general way to the statements of 8:1b-8. See further 5:12-13; 6:1-2; 8:10.

15. A similar conception of the heart's function is expounded in the Egyptian "Memphite Theology": "Sight, hearing, breathing—they report to the heart, and it makes every understanding come forth. As to the tongue, it repeats what the heart has devised" (*AEL* I, p. 54). The senses (Qohelet, less specifically, says "I") transmit sensations to the heart, which organizes them into knowledge; the heart then passes this knowledge to the tongue (again, Qohelet says "I"), which speaks what it is told. Since Qohelet is more concerned with understanding, whose agent is the heart, than with the senses and speech, he subsumes the eyes, ears, and tongue to the "I", while frequently distinguishing the heart from the person.

Testimony is effective only if the audience accepts the speaker's credibility, his rhetorical ethos. Qohelet tries to strengthen his credibility by reiterating and emphasizing that his ideas are all first-hand perceptions: I saw this; or better: *I* saw this. The frequent redundant first person pronoun focuses attention on the perceiver: *paniti 'ăni, ra'iti 'ăni, šabti 'ăni wa'er'eh*, and so on (Muraoka, 1985:48f.). On Qohelet's introspective reporting see §3.22.

Qohelet also uses experience as *validation*, basing propositions on publicly observable facts. An example of validation is 2:21-23, where Qohelet argues that toil is absurd by pointing to the fact that at death (if not before) a toiler passes his wealth on to another person, one who did not toil for it. Qohelet takes this publicly observed fact as a premise. A similar, but more complex example of validation is the description of natural phenomena, which recur endlessly (1:4-7). This description serves to justify the conclusion, "That which happens is that which shall happen, and that which occurs is that which shall occur, and there is nothing at all new under the sun" (1:9). This conclusion in turn validates 1:3: man is not adequately compensated for his toil. The implicit rationale is that if even the powerful, incessant forces of nature can achieve nothing new, certainly human toiling can not do so. The fate of human toil is subsumed to a universal rule, which is learned from and validated by observations of particulars. Another example of empirical validation is 5:7f., where Qohelet explains the existence of "oppression of the poor and robbery of justice and right in the state" by the observation (whose validity he assumes the reader will grant) that one person of rank watches over another. (The usual Wisdom approach would be to point to consequences rather than causes, to teach, for example: If you see oppression of the poor, etc., know well that the oppressors shall be punished.) The importance Qohelet gives to validation is unique in Wisdom Literature.

Qohelet's argumentation is not, it should be stressed, always valid. Its main flaws are those to which all induction is susceptible: generalization from too few examples and transference of conclusions to inapplicable categories. His argumentation is, however, significant because of what it *attempts* to do: to prove the propositions of wisdom from experiential evidence.

§3.213 *Comparison with other Wisdom Literature*

The procedure of discovery and the forms of argumentation of other Wisdom Literature differ significantly from Qohelet's. Contrary to a widespread assumption, Wisdom's epistemology is not empirical. To be sure, many of the sages' teachings undoubtedly derive from the observations of generations of wise men (though always shaped in accordance with prior ethical-religious principles).[16] My concern, however, is not with what the authors of Wisdom or other sages actually did—this is at any rate unrecoverable—but with what they *present themselves* as doing, in other words, with their epistemological self-portrait. For the way they present themselves shows their theory and ideal of what a wise man does, and thus reveals their conception of wisdom. And the fact is that whatever the teachings' actual derivation, the sages do not offer their experience as the source of new knowledge, and they rarely invoke experiential arguments on its behalf. Nor do they even refer to the experiences of predecessors.

In a few passages, the teacher in conventional didactic Wisdom does refer to something he saw, giving an appearance of empiricism. But that is for the most part a rhetorical strategy, not, as in the case of Qohelet, a fundamental methodological principle.[17] In didactic Wisdom, reporting of individual experience is used to engage the pupil's attention and inspire him to obey the teachings.

The author of Prov 24:30-34 says that he "saw" what happened to a lazy man's field; the sage of Proverbs 7 "saw" a woman entice a

16. The same can be said for teachings that present themselves as revelatory in origin, e.g., the Covenant Code; yet no one would think of them as empirical.

17. Rhetoric is, to be sure, an expression and manifestation of an underlying epistemology.

The rhetoric of Wisdom Literature has been neglected. Crenshaw (1981b) has sketched some lines of Wisdom rhetoric under the rubrics of ethos, pathos, and logos (i.e., logic) (these "warrants", as Crenshaw calls them, are of course present in all rhetoric; the question is just how they are realized in specific texts). As the form of "logos" characteristic in Israelite Wisdom, Crenshaw mentions argument from consensus. This is likewise a way to strengthen ethos, since, as Crenshaw observes, ethos in Wisdom Literature derives from community. In fact, the seemingly empirical arguments in Wisdom Literature are primarily ways of strengthening ethos by creating consensus.

youth to fornication.[18] These passages may well report actual experiences, but the experiences are not claimed as the source of new knowledge or even as its proof. In Prov 7:6-20, the teacher reports seeing the seduction but does not even claim to have observed the consequences; those he already *knows*. In Prov 24:30-34, a lesson follows upon an observation, but a truth is only called to mind, rather than being discovered or inferred. The sage does not say that he saw a field gone wild, looked for the cause, and found that its owner was lazy, nor does he claim to have looked at lazy farmers and observed what happens to their fields. Rather he came across a field gone wild, and this sparked a meditation on its causes. Experience is simply an occasion for thought. Likewise, when a sage tells the pupil to go to the ant (6:6-8), in a passage often considered a prime example of Hebrew *Naturwissenschaft*, he uses the ant as a teaching device, an illustration of diligence. He does not use the observable facts about ant behavior to prove a point, but merely to make his point more emphatic. And note, the sage does not himself go to the ant—he does not have to—but just sends the pupil.

A sage may also make general reference to his life-experiences in order to strengthen his ethos. Ben Sira speaks of experiences that enriched his sagacity and gave him the cunning to escape danger (34:9-12). He does not, however, claim that these are the basis of the wisdom he teaches. Another case of experience mustered to reinforce the speaker's ethos is Ahiqar l. 111, "I have carried sand and hauled salt, but there is nothing more burdensome than debt" (similarly ll. 105a and 112).[19]

These passages are as close as didactic Wisdom gets to empiricism, and they are rare. We might even say that the empirical garb of these teachings is necessary only for the callow youth to whom they are

18. LXX has the *woman* looking through the window in 7:6-7, but that accords poorly with v. 10, because *w^ehinneh* in that verse must introduce what is seen from the perspective of someone other than the woman in question.

19. Von Rad (1970:56-58) recognizes the essentially rhetorical function of the "autobiographical style" in Wisdom Literature, a style he considers a "traditionelle Stilform" (p. 57). He observes that in these passages there is a tension between the form, which implies personal experience, and the content, which is impersonal and general. In this way the teacher shows that such knowledge must be anchored in the life of the individual.

directed. A wise, mature man would not need such extraneous reinforcement of belief.

Personal experience is more often cited in theodicy, by both the sufferer and the defenders of divine justice.[20] The sufferer in particular draws inferences from what he has undergone (though we cannot assume that all his statements are to be understood as knowledge from the *author's* point of view). The defender too, whether in dialogue or in argumentative soliloquy, sometimes appeals to experience to support his tenets. For example, the psalmist of Psalm 37 claims that he never saw a righteous man abandoned (v. 25), whereas he did see the wicked cut down (vv. 35-36). Eliphaz says he observed evildoers reaping what they sowed (Job 4:8). Ben Sira uses personal testimony in the same cause: "Many such things my eyes have seen, and mightier things than these my ears have heard" (16:5). Note that the events he recounts in vv. 8-10 are examples of punishment in ancient times, things "heard" rather than "seen". Observation in theodicy testifies to old truths; it does not uncover or argue for new ones. Sounding a note of exasperation, the psalmist and Eliphaz mention their experiences in order to emphasize the obvious. Qohelet's use of experience does have certain parallels in theodicy both in the sufferers' complaints and in the defenders' theodicy. He differs in the greater importance he gives to the "I" and, more significantly, in the reasons for which he appeals to the ego. While the sufferers and defenders try to understand what they observe, they, unlike Qohelet, do not observe *in order* to gain knowledge.

§3.22 *Reporting discoveries*

The last step in Qohelet's procedure is to report his discoveries. This he often does in an unusual way, relating them introspectively. Instead of simply stating truths, he looks back and tells what he earlier "saw", "realized" (*yada'*), "found" or "apprehended" (*maṣa'*), and "said" (i.e., thought; at that stage he was speaking to himself). Concerning the wise man and the fool, for example, he says: "But I also realized that the very same fate befalls them both" (2:14) (not only: "but the very same fate befalls them both"); "I next saw that under the sun the race does not necessarily go to the swift..." (9:11)

20. Höffken (1985:123f.) describes well the various functions of the "I" in first-person discourse in Job.

(and not: "Under the sun the race does not necessarily go to the swift").

In line with this type of introspective reporting, Qohelet often evaluates situations and activities not by an independent external standard but by their effect on him. "Of amusement I said, 'Inane!' and of pleasure, 'What does this accomplish?'" (2:2). Thinking about the unfairness of death made him "disgusted" with life (2:17). He "found" woman to be more bitter than death (7:26). An event he "saw" (a wise man saving a city) he considered significant (as he puts it, "it was great upon me"; 9:13). The *hebel*-judgment too describes a psychological datum, for absurdity exists only as presented to the mind. Qohelet constantly interposes his consciousness between the reality observed and the reader. It seems important to him that the reader not only know what the truth is, but also be aware that he, Qohelet, saw this, felt this, realized this. He is reflexively observing the psychological process of discovery as well as reporting the discoveries themselves.[21]

§3.221 *Other Wisdom Literature*

Qohelet's introspective reporting has no close parallels in other Wisdom Literature. To be sure, a sage may occasionally say "I saw" something, or even report an experience at greater length (this happens most often in theodicy, e.g., Job 4:12-21; Ps 73:13-28). The best parallels are in the Individual Lament psalms. There is, however, a fundamental difference: the speakers in those psalms report, for the most part, their personal pains and misfortunes, not (with rare exceptions) facts about the world at large. Qohelet reports his personal discomfort but also, and mainly, draws conclusions about the external world. Furthermore, the lamenters are not looking inward in order to find knowledge, but have had it thrust upon their consciousness by experience, whereas Qohelet sets knowledge as his conscious goal. In any case, none of the sages or psalmists speaks about or refers to (as opposed to expressing) his perceptions and

21. In his perceptive study of the role of the ego in Wisdom Literature, Höffken (1985:125f.) points out the unusual importance Qohelet gives the ego and explains its role as criterial—Qohelet will evaluate transmitted teachings (*Bildungsgut*) by the measure of his own experiences. In my view, however, Qohelet is only occasionally and incidentally concerned with evaluating or testing ideas of others.

feelings as frequently and as systematically as Qohelet. His intense concern with the process of perception is a concomitant of his conception of the ontology of knowledge.

§3.23 *The ontology of knowledge*

Qohelet conceives of knowledge as a product of thought and discovery, not as an entity independent of the individual mind. He does not phrase his idea in this way, of course, but such a notion is implied by his description of what happens when he reaches the boundaries of knowledge. Having surpassed his predecessors in wisdom, he sets out on his own "to investigate and explore with wisdom all that occurs under the heavens" (1:13). He pursues knowledge not merely by absorbing existing wisdom and elaborating on it or applying it intelligently, but by pushing back the frontiers of wisdom, creating knowledge that did not exist before his investigation. Thus he determined to try out pleasure, "*so that* I might see (*'ad 'ăšer 'er'eh*) what is good . . .". (2:3). Knowledge is subsequent to and dependent upon observation. In one verse Qohelet does speak of *ḥokmah* and *da'at* being given by God to a favored man (2:26). That, however, surely refers to wisdom in the sense of a disposition to do what is wise, in other words, to the faculty of reason. It is not a statement about the source of knowledge in general. *Ḥokmah* and *da'at* here do not refer to a deeper understanding of life such as Qohelet sought, for that type of wisdom brings misery (1:16-18), hardly an expression of divine favor.

It is of course possible for an individual to increase his wisdom by receiving knowledge from others. Qohelet introduces himself as one who excelled at that in the past (1:16). But he believes that as well as receiving truths, an individual can produce fundamentally new knowledge—truths never before known, and not only transmitted knowledge. Within the investigation that Qohelet reports in his monologue, he does not picture himself as learning facts others already know, but as discovering truths that would not otherwise be known. Above all, his awareness that "all is absurd", which encompasses many of his other conclusions, is a fundamentally new perception. He never suggests that anything but his own investigations contributed to that discovery. Much wisdom, he implies, already exists, but wisdom in its totality does not.

Qohelet's new wisdom he calls *da'at* and *ḥokmah* (1:17-18), just like the wisdom he believes others can have (1:16; 2:12-14; etc.). This newly acquired wisdom is wisdom as knowledge—the sort of wisdom that can be increased through study and observation—rather than wisdom as reason. He does not speak of the development of reasoning powers; these he already possessed at the beginning of his inquiry. Knowledge, on the other hand, comes into existence by the process of thought and discovery.

Qohelet clearly perceives at least some of his most important findings to be fundamentally new knowledge, not merely truths long known that he might have garnered from others' wisdom. He does not bring this perception into confrontation with his statement that "there is nothing at all new under the sun" (1:9), but the two ideas do not necessarily contradict each other. The statement in 1:9 refers to events (*mah šehayah*, *mah šenna'ăśah*; see commentary), and it is unlikely that Qohelet would apply it to anything as abstract as thoughts or items of knowledge. If, however, he does intend to assert that ideas cannot be innovative, he is first of all contradicting himself—which Qohelet is quite capable of doing—and second, he is simply wrong, as his book itself illustrates.

Qohelet's epistemology makes knowledge (at least knowledge of the sort that interested the sages) dependent on the knower's perceiving it. For Qohelet there is no body of truth standing above the individual and demanding assent, no Dame Wisdom who was created before mankind and who would exist even if all humans were fools. For Qohelet, wisdom must be justified through the individual's experience and reason. Qohelet alone of the sages speaks with "a voice that justifies itself by reference to the good sense of the individual's reflections on his experiences" (J. G. Williams, 1981:85). But argumentation based on justification of that sort could well turn against the speaker, weakening the rhetorical ethos it is meant to strengthen. After all, what right does the individual have to look about and within himself and come up with things not known to contemporary wise men, let alone to the wise men of old?

By making knowledge relative to the knower, Qohelet sacrifices the right to claim certainty or built-in authority for the wisdom he teaches. This loss may exacerbate his frustration at the impossibility of attaining the kind of certainty he longs for (7:23-24; 8:16-17).

The belief that knowledge proceeds from perception may also produce philosophical skepticism, for the subject is likely to recognize the inherent fallibility and unverifiability of his own knowledge. In 6:12 Qohelet seems to do just that. He ironically undermines his own—quite serious—series of statements about what is "good" (7:1-12) by first denying the possibility of knowing "what is good for man". This is not radical epistemological skepticism; Qohelet believes his knowledge is genuine. It is, however, an awareness that one's knowledge cannot lay claim to certainty. This reflexive skepticism is more dangerous to Wisdom beliefs than are remarks about the limitations of wisdom (see §3.24), for it undercuts certainty, not only with regard to specific items of knowledge, but with regard to knowledge itself. Not only is there much that man cannot know (with this all would agree), but even what he *does* know is uncertain and unverifiable. Other sages revealed no such self-doubt; they would, I believe, have found it incomprehensible.

One means of strengthening the ethos endangered by Qohelet's conception of knowledge is the Solomonic fiction, which bestows on the book the prestige attached to that archetypal wise man. Additionally, the epilogist (who I think is the author; see Excursus III) tries to blunt the brashness of this claim by speaking in the traditional stance of a father transmitting wisdom to his son (12:12). The epilogue informs the readers that the words have been channeled through the pipeline of tradition *from* Qohelet if not to him, and transmission in itself has legitimizing force. Finally, the introspective report, though contrary to the usual claim of traditional authority, strengthens the speaker's ethos. Qohelet interposes his consciousness between the facts and his readers, for he seeks to persuade by empathy. He bares his soul in all its twistings and turnings, ups and downs, asking his readers to join him on an exhausting journey to knowledge. His new episemology has led to a new rhetoric. If the readers can replicate the flow of perception and recognition as it developed for Qohelet, they will be more open to accepting the author's conclusions as their own.

§3.231 *Other Wisdom Literature*

In the usual Wisdom conception, wisdom—in both its aspects, knowledge and reason—exists essentially independent of the individual mind. What the individual knows would be known even without him. Knowledge exists "out there", waiting for man to appropriate. It need not be proved, only found and applied. This notion is nowhere stated, but it is implicit in the way wisdom is personified and by the way the sages speak about the process of gaining wisdom.

The images of wisdom in Proverbs (1:20-33; 8:1-36; 9:1-12) and Ben Sira (14:20-15:8; 24:1-29) are a configuration of the same wisdom that is taught and praised elsewhere in the wisdom texts. If personified wisdom represented something fundamentally different,[22] the image of wisdom as a person would communicate nothing about the wisdom the sages were trying to inculcate.[23] These personifications show that knowledge is thought of as existing, in essence if not in specifics, before mankind. The preexistence of the substance of wisdom—knowledge itself—is expressed most clearly by Ben Sira. He says that wisdom proceeded (at creation) from the mouth of God (24:3), and that those who desire wisdom need only come to her and satisfy themselves from her produce (24:19-22). She was present at the first and available to the first man (24:28; cf. Job 15:7). What place can there be in such a conception for the individual to increase the total store of knowledge in the world by observing life and watching his own reactions? A human being, whether as wisdom's plaything (Prov 8:31) or as a passer-by invited to her noble banquet (Prov 9:1-7) can hardly expect to make significant additions to this awesome force, but can, at most, seek to refine and express it in new ways.[24]

The conception of wisdom as a static entity, independent of the human mind, is manifest also in the sapiential idea of the way

22. Such as the world-order or the "self-revelation of Creation", as von Rad understands it (1970:189-228). I cannot agree with him that "[d]iese 'Weisheit', 'Vernunft' muß also etwas wie den von Gott der Schöpfung eingesenkten 'Sinn', ihr göttliches Schöpfungsgeheimnis bedeuten..." (pp. 193-94). Contrary to von Rad, wisdom is not "die der Welt von Gott eingegebene Ordnung" (p. 194), but rather knowledge *about* that order. The personification texts do not suggest that knowledge can be extracted from the created order by observation. In fact, Job 28 (which von Rad brings in, perhaps improperly, as an example of personification) teaches that it *cannot* be.

23. In identifying personified wisdom with Torah, Ben Sira is not redefining wisdom, but subsuming the wisdom taught in his book (and elsewhere) to the concept of Torah. It is the concept of Torah, not wisdom, that is being redefined by radical expansion.

24. Ben Sira says, "If a man of understanding hears a wise saying, he will praise it and add to it" (21:15). This means that the essence of the saying, the idea it teaches, is already there, and the wise man elaborates it.

wisdom is gained. One gains wisdom by absorbing and applying existing knowledge. The sages prided themselves not on having created knowledge but on having taken it to themselves. Whereas Qohelet's favorite verb of perception is "seeing", theirs is "hearing".[25] The Egyptian sage Ptahhotep describes the pupil's duty as "hearing" his father's teaching in order to recount it to *his* children, thereby "renewing the teaching of his father" (ll. 588-95). The teacher in Proverbs 1-9 (where alone in Proverbs we find much reflection on the process of acquiring and transmitting wisdom) enjoins the pupil to "hear" and "keep" his father's wisdom. Whereas for Qohelet "seeking" and "finding" wisdom refer to exploration and discovery, in Proverbs these concepts imply striving and succeeding in absorbing and understanding existing truths. For the most part, the sages of didactic Wisdom sought not to discover truths but to inculcate them. This sapiential attitude is attested in Wisdom Literature from its beginnings in the Egypt of the Old Kingdom down to the Demotic Wisdom books and Pirqe Avot.

Since knowledge, in the sapiential view, is not created through the individual's thought, its truth and authority need not be established by argumentation. Wisdom Literature, as noted earlier, uses argumentation less to prove its propositions than to establish the speaker's ethos and to motivate the pupil. Mainly Wisdom argues deductively, inferring truths from axioms or extending the application of given concepts.[26] Wisdom Literature shows very little attempt at argumentation from individual experience. In fact, there is little argumentation of any sort. The sage need not prove the truth of his wisdom, because if it *is* wisdom, it is not essentially his. He has partaken of it, not produced it. He does not know everything, of course, and he may be mistaken in what he thinks he knows, but the

25. "Seeing" denotes immediate experience, not necessarily visual; "hearing" means mediated, reported knowledge (Job 42:5).

26. Höffken (1985:122) says that in traditional Wisdom Literature (in particular, Proverbs, Ps 37, and the friends' speeches in Job), the primary functions of the teacher's ego are deduction (as in Prov 24:30-34) and affirmation. As I see it, although deduction is the main form of reasoning in Wisdom Literature, virtually the only function of the interposition of the teacher's ego in didactic Wisdom is (in Höffken's terminology) *affirmation*, i.e., the strengthening of traditional teachings by appeal to the "geballte Lebenserfahrung des Ego" (p. 122).

knowledge he does have, certified by its conformity to tradition, is secure.

Job 28 presents a divergent concept of wisdom. The poem asks: where can wisdom be found? and answers: it cannot be *found*; it cannot be bought. God alone knows the way to it. Thus man can partake of wisdom only through God's mediation (v. 28). Fearing God, man will do what is wise. Proverbs too asserts that fear of God is the path to wisdom (1:7; 2:5f.; 8:13; 9:10), but Proverbs also requires the individual to participate in the process of acquiring wisdom; fear of God is only a starting point. The implicit starting definition of wisdom in Job 28 resembles Qohelet's concept of wisdom as the product of discovery, but the author of the former presents this concept only in order to insist on the invalidity of such an approach. Westermann (1977:132) correctly calls Job 28 radical and polemical. It is, in a sense, more skeptical than Qohelet, for it insists that whatever man can attain by his skills and efforts is not to be reckoned as wisdom, whereas Qohelet grants that the knowledge the human intellect is able to grasp is truly wisdom, though the limits of this wisdom are strict and oppressive.[27]

In contrast to Qohelet and Job 28, most Wisdom Literature conceives of wisdom as existing independently of the human mind and always available for appropriation. In brief, if one could ask a

27. Job 28 has been ascribed variously to a later hand, to the author of Job at an earlier stage (Gordis, 1965:101-103) or a later stage (Driver and Gray, and many), and to the author of Job at this stage (Andersen; Westermann, 1977:130-33; by the latter view, the poem is authoritative within the world of the text).

As an authorial statement this chapter is awkwardly placed. It proposes a solution to the crisis—fear of God—but this comes too soon to be the author's solution and vitiates the actual climax. Moreover, it sides too strongly with the friends' attitude: the only wisdom is self-effacing affirmation of God's justice. Although Job does in the end choose this path, at least in part (42:5f.), this is not the point of God's message, nor is it the author's "solution". Only for the friends is this an adequate solution to Job's dilemma.

I believe that we should reconsider the thesis of Graetz (1872) that Job 28 is a continuation of Zophar's third speech, begun in 27:7. (The introduction of the speaker has been lost before this speech, as most commentators realize; 27:11f. should perhaps, but not necessarily, be ascribed to Job.) 27:13

more conventional sage, "How do you know this?" he would, I believe, answer: "Because I learned it". To this question Qohelet would reply: "Because I saw it". The shift is profound.

§3.24 *The scope of wisdom*

In sharp contrast to didactic Wisdom Literature, Qohelet emphasizes the limitations and vulnerabilities of wisdom. This emphasis on the negative has led commentators to view the book as an attack on wisdom or a polemic against those who ascribe to wisdom powers that, in Qohelet's view, it lacks. Such an attack would be a polemic against Wisdom (whether perceived as a "school" or only as a way of thinking accompanying a literary genre), for Wisdom Literature above all praises wisdom and promises great benefits to those who possess it.

The following sections (§§3.241-3.32) seek to describe Qohelet's evaluation of wisdom—the pluses and minuses he sees in it—and to compare this with the ideas expressed in other Wisdom Literature. This description will put us in a better position to decide if Qohelet is indeed a polemic against the sages—the authors and teachers of

repeats Zophar's words in the second dialogue, 20:29. Job 27:1-4 is Job's brief and eloquent assertion of innocence, appropriately short in view of his lengthy apologia in chs. 29-31. Like others of the friends' speeches, 27:7-28:28 is compounded of threats and a bit of *Schadenfreude* alongside an apparently sympathetic call to humble piety. Job 28 is entirely in accord with the sort of tactical skepticism Zophar propounds in 11:5-8, asserting that wisdom is hidden with God. It is deeper than Sheol and broader than the earth, and thus hopelessly beyond human reach.

The main argument used against the ascription of Job 28 to Zophar is aesthetic. The poem seems too subtle and eloquent for Zophar (Rowley, 1963:166f.; Gordis, 1965:102). It is indeed eloquent, but it is also somewhat banal and more than a little irrelevant to Job's plight. In any case, much that the friends say (including ch. 11 and not excluding some of their nastier moments) would be reckoned magnificent and inspirational if it were found (as similar material indeed is) in Proverbs, Psalms, or the Prophets. The friends are not straw men; they are wise, and they are often eloquent. This eloquence is, of course, the author's, and is not to be taken as validating the friends' position.

Wisdom Literature—as many commentators believe.[28]

Again, the biblical concept of wisdom includes both knowledge and reason. While a particular passage may emphasize one or the other of these aspects, the distinction is not lexicalized. For Qohelet, as for the other sages, the denotations of *ḥokmah* and *da'at* are virtually coextensive. When Qohelet speaks of the limitations of knowledge or the power of reason, he is referring to the scope and abilities of human wisdom.

In Qohelet's evaluation of wisdom we may distinguish two issues: wisdom's scope—what can and what cannot be known (§3.2)—and its utility—what benefits it provides its possessors and in what ways it fails them (§3.3). In both these matters, Qohelet's attitude toward wisdom is complex and nuanced, not merely a pro or con stance.

Qohelet denies the possibility of two types of wisdom: the knowledge of the future and the understanding of life. But alongside these negations, he also affirms wisdom's essential validity.

§3.241 *Knowledge of the future*

Qohelet insists repeatedly that man cannot know what will happen. The issue is not, of course, the validity of prophecy; the possibility of divine communication through dreams or visions is not touched upon in Qohelet and scarcely mentioned in earlier Wisdom Literature. The issue for Qohelet is the possibility of extrapolating the future from facts of everyday life in order to know the consequences of plans and deeds. Without such foreknowledge (and in the absence of

28. Many interpreters (e.g., Zimmerli, 1962:132-35) have said or implied that Qohelet is a polemic against Wisdom (or the Wisdom "School"). Fichtner (1933:8) says that Qohelet undertakes "eine radikale Kritik an dem Wert der Weisheit". Von Rad says: "Daß sich Kohelet gegen die herrschenden Lehren wendet, ist nicht zu bezweifeln" (1970:301); and ". . . sich Kohelet ja nicht nur gegen Auswüchse der traditionellen Lehre wendet, sondern gegen das ganze Unternehmen". The main conclusion of Loader is that ". . . Qohelet is constantly polemizing [sic] against general *ḥokmā* by turning its own topoi against it, by using its own forms and types with antichokmatic function and by categorically opposing the very heart of chokmatic optimism" (1979:117). Schmid says that it is generally granted that Qohelet takes a stance critical of wisdom (1966:186; see p. 186 n. 218 and p. 194 nn. 260-62 for further references). Kroeber (p. 270) is one of the few who denies that the purpose of the book is polemical. He understands the dialectic with the older world view to be itself a form of wisdom.

another source of knowledge, which Qohelet does not mention), man cannot "know what is good" for him (6:12).

Several times Qohelet declares flatly that "no one can enable (man) to see what will happen afterwards (*'aḥărayw*)"[29] (variants of the formula use the verbs "see", "find", and "tell"; 3:22b; 6:12; 7:14; 10:14; cf. 8:7). *'aḥărayw* usually refers to the future within an individual's life (6:12b; 7:14; 8:7; 10:14a). In 3:22b this word seems to mean "afterwards", referring to the time after death (cf. 3:21).

Qohelet uses similar vocabulary in denying the possibility of knowing one's "time" (i.e., time of death; 9:12), and of knowing what happens after death (3:21), what misfortunes will occur (11:2) and which planting will succeed (11:6).

In spite of these denials, Qohelet assumes that some things *can* be known about the future. He makes statements about the expected consequences of various deeds, as in 7:1-7, 11-12; 8:1b, 5; 10:8-9, 12b-13, 20; 11:1, 4. He asserts that God will judge (3:17), that it will go well with the righteous and ill with the evildoer (8:12-13a; 7:17), and that God may punish rash vows (5:5). Qohelet also believes it possible to know what *types* of events will inevitably come to pass. Because nothing new ever occurs (1:9f.; 3:15), the future must echo the past. The fact that "everything has a time" (3:1-8) means that "everything"—every type of event—will occur and recur. In this sense, we do indeed know what will happen in the future.

The tension between Qohelet's assertions of knowledge and his blanket statements of ignorance (especially 7:14) can be explained, though not eliminated, by defining more closely just what kind of foreknowledge he considers impossible.

Not to know what will happen means, in Qohelet's view, to lack foreknowledge that is both certain and specific. In 8:7 he says that the reason man is ignorant of "what will happen" (*mah šeyyihyeh*) is that he does not know "when it will happen". Knowing "what" is dependent on knowing "when". From this we learn that knowledge of "what will happen" does not mean knowing the expected result of behavior; for example, the fact that God will punish the careless oath-taker, or that one who digs a pit will probably fall into it, or that death will occur—for it is possible to know a general truth without knowing when a particular manifestation of it will take place. "What will happen" in 8:7 means a specific occurrence, such as a certain

29. The rhetorical question serves as a negative.

person's undergoing judgment, an individual's death, the outbreak of a specific war. A man knows he will die; but because he does not know the time of his death, he cannot, in Qohelet's terminology, be said to know "what will happen".[30] Qoh 10:8-14 supports this explanation of what it means to know "what will happen". In 10:8-13 Qohelet makes some statements about certain ironic reversals that can be expected to occur and teaches or implies the importance of taking precautions (10:10-11). Such statements assume an ability to estimate the effects of present actions. Yet in encapsulating this unit his conclusion is: "Man does not know what will happen, for who can tell him what will happen afterwards?" (10:14).[31] The fact that Qohelet believes that ironic reversals demonstrate ignorance rather than knowledge shows that "knowing" here means awareness of the particulars of an individual's fate. Such knowledge is, of course, impossible, but the principle—one's deeds may rebound on him—is accessible.

In any particular case, there can be no certainty even about the broad outlines of the future, except with regard to the universal fact of death (9:5). Man cannot know whether a certain person will prosper or suffer, live long or die young, for there are always exceptions to the rules that would predict these things (7:15; 8:11-14). Man cannot even know whether wisdom and diligence will bring prosperity, for though they may be expected to do so, wealth can easily perish in an unfortunate incident. Conversely, while one's folly usually harms him, it may happen that a fool gains a wise man's wealth (2:19) or is appointed to high office (10:6). Although wisdom will usually bring wealth, the wise cannot be said truly to possess property, because *'et wapega'*, lit., "time-and-accident" (9:11), in other words, happenstance, may sever deed from outcome.

As different as Qohelet's vision of the world is from other Wisdom

30. The Instruction for Kagemeni uses the phrase "what will happen" in the same way: "One knows not what may happen, what god does when he punishes" (Pap. Prisse 2,1; *AEL*, I, p. 60). "What may happen" refers to the particular punishment awaiting an individual. The man spoken of in this passage thinks he has the future under control but may be in for a surprise. On the other hand the principle—divine retribution—is indeed known. Sir 9:11 and 11:4 show the same concept of "not knowing" the future.

31. *Me'aḥărayw* is ambiguous but probably refers to the future in general, including the future within an individual's life; see comment on 10:14.

Literature, his skepticism about the future is not in itself a radical *conceptual* break from other Wisdom Literature. He still assumes the existence of patterns and principles, and these are accessible and do allow *probable* knowledge of the future. They are not, however, inviolable. While man can discern what types of consequence will probably ensue from deeds, he cannot have knowledge of the specifics of future occurrences. Again: some knowledge, some ignorance; but for Qohelet it is the latter that defines the quality of human powers.

The sages manifestly believed that they were able to predict what *kind* of consequences moral character (if not specific acts) would produce, at least in the long run: "Righteousness delivers from death" (Prov 10:2); "The fear of the Lord increases one's lifetime" (10:27); "Honor the Lord from your wealth, from the first fruits of all your produce, and your barns will be full of provisions, your vats will overflow with new wine" (3:9f.). Almost every saying in didactic Wisdom displays confidence in man's ability to forecast the types of effect human behavior will have.

Nevertheless, the conventional sages too taught that the future is hidden. It is hidden first of all from an individual whose plans violate the moral working of the world. The consequences of his behavior are different from what *he* expected. He falls into the pit he dug for another.[32]

More fundamentally, the sages taught that there can never be certainty about the future in any specific case. No one can know the outcome of his plans. Several Egyptian sayings teach this; for example: "There is no one who knows (the outcome of) his plans, that he might plan the morrow".[33] The book of Proverbs similarly warns: "Do not boast about the morrow, for you do not know what the day will bring forth" (27:1); "From the Lord are a man's steps, so [*w*^{e}-] how can a man understand where he is headed [*darko*]?" (20:24). Further examples of proverbs that speak of the obscurity of the future are Prov 14:12; 16:1, 9, 25; 19:21; 20:24; 27:1; Sir 9:11; 11:4. Wisdom Literature manifests a sense of the contingency of

32. This topos is widespread in Wisdom Literature. Variant formulations appear in Prov 26:27; Pss 7:16; 9:16; Sir 27:26; *Qoh Rab* 7:21; Onchsheshonqy 22,5; Petubastis 26-27 (quoted in Lichtheim, 1983:29f.).

33. Ptahhotep l. 345 (*AEL*, I, p. 69); similarly "Eloquent Peasant" B 1, 183 (*AEL*, I, p. 177); Amenemopet 19,13 (*AEL*, II, p. 157).

events and a respect for the unpredictability of God's will.

J. G. Williams has observed that proverbs asserting retribution should be understood as speaking of typical cases, as teaching that "*usually* or *typically* one obtains results in terms of what one gives and how one takes a stance toward others" (1981:18). Proverbial statements are principles, not strict predictive formulae. The sages were aware of exceptions, although they rarely mention them in didactic Wisdom, whose purpose, after all, was inculcating proper behavior, not addressing existential or epistemological problems (a task that few besides Qohelet took on themselves). Theodicy, of course, does wrestle with the implications of exceptions to the principles Wisdom teaches. The answers are too various to summarize, but one of the basic postulates of theodicy (put forward by both the author of the book of Job and by Job's friends) is that man is indeed ignorant—not of the principles of God's rule but of the way these work out in reality. Thus human ignorance is made to serve as a buffer to human knowledge. The exceptions move from being the problem to being part of the solution.

In the matter of knowledge of the future, Qohelet does not differ conceptually from didactic Wisdom Literature. The difference—and this is a significant one—is in the greater emphasis Qohelet places on the inevitability of human ignorance.

Qohelet alone is troubled by the limitations on knowledge of the future. He alone is burdened by the inability to know when one will die (one's "time")—a limitation the other sages seem to have accepted easily enough, or at least did not brood over. Qohelet thinks that the lack of this knowledge makes man as helpless as a trapped fish or bird (9:12). Now we might object that knowing when we will die would still not make us less helpless in the face of death. But not only helplessness bothers Qohelet. Ignorance in itself, apart from its actual consequences, oppresses him, as if knowledge of the time of death would make the thought of death easier to bear.

When Qohelet denies the possibility of foreknowledge, he is implicitly defining knowledge as both certain and specific.[34] He does

34. The assumption that knowledge must be certain enters into the conundrum of Western skepticism as well: if knowledge is justified true belief, we cannot *know* that something will happen until it has happened. But if I believed that something would happen, and it does, did I not *know* it would happen?

not apply this conception consistently, but it does inform his statements about foreknowledge. For him, anything less than certainty is ignorance; a grasp of patterns and probabilities does not qualify as knowledge. Qohelet experiences disappointment because he expects of wisdom more than it can deliver, more even than it was thought to deliver.

None of this places Qohelet in the ranks of the orthodox. The different emphasis results in a book unlike any other Wisdom text. The other sages saw the same realities as Qohelet (how could one avoid being aware of the injustices he points out?), but he responds to them and interprets them differently.

Qohelet desires knowledge, in particular a knowledge of the consequences of deeds. An intense desire for knowledge, knowledge defined most stringently, rather than a contemptuous rejection of someone else's claim to have it, is the source of Qohelet's obsession with ignorance of the future.

Qohelet seems to start with the expectation that reason can provide certainty, and when he sees that it does not, he is struck by its frailty. The other sages seem more comfortable with the limitations of knowledge. A belief in God's beneficence allows them to trust in his guidance of human affairs even when humans cannot see clearly where they are going, and moreover to feel that this is all to the good.[35] Qohelet does not have a confidence in God's benevolence that could make his awareness of ignorance more bearable.

§3.242 *Understanding of life*

Besides seeking to know what will happen, man desires to understand life, but this, Qohelet says, is denied him. Yet in some ways Qohelet attributes to the human intellect potentials and prerogatives far beyond what the other sages allowed for.

To refer to the type of understanding denied man, Qohelet uses much the same vocabulary as he used in denying knowledge of the

35. This, as well as the infirmity of human planning, is the lesson of Prov 16:9: "A man's heart plans his way, but God establishes his step". In other words, whether a man will succeed, will walk securely to his goal, ultimately depends on God. But since God's favor can be secured by proper behavior, the outcome can be influenced by humans, even though individuals cannot know just how their plans will eventuate.

future, usually the verbs *maṣa'* and *yada'*, both of which sometimes mean "understand". The near synonymy of *maṣa'* and *yada'* is seen in 8:17b: even if the wise man intends to "know" (YD'), he cannot "find" (MṢ'). *Yad'a* clearly means "understand" in Prov 30:18. Examples of *maṣa'* in a closely related sense are Judg 14:18b; Job 11:7; 37:23. *Maṣa'* always refers to the result of a process, usually a deliberate search, such as Qohelet's own investigation (see the interplay of *baqqeš* and *maṣa'* in 7:23-8:1; 8:17). *Maṣa'* signifies attaining the understanding designated by *yada'*. We can often translate *maṣa'* as "come to an understanding of", or "apprehend", as in Judg 14:18b (*m^eṣa'tem ḥiddati* = "come to understand my riddle", i.e., solve it) and Sir 31:22 (*tmṣ' 'mry* = "understand my words"; *tśyg 'mry* in the doublet). (Qohelet does not use *hebin*, the word most commonly translated "understand".)

To designate the objects of the desired understanding, Qohelet uses the phrases *mah šehayah*, *ma'ăśeh ha'ĕlohim*, *hamma'ăśeh 'ăšer na'ăśah taḥat haššemeš* (and variants). These phrases all signify the events of life. *Ma'ăśeh ha'ĕlohim* means "God's work" in the sense of the events that he brings to pass. This is the same as "that which occurs [*na'ăśah*] under the sun", inasmuch as God "makes everything happen" (11.5; similarly 3:11); see §§5.11, 5.13. *'aśah* in 3:11 does not refer to Creation, which would be irrelevant to this context, but to events in human life, such as summarized by the "catalogue" of 3:1-8. Qohelet's claim is that no one can understand what God brings to pass, in other words, what happens in life (3:11; 7:23-24; 8:16-9:2; 11:5).

Man's inability to understand what happens on earth is, in Qohelet's view, equivalent to the incomprehensibility of God's will. This is clear in 8:17, where *ma'ăśeh ha'ĕlohim*, "the events that God brings to pass", is rephrased as "the events that occur under the sun" (see commentary). These are what man cannot understand.

Just what type of understanding is denied man? He is not denied understanding entirely. It is, for example, possible to understand that wisdom is of great value (7:11-12) or that bribes will corrupt judges (7:7). The understanding impossible for man is of the sort Qohelet set out to find (1:13) but found stymied by life's absurdity (1:14).

Qohelet's insistence on the incomprehensibility of life is another expression of his assertion of life's absurdity, as the restatement, in very similar phraseology, of Qoh 1:13-14 by 8:16-17 shows. Both speak of Qohelet's inquiry and its failure—the first describing life's absurdity, the second its incomprehensibility. It is the absurdity of life—the divorce between expected and actual consequences—that makes it incomprehensible and prevents knowledge of the future. Thus both limitations on human wisdom result from the same quality of reality. Not everything in life is absurd, but enough is absurd that this becomes the salient characteristic of the totality, and that characteristic prevents the understanding of life and God's will.

By looking at the phenomena that proved counter-rational and thus incomprehensible, we see examples of the kind of understanding Qohelet sought. Qohelet desired to understand the relation between toil and consequences, between people's moral quality and the length of their lives, between a person's wisdom and his possession of wealth, and so on. In other words, Qohelet sought to grasp the rationale of events in human life, to know the logical connection between behavior and outcome. When he could not find a logical, infallible connection, he pronounced the phenomena he observed, and life as a whole, absurd.

This insistence on the absurdity of life, which is to say, its incomprehensibility, is not an attack on human intellect so much as a complaint against the barriers placed upon it. Even if the power of human intellect were vastly increased, it would face the ineluctable irrationality of life. The limitations of human wisdom are thus rooted in the very nature of the world.

Even while pointing out these barriers, Qohelet reveals a sense of the mind's power to grasp widely and deeply. He maintains the essential epistemological validity of wisdom, believing that human wisdom is truly knowledge. He manifests this belief first of all in stating that he possessed and used much wisdom (1:13, 16) and then declaring, with a certitude rivaling that of Job's friends, the conclusions to which his wisdom led him.

The validity of wisdom is revealed in one of its severe shortcomings: it exposes painful truths (1:17f.; 7:15f.). When Qohelet warns of the dangers of growing too wise (as he does in 7:15f.), he assumes the epistemological (and not merely the practical) validity of wisdom. It is important to remember that Qohelet considers the unpleasant truths he discovered to be wisdom no less than the conventional counsels he offers.

With regard to the attempt to understand the logic of events Qohelet is indeed critical of the wise, but the nature of this criticism needs to be defined. He is not attacking the teachers of Wisdom Literature for extravagant claims. Rather, in asserting the hopelessness of speculation such as he himself undertook, Qohelet is chiding anyone who makes such an attempt. Wisdom is properly used in such an investigation (1:13), and the wise man is the person best equipped for the task (8:16-17), though others too may attempt it (8:17 speaks of "the wise man" as one type of person who might try to comprehend the events of life). The wise man in question is not perceived as a member of a "school" or "profession" or as an author of didactic Wisdom Literature. While authors of speculative Wisdom (such as the book of Job) might be included, Qohelet's remarks are not directed specifically at people who write or teach about the rationale of the events of life. The wise man that Qohelet is representing and addressing is anyone who sets out to "investigate and to explore with wisdom all that occurs under the heavens".[36] In any case, the criticism is not polemical, because Qohelet does not say it is *wrong* to do this, only that such thinkers weary themselves out in a hopeless task. This criticism, which is really more in the nature of a warning, is incidental to his belief that it is unfair for such understanding to be withheld.

Qohelet's recognition of the futility of speculation is not unique. Agur declares that wisdom—defined by the parallel stich as "knowledge of Holiness" (i.e., God or God's will)—is beyond him (Prov 30:3-4). Ben Sira says, "Who has seen [God] and can tell about it? Who can extol him as he is? There is much hidden that is greater than these things, for we see but little of His works" (43:31-32; cf. 11:4b; 16:20-22; 18:4-7). In a similar vein Zophar asks: "Can you discover the mystery of God? Can you discover the limit of the Almighty? It is higher than heaven—what can you do? It is deeper than Sheol—what can you know?" (Job 11:7f.).

Didactic Wisdom Literature does not attempt the kind of investigation that Qohelet criticizes. The field of vision that didactic

36. Gordis (pp. 25-28) distinguishes between "practical" wisdom and "speculative" wisdom, the latter comprising Job, Qohelet, and Agur (Prov 30). It would be better to distinguish two (among the many) different *applications* of wisdom: speculation and practical ethics. There is no reason whatsoever to associate these two activities with different "schools".

Wisdom Literature chooses for itself is modest enough. It never claims to fathom the mysteries of Providence, never even tries to do so. It is rarely speculative and never esoteric. When it speaks about Creation (in particular in Prov 8), it identifies the primordial wisdom with the wisdom manifest in daily life and accessible to everyone. In fact, the book of Proverbs as a whole, and probably all of Wisdom Literature, understands true wisdom not as comprehension of life's mysteries, but simply as piety and everyday good sense. The sages repeatedly define wisdom by equating it with attitudes and actions that are within the individual's control—fearing God, staying away from another man's wife, speaking honestly, bridling one's temper, and so on—as if to assure the reader that everyday morality and sensible behavior is ample wisdom, and no deeper understanding of life is necessary. This is close to the message of Job 28 and of the proverbs that identify wisdom with fear of the Lord and moral behavior. And it is not far from the teaching of Qohelet. Qohelet is a speculative thinker who warns against the futility—not the legitimacy—of speculation.

While Qohelet is at one with the Wisdom tradition in insisting on the mystery of God's work, two deep differences divide him from the other sages.

First, the others are not troubled by the limitations on human reason. They believe that what knowledge is accessible to humanity is quite adequate, and they feel no need to push beyond this. Qohelet, in contrast, feels just such a need, and tries to push beyond, then feels hemmed in by the barriers to wisdom. and is oppressed by the limitations of his knowledge. Again we see Qohelet's fierce demands on wisdom: if it is unable to apprehend the fundamental rationale of events, it has not achieved what it should have.

Second, Qohelet chooses a perspective far broader than the authors of didactic wisdom, wider even than that of other speculative wisdom, such as Job. Qohelet extends wisdom's horizon by undertaking an inquiry of a scope unparalleled in earlier Wisdom. As von Rad observed, Qohelet views life in its totality:

> Ihm geht es weniger um die Fixierung und die Diskussion von Einzelerfahrungen als um das Lebensganze und um ein abschliessendes Urteil darüber. Darin also ist Kohelet in theologischer Hinsicht viel anspruchsvoller geworden (1970:293).

Didactic Wisdom evaluated human actions, confining itself to informing the pupil and reader which behaviors win "favor and a good opinion in the eyes of God and man" (Prov 3:4) and which provoke disfavor. Qohelet alone tries to think about life in its totality. Not only that, he also dares to *judge* it (others might do so only to the extent of echoing God's primordial declaration of the world's goodness). The book of Job comes closest to the breadth of Qohelet's field of vision yet seems finally to veer away from a global judgment. Though Qohelet believes himself unable to understand life and God's ways, he does not draw back from evaluating them. One cannot understand things that are absurd, but he can know them to be so.

Qohelet assumes that the individual has the ability and the right to discover certain fundamental and disturbing truths. God can prevent man from knowing the particulars of the events to come in the drama of human life and from making sense of the events in it, but he cannot keep man from judging the play. Qohelet thus arrives at a peculiar combination of humility and arrogance in his attitude toward the scope of knowledge: you cannot know the particulars of the events that God will bring to pass, and you cannot understand their reason or nature, but you *can* know about—can, indeed, pass judgment on—the rationality of God's behavior. And this judgment too is wisdom: knowledge attained by a wise man through the exercise of *ḥokmah* (1:13). Man's power of moral judgment can assess realities his intellectual powers could not untangle.

These differences, significant as they are, do not constitute a dispute, an argument *against* someone. In exposing the limitations of reason, Qohelet is not attacking the wise (or the sages) for overstepping boundaries or for pretending to greater knowledge than they have. He does not do this even in Qoh 8:17, which is commonly thought to be rebuking the sages for their pretensions to knowledge. Zimmerli, for example, invokes this verse to depict Qohelet as a polemicist:

> All seine [sc., Qohelet's] Bemühung ist im Grunde ein großes Kampfgespräch mit der Weisheit, die meint, die Dinge der Welt in ihren Zusammenhängen, und damit auch Gott, verstehen zu können und die darauf ihre zuversichtliche Lebenskunde baut (1962:223).

But this verse does not rebuke the wise man. When Qohelet says, "And even if the wise man intends [not 'claims'—see commentary] to understand it, he is not able to apprehend it [sc., what God brings to pass]" (8:17b), he is not blaming or mocking the wise man for presumptuous claims, but rather heightening the complaint of 8:17a. No one, *not even* the wise man—the one most able to gain understanding and most deserving of it—can discover the rationale of what happens in life. There is a note of sadness and even indignation here, a feeling that it is unfair to deprive one of the knowledge he desires, a desire imposed on him by God (3:11). Qohelet is indignant that the wise man does not receive the full rewards of his wisdom, just as he is irritated that a toiler may not get the full benefits of his earnings (6:1-6) or that the rich may have to "sit in lowly places" (10:6).

Qohelet's distress at the inevitability of ignorance is not polemical. He does not say: wise men think that their wisdom shows them what will happen, but *I* say that the future is hidden. He says: using wisdom, I came to realize that the future is hidden. He does not criticize the wise for speaking about the future. It is not they, but the foolish, that dare to speak much about what will happen (10:14). Qohelet assumes that the wise man knows better; indeed, one who did not know better would not be wise. Likewise he does not set his knowledge against that of the wise, but takes his own wisdom, whose validity he assumes, to show the limits placed about human knowledge.

In complaining about the limits of wisdom, then, Qohelet's stance is not polemical but protective. He himself is a wise man and a sage, and he shares the sages' esteem of wisdom. Therefore he feels chagrin at the world—and thus, indirectly, at God—for denying wisdom its just rewards.

§3.3 *What good is wisdom? The pragmatics of wisdom*

Modern commentators, in emphasizing (quite rightly) Qohelet's statements about the shortcomings of wisdom, tend to push his affirmations of wisdom's benefits far to the periphery, taking them as minor concessions to wisdom's "relative" or (merely) practical value (see n. 38). Qohelet is believed to be denying the speculative, philosophical value of wisdom, conceding to it only a modest, restricted usefulness. Traditional exegesis, on the other hand (like the epilogue itself), focused on the affirmations of wisdom, playing down Qohelet's observations of its violability by viewing them as admissions of the failure of certain types of wisdom (in particular, practical cunning) in certain circumstances. This section will compare the negative with the positive in order to achieve a more precise understanding of Qohelet's attitude and to see where his emphasis lies.

§3.31 *The benefits of wisdom*

Qohelet asserts the practical value of wisdom frequently and emphatically. He says that wisdom is superior to folly. We may call this advantage "relative", but it is certainly not a marginal one; it is as extreme as the advantage of light over darkness (2:13). For the wise man has eyes to see where he is going and can maneuver through life, while the fool stumbles about in the darkness of ignorance (2:14a). Nothing Qohelet says ever contradicts this estimation of the advantage of wisdom.

The benefits of wisdom are vast. It may bring a man wealth (7:11-12a), the showcase example being, of course, Qohelet himself, who grew rich by laboring in wisdom (2:9, 19, 21). The wise man's mind ("heart") helps him, the fool's harms him (10:2-3). The wise man's mouth gains him favor, while the fool's destroys him (10:12). Wisdom guides a man to correct and careful behavior in the presence of a ruler (8:1b). Wisdom's aid is more valuable than the wealth of a city's rulers (7:19; see comment). Wisdom can save a city (9:14f.), for it is more powerful than a warrior's might (9:16) or than weapons of war (9:18). It can bring a poor youth from prison to kingship (4:13f.). The softly spoken command of a wise man has a greater effect than a ruler's shout among fools (9:17). The rebuke of the wise improves one's mind (7:3). Wisdom even keeps its possessor alive (7:12). All these are benefits of the highest magnitude.

§3.32 *The failings of wisdom*

Among the blessings Qohelet praises wisdom for conferring, one benefit conspicuously lacking is happiness. Wisdom, at least in high degree, may in fact be a source of unhappiness and disappointment. It may also fail to provide other promised advantages.

Wisdom causes unhappiness first of all by revealing bitter realities. This is a lesson of Qohelet's experience, discovered when he set out "to investigate and to explore with wisdom all that occurs under the heavens" (1:13). As Qohelet's wisdom increased (1:16), so did his misery (1:17-18). The cause for his misery, stated earlier, is the world's absurdity and perversity (1:14-15). The wise man, who "has his eyes in his head" (2:14), sees this and is distressed; if he pushes his wisdom too far, he may become "dumbfounded" (7:16).

Second, wisdom's efficacy is uncertain. It is too vulnerable to life's exigencies to guarantee the benefits promised by the wise men (Qohelet among them). As valuable as wisdom is (9:13-15a), people respect wealth more, often holding the wisdom of a poor man in contempt (9:16b). And if they heed it, they quickly forget the wise man himself, even if his wisdom saved their city (9:13-15). One offender (9:18), one offense (10:1), can undo much wisdom. Wisdom can indeed be expected to produce wealth, yet a fool may come into a wise man's property without effort (2:19). Though wisdom may make a man king, he too will be replaced and forgotten (4:14-16). The wise cannot secure their bread, wealth, or favor (9:11), because all efforts and talents are buffeted about by the vagaries of chance (v. 12).

Qohelet bemoans the treatment the wise receive at the hand of God and man. "How the wise man dies just like the fool!" (2:16) is a lament, and "to what purpose, then, have I become so very wise?" (2:15) is a complaint.[37] Qohelet feels cheated; the equal treatment of wise man and fool is a severe injustice. But this does not make Qohelet repudiate wisdom any more than the undeserved fate of the righteous (7:14) makes him repudiate righteousness. The injustices wrought upon wisdom do not obviate the qualitative difference between wisdom and folly; rather, the difference exacerbates the absurdity.

In comparing Qohelet's view of wisdom's benefits with that of other Wisdom Literature, we may consider one common formulation of Qohelet's ideas. It is often stated, by way of resolving the tension within Qohelet's evaluations of wisdom, that he grants wisdom a "relative" value, or a merely practical value (hence his "positive" evaluations), but not an absolute value (hence his "negative"

37. R. E. Murphy (1979:237) points out that 2:15-16 is not a rejection of wisdom but a complaint about its failure to deliver. The complaint is against a wrong *done to* wisdom and presumes that wisdom is intrinsically valuable.

evaluations). This is thought to distinguish him from conventional Wisdom Literature, which supposedly absolutized the value of wisdom.[38]

We must ask what it means to ascribe a relative value to wisdom. It could mean that wisdom is valuable only by comparison with folly, but not in and of itself. But this formulation characterizes neither Qohelet nor the other sages. First, all values are relative in the sense of being determined by the relation between qualities on the same scale. The issue is where one places the qualities in question. The sages placed wisdom and folly on two extremes of the moral-intellectual scale, and Qohelet did the same. He taught that wisdom is at the opposite extreme from folly, no less than light is from darkness (7:11); wisdom is life-preserving (7:11-12). This is no begrudging admission of a small relative value, but an insistence on a vast relative value.

Alternatively, to say that wisdom has a "relative value" may mean that it is (intrinsically) useful but not invariably so; it may not succeed in all ways and in all circumstances. In this sense, Qohelet

38. See, for example, the comments of Hertzberg, Zimmerli, and Lauha on Qoh 2:13-15. A distinction of this sort seems to be the solution advocated by Loader (1979). He summarizes the "polar structure" of 1:12-2:16 as follows:

Pole: General *ḥokmā* Contra-pole: Folly
Tension: Relative advantage of the general *ḥokmā*

Pole: General *ḥokmā* Contra-pole: Occur[r]ences of life
Tension: Worthlessness of the *ḥokmā* (pp. 42, 35-66, *passim*)

It is not clear how "occur[r]ences of life" are the "contra-pole" of "general *ḥokmā*", and it does not seem that what Loader calls "tensions" are really that (perhaps he means "resolutions"). Throughout his book Loader seems to argue that Qohelet sets up tensions between opposites (and complements) of various sorts and resolves them either by rejecting one pole or by judging one pole preferable. (I am not certain that this is Loader's point. He is extremely unclear on the nature of his "poles" and "tensions".) If by the second "tension" Loader means that Qohelet regards wisdom as vulnerable to mishaps, that is certainly correct. But such vulnerability does not make wisdom ("general" or otherwise) "worthless". In any case, if wisdom has an advantage "relative to" anything, it is not worthless. (It is not clear what Loader means by "relative to" in his description of the second polar structure.)

does indeed regard wisdom as a relative value (it would be better to call it a "contingent" value). But in this same sense wisdom is a relative or contingent value in all Wisdom Literature. Though this is rarely stressed in didactic Wisdom (probably for pedagogic rather than ideological reasons), the sages recognized that success cannot be secured perfectly; wisdom cannot overcome all of life's contingencies or the unpredictable turns of God's will. (This has been shown by von Rad, 1970:131-48.) Qohelet does not differ from the conventional sages in recognizing that wisdom is powerless before the inevitability of death, just as he agrees with them in his belief that wisdom (and the attendant piety) can save one from a premature death (thus we are to interpret the promises in Qoh 7:12; Prov 11:4; etc.). But certainly Qohelet departs sharply from the other sages in emphasizing the contingency of wisdom's effectiveness. The difference is once again that Qohelet is disturbed by a fact that was generally recognized but, for the most part, taken for granted.[39] He will not dismiss impingements on wisdom's efficacy as temporary or localized anomalies, but interprets them as further evidence of universal injustice and absurdity.

Qohelet believes that wisdom can grasp significant truths, but these do not include an understanding of the rationale of events, for an absurd world defies such insight. He believes that wisdom has great value, but that this value is often undermined by the accidents and injustices of an absurd world.

Qohelet diverges from didactic Wisdom also in recognizing that knowledge—genuine knowledge, and not just opinion—could cause unhappiness (the authors of Job and Ps 49 knew this, but they believed that painful knowledge could be subordinated to a broader perspective). There may be some dissent in this divergence; Qohelet may be implying: wise men think that knowledge (i.e., wisdom) makes one happy, but in my superior wisdom I discovered that it can cause discomfort as well. Yet the first part of this statement is not heard in Qohelet, so although he may be consciously moving away from a common opinion, he is not *attacking* it or the people who hold to it. He is certainly not directing a polemic against wisdom or Wisdom teachings, any more than a moralist is attacking ethical

39. An exception is the author of Ps 49, who is troubled to see the wise dying like the foolish and leaving their wealth to others (vv. 11f.), though he does hint obscurely at a solution (v. 16).

philosophy by recognizing that moral people often know disappointment and failure, and that they may even be especially sensitive to the pain of human suffering. Qohelet knows that wisdom is vulnerable, and he emphasizes this more than most sages, but he does not treasure wisdom less for recognizing—and complaining about—its vulnerability.

§3.4 *The wisdom imperative*

Wisdom, Qohelet believes, is to be pursued for its own sake, apart from any utilitarian motivations. It is, in fact, sometimes the opposite of useful, but its value, whatever its failings, is fundamental. This valuation of wisdom is not so much a teaching, expressed in observations or words of counsel, as an attitude, an unspoken ethic, manifest more in what Qohelet does than in what he says about wisdom. On the deepest level, Qohelet feels it imperative to pursue the truth.

The wisdom imperative makes itself felt even (and perhaps especially) when Qohelet is not praising wisdom. It comes to expression when he explains that people imagine an event to be new only because they forget the past (1:11). He is certainly not saying this with a sigh of relief. This verse is part of a gloomy passage whose tone of weary resignation is sounded by 1:3 and 8. Qohelet is annoyed at people's unawareness of reality. Underlying this annoyance is a feeling that they *should* be aware of the fact that there is nothing new under the sun, although that truth is vexing and not particularly useful. The praise of wisdom in 2:13-14 may also reveal this attitude: the wise man's seeing and walking in light may signify not only that he manages better in life, but that he alone sees reality. If so, the verse does not praise wisdom for its practical utility so much as for its grasp on truths, including unpleasant ones such as Qohelet rakes up in this very unit—the absurdity of toil and the leveling of the wise and the foolish by death.[40] Qohelet believes that it is better to live with open eyes, whatever one may see.

Qohelet again reveals the value he places on knowledge for its own sake when he advises the reader to pursue life's activities, because

40. Thus Plumptre interprets 2:13-14: "A man is conscious of being more truly man when he looks before and after, and knows how to observe". Plumptre compares the *Iliad*, xvii 647: "And if our fate be death, give light, and let us die" (similarly Barton).

"there is no activity or calculation or knowledge or wisdom in Sheol, where you are headed" (9:10). You should embrace these things while they are still possible, even if the effort is futile and the knowledge oppressive. The intrinsic value of knowledge gives the living, however unhappy, at least one advantage over the dead: "the living know that they will die"—a most painful awareness—"while the dead know nothing" (9:5). The living should keep this disturbing truth ever in mind (7:2); thus the thoughts of the wise man dwell in the house of mourning (7:4). Qohelet does not tell us just what "good" this will do. Some truths have slipped through the barriers God placed before human knowledge. The fact of death is one, and it should not be avoided.

More fundamentally, we may ask to what end Qohelet reports the maddening inequities and absurdities he sees in life. Why does he tell us of the oppression and the callousness he observed, or of the unfair treatment of the wicked and righteous at death, or of the righteous dying young? Or, for that matter, why does he harp on the absurdity of life itself? He proposes no remedies for these inequities. He recommends the balm of pleasure to soothe the observer, but if soothing was his main concern, why rake up the disturbing facts in the first place? Qohelet reports the injustices he sees because he feels that the reader *should* know these truths.

Once, to be sure, Qohelet seems to advocate a blurring of consciousness as a way of dulling the pain of awareness. In 5:19 (and only there), he explains why pleasure is useful. A person allowed to steep himself in pleasure "will not much call to mind the days of his life, since God is keeping him occupied with his heart's pleasures". Pleasure is an anodyne for the pain of consciousness, but it has not worked for Qohelet, who, by persisting in his search for knowledge, shows that he considers it more important to achieve wisdom than to eliminate the attendant discomfort. In any case, the remark in 5:19 is contradicted by the emphatic teaching in 7:2-4, that it is better to go to a house of mourning, so as to keep death in mind, than to go to a place of festivity (*beyt mišteh*, also called *beyt śimḥah*).

In 7:16 Qohelet warns us against going so far in wisdom as to be dumbfounded. The wisdom he is cautioning about here, the wisdom that might dumbfound you, can only be the honest, unflinching exercise of reason, the willingness to face facts such as he reports in 7:15, namely that there are just people who die young and wicked people who live long. To see such inequities is *l^ehithakkem yoter*, "to become exceedingly wise". But this advice (like his warning against great righteousness) should not be isolated and elevated to the status of a fundamental principle. Although he here warns of the consequences of pushing too hard for wisdom, he himself pursues just this sort of wisdom throughout the book, showing that he values wisdom even while aware of the price it exacts.

The compulsion for knowledge that Qohelet recognizes in himself, he considers divinely imposed upon him and upon mankind generally. He describes his exploration of "all that occurs under the heavens" as "an unfortunate business that God has given people to busy themselves with" (1:13b). God has put "toil" (reading *he'amal*) in man's heart, this toil being the hopeless task of seeking to "apprehend [*maṣa'*] ... that which God has brought to pass" (3:11). Once implanted, however, that compulsion becomes part of human volition, so Qohelet can say that he took it upon himself to investigate all that happens in life (1:13a).

For Qohelet, wisdom means lucidity, the virtue Camus calls *clairvoyance*. Man's knowledge, as Qohelet sees it, is hemmed in by a jealous deity, and man's achievements are undermined by God's inexplicable, apparently arbitrary, rule. But through wisdom man may rise above his helplessness, look at the world and at God from a certain distance, and judge both. Yet this lucidity is not for Qohelet (as it is for Camus's hero of the absurd) an act of rebellion, at least not deliberate rebellion. Qohelet neither challenges God nor hopes for change. Human freedom resides not in action but in wisdom: the observation of life by independent human reason. Qohelet, the archetypal wise man, is a Sisyphus, ever condemned to pushing a rock to the top of a mountain knowing that it will immediately roll back down. For Camus, the moment of lucidity at the top of the mountain, before the rock rolls back, constitutes Sisyphus's triumph over his fate; indeed, in this lucidity, Sisyphus the rebel triumphs over the gods. For Qohelet, on the other hand, an authentic life is not a rebellion, nor is lucidity man's triumph over divinity (it may, on the contrary, be another divine affliction). Yet Qohelet too affirms lucidity apart from its practical benefits. By relentlessly pursuing a truth that does him no "good" to discover, subordinating every other consideration to this "unfortunate business" (1:13), Qohelet shows that he cherishes wisdom, wherever it leads, above the pleasures he often praises. Qohelet is a Sisyphus aware of his fate but unaware of his triumph.

Qohelet undoubtedly differs from other Wisdom texts in many ways, more radically, I believe, in his epistemology than in his specific conclusions. But he does not attack Wisdom Literature or the wisdom it teaches. He regards his own thought as wisdom and of a piece with the wisdom of his predecessors. He never draws a distinction between wisdom of his type and that claimed or practiced by the other sages. He never sets up a proposition maintained by other sages in order to refute it. Roland Murphy has described the book of Qohelet as a bold extension of Wisdom (1979:235-45). That is precisely what Qohelet says his investigation was. He took existing wisdom to himself—not to attack it, but to make it his own; in this he was like all the wise. But then he proceeded to extend it boldly by seeking new knowledge in new ways in new frontiers.

> Pour un homme sans œillères, il n'est pas de plus beau spectacle que celui de l'intelligence aux prises avec une réalité qui le dépasse.
>
> Camus, *Le Mythe de Sisyphe*, p. 78

Chapter 4

JUSTICE AND THEODICY

> [Le révolté métaphysique] oppose le principe de justice qui est en lui au principe d'injustice qu'il voit à l'œuvre dans le monde. Il ne veut donc rien d'autre, primitivement, que résoudre cette contradiction.[1]
>
> Camus, *L'Homme révolté*, p. 40

§4.0 *The problem*

Qohelet both affirms divine justice and complains of the injustices that God allows. The contradiction is most blatant in 8:10b-14, where Qohelet says that the righteous live long and the wicked die young (8:12b-13) *and* that the opposite sometimes occurs (8:10b-12a + 14).

The techniques for eliminating contradictions have been exercised most vigorously on Qohelet's statements on justice. Inconsistencies have been harmonized and various sentences tagged as orthodox glosses or quotations (see Excursus I for discussion and examples). But this contradiction appears too often, too prominently, and too well-integrated into context to be convincingly harmonized. The addition-hypothesis requires deciding in advance that Qohelet believes one side or the other of the contradiction, though both are well represented. And it is equally arbitrary to identify one opinion as a quotation, for nothing in the passages at issue attributes one of the contradictory ideas to another voice.

The contradiction in Qohelet's statements on justice should not be harmonized or excised, for he himself recognizes it. He bemoans it but does not resolve it, for he is describing a paradox he sees in the world about him: God is a just judge who allows inexplicable

1. The continuation of the sentence cannot be well applied to Qohelet: "... instaurer le règne unitaire de la justice, s'il le peut [Qohelet does not attempt theodicy] ou de l'injustice, si on le pousse à bout [Qohelet's despair does not dislodge his insistence on the primacy of the value of justice]. En attendant, il dénonce la contradiction". [This Qohelet does do.]

inequities. This is truly a contradiction, thus an absurdity, for "l'absurde en lui-même est contradiction".[2]

§4.1 *Terminology*

Let us distinguish between judgment and justice, formulating working definitions for terms of extraordinary philosophical complexity. *Judgment* is an instrumental act comprised of a judicial decision together with the execution of that decision (both are denoted by ŠPṬ in its various forms).[3] Just judgment punishes the guilty and rewards the righteous in order to bring about *justice*, an equipoise between behavior and its consequences. Justice is ideally distributive: the ledger of every individual life must balance, with happiness or misfortune poised precisely against the goodness or evil each person has done. We may call such a state of complete justice equity. Acts of justice and just judgment promote equity but do not necessarily achieve it. Just judgment issues in retribution, but judgment, even a just judgment, may fail to restore equity. A human court system offers judgment, and when it works well we may say that justice is done. This is often a poor substitute for equity, but it is the best that humans can achieve. If an omnipotent being is just, he must bring about equity. Qohelet believes that God is just, and that he will judge, but he doubts that this will restore equity.

The central problems in this issue can be discussed without determining the precise sense of the Hebrew terms associated with it, for the contradiction in Qohelet does not depend on the niceties of definition, and redefinition will not remove them. The exact meaning of the derivatives of ṢDQ (*ṣaddiq*, *ṣedeq*, and *ṣᵉdaqah*) does not bear directly on the problem of divine justice. It is enough to know that *ṣedeq* is a moral good to realize that for a *ṣaddiq* to die young is an injustice. For the most part we can follow Fahlgren's broad definition (or, perhaps, characterization) of these concepts:

> [*Ṣᵉdaqah*] und verwandte Begriffe im Alten Testament sind sämtlich Ausdrücke für das Gute, das Rechte und Richtige, mag es sich nun um das Verhältnis der Menschen zueinander oder um ihre Stellung zu Gott handeln. Sie bezeichnen die rechten Gedanken,

2. Camus, *L'Homme révolté*, p. 18.

3. This is the "richterliche Instanz" that Koch (1972 [orig., 1955]:133) regards as constitutive of "Vergeltung" (retribution), a concept he considers foreign to the HB. See below, n. 5.

> Worte und Handlungen, die Harmonie im einzelnen Menschen, in der Familie und in der Gemeinschaft, Reichtum, Ehre und Erfolg, mit einem Worte: das Leben selbst in all seinem Reichtum und seiner Fülle. Sie sind also positiv im eigentlichsten Sinne dieses Wortes (1932:1).

The words *šapaṭ* and *mišpaṭ* too are significant in Qohelet's remarks on justice. We do not have to discover the "Grundbedeutung" of these wide-ranging terms; it is enough to consider the senses the terms have in Qohelet, in particular where they refer to God's activity. (On human *mišpaṭ-ṣedeq* see 3:16; 5:7.)

Verses 12:14, 3:17, and 11:9b use ŠPṬ as a forensic concept and refer to God's judgment as a future event. God's judging is not something that goes on at all times, but an event in the future within an individual's life. In this judgment God distinguishes between good and bad deeds, between righteous and wicked people, and calls everyone to account. Whether or not ŠPṬ denotes the execution of the judgment (as it seems to do), certainly in the case of divine judgment there can be no gap between decision and fulfillment. For God to judge means that he will give each person his due, setting things aright.[4]

The words *'et umišpaṭ* in 8:5 and 6 are problematic (though *umišpaṭ* in v. 6 should probably be omitted; see commentary). According to these verses, the wise man will know *'et umišpaṭ*, because every matter has a time. For reasons explained in the commentary, I understand this phrase to mean "the time of (divine) judgment", in this case, the time when the despot will be judged and thus punished for his deeds.

§4.2 *Qohelet's belief in God's justice*

Several times Qohelet speaks of retribution, both reward and punishment (but mostly punishment), almost in a tone of pious confidence. His belief in the justice of God's rule underlies many of his statements. When Qohelet says that God makes everything happen appropriately (*yapeh*) in its time, he is affirming the fundamental justice of divine rule. When he praises the benefits of

4. "Setting right" comes close to the "Grundbedeutung" of *šapaṭ*, which is to say, the concept common to the greatest number of its uses. Administrators, military leaders, and judges all, in principle, exercise *mišpaṭ*-law and *mišpaṭ*-judgment to bring about the right state of affairs, also *mišpaṭ*.

wisdom and warns of the dangers of folly, he implies that virtues have their rewards, moral failings their punishments. Occasionally his affirmation of divine justice is explicit.

Following a common Wisdom usage, Qohelet pictures retribution in images of natural causality in 10:8-11:

> (8) He who digs a pit will fall into it, and he who breaks through a wall will be bitten by a snake. (9) He who moves stones will be hurt by them, and he who splits wood will be endangered by it. (10) If the iron is dull and he does not sharpen the edge, then [the axeman] must exert more force; but the advantage of the skilled man is wisdom. (11) If a snake bites for lack of a charm, what gain does the snake charmer have?

The Wisdom topos of falling into the pit one dug usually serves to teach the principle of peripety: a man's own evils rebound upon him (see commentary). Though this principle is usually formulated as a natural process, its working is felt to evidence God's ongoing intervention in the world's affairs. Ps 9:17 confirms this interpretation by identifying the nations' sinking in their own pit (v. 16) as Yahweh's judgment (v. 17). Similarly, Psalm 7 identifies natural retribution with God's judgment: the psalmist declares that God is a righteous judge (vv. 11-14) and illustrates this judgment by the pit-topos (vv. 15f.). He then interprets the image as signifying the recoiling of wickedness upon the one who plans to do it (v. 17).

In Qohelet, digging a pit is one of four actions of the sort included in everyday chores. The main point of these proverbs in this context is not that evil is punished, but that deeds may have unexpected consequences; 10:14 recapitulates this idea. (That Qohelet is describing probabilities or typical cases, not absolute causal linkages, is shown by v. 9, which speaks of *danger*, not of certain harm.) Nevertheless, this topos, even as Qohelet uses it, does imply retribution, for it shows dangerous actions producing undesirable consequences, and the principle naturally applies to evil actions as well.

Qohelet's belief in retribution also comes to expression when he warns against failure to pay vows "... lest God get angry at your voice [that made the hasty vow] and destroy the work of your hands" (5:5). The punishment fits the crime: God damages the possessions of the man who deprives God of the possessions due *him*. This tit-for-tat punishment is not an inevitable effect of the deed, part of a

"Tat-Ergehen-Zusammenhang"[5] but follows upon God's displeasure (5:3bα). God's "getting angry"—an independent divine decision—links act to consequence. Again, the warning introduced by "lest" (*lammah*) implies a danger, not a certainty, that God will retaliate in this way.

The form of retribution most clearly specified is premature death, as in 7:17: "Do not be very wicked nor act the fool, lest you die before your time [*bĕlo' 'itteka*]". Qohelet warns the reader that an early death may ensue from wickedness, but, again, he does not declare flatly that this punishment *will* come. Qohelet has, after all, just told the reader that there is "a wicked man who lives long in his wickedness" (7:15). He expects an early death to befall the wicked, but he is quite aware that this does not necessarily happen. These views are no more contradictory than a belief that drunk drivers endanger themselves contradicts a recognition that they often escape

5. In an influential article, K. Koch (1972) argues that there is no concept of retribution ("Vergeltung") in the Hebrew Bible. He defines "Vergeltung" narrowly: ". . . zum Gedanken der *Vergeltung* gehört, daß eine *richterliche Instanz* dem Täter, dessen persönliche Freiheit und wirtschaftliche Stellung durch seine Tat keineswegs verändert ist, eine solche 'Veränderung' seines Besitzes, seiner Freiheit oder gar seines Lebens auferlegt als 'Lohn' oder 'Strafe'. *Strafe wie Lohn sind dabei sowohl dem Wesen des Täters wie dem Akt seiner Tat fremd*, werden ihm von einer übergeordneten Größe zugemessen und gleichsam von außen an ihn herangetragen" (p. 133; italics in original). I cannot agree that the "Tat-Ergehen-Zusammenhang" is the dominant, let alone exclusive, principle of justice in the HB. Koch argues for his thesis by a rather forced exegesis. Indeed, many verses he discusses, such as "wait for the Lord and he will save you" (Prov 20:22b), show God doing more than merely facilitating a natural causal process. Even Prov 24:12, ". . . Surely he who weighs hearts understands [sc., the truth], and he who keeps your soul knows [it], and he will requite [*hešib*] a man according to his actions", makes the requital depend upon God's knowing what happened. Koch goes so far as to deny that the verb *šapaṭ* shows juridical retribution and that Prov 12:2; 16:5; 22:23 have no explicit juridical terminology (pp. 138f.), despite the presence of the juridical terms *yaršia'*, *yinnaqeh*, and *yarib*). Certainly prophets and psalmists believe that God's judgment intervenes in natural historical processes and supersedes them. Finally, it is hard to see what sort of statement Koch's protean exegesis would be unable to interpret as a "Tat-Ergehen Zusammenhang". (Contrast the more careful exegesis of P. D. Miller, Jr. [1982:121-39], who reveals more complexity and variation in the

the consequences of their actions.[6] The contradiction lies rather in God's nature: why does God, who could bring about full equity in all cases, make do with merely probable, and not necessarily full, recompense?

In 8:12b-13, in the midst of remarking on the unjust fate that some people suffer (see below on 8:11-12a + 14), Qohelet declares that peoples' lifespans will match their merits:

> (12b) . . . I know too that it will go well with God-fearing people, because they are afraid of him, (13) and that it will not go well with

formulation and presuppositions of the passages supposed to show the "Tat-Ergehen-Zusammenhang".) Even a judgment in a human court could be described in Koch's terms, with the judge being considered a "midwife" who is merely carrying to completion a process begun with the crime. One factor that Koch considers criterial for retribution—preestablished norms for the assignment of punishment (p. 133)—may indeed be lacking in some formulations of divine judgment, but if so, this judgment fails to be retribution only by Koch's arbitrarily restrictive definition. Miller, however, observes that a norm is present in the notion of talion and sometimes in a reference or allusion to legal statutes and covenant (1982:136).

Rather than excluding divine judgment, the "Tat-Ergehen" formulation emphasizes the omnipresence and immediacy of God's retributive activity in human affairs. Since God is omnipotent, any deserved consequence can be regarded as divine judgment (thus in Pss 7:11-14; 9:16f.; see above). In other words, God's judgment subsumes natural causality rather than the other way around.

Gese (1958:45-50) shows that the "Tat-Ergehen-Zusammenhang" is not the only one in Proverbs, but he assumes—without adequate evidence—a historical development from the assumption of a "schicksalwirkende Tatsphäre" to the belief in God's free intervention in human affairs, which is supposedly a Yahwistic "Sondergut". Miller (1982:121-39) demonstrates that Koch's analysis is highly oversimplified and often erroneous. Miller's conclusions include a recognition that many passages Koch brings as evidence for his theory do not suggest an internal relation between deed and consequence, and that many of these emphasize the *correspondence* between sin and punishment rather than consequentiality. Furthermore, there is a sharp sense of judgment as retribution, in which the link between sin and punishment is made by Yahweh's decision to punish.

6. The warning in 7:17 should not be removed as a pietistic addition, for that would leave v. 16 unpaired in a passage that requires two types of behavior—and v. 16, with its peculiar, heterodox advice, can hardly be a later addition.

> the wicked man, and, like a shadow, he will not live long, because he is not afraid of God.

"Going well" and "not going well" refer to life and death, the respective fates of the God-fearing and the wicked.

Qohelet may indeed be citing conventional wisdom in these sentences (thus Gordis; see Excursus I), but if so, he states it as something he knows, as a fact rather than an opinion of which he is aware. He gives no sign that he rejects that piece of knowledge any more than he signals rejection of the facts he states in 8:11-12a + 14. Hertzberg regards 8:12b-13 as the concessive element in a "Zwar-Aber Tatsache". Although we may grant that 8:11-12a + 14 limits the universality of the affirmation of justice, 8:12b-13 does not, contrary to Hertzberg, express an attitude from which Qohelet is distancing himself. Nor does it assert an absolute correlation between virtue and lifespan, supposedly the popular notion that Qohelet rejects. Even in the most orthodox Wisdom Literature, a statement like 8:12b-13 would be understood as formulating a principle or the typical case (see below, §4.4), and this is the way most of the traditional interpreters take it.[7]

Beyond the ongoing execution of justice that everyone may, and probably will, undergo in the course of life, there will come a special time of judgment for everyone. Such a judgment should right the remaining wrongs. After observing wickedness in the courts, where just judgment should reign, Qohelet reminds himself that God will judge the righteous and the wicked, "for there is a time for every matter, and upon every deed . . . " (3:17). Judgment *must* come, Qohelet believes, because it has a time, a claim on occurrence. Qohelet never repudiates this affirmation of the certainty of judgment.

In 8:5-6a, a difficult passage, Qohelet again declares the certainty of future judgment:

> (5) He who keeps a command will experience no misfortune, and the wise man's heart should be aware of the time of judgment,
> (6a) (for every matter has a time . . .).

7. Among the passages at issue, Hertzberg interprets 3:17-20 as well as 8:5-6 + 8b as instances of the "Zwar-Aber Tatsache". There are further objections to formulating the relation between the sentences in tension as "zwar-aber"; see Excursus I.

The command referred to in 8:5 is the king's, mentioned in v. 4, not God's. Seen in context, v. 5 promises not that the wise man will never suffer *anything* bad (something never claimed by even the most sanguine sages), but rather that a man obedient to the king's command will not suffer the king's anger (implied in v. 3: note the recurrence of *dabar ra'*). The wise man can patiently bear up under the ruler's wrath, because he is aware that everything, including the ruler's behavior, has a time of judgment.

Qoh 11:9b too affirms divine judgment: "And know that for all these things [sc., the pleasures of youth] God will bring you to judgment".

The book concludes with an affirmation of the certainty of divine judgment (Qoh 12:14): "For God will bring every deed into judgment, (judging even) every secret deed, as whether it is good or evil". This verse, whether written by an editor or by the author (see Excursus III), does not conflict with anything in the body of the book. Although more emphatic and confident in tone than most of Qohelet's affirmations of justice, 12:14 is no more categorical than 3:17 or 11:9b. The difference between the epilogue and the rest of the book is that the epilogue emphasizes God's judgment without raising the problem of delay in judgment.

Qoh 2:26 may seem to be a simple affirmation of divine retribution, since Qohelet calls the toiler "the one who is offensive" (*ḥote'*, a term that almost always implies sinfulness) and the recipient of the toiler's wealth is called "the one whom God likes". But the verse should not be so read, because if the situation described in 2:26 were simply the case of the righteous man enjoying God's favor and the wicked one suffering his wrath, it could not be called an absurdity and would not disturb Qohelet. The terminology of this verse reflects Qohelet's belief that the person God likes is "good before God" (whatever the reason) and the one God dislikes is somehow offensive to him (without necessarily having sinned). Qohelet uses moralistic terminology here to describe people from the perspective of what befalls them. This verse thus describes an inequity, not an act of justice.

Qohelet uses similar language in declaring that "the one who is offensive" will be trapped by a woman, while the God-favored man will escape her wiles (7:26). This is Qohelet's sardonic way of accentuating the miseries of being thus ensnared: so harsh a fate must reflect divine annoyance. Whether the "offender" has done something to deserve his fate is not stated.

In sum, justice will usually, but not always, be done in life. It is, however, a certainty that God will judge. Will that judgment then repair the inequities that chance allows?

§4.3 *Qohelet's doubts about equity*

Qohelet believes in divine judgment, but he recognizes that judgment sometimes comes too late to rectify wrongs. Equity is a matter of timing: does God execute judgment soon enough? In spite of the assurance that God "makes everything happen appropriately in its time", Qohelet is aware that this is not always the case.

We must first make a distinction that is assumed but not drawn too clearly in Wisdom texts, including Qohelet, a distinction between the sentence of death and death itself. Death is, of course, universal, but one might die before the appointed or expected time. Death as a punishment means premature death, just as life as a reward means an extension of one's lifetime. To say, for example, that "righteousness saves one from death" (Prov 11:4b) does not mean that righteousness bestows immortality, but rather that the righteous will be spared the death that befalls the wicked in a "day of wrath" (v. 4a). There is a distinction between the normal, proper day of death, which awaits the righteous, and the "day of wrath", the time when the wicked are judged and punished by premature death. The concepts of premature death and extended lifetime presuppose the notion that everyone has "his time", a determined, or at least an appropriate, time of death. Qohelet expresses this assumption in 8:12b-13; 9:12; and, most clearly, 7:17.

Ginsberg considers the "judgment" mentioned in 3:17 and 8:5 to be the bare fact of death. This would be a twist on the usual idea of (untimely) death as a punishment. Such a twist would be possible in itself, but it certainly would require more guidance to the reader than Qohelet gives. To be sure, in 3:18-21 Qohelet speaks about the fact that man and beast die alike, but he does not call this a "judgment". (To the contrary, this fact nullifies the significance of the judgment.) Likewise in 8:8-9 he declares death's inevitability (after first speaking of human ignorance of the future), but without connecting this with the "time of judgment" of v. 5. Qohelet considers it significant that everyone, including the despot, will die, but eventual death is not in itself the judgment that the wise man will know about. Qohelet's belief that death as punishment means premature death, not death in itself, is shown by the warning of 7:17b: "lest you die before your time".

God's judgment cannot reach beyond the grave. Or can it? This unspoken question is heard in the answer: since no one knows the fate of humans after death (3:21), the question is moot. A mere possibility cannot ease Qohelet's sense of injustice. But the possibility has been raised, and his rhetorical question tacitly concedes that knowledge of an afterlife, were that possible, would allay our fears about the failure of justice. For then we could hope for a future restoration of equity in cases where it is manifestly absent in this life. But since we cannot know if the life-spirit exists beyond death, we cannot factor that possibility into the equation of equity.

The problem of delay in judgment burdens Qohelet in 8:5-7. He first affirms that a time of judgment awaits the despot (8:5-6a; see above). Judgment, he says, will come, because everything has a time,

> (6b) . . . for man's evil weighs heavy upon him. (7) For he does not know *what* will happen, for none can tell him *when* it will happen.

Again the problem lies in the timing: man can know that judgment will take place but not when.

In a concentrated discussion of the problem of retribution, 8:10b-14, Qohelet complains that delay of punishment encourages people to do evil:

> (10b) This too is an absurdity: (11) the sentence for a wicked deed is not carried out quickly; for which reason people's hearts are intent on doing evil. (12a) For an offender may do evil for years but live long . . .

Qohelet next reaffirms the principle of retribution (8:12b-13), but then, in v. 14, restates the disturbing fact noted in v. 12a, along with its obverse:

> (14) There is an absurdity that happens on the earth: there are righteous people who receive what is appropriate to the deeds of the wicked, and there are wicked people who receive what is appropriate to the deeds of the righteous. I said that this too is an absurdity.

Qohelet "knows" that such things happen, although he *also* knows that the God-fearing will have good fortune while the wicked will die before their time (8:12b-13). Qohelet takes it for granted that the evildoer's sentence will eventually be carried out (8:11a), yet he is troubled that it may be delayed. The rule stands: righteousness produces (long) life, wickedness produces (early) death. But there are exceptions.

The formulation "there are" (*yeš*) shows that Qohelet is pointing to anomalies, not stating an additional (and, if taken absolutely, completely incompatible) principle. Ibn Ezra (commenting on 7:3) says that 8:13a states the usual case, while 7:15bβ tells what happens on rare occasions (*lipraqim mĕʻaṭim*).[8] Ibn Ezra's interpretation is correct and does soften the logical contradiction within Qohelet's words, but it does not solve the fundamental tension between justice and injustice, for the exceptions *are* the problem. No matter how rare early death may be (and it is not so rare, as we know, the sages knew, and Qohelet knew), each unjustifiably early death speaks against God's justice.[9]

The violations of equity vitiate the moral impact of retribution by leading people to think that there is no justice whatsoever. Even if it is true, say, that habitual criminals tend to die younger than law-abiding citizens (a fact that can be expressed in terms of either theological or natural causation), nevertheless, when people see even a few mobsters growing old and rich, they may conclude that there is no justice. And what does it matter if criminals eventually do meet the death due them? People are not deterred from crime by seeing an eighty-year-old mobster gunned down (or worse, dying of illness) after a life of prosperity. It may be justice for him to die by the violence by which he lived, but "judgment" of this sort leaves inequity. And the inequity is sometimes pushed even further; there are cases when not only do the righteous and the wicked fail to receive their respective reward and punishment, they get the *opposite* of what they deserve. This is surely an absurdity.

8. Barton too, though attributing 8:11-13 to a Wisdom glossator, understands 8:13a in this way.

9. Zer-Kavod, who seeks to make Qohelet conventional as well as consistent, believes that Qohelet is humbly admitting his incomprehension of the exceptional cases while declaring (in 3:17) his faith that judgment will eventually come (p. 36). But again, the delay is what Qohelet considers inequitable.

§4.4 *Justice and its violation according to Wisdom Literature*

The sages of Wisdom Literature did, of course, most emphatically believe in retribution: a good person will—sooner or later—receive the proper measure of good fortune, while a bad person will—sooner or later—undergo appropriate misfortune. The sages commonly speak of retribution as a natural, automatic result of behavior, believing that in the normal course of events a person's deeds are adequately punished or rewarded by their effects upon him. God has created an orderly world in which good deeds typically have good effects, bad deeds bad effects. But since the natural order does not necessarily bring about retribution, there is an opening for injustice, the possibility for a disharmony between a person's deserts and his fate. In such cases God's judgment, the sages believed, will intervene to right the wrong.

Throughout the HB, injustice provokes complaints paralleling Qohelet's in content and equaling them in severity.[10] Jeremiah puts it most sharply: "Why are the wicked successful, and the treacherous at ease? You planted them and they have taken root; they give ever more fruit" (Jer 12:1b-2a).[11] Many Wisdom texts too wrestle with the problem of injustices. This is most obviously true of Job, but even very orthodox Wisdom Literature, in which God's justice is undeniably affirmed, recognizes the same facts as Qohelet. The

10. Crenshaw (1970) discusses "popular questioning of justice" in ancient Israel. He includes in the "questioning of justice" two very different categories without adequately distinguishing them: outcries against injustices from people who believe in God's justice, as in Jeremiah, Psalms, Job, and Qohelet; and putative quotation of remarks that express a cynical attitude about God's justice (e.g., Mal 1:7; 2:17; 3:12, 14-15; cf. Ezek 8:12; Ps 10:11; Job 22:13-14).

11. No one finds it necessary to attribute Jer 12:1a to an orthodox glossator or to a quoted voice, though Jeremiah contradicts himself in Jer 12:1-4 no less than Qohelet does in 8:11-14. The prophet claims that God is just while complaining that he allows injustices. (Jeremiah is not merely saying that God will win the dispute; *ṣaddiq*—unlike the verb *ṣadaq*—never refers to purely formal, juridical vindication; *pace* Holladay 1962:49-51). Jeremiah, in arguing with God, points out a contradiction he observes: since you are just, how can you tolerate injustices? The answer he gets is an admonition to be patient, with a hint that a future judgment will come (cf. Hab 1:13; 2:3).

speaker in Psalm 73, a Wisdom Psalm,[12] comes to believe that God will destroy the wicked (vv. 18-19), though he does not cease to be aware that the wicked may prosper (vv. 2-5) and even be "ever at ease" (*šalwey 'olam*; v. 12). (The revelation he receives is a solution to his consternation, not a repudiation of the observations that troubled him.) The writer of Psalm 49 knows that the wise may die (sc., young) and leave their wealth to others (v. 11). And even didactic Wisdom Literature, which comes closest to a dogmatic, formulaic assertion of retribution, is aware of exceptions to the rule of recompense.

The pedagogical rhetoric of didactic Wisdom does, to be sure, tend toward categorical formulations of retribution. The dicta "Righteousness saves one from death" (Prov 10:2b) and "The hand of the diligent will prosper" (Prov 10:4b) are, after all, more impressive and memorable than more restrained statements such as "Righteousness usually saves one from early death" or "The hand of the diligent will, barring unforeseen circumstances, generally bring prosperity". Most proverbs do not hedge their promises of retribution; for example: "The fear of the Lord increases one's lifetime, while the years of the wicked are cut short" (Prov 10:27); "A righteous man will never totter, while the wicked will not inhabit the earth" (Prov 10:30); "No evil will befall the righteous, while the wicked are full of misfortune" (Prov 12:21); and so on throughout most of the book of Proverbs. Such absolutistic rhetoric gives an impression, not entirely unjustified, of self-assured dogmatism.

But closer examination shows that Wisdom Literature, in spite of this dogmatic cast, does not assume strict and exclusive causal links between a deed and its recompense. As J. G. Williams (1981:18f.)

12. A psalm is more or less sapiential to the degree that it has a higher or lower concentration of terminology and ideas characteristic of didactic wisdom. The precise delineation of this genre is not crucial to the issue at hand, because there is no reason to think that Qohelet was any more or less familiar with "Wisdom Psalms" than with other types. We need not suppose a special life-setting for such psalms or an origin in a special class or professional group. Murphy (1962) includes the following psalms in this category: 1; 32; 34; 37; 49; 112; 128. Sabourin (1974:369-71) includes: 1; 37; 49; 73; 91; 112; 119; 127; 128; 133; 139. The overlap of lists shows the psalms that clearly belong to the Wisdom category. I would follow Sabourin in including Ps 73, which, like Ps 49, resembles the book of Job in brooding on the problem of retribution (rather than simply lamenting injustices).

observes, biblical Wisdom (and, we may add, its Egyptian predecessors) speaks of *typical* cases, not absolute causal patterns. This is true of proverbial sayings in general. Wisdom's ideology (as opposed to its rhetoric) does not insist that "all X leads to Y" and "Y is always the result of X" (*ibid.*).

Intermixed with the proverbs formulated as absolutes are numerous sayings describing cases where the circumstances of one's life do not accord with the moral quality of one's behavior. For although the writers of didactic wisdom emphasize the positive—which is what they think usually happens—they are well aware of exceptions: a good or industrious man may be poor or ill or mocked; a wicked or lazy one may be prosperous or respected. This is the insight of Prov 11:24: "There is[13] one who scatters (his money) about and yet gets more, and one who saves out of honesty yet ends up needy";[14] similarly Sir 11:11-12. Furthermore, if the authors of Proverbs believed in a strict causal connection between one's merits and wealth, they would not so earnestly urge mercy toward the poor.[15]

The book of Proverbs occasionally mentions anomalies in the working of justice.[16] Retributive paradoxes (more precisely, literary indications of retributive paradox; see Williams, 1981:43) should be distinguished from surprising events (the "pit" topos, for example) in

13. Note the use of *yeš* to introduce anomalies, as in Qoh 2:21; 6:1; 7:15; 8:14.

14. Even if Prov 11:24a is to be construed as a reference to almsgiving (thus NJV), v. 24b is clearly paradoxical. However, *m^{e}pazzer* with no further modification (such as it has in Ps 112:9) does not elsewhere mean almsgiving. The above interpretation is supported by Sir 11:11f., a reworking of this proverb.

15. As they do in 14:21, 31; 17:5; 19:17; etc.; see Gese, 1958:38. Ben Sira specifically excludes the ungodly poor as objects of charity (12:4-5).

16. See the discussion by von Rad (1970:166-70). Gladson (1978) examines at length proverbs in Prov 10-29 that show recognition of injustices. He brings extensive evidence demonstrating that the sages of all times and places were quite aware of the existence of injustices. He is too quick, however, to explain "retributive paradoxes" as dissent from the dominant Wisdom doctrine of retribution, and thus as evidence for diversity of thought within Wisdom. The most orthodox believer could not deny that injustices occur. There can hardly be a doctrine of retribution without recognition that there exist wrongs to be punished. Dissent begins only when these wrongs are held to contradict the rule of justice.

which justice is manifestly served, for the latter are paradoxical only to the shortsighted.

The sages knew that even in this orderly world vicissitudes of fortune often do not correspond to personal merit. It is, in fact, important to be aware of such events, lest one view every poor person as sinful or indolent, or become haughty in prosperity. As one widespread teaching puts it: "Do not boast of the morrow, for you do not know what the next day will bring" (Prov 27:1). The Egyptian sage Anii says:

> Do not eat food while another stands by, failing to stretch out your hand for him to the food. What is there that endures forever? It is man who does not last. One may be rich, while another is poor. Does food remain? May it not pass away?[17]

Anii does not say: be generous to others *in order to* ensure your wealth; but rather: because you cannot ensure your wealth, be generous to others as a hedge against future vicissitudes. Wealth is, we might say, subject to "time and accident" or—what amounts to the same thing—to God's not entirely predictable will.[18]

While undeserved poverty is not necessarily a calamity (after all, "better a little [gained] with righteousness than great harvests [gained] without justice", Prov 16:8; cf. 15:16f.), the death of the innocent most certainly is one. It is a severe injustice, the possibility of which the sages rarely mentioned but of which they were undoubtedly aware. The highwaymen's plan to "lie in wait for the innocent" (Prov 1:11) may be expected to backfire, but it does not always do so. Since there are people guilty of spilling innocent blood, blood has been shed unjustly, whatever the consequences for the wicked. In fact, the sages concede the existence of injustices every time they condemn the wicked for perpetrating them.

17. Translation based on Volten, 1937:117-26.

18. Contrary to Gese (1958:45-50), the idea that God determines the outcome of deeds independently of human action is not a Yahwistic invention. The sayings that Gese regards as declaring God's control of the "world order" do indeed make such a declaration, but nothing in any Wisdom book denies this control. The world order assumed by Wisdom is not a rigid set of causal formulas (nor does "Ma'at" have that meaning in Egyptian Wisdom). It is the generally orderly working of justice in natural processes, guaranteed by the supervision and intervention of divinity.

Because speculation on injustices would not serve the educational goals of didactic Wisdom Literature, the sages kept the awareness of such evils well in the background of their teachings. But occasionally this awareness breaks through, as in Prov 13:23: "The tillage [*nir*] of the poor[19] [produces] much food, but there are some people who are swept away unjustly". The first stich is a pun, for *nir* can mean offspring (1 Kgs 11:36; 2 Kgs 8:19), and the stich can be translated, "The offspring of the poor possess much food", in other words, the house of the poor man will eventually come into prosperity. In this way v. 23a reiterates the preceding verse: "The good man will pass on an inheritance to his son's sons, while the wealth of the offender is stored up for the righteous". Justice *will* be done, even if it must wait until the next generation. But, v. 23b concedes, there are (*yeš*) people who die unjustly. Likewise, "Those who are taken to death", whom we are admonished to rescue (Prov 24:11f.), are certainly not criminals sentenced to capital punishment, but innocent people wrongly condemned.

On rare occasion we hear a note of indignation as the sages observe violations of the proper order—indignation directed not, as usual, at the violators, but at the occurrence of the violation itself. In this case the teacher is not simply saying that people should not do this or that, but that such things should not happen; thus: "A muddied spring and a polluted well: a righteous man crumbling before a wicked man!" (Prov 25:26). In other words, dirty things happen in life. (Note that the images represent the event, not the person.)

The sages also complain of disruptions of the social order which (to the sages) are improper if not immoral:

> Under three things the world shudders,
> of four it cannot bear the burden:
> a slave being in power,[20]
> a knave being sated with food,
> a loathsome woman getting married,
> a slave-girl inheriting in place of her mistress
> (Prov 30:21-23).[21]

19. LXX's δίκαιοι does not witness to Hebrew *yěšarim* (contrary to BHS), because the Greek rendering of this verse is too paraphrastic to allow secure retroversion. The LXX turns the verse into theodicy, as do various modern commentators.

20. Cf. Qoh 10:6f.

21. These sentences are all nominalized clauses with proleptic subjects (cf. Qoh 6:2); lit., "a slave, that he rules" = "that a slave rule", etc.

Throughout biblical literature, even in didactic Wisdom, we find clear recognition that injustices, even severe ones, do occur. Qohelet's observation of them is not a conceptual innovation. Again, his innovation is in his reaction and emphasis.

§4.5 *Theodicy and its inadequacy*

Only the most resolute naivety or dogmatism could blind one to anomalies in the working of justice, and, as emphasized above (§4.4), this does not happen in Wisdom Literature. Wisdom's response is rather to develop theodicies that subsume anomalies to a broader perspective in which they are revealed to be either insignificant or part of a greater, meaningful whole. In a perspective broadened to include psychology, for example, some injustices may be outweighed by an interior good (such as in the case of a righteous man who lives in poverty but is at peace with his household: Prov 17:1). Eliphaz, invoking the wisdom of the ancients, insists that the wicked live in constant fear (Job 15:20-24). Theodicy may also justify God by insisting on human insignificance and native corruption, so that injustices done to humans appear trivial or even justified *a priori* (Eliphaz takes this tack in Job 4:17-21). Or theodicy may appeal to a greater temporal perspective, insisting that retribution will come at some later time, whether in the individual lifetime or beyond it. Ben Sira uses this line of reasoning in 39:16-34. "None can say, 'This–why is this?', for everything was created[22] for its need" (39.21; see variants in vv. 17 and 34).

A wise man can, in Wisdom's view, usually incorporate anomalies into his greater breadth of vision. But even when he cannot explain them, he can infer the existence of a non-observable order from the wonders of observable creation (Job was taught to do that). Even without such an inference, the wise man is at least confident that there *is* a perspective from which anomalies make sense (the reader of Job learns this in the prologue).

Even when God allows injustices, he is in control of justice on a larger scale, and divine intervention, the sages believe, will eventually right matters. Justice will surely come, and the faithful will wait for

22. Thus Greek. Hebrew: *nibḥar*, "chosen". Rabbinic evidence (*b. Shab.* 77b; *y. Ber.* 9:2) supports the Greek; see Segal, 1958:263.

it.[23] This theodicy is inseparable from the belief it undergirds—the promise of future rectification. The promise becomes theodicy when it is used not in motivating behavior but in explaining a current injustice. The promised judgment may be either individual or collective. In Wisdom Literature, including Qohelet, it is almost always individual. Life and death—i.e., long life for the innocent and untimely death for the wicked—are the forms of recompense most often promised; for example:[24] "Wealth will be of no avail in the day of wrath, but righteousness saves one from death" (Prov 14:4); "When the storm has passed the wicked is no more, but the righteous man is firmly established forever" (Prov 11:25); "Thus righteousness (leads) to life, but as for him who pursues evil—it (leads) to his death" (Prov 11:19). This is likewise the promise of Psalm 37: when you see the prosperity of the wicked man, remember that "his day" (v. 13), i.e., the day of his death, awaits him. The righteous may have their ups and downs, the psalmist grants, but the wicked will be extirpated. Ps 34:20 offers similar assurance: "Many are the afflictions of the righteous, but God will save him from them all". Psalm 92 likewise uses the "long run" explanation, insisting that only the fool does not see its validity.

In Proverbs, the belief in future rectification is stated as something that can be taken for granted, not as an insight won by faith through a struggle with the fact of inequity. Elsewhere this form of theodicy often manifests itself as an act of faith, asserted with a vehemence matching the severity of the doubt that provoked it. The psalmist of Psalm 73 is almost overwhelmed by observing the prosperity of the wicked and by his own suffering, but then he sees the solution: the wicked will die suddenly (vv. 17ff.). He seems to know that this

23. As Crenshaw says, "Perhaps the most natural response to the incursion of evil into unexpected circumstances is the surrender of the present moment in favor of future rectification" (1983b:7). There is indeed "surrender" in this type of theodicy, for while it grants that equity has failed in the present, it insists on subordinating the significance of the present moment to a possible future resolution.

24. "Life" often connotes a full, happy life (*TWOT* 334f.), and "death" may imply misery preceding death (Bailey, 1979:40f.), but rarely, if ever, are these terms demonstrably only metaphors for qualities of living. They almost always denote biological life and death. In any case, Wisdom Literature clearly promises long life as reward and threatens early death (and not only a better or worse quality of life) as punishment.

cannot be proved, since he presents it as a revelation, but he is satisfied with the expectation that sudden death awaits the wicked.

When rectification comes, the state of justice, unlike the temporary inequity, will be permanent: "The righteous man may fall seven times, but he rises. But the wicked will founder in evil" (Prov 24:16; cf. Ps 37:24). The seven falls of the righteous man are outweighed by his ultimate rising. The evildoer's fall may be delayed, but it is final and cancels out any earlier good fortune.

The theodicy of the book of Job does not overturn the retribution ideas of conventional (didactic) Wisdom Literature. It *protects* them by broadening the perspective for viewing justice. The author of Job (unlike the friends, with their formulaic view of retribution) holds essentially the same idea of the economy of divine justice as the authors of didactic Wisdom. He has written (or has chosen to incorporate) a narrative framework that presumes that God *usually* gives people the life they deserve. This was the way God was running things before Satan's challenge. God had (as Satan says and God tacitly concedes) shielded Job and made him prosper, and God eventually rewards Job and restores him to the state he deserves. Job's suffering (as Satan, God, and the reader know) was an exception—one of many such, perhaps, but still a temporary aberration in a just order, a local disturbance that served purposes unknown to the sufferer.

Qohelet, in his dogged if erratic empiricism, will not subordinate the anomalies he observes to axioms, not even to ones he accepts. Injustices are intractable distortions (1:15; 7:13) that warp the larger pattern (1:14) rather than blending into it. On the other hand, Qohelet presumes that God is just and that he will judge. Qohelet's peculiarity, then, lies not in being a more acute or realistic observer, or even in being skeptical about doctrines, but in being unable to regard the promise of eventual judgment as satisfactory theodicy (even Job would have been satisfied with eventual judicial vindication). Qohelet believes in divine justice but lacks a theodicy to undergird his belief.

If Qohelet agrees with other sages on the principle of divine justice and the fact of injustice, he differs profoundly in his response to these givens. What are the underlying attitudes that distinguish Qohelet from other sages (as well as from thinkers outside the Wisdom tradition) and call forth his peculiar response?

(1) Qohelet speaks of life and death as a simple dichotomy without gradations of severity. Elsewhere in the HB there is the concept of a "bad death". This is the fate of a person who dies prematurely or violently or without heirs. Conversely a "good death" is the lot of one who dies at a ripe age, at peace, leaving behind heirs (Bailey, 1979:48-51). Varying combinations of these factors might be invoked to rationalize an inappropriate life span or to help explain why (as Ben Sira puts it) "it is easy in the Lord's sight to repay a man on his last day according to his ways" (11:26; see below). But Qohelet simply does not raise the possibility that the death-judgment allows for such distinctions, perhaps because simple observation shows that this is not so, perhaps because distinctions between different kinds of death are lost in the void beyond life. Death, as Qohelet sees it, is a trap for everyone, not just the wicked. It snaps shut suddenly on everybody (9:12).[25] Nothing blunts its violence. Other sages promise that the memory of the righteous will live on beyond life, while the wicked are forgotten or remembered only as a curse (Prov 10:7; Job 18:17; Sir 41:11). Qohelet does not believe that *anyone* is remembered (Qoh 2:16; 9:5). Qohelet feels that memory is usually unreliable (cf. 1:11), though his weighs heavy upon him.

(2) Qohelet's peculiar fixation on anomalies derives in part from a different attitude toward time and memory. The problem is: how does the past weigh in the scales of equity? Conventional Wisdom instructions (and many psalms) evaluate a person's life by its outcome; the latest moment is decisive. When retribution arrives, wrongs are righted retroactively, for previous experience—good and bad—no longer exists.[26] Thus in the prose framework of the book of Job, the two-fold restoration of Job's fortunes wipes away his suffering and (we are to feel) restores equity. In Qohelet's view, on the contrary, later experiences in a person's life do not cancel the

25. The concept of suddenness consistently implies disaster; see Daube, 1964:1-8 and *passim*.

26. We hear a similar emphasis on the present moment in Ezek 3 and 18. Ezekiel teaches that a person's latest deeds determine his moral character and thus his fate (see Brin, 1975:83-93). Ezekiel is concerned less with the justice of what befalls people than with the question of how they determine the course of their lives. Yet his focus on the individual and on the value of the present moment is comparable to the attitudes dominant in Wisdom Literature.

earlier ones. A certain amount of good fortune might counterbalance an equal amount of undeserved misery, and later misery might outweigh some undeserved good fortune; but for that to happen justice must come early enough to allow for a sufficiently long period of rectification, and often it does not.

The crucial factor is memory. Does memory live on as a factor in present emotion? Qohelet knows that people often forget the past (1:11). Logically, then, he might have concluded that for them the latest moment is decisive. But his belief that time is static blocks this line of thought. For Qohelet, the eternal repetitiveness of events presses down on every moment. When he speaks of people forgetting the past (1:11), he shows that he himself does not do so. This sense of the ongoing presence of the past will not allow him to see the slate wiped clean in a moment of judgment.

(3) Qohelet lacks hope that human action can correct or even ameliorate wrongs. Such an attitude is foreign not only to prophecy and law, but also to Wisdom Literature, which demands justice and charity and assumes that the individual can promote social justice (e.g., Prov 14:31; 19:17; 22:9, 22; 24:11-12; 29:14; 31:9).

When Qohelet remarks that the oppressed lack a comforter (4:1), he does not urge the reader to strive against oppression or even to avoid oppressing others. He does not even urge us to extend the solace that is lacking. All that he can think to do is to bemoan what he sees—or, more precisely, to bemoan the fact that he must see it—and to envy the unborn for being spared the unpleasant vision. When he considers political corruption and persecution, he merely tells us not to be surprised (5:7). Again, social injustice is an inalterable reality; all that people can affect is their own emotional response to it. When he speaks of despots (8:1b-9), he reminds us that their day of reckoning will come, but for the present he does not tell the despots to change their ways, nor does he suggest how to ease the lot of those who suffer at their hand. He only teaches us how to minimize harm to ourselves when encountering the ruler's wrath (8:1b-2, 5b; 10:4). When Qohelet observes judicial injustices (3:16), he does not demand justice in judgment. He does not even chastise the unjust judges. He merely reminds himself that God will eventually judge the innocent and the guilty (3:17). But having deferred all hope of divine judgment till the indefinite future, he finds that this will not achieve rectification (3:18-22). Distortions of justice are a fact of life, and "nothing twisted can be straightened out" (1:15).

(4) Qohelet differs from most other sages in focusing on manifestations of injustice rather than justice, a shift that diffracts his entire world-view. Consider how the effect of 8:11-14 would differ if Qohelet had made the same observations in a different sequence, if he had said:

> (8:10b) This too is an absurdity: (11) the sentence for a wicked deed is not carried out quickly; for which reason peoples' hearts are intent on doing evil, (12a) for an offender may do evil for years but live long. (14) There is an absurdity that happens on the earth: there are righteous people who receive what is appropriate to the deeds of the wicked, and there are wicked people who receive what is appropriate to the deeds of the righteous. I said that this too is an absurdity, (12b) although I know too that it shall go well with God-fearing people, because they are afraid of him, (13) and that it will not go well with the wicked man and, like a shadow, he will not live long, because he is not afraid of God.

Without changing the substance of the observations, the rewritten version grants the existence of anomalies while making the eventual judgment decisive in determining whether justice has been done. Qohelet's actual statement grants that there will be judgment, but makes the anomalies decisive; thus he judges the world absurd. A similar effect can be produced by putting 3:17 after 3:21 or 8:5-6a after 8:7. In this arrangement, stubborn faith in the inevitability of judgment overcomes uncertainty about justice. But Qohelet does not affirm divine justice *in spite* of life's injustices; he is not a hero of faith, defying logic in favor of a deeper loyalty. He does not declare divine justice obscure then bravely hold fast to it. Such a stance would require declarations like the reformulated version of 8:12-14, with an emphasis on the assertions of justice, and it would not allow for complaints about the world's irrationality. For Qohelet, divine justice is a truly unquestioned assumption upon whose essential validity the exceptions seem scarcely to impinge. And yet this assumption cannot dislodge the exceptions from the center of Qohelet's consciousness.

When Qohelet considers life he sees it colored by the exceptions rather than the rule. It is a matter of weighting premises. One person might infer from the fact that most babies are born healthy that God is beneficent and life is orderly and meaningful. This is the religious temperament of the other Wisdom writers—the author of Job included. Another might infer from the fact that babies are occasionally born schizophrenic that God's ways are arbitrary. This is the religious temperament of Qohelet. Though commonly thought to be attacking the rigidity of conventional sages, Qohelet is in fact the rigid one. The generally orderly working of the universe was enough to convince the others that God's order extended even to areas where it is not visible. For Qohelet, the absoluteness of God's control means that each individual case is an ethical microcosm, so that the local absurdities—and there are many—are irreducible. Qohelet generalizes from them no less than from acts of divine justice. As a result, no matter how much right order we see, the absurdities undermine the coherence of the entire system.

The above is a description, not an etiology, of Qohelet's vision. There have been, of course, attempts to explain its external causes. Most recently, Crüsemann (1979:83-88) has sought to describe the breakdown of the "Tat-Ergehen-Zusammenhang" belief against the background of the exile, the end of the old, stable economic order, and the economic oscillations of the hellenistic period. According to Crüseman (pp. 87f.), in the third century BCE a connection between deed and result is no longer in evidence.The traditional norms of thought and action no longer accord with economic realities, and the world becomes incomprehensible. I am, however, skeptical about attempts to find external "causes" for an individual's thought. Although historical and material realities can provide the *context* in which an individual's thought develops and to which it responds, these realities cannot explain it. The types of economic and social dislocations Qohelet complains of, such as social oppression (4:1f.), corrupt officialdom (5:7), abuse of power (9:9), and appointment of the unworthy to high office (10:6), were hardly unknown during the First Commonwealth, as the prophets loudly testify. Conversely, the possibility for economic advancement and security did not disappear in hellenistic times. Qohelet's complaints do not reflect specific historical-social conditions. Conversely, the conditions that supposedly spawned Qohelet's crisis had no such effect on Ben Sira, whose confidence and sense of security at least rival, and perhaps surpass, those of preexilic Wisdom. Violations of the "Tat-Ergehen-Zusammenhang" were always a reality and always recognized, but divine justice was and remained a standard doctrine in Judaism, shaken by neither the first nor the second exile.

Qohelet's discomforts and doubts are commonly thought to indicate a crisis in Wisdom Literature. It is not clear whether he is supposed to have initiated a crisis or to reflect an existing one. If he *reflects* a crisis, where in Wisdom Literature do we see it prior to Qohelet? We can hardly view the book of Job as Qohelet's predecessor in this crisis, for Qohelet addresses different questions (the absurdity of the human situation in general rather than the problem of unjust suffering), shows no signs of being influenced by Job in ideas or phraseology, and rejects Job's solution (for Qohelet, the fact of God's power and mystery is no solution to human helplessness and ignorance). If he initiated a crisis, did he have followers, or was the crisis his alone?

William James's classic dichotomy between the temperament of the "healthy minded" and that of the "sick soul" (1902:77-162), though schematic, captures the difference between Qohelet and the other sages. James's description of the two religious temperaments does not give the *cause* of this difference, but it does help describe its manifestations. (It would be circular to invoke the "temperament" of unknown individuals to explain attitudes that are the only extant manifestations of their temperaments.) According to James, the religion of the healthy minded

> ...directs him to settle his scores with the more evil aspects of the universe by systematically declining to lay them to heart or make much of them, by ignoring them in his reflective calculations, or even, on occasion, by denying outright that they exist (p. 125).

In contrast to the healthy-minded way of deliberately minimizing evil stands

> a radically opposite view, a way of maximizing evil, if you please so to call it, based on the persuasion that the evil aspects of our life are of its very essence, and that the world's meaning most comes home to us when we lay them most to heart (p. 129).
>
> For the healthy minded, evil is incidental and accidental, and thus curable on the natural plane, while for the sick soul evil is radical and essential, not curable by any alteration of circumstances. To the sick soul, simple happiness and well-being are no solution to the "joy-destroying chill":
>
> Our troubles lie too deep for *that* cure. The fact that we *can* die, that we *can* be ill at all, is what perplexes us; the fact that we now for a moment live and are well is irrelevant to that perplexity (p. 137).

The problem for Qohelet is not the concrete case of a righteous person dying young or an evildoer living long, but an abstraction, namely the fact that *there are* people who suffer the wrong fate. And beyond that elemental injustice stands the ultimate injustice of death. James quotes Qohelet to epitomize the sick soul's consciousness of all-vitiating death, and summarizes:

> In short, life and its negation are beaten up inextricably together. But if the life be good, the negation of it must be bad. Yet the two are equally essential facts of existence; and *all natural happiness thus seems infected with a contradiction*. The breath of the sepulchre surrounds it (pp. 136f.; my italics).

If Qohelet is inconsistent, he is not erratic, now declaring faith in divine judgment, now deciding there is none. He maintains a single view of the problem of justice. Qohelet asks: how can there be injustices (as there are) if God is just (as he is)? Qohelet sees no answer. He believes that God is just (thus retribution is the rule; thus God will judge) but that he allows injustices. This, Qohelet knows, is contradictory, absurd. He is not merely complaining about injustices, he is complaining about the irrationality of injustices.

By observing a contradiction and continuing to hold to both of the contradictory propositions, Qohelet *is* contradicting himself. Philosophical consistency would require resolving the tension. Qohelet might have achieved logical consistency simply by abandoning belief in God's justice or omnipotence,[27] or by subordinating the injustices to a larger temporal or theological perspective. He does not choose any of these paths, but simply registers his dismay at the violations he observes. He is at a dead-end. He does not even try to solve the problem, but teaches how to live with it. Loader (1979:123) rightly states that unlike other "crisis literature" (e.g., Job), Qohelet does not "discharge" the tension in his discussion of retribution, but resolutely maintains it. But contrary to Loader, the tension is not between "protesting wisdom" and "dogmatized wisdom"; nor does Qohelet "combat" the doctrine of retribution and deny it completely (*ibid.*). The tension is between two beliefs, both of which Qohelet presents as equally his own, and neither of which he ascribes to another form of wisdom.

27. A polytheistic or dualistic system allows for this explanation, though in the ancient Near East the activity of gods of chaos and death was rarely invoked to rationalize unjustified misfortune or prosperity.

The poles of the tension are not such that they could not coexist in the mind of a reasonably coherent thinker. Many a modern believer takes the same course, holding faith in a just God who runs an unjust world. But believing in God's justice while conscious of irreducible inequities undeniably produces an unstable equilibrium which seems to tilt as we look from one side of the balance to another.

§4.6 *"These too are by the sages"*

Qohelet's obsession with the violations of the principle of retribution is not polemical. He does not engage in a "sustained argument against the doctrine of retributive justice" (contrary to Williams, 1981:20). He is not even *skeptical* about these doctrines, in the sense of doubting their validity, but, on the contrary, stubbornly holds to belief in retributive justice. To differ is not to attack. Qohelet does not attack or cast doubt upon any teaching of Wisdom. He shows no awareness that his observations clash with the beliefs of other sages—and, except in emphasis, they do not. He distinguishes his wisdom from others' only by its greater degree.

To be sure, if Wisdom Literature deliberately denied, as a point of ideology, the existence of injustice, then for Qohelet to mention injustices would indeed be an attack on Wisdom, or at least a symptom of a "crisis" brought on by a sudden awareness that the old rules have exceptions. But Wisdom Literature makes no such denial. Nor are Qohelet's observations a struggle against a theodicy. He treats the inequities he observes as a frustrating problem, not as evidence for or against a particular solution.[28] He does not find the

28. Contrary to Eichrodt's influential article, "Vorsehungsglaube und Theodizee" (1934). Eichrodt defines theodicy as an attempt to balance the present state of the world with the all-inclusive government of a just and beneficent God; theodicy thus defined is an attempt to master the *world's* contradictions. This concern he believes is an invention of "Spätjudentum". The only texts he mentions as exhibiting this mechanical theodicy are Chronicles, a few verses in Nehemiah, and Pss 17; 26; 59. Job's friends are also said to exemplify this ("spätjüdisch"?) theology. But then, he says, came a "Durchbruch von dem Gott der vernünftigen Abstraktion zu dem lebendigen Gott der Offenbarung" (p. 64), a movement he finds in texts which "alle Krücken der Theodizee von sich warf" (*ibid.*). These texts are Pss 22, 73, Job, and Qohelet. (Eichrodt's literary-historical chronology is rather murky.)

promise of future judgment a satisfactory theodicy, and he tries no other solution.

Qohelet is a middle term between the earlier theodicy, which simply asserted future mundane judgment, on the one hand, and the complex theodicies of later wisdom texts, which develop multiple perspectives to explain apparent injustices, on the other.

Ben Sira recognizes and responds to the problem of delays in judgment.[29] He asserts that "with him who fears the Lord it will go well at the end; on his final day he will be blessed" (1:13; cf. 9:11; 18:22, 24). At that time, forgetfulness will erase the significance of earlier injustices.

Eichrodt's definition of theodicy is idiosyncratic. Theodicy is commonly understood as any attempt to maintain God's justice in the face of evil. It is not, as Eichrodt would have it, a particular solution, namely an insistence on the formulaic balancing of deed and recompense, "die unparteiische Verteilung von Lohn und Strafe nach der Norm des Gesetzes, die justitia distributiva . . ." (p. 63). Nor does theodicy necessarily try to justify the present state of the world; it may, for example, view that state as illusory or defer justice to the indefinite future.

At any rate, Eichrodt's history of theodicy is artificial. First of all, theodicy is present in the pre-exilic prophets, because prophetic eschatology *is* a form of theodicy; in any case, the "eschatological solution" was hardly abandoned in "Spätjudentum". Conversely, the "Streben nach einer eigentlichen Theodizee" (*ibid.*), however the concept is defined, emerges well before Ezekiel. Both Proverbs (and its Egyptian forebears) and the deuteronomic writings teach a distributive justice of the sort that Eichrodt identifies with theodicy. Eichrodt, like so many theologians who find a hardening, a "verhängnisvolle Verengung des Gesichtskreises" (*ibid.*), in postexilic Judaism, does so by ignoring evidence for the phenomenon in question in preexilic texts while emphasizing similar features in documents considered post-exilic. Contrary ideas that are recognized in "late" texts are explained as signs of a struggle against the prevailing attitude. (The relative dating of a text is itself often circular, the criterion used being the text's place in the hypothesized scheme of development.)

29. On the issue of theodicy in Sira, see Crenshaw, 1975:47-64. On the problem of delay of judgment, see *ibid.*, pp. 55-60.

> (11:25) A day's good fortune makes (earlier) misfortune forgotten, and a day's misfortune makes (earlier) good fortune forgotten, and a man's end will be upon him.[30] (26) For it is easy in the sight of the Lord to reward a man on the day of his death according to his conduct.[31] (27) A time of misfortune makes pleasures forgotten, and the end of a man will tell about him.[32] (28) Call no man happy before his death, for a man is known by his end.

Ben Sira also tries to account for the time *before* a person's end. All mankind suffers malaise, but the wicked are afflicted by anxiety seven-fold (40:1-11).[33] Although the godly may be poor, God can suddenly make a man rich (11:21), and only the wealth of the godly endures (11:17). The Wisdom of Solomon also strongly endorses the psychological solution (17:2-6, 14-16),[34] as well as rationalizing the early death of the righteous by various ad hoc, sophistical suppositions, such as the possibility that God wished to extricate a righteous person from a potentially corrupting environment (4:14-15).

The complicated (if not convoluted) theodicy of these two works may have been called forth by Qohelet's scrutiny of the problem of justice. That is not to say that they attack his views, or even that they consciously respond specifically to him. Crenshaw, to be sure, argues that Ben Sira's theodicy is a polemic against actual opponents, namely "a vocal group bent on attacking divine justice" (1975:47). But while there are always people who attack divine justice, usually in anger and disappointment at not seeing it fulfilled, that opinion need not be associated with a definable group. Ben Sira does not attack or criticize any of his predecessors, certainly not Qohelet, but rather attempts to strengthen earlier beliefs by elaborating them and clarifying matters that might be misinterpreted. He is tending the same vineyard.

30. Segal (1958:73) explains the existing text thus: "The end of a man will be and will remain on him, and he must be evaluated according to his end". But Segal prefers to emend *yhyh* to *yḥwh*, "tell" and to take 25c as a doublet of 27b.

31. Thus Greek; in MS A this follows v. 24 (now missing).

32. Sc., whether he is fortunate or not. After v. 27, MS A has a doublet of v. 28.

33. See Crenshaw (1975:57) for this interpretation of 40:8. According to him, "the marginal situations of life, particularly sleep, fantasy, and death, become occasions of divine vengeance" (p. 60).

34. *Ibid.*, p. 63.

The Wisdom of Solomon, although more polemic than Ben Sira, probably does not include Qohelet among its opponents—"the ungodly men" (1:16) whose thoughts are quoted in 2:1-20. First of all, the Solomonic authorship of Qohelet must have been taken for granted by that time, and no one would imagine Solomon advocating debauchery and wanton persecution of the righteous. Moreover, the thoughts attributed to the wicked are so distant from anything Qohelet says that they would not be recognized as his, and the polemic would miss its mark.[35] The thoughts of the wicked in these verses are best explained as a construction of what the wicked can be assumed to think, a device with precedents in prophecy and psalmody.[36]

The writer of the epilogue to the book of Qohelet, who speaks as a pious and cautious sage, regards Qohelet as remaining well within the scope of legitimate Wisdom activity (thus Murphy, 1979:242f.). To be sure, the epilogist may be seeking to blunt the thorn of Qohelet's words, but he must have expected the reader to be able to accept Qohelet as a teacher of Wisdom. The epilogist describes Qohelet as a sage doing what sages generally do: weighing and composing proverbs, writing words of truth, and teaching the people knowledge. And this view is accurate. Qohelet is less conventional than most sages but stands within the same tradition.

Certain Tannaim are reported to have expressed concern that the words of Qohelet might "cause an inclination to heresy" (*Qoh. Rab.* 1.4[37]). Significantly, the verses they quote as examples of this danger, Qoh 11:9aβ and 1:3, are not the ones modern commentators consider most radical. The rabbis in question apparently feared that 11:9aβ (" . . . and follow your heart, and the sight of your eyes") might be conducive to licentiousness (see comment ad loc.), and that the "toil" decried in 1:3 ("What adequate gain has man in all his toil at which he labors under the sun?") might be thought to include the study of Torah. In both cases, the danger envisioned lies not in an attack upon

35. Skehan (1938:9-37) argues persuasively that Wisdom of Solomon is not attacking Qohelet or even referring to him.

36. E.g., Jer 2:20, 25; Ezek 8:12; Pss 10:6, 11; 41:6; 71:10f.; and often. See Wolff's analysis of imaginary citations in the Bible (1937:43-51).

37. *Maṣĕ'u bo dĕbarim maṭṭim lĕṣad miynut*. The variant in *Lev. Rab.* 28.1 reads *noṭin*, sc., "incline" (intrans.) instead of *maṭṭim*, "make incline".

doctrine but in the susceptibility of these verses to misinterpretations that might have practical consequences.[38]

That is not to say that Qohelet's views are quite ordinary and comfortable. On the contrary, he was one of the wise, and, the epilogist tells us, the words of the wise can prick like ox goads or nails (Qoh 12:10), or (as Rabbi Eliezer b. Hyrcanus was later to put it) burn like fiery coals, bite like jackals, sting like scorpions (*Avot* 2:15).

38. For this reason, *maṭṭim* (*Qoh. Rab.* 1.4) is the better reading. The sentences the rabbis discussed are never suspected of being in themselves heretical, but of being liable to lead others astray.

Chapter 5

COMMENTARY

§5.0 *Purpose of this chapter*
This chapter is not a complete commentary on Qohelet, for it bypasses many exegetical problems and does not attempt to survey earlier interpretations or theories. On the matter of dating, suffice it to say that I accept the nearly universal placement of Qohelet in the fourth to third centuries BCE, primarily on linguistic grounds. This chapter consists of introductory remarks on key words in Qohelet (§5.1), Qohelet's language (§5.2), literary structure (§5.3), a mention of other commentaries on Qohelet (§5.4), discussion of the Greek and Syriac translations (§5.5), and remarks on my translations (§5.6). These are followed (in §5.7) by exegesis dealing with (a) the delineation and internal structure of the larger literary units (see also §5.3); (b) specific exegetical, philological, and textual difficulties; and (c) some broader interpretive issues. A paraphrastic translation at the end (§5.8) serves to summarize the exegesis.

§5.1 *Some key words*
§5.11 HYH (*hayah*). This verb is often best translated "to happen". This is a well-established sense of *hayah* (BDB, pp. 224f.). The concept of "being" is not, of course, entirely distinct from "happening", and often a translation can use either verb. In 1 Sam 4:17a, for example, we can translate "there has been a great slaughter among the people" as well as "has happened . . .". "To happen" (or "occur") is the better rendering when the author is not speaking of simple existence. In Qoh 1:9, *mah šehayah hu' šeyyihyeh* (usually translated "That which has been is that which shall be") does not mean that a certain entity will once again come into existence, a notion quite foreign to Qohelet. It means that *types of events* recur *ad infinitum*. The types of events he has in mind are illustrated in 3:1-8, the "Catalogue of Times", whose idea is recapitulated in 3:15: "Whatever happens [*hayah*] already has happened, and what is to happen

[*lihyot*] already has happened [*hayah*] . . .". The rendering of *hayah* as "to be" could lead to misunderstandings, as it has in 3:14, where the translation "whatever God has made will be forever" may be read to imply the eternity of the created world, a notion unparalleled in Qohelet and not relevant to context.

§5.12 'NH (*'anah* and *'inyan*). Words from this root mean "activity", "business", and corresponding verbal notions. *'inyan* is nearly synonymous with *ma'ăśeh*, signifying both "deed" and "event" (e.g., 1:13; 5:13; 8:16f.). In 2:23 and 5:2 it refers to mental activity. "Business" or "be busy with", with attention to the etymological sense, "busy-ness", is usually a good English equivalent. When the activity or business is imposed on someone, "task" is an appropriate translation, but the notion of imposition or requirement is drawn from the context, not from the word's denotation.

§5.13 'ŚH (*ma'ăśeh*, *na'ăśah*, and *'aśah*). On 'ŚH meaning "acquire", "acquisitions" see §2.111. Here I will consider a different area of ambiguity: doing and happening. Ginsberg's discussion of Qohelet's key terms (1961:15-16) includes an observation of prime importance for the understanding of the book: words from the root 'ŚH denote *happening* as well as *doing*. Thus *na'ăśah* means "happen", "occur"; *'aśah*—when God is the subject—almost always means "make happen"; and *ma'ăśeh* usually means "event" or, as a collective, "events". When the subject of the verbal notion implied by *ma'ăśeh* is human, it means "deed(s)", "activity", etc. Furthermore, *ma'ăśim* may refer to the product of work, i.e., "property", "acquisitions". Ginsberg does not, however, bring adequate evidence for his interpretation of the derivatives of 'ŚH. In the course of the commentary I will examine the meaning of these words in all problematic cases. On the distinction between "deed" and "event" see §1.12, n. 12.

The recurrent phrase (*hamma'ăśeh 'ăšer*) *na'ăśah taḥat haššemeš* means "(the events that) occur under the sun". *Ma'ăśeh ha'ĕlohim* is "the work of God" in the sense of the events that he brings to pass (*ma'ăśeh*-"work" designating the product of the activity, not the activity itself). The usual translation, "work of God", is not incorrect, but it might be understood to refer to types of activities that Qohelet does not seem to have in mind. As von Rad (1966) has observed, *ma'ăśeh ha'ĕlohim* in Qohelet, contrary to the earlier use of "the work of Yahweh" (and related phrases), does not refer to acts of creation or to specific acts of God in history (or, we may add, to created things and beings). Von Rad is wrong, however, in understanding its sense in Qohelet as "divine rule"—an abstract concept von Rad contrasts to the earlier usage, which applied the concept to specific divine deeds in creation or history, past and future (pp. 295f.).[1] Examination of this word in context will show that in Qohelet *ma'ăśeh ha'ĕlohim* (a collective, equivalent to the plural) refers not to God's rule but to the totality of the events he makes happen; thus the translation, "the events God brings to pass". These events, of course, reflect his control of the world, but they are not identical to it.

The senses of 'ŚH are distributed as follows:

(1) "Happening"
- (a) *na'ăśah* meaning "to happen": 1:13, 14; 2:17; 8:9, 14, 17; 9:3, 6
- (b) *'aśah* meaning "make happen": 3:11 (2×), 14 (2×); 7:14; 11:5
- (c) *ma'ăśeh* meaning "event": 2:17; 3:11; 7:13; 8:9, 17 (2×); 11:5

(2) "Doing", "making"
- (a) *'aśah* meaning "to do", "make", etc.: 2:2; 3:9, 12; 4:17; 7:20, 29; 8:3, 4, 10, 12; 9:10 (2×); 10:19; 12:12
- (b) *na'ăśah* meaning "be done": 8:11, 16
- (c) *ma'ăśeh* meaning "deed", "action": 3:17; 4:4; 8:11, 14 (2×); 9:7, 10; 12:14

(3) "Acquiring", "property", etc.
- (a) *ma'ăśeh* meaning "earnings", "property": 5:5 (*ma'ăśey yad-*)
- (b) *'aśah* meaning "earn": 2:12 (?)

  Ambiguous, a or b: 1:9 (2×); 4:1, 3 (2×)

  Ambiguous, a or b: 2:4, 5, 6, 8; 2:11; 3:22

1. Von Rad adduces only three verses outside Qohelet as evidence for the abstract sense of God's *ma'ăśeh*, in each of which the abstract sense is doubtful. In Ps 145:17, "deeds" certainly refers to specific acts of kindness and power such as mentioned throughout the psalm—the sense it has in v. 4, where it is parallel to *g^{e}buroteyka*, "your mighty acts". Job 37:7 is obscure, but *ma'ăśehu* seems to refer collectively to God's activities in nature, examples of which Elihu lists in this speech. And the "work" mentioned in Sir 38:8 is almost certainly the physician's (this is clearly the antecedent in the Greek), not God's (God's *rule* would hardly cease in the absence of medicine; it is rather his creation, man, who might die without medical help). I do not think that the *ma'ăśeh* of God ever refers to divine rule in the abstract. Since God's rule is manifest in his *ma'ăśim*, his deeds, some passages might allow that understanding, but none require it.

The meaning in several occurrences, in addition to those listed as ambiguous, is debatable, but there are enough clear examples of each usage to establish the existence of all of them.

§5.2 *Qohelet's language*

With most commentators, I treat Qohelet's Hebrew as transitional between classical BH and mishnaic Hebrew.[1a] Against Dahood's theory that Qohelet was written in Phoenician orthography (Dahood 1952, 1962), the arguments of Gordis (pp. 402f.), Ginsberg (pp. 42-49), Piotti (1977a), and Whitley (1979:111-18) are persuasive and need not be repeated here. In addition we may consider that all the "Phoenician" characteristics Dahood finds in Qohelet, he and his students have claimed to have discovered throughout the HB. To the extent that this latter methodology succeeds, it is its own best argument against a special Phoenician provenance for Qohelet, for it shows that BH shares many characteristics with its sister-dialects to the north. Furthermore, Barr's critique of Freedman, who argued for the presence of many northern or Phoenicianizing spellings in Job (Freedman, 1969), is applicable to Dahood's treatment of Qohelet as well: MT spellings may have nothing to do with the book's origins (Barr, 1985).

1a. D Fredericks (1988) has recently argued that Qohelet's language is not postexilic. To do this he must ascribe to Qohelet a highly vernacular character with heavy northern-Israelite influence. One might wonder why these presumed vernacular, northern features (if that is indeed what they are) would emerge in notable concentrations in a preexilic Qohelet and remain largely dormant until MH. Fredricks also thinks that Qohelet's peculiarities can be explained by his "unique genre". But most of the individual generic features of the book are paralleled elsewhere in biblical literature, especially in Wisdom Literature, and none of Qohelet's literary-philosophical peculiarities require the morpho-syntactic usages that give his language a late character, e.g., the high frequency of ^{e}- (of course it *existed* in preexilic Hebrew, but it was extremely rare). Fredericks' approach is to take each feature individually and try to show that it *could* have existed in preexilic times—assuming that Qohelet wrote an unparalleled form of Hebrew. Fredericks succeeds in showing that some linguistic features are early; in other cases he is not convincing. This suggests that Qohelet is, as has often been observed, in a "transition stage" between preexilic Hebrew and MH (this has nothing to do with MH "influence", as Fredericks puts it). Qohelet's Hebrew is certainly not the language known from definitely preexilic sources, and it is gratuitous to explain its peculiarities from unknowns.

On the other hand, I am attracted to Zimmermann's and Ginsberg's theory that the Hebrew text is a translation from Aramaic (Zimmermann, 1973:98-122; Ginsberg, pp. 28-42)—more so in Ginsberg's presentation than in Zimmermann's. The theory is not implausible and eases interpretation at many points (and see my remark on 9:1). Nevertheless I do not make use of it as an exegetical tool, for two reasons. First, while the arguments against the theory (Gordis, pp. 399f.; Whitley, 1979:106-10) have not disproved it, they are effective in many individual matters and have shown that the case for an Aramaic original has not yet been made convincingly—and the burden of proof rests, of course, on the theory. The main problem with the theory is that most of the features used as evidence can be explained as calques rather than as translations from the Aramaic. It is, in fact, impossible to distinguish a translation-equivalent from what may be called a "natural" calque. After all, even if the Hebrew word in question is a mechanical rendering of the Aramaic, it is *also* a calque, since the translator considered that word to be comprehensible Hebrew. Second, even if the theory is correct, I doubt that in retroverting to Aramaic we would have much chance of hitting upon the original text, especially in cases where the retroversion rests on an emendation of the hypothetical Aramaic or of the actual Hebrew text.[2] The (presumed) original translator was more likely to get it right than we are. As an exegetical strategy I interpret MT (except when emendation, based on the usual text-critical procedures, is necessary). The interpreter is simply less apt to go astray by working from the existing text, even if it is a translation. After all, the translator would have been an Aramaic speaker and more likely than we to have understood the original text, and he would have known Hebrew well enough to create a translation of undeniable literary power.

§5.3 *Literary structure*

Numerous scholars have attempted to discover a comprehensive literary design in the book of Qohelet.[3] The most determined structural analysis is that of A. Wright, "The Riddle of the Sphinx"

2. E.g., 5:5 (Ginsberg, p. 41); 6:10 (*ibid.*, p. 38); 6:12; 8:13 (*ibid.*, p. 39f.); 8:8 (*ibid.*, p. 41).

3. These are conveniently summarized in Wright, 1968:315-17.

(1968).[4] The main outline, supposedly revealed in various verbal repetitions, is:

Initial poem (1:2-11)
I. Qohelet's investigation of life (1:12-6:9)
II. Qohelet's conclusions (6:10-11:6)
Introduction (6:10-12)
A. Man cannot find out what is good for him to do (7:1-8:17)
B. Man does not know what will come after him (9:1-11:6)
Concluding poem (11:7-12:8)
Epilogue (12:9-14)

These parts are subdivided, yielding an intricate, well articulated, hierarchical design. Wright's article should be consulted for details and argumentation.

Wright's analysis suffers from certain fundamental flaws common to many so-called "rhetorical" analyses (he identifies his methodology with the New Criticism). The following objections to Wright's methodology apply in principle to other such attempts as well.[5]

(1) The markers of unit division (particularly in part II) are not well-defined phrases, but word-groups of dubious cohesiveness, such as "not knowing". Wright obscures the looseness of these phrases by citing them in English. In any case, "inclusios", which the phrases are said to form, do not prove the boundaries of literary units, for an expression (root, word, phrase, etc.) can be repeated within a unit and can recur beyond it. Consequently we can know that a repeated expression *is* an inclusio only after we find it occurring at the beginning and end of a unit demarcated by other means. Then we may point to the inclusio to show how the author effects closure.

(2) The words and phrases chosen as unit markers are not always the most prominent. The marker in part I is said to be *hebel*

4. In his studies of 1980 and 1983, Wright additionally argued that the work is built on intricate, hidden numerological patterns. It is not clear why Qohelet would play such games. It is more likely that a determined scholar can extract patterns of some sort even from random material.

5. Schoors (1982b:97f.) raises the following objections to Wright's schema: (1) The closing formulas are not always clear and are not always at the end of the unit. (2) There are other formulas that Wright does not take into account. (3) The units are of very unequal length. (4) Units marked out by the same formula are not always on the same level of structure. (5) The proposed structure does not accord with the content.

w^e ra'yon/r^e'ut ruaḥ, but since the presence of *hebel* is optional, the marker is actually only *ra'yon/r^e'ut ruaḥ*. Yet the reader's attention certainly focuses on *hebel*, which 1:2 sets forth as the book's leitmotif, rather than on *ra'yon/r^e'ut ruaḥ*. If we use *hebel* as the unit marker, we get quite a different division.

(3) The key phrases are frequently not where we would expect them according to Wright's schema. For example, the end-marking phrases in 1:15; 1:17; 2:10; 9:5; 10:12, 14 are followed by one sentence or more before the unit ends, while the beginning-markers in 1:14; 2:3; 2:4; 2:21; 5:1; 9:16f.; 11:4 are each preceded by a sentence or two. How is the reader to get a sense of bracketing if the unit begins before or extends beyond the phrase that is supposed to mark its boundaries?

(4) The plan does not match the thought. Wright frequently gathers a variety of topics under an inappropriate or vague rubric. For example, 4:17-6:9 is supposed to teach that "one can lose all that one accumulates", but this theme cannot subsume all the topics discussed there. Conversely, Wright passes over or subordinates major unit divisions that are clear and significant even though not formally marked; e.g., after 3:22; 5:6; 7:12;[6] 7:22; 10:3; 10:20. If unit divisions are of any rhetorical significance, the reader should be able to sense their presence even without the type of analysis that Wright undertakes. The structure Wright outlines pertains only to the artificial units that he delineated in order to produce a structure.[7]

Wright claims to have solved the Riddle of the Sphinx. But perhaps there is no riddle, no hidden structural code to be "cracked". The book does not progress in an organized fashion from start to finish but rather wanders about, finally leading back (in 12:8) to the starting point.

Wittgenstein, an intensely systematic thinker, described the structure of his *Philosophical Investigations* thus:

> The thoughts which I publish in what follows are the precipitate of philosophical investigations which have occupied me for the last sixteen years. They concern many subjects: . . . I have written

6. Or 7:19, if that verse is placed after v. 12, as I have done.
7. See further the critique by Mulder (1982), whose objections in part overlap the above. Mulder, however, accepts certain elements of Wright's structure.

> down all these thoughts as *remarks*, short paragraphs, of which there is sometimes a fairly long chain about the same subject, while I sometimes make a sudden change, jumping from one topic to another. — It was my intention at first to bring all this together in a book whose form I pictured differently at different times. But the essential thing was that the thoughts should proceed from one subject to another in a natural order and without breaks.
> After several unsuccessful attempts to weld my results together into such a whole, I realized that I should never succeed. The best that I could write would never be more than philosophical remarks; my thoughts were soon crippled if I tried to force them on in any single direction against their natural inclination. — And this was, of course, connected with the very nature of the investigation. For this compels us to travel over a wide field of thought criss-cross in every direction. — The philosophical remarks in this book are, as it were, a number of sketches of landscapes which were made in the course of these long and involved journeyings (1968:ix).

The type of composition that Wittgenstein sees in his own work is strikingly akin to that of Qohelet's "philosophical investigations". The surface of the text shows little structuration not because the author was incapable of creating it, but because the book is a report of a journey of a consciousness over the landscape of experience (1:13), a landscape generally lacking highways and signposts, order and progression.

Yet the book of Qohelet does not lack coherence. On the contrary, if we step back from the literary surface and consider Qohelet's methodology of discovery and reporting (discussed in §3.22), we find a fair degree of conceptual organization. The body of the book from 1:3 to 12:7, taken as a whole, serves to establish a single proposition: "all is absurd". The book opens with a central thesis and proceeds to establish it by reporting on Qohelet's quest for knowledge, deliberately undertaken, which led to and validated this thesis. In pursuing a single idea from start to finish, the book, for all its bumpiness, is unusually systematic for an ancient Wisdom text.[8] This conceptual organization is reinforced by uniformity in the book's tone, ideas, and style. This uniformity has been adequately demonstrated by

8. Pedersen notes the uniqueness of Qohelet's approach of stating a thesis and defending it. "Toute son œuvre est la défense d'une seule conception" (1930:317).

Loretz (1964:212-17, cf. 135-217 *passim*) and by the discussions of Qohelet's style in various commentaries. The stylistic texture is unmistakably consistent.

The book's cohesiveness inheres above all in the constant presence of a single brooding consciousness which provides a framework of perception. Everything seen and taught in the body of the book is filtered through this one consciousness (see §3.22).

This form of presentation is a development of the mode of composition of many ancient Near Eastern Wisdom books. All Egyptian Wisdom Instructions, from the Old Kingdom Hardjedef to the Ptolemaic Demotic Wisdom Book, present themselves as the teaching of individuals, not as proverb collections. They begin by introducing the speaker (usually in the third person) and often close with a third-person biographical retrospective. The teachings themselves are organized in various ways. The classical, pre-Demotic Instructions are composed of short discourses on different topics, these being strung together without any overall principle of organization. The Demotic Instructions are composed of independent monostich sayings, but in Phebhor, and to a lesser degree in Onchsheshonqy, these are grouped thematically. In Ben Sira too the central units comprise a mixture of proverbs and short discourses on various themes (themselves including proverbs) proceeding without an overall principle of organization. (Sira's thematic introduction [1:1–3:31] and the concluding units—the historical panegyric [44:1-50:24] and the autobiographical conclusion [51:1-30]—are, of course, placed where they logically belong.)

The book of Qohelet goes far beyond its predecessors in the importance it gives to the organizing consciousness of the sage. In other books, few sentences seem to reflect the situation or personality of a particular teacher.[9] In most, the person of the sage disappears almost entirely, and we rarely if ever hear his "I" again, at least not until the epilogue. The teacher's "I" is more pronounced in Proverbs 1-9, though it is in the person of a "generic" wise man—a father with

9. Examples of sentences that seem especially appropriate to the sage who speaks in the work are Onchsheshonqy 8,9-10; 26,1-8; 28,10 and Ahiqar §§50, 76, 80. But the apparent relevance of such sayings to the narrative may be accidental or secondary. Lindenberger (1983:17-18 and *passim*) argues that the narrative of Ahiqar was joined to the proverbs secondarily and that these three sayings are editorial additions.

the requisite intellectual and moral virtues who is instructing his son, not an individual with experiences and attitudes distinct from those of other sages. The person of the specific teacher is prominent in the body of the instructions only in Amenemhet and Merikare (in the former the authorship is clearly fictional, since the speaker is dead). Amenemhet and Merikare are organized largely according to the sequence of events in the lives of the speakers. Their teachings derive from their past experiences but not from a deliberate attempt to sift experience through consciousness. The person of the teacher is more significant in Ben Sira than in most Wisdom books, and he is one of the few who project a clear image of their personality. But he too does not constantly state facts as things he "saw" or describe their effect on him.

The pervasiveness of the teacher's consciousness in the book of Qohelet is the main source of its cohesiveness. It may also help explain why modern scholars have often been disconcerted by the lack of an overall plan. Since an individual consciousness gives a framework of continuity to the topics, we expect more intrinsic connection between one topic and the next than we do when reading a mere collection of proverbs.[10] Moreover, Qohelet presents himself as a systematic thinker: he begins with a broad thematic prelude, introduces himself, describes his task, gives a preview of his results, and proceeds to the first stage of his investigation. This opening, together with the constant reflexive reporting, arouses expectations of a more structured discursive rhetoric, and these are quickly frustrated by the haphazard arrangement in most of the book. This lack of sequential organization is not a "riddle" but simply a characteristic of style. It may perhaps be adjudged a literary flaw, but it need not be overcome by scholarly ingenuity. Very likely the tension between sequential disorganization and perspectival cohesiveness arises from the fact that the book of Qohelet uses an ancient form, the Wisdom Instruction, for a philosophical discourse of a new kind, without fully adapting the old form to the new need.

In the commentary to follow I am less concerned with discovering hierarchical and symmetrical patterns than with tracing the movement of thought within the units. At the beginning of a unit that is not simply aphoristic, I trace, by outline or paraphrase, the structure of

10. Qohelet has also been compared to a journal or "confession", like Pascal's *Pensées* (Murphy, 1955) or Marcus Aurelius' *Meditations* (Rudolph).

argumentation found in it. Sometimes I employ indentation to show levels of logical subordination. The purpose of letters and primes is to draw attention to repetitions of ideas or phraseology.

Often no balanced hierarchies or symmetrical patterns appear (such as envelope structures, inversions, chiasms, mirror patterns, and the like). It is puzzling that scholars, especially those identifying with "rhetorical criticism" or "literary criticism", have come to assume that literary-rhetorical analysis has not done its job until it has dredged up some symmetrical design, as if this were the *sine qua non* of artistry or persuasiveness. An argument may proceed in a quite disorganized fashion while remaining reasonable and persuasive. Nor is it essential that the rhetorical movement ("argument") coincide with the literary structure or section division. A single section, even a single sentence, can make more than one point, or make a point and argue for it, while a single step in an argument can extend over two or more sections that are clearly marked off by syntax or theme (as in 12:1-8). In rhetoric, at least in reasoned argumentation such as Qohelet usually offers, the relationships between propositions and arguments are far more important—and intricate—than verbal patterns of the sort that have received so much attention in the last two decades and may be, at least in part, independent of the patterns. Thus my sketch of the "argument" of a unit or section sometimes suggests a different breakdown from the one reflected in the subsection division I propose or reveal in the formatting of the translation. In 1:13-18, for example, the process of argumentation generally accords with the section divisions. Verse 17, however, both includes a description of the process of inquiry and begins a reflection on the inquiry; yet this verse—a single sentence—can hardly be divided into two sections. Similarly, in 8:16-9:6, 9:1 is syntactically and logically bound to 9:2, yet at the same time 9:1 continues Qohelet's reflection on the profundity of human ignorance begun in 8:16.

As for the existence of an overall design in the book, I agree with Zimmerli (1974) and Schoors (1982b), among others, in viewing Qohelet as standing at neither extreme of the continuum between an organized treatise and a mere collection of sayings. Schoors emphasizes the importance of associative connections and linking words (*mots-crochets*) in determining the book's organization. With this too I am basically in agreement, except that I do not consider associative connections adequate evidence of structure. It is unlikely that any human discourse can be truly random, for *unstructured* thought inevitably proceeds by associations. In any case, I believe that logical or rhetorical considerations determine the progression from unit to unit more than Schoors's analysis shows. Moreover, I do not see the slightest evidence that any of the linkages between units are necessarily redactional (on the question of redaction, see Excursus III). Still, my unit division, developed independently, is largely in accord with his—and with those of many other interpreters. Ellermeier's synopsis of the unit division proposed by eight major commentators (1967:131-41) shows considerable agreement on the placement of the breaks. This agreement suggests that the segmentation of the book is reasonably clear, in other words, that readers tend to pause at the same places. I doubt that any complex hierarchical organization registers in the consciousness of the reader, even after many readings. Therefore, an intricate, multileveled design of the sort Wright sees, even if it did exist, would be rhetorically irrelevant.

The boundaries between units are not absolute; one passage inevitably affects the way we read the following one. The purpose of unit demarcation is more to link material than to segment it. The guiding question is: what are the minimal passages that may be read in isolation without distorting the contextual meaning of the material? It is better to be too inclusive than too restrictive. If we include too much in a single unit, the distortion is unlikely to be severe, since all the material belongs to the same book and is part of a single overall argument. Break-up of integral units, on the other hand, is likely to distort the meaning of the parts. There are no *a priori* rules and few *a priori* guides to such demarcation. Unit division must be based on a convergence of features, both in form and in content (and these *are* distinguishable in analysis). The most important feature is the relations among the ideas of the argument, since the argument is primary, and most formal features are developed to help communicate it.

§5.4 *Commentaries*

No matter how carefully Bible scholars reference their ideas, they cannot do justice to all who influenced them. We appropriate earlier ideas, weaving them into our own, often without knowing it, or knowing it but giving those ideas a new twist that makes it awkward, if not impossible, to separate what is borrowed from what is created.

This fact is a source of encouragement, not only an excuse. It means that even ideas that are less than revolutionary may contribute to the progress of our common enterprise. The threads we spin may in turn be woven into the tapestry of Bible scholarship and take their place in the ever-emerging design, one that might be unrecognizable from up close and quite different from what the individual contributors intended.

While I try to reference adequately the sources of ideas I mention (which may not, however, be the origins of the ideas), certain commentaries have been of importance in my study of this book beyond what the number of references to them may suggest:

> Émile Podechard's patient, even picky, analysis of text, grammar, and vocabulary makes his work, in my view, the best all-around modern commentary. Much more dated, however, is his allocation of numerous verses to a "*ḥasid*" and a "*ḥakam*". Even if we could identify certain glosses, we could not credibly associate them with specific types of thought.
>
> Franz Delitzsch resolutely interprets the text from a conservative stance within the well-established perimeters of classical Hebrew grammar and lexicography, and this is where all exegesis should begin. The virtues of his commentary are at the same time its limitations.
>
> Robert Gordis's balanced, level-headed evaluation of exegetical problems has made his commentary a standard reference work.
>
> H. L. Ginsberg's short Hebrew commentary is full of flashes of insight. Many of these insights—some packed into single sentences—have considerable significance for the meaning of the book of Qohelet in its entirety. I see certain of my contributions as attempts to argue in detail for some of the ideas that Ginsberg states in an apodictic, even off-hand, fashion, and to draw their broader implications for interpretation.

These books, and even many with more modest contributions to the subject at hand, disprove Qohelet's contention that there is nothing new under the sun (1:9) and the epilogue's belief that making many books is pointless (12:12). They have well repaid the "weariness of flesh" that comes with "much study" (12:12).

§5.5 The Greek and Syriac translations of Qohelet

The highly literal character of the "Septuagint" translation of Qohelet and, above all, its propensity to render *'et* by σύν, led Graetz (1875) to suggest that the version preserved in LXX was the "first edition" of Aquila ("Aq") mentioned by Jerome, while the fragments that Origen identified as Aquilan represent Aquila's "second edition". McNeile's detailed study (1904:115-34) supports the hypothesis that LXX-Qoh is indeed Aquilan in character. Jerome does not, however, mention two Aquilan editions of Qohelet. This fact, together with a careful examination of some of the stylistic traits of Aquila (in particular the ways he typically handles the *nota accusativi* in various syntactic environments), led Barthélemy (1963:21-30) to conclude that the "Septuagint" to Qohelet is Aquila's *only* edition, while the fragments Origen identified as Aquilan are not his, but probably belong to Symmachus.[11] Hyvärinen (1977:88-99, 112) points to significant deviations in LXX-Qoh from Aquilan techniques in lexical and syntactical matters and argues against an Aquilan origin for LXX-Qoh, observing that Aquila's *Vorlage* elsewhere diverges less from MT than does that of LXX-Qoh, which shows at least thirty consonantal variants (one for every seven or eight verses).

I will refer to the Greek translation of Qoh by the conventional designation "LXX", and to the putative Aquilan fragments as "Aquila". Whether or not LXX-Qoh is Aquilan, it is an Aquilan-type translation, with a precise word-to-word and (for the most part) particle-to-particle mapping. We may therefore usually retrovert from the Greek with confidence and view many of the resulting variants as hyparchetypes having, in principle, equal status with MT.[12] Unless otherwise noted, my references to "LXX" follow Rahlfs.

11. Salzberger (mentioned by McNeile, p. 115) already suggested in 1873 that the present Greek, but not the Aquilan column of the Hexapla, is by Aquila. McNeile mentions this idea in a footnote (p. 115) but curtly rejects it.

12. For this concept see Goshen-Gottstein (1957), and note in particular the principle: "Unless and until we are forced by strict philological evidence to regard a certain reading as secondary or corrupt, we have to look upon conflicting readings in our primary sources as alternative readings, none of which must be considered as superior to the other, simply because it is contained in one special tradition . . ." (p. 198).

The Peshiṭta (Syr) to Qohelet is likewise highly literal. In determining the correct readings in Syr and its *Vorlage* (where this differs from MT) I have made use of Kamenetzky's text-critical study of the Syriac translation of Qohelet (1904). Euringer (1890) continues to be of value. A. Schoors (1985b) has shown that Syr was translated from the Hebrew with the aid of the LXX in difficult passages and was later revised under the influence of the LXX (specifically the B and S texts).

"Syr(iac)" refers to the base text of the Leyden Peshiṭta, which, in the case of Qohelet, is the Ambrosian MS. In a survey of the manuscripts used for the Leyden Peshiṭta, Lane (1979) says that the manuscript tradition for Qohelet is homogeneous, showing only minor variations. He also notes evidence (in doublets) for different understandings of a single underlying text rather than for later assimilation to the Hebrew.

§5.6 *The translations, literal and paraphrastic*

In conjunction with the comments on each unit I give a literal translation. A paraphrastic rendering follows the commentary (§5.8). When quoting Qohelet elsewhere I use the literal translation, except when a slightly different form serves to bring out certain features of the passage in question or to highlight other interpretations. Both translations are meant as interpretive aids to be used in conjunction with the Hebrew, not as substitutes for it.

The literal translation is not on the extreme of the scale of literalness (mechanical representations, where necessary, are left to the remarks in the commentary) and does not aim at strict English-Hebrew concordance. It does attempt to render the theme words consistently, but not even this can always be achieved without violence to the meaning. In the literal translation I usually maintain ambiguities present in the Hebrew text, so that the reader will see immediately some of the problems the commentary must address. Disambiguation is left for the comments and the paraphrastic translation.

The paraphrastic translation is a form of commentary. Like any paraphrase, it does not give "the" meaning of the book; it clarifies one type of meaning—the propositional content (as I understand it)—at the expense of the others. This translation disambiguates the antecedents of ambiguous pronouns, supplies connectives between the thoughts, moves verses within a section to provide a smoother flow, adds occasional explanatory "glosses", and converts metaphors into literal statements when necessary for clarity. It attempts to provide an unambiguous, prosaic rendering even where the meaning is very uncertain. (This is almost impossible in 12:2-6.)

The paraphrastic rendering usually transforms rhetorical questions into negative statements; the literal translation does so only when a negative is required in English, as in motive clauses. Though gaining in clarity, the paraphrase dampens the force of the rhetorical questions. A rhetorical question may be a challenge, as if to say: "Answer me if you can! Is there any advantage in toil? Tell me what it is!" Sometimes the rhetorical question is a groan: "Why oh why have I become wiser than the fool?" (2:15). The rhetorical questions are often a way of throwing up the hands in despair and of inviting the reader's participation in Qohelet's exasperation.[13] Of course, much in the way of subtlety, connotation, and deliberate ambiguity is lost in such a rendering, but its purpose is to convey only one aspect of Qohelet's meaning—its literal, propositional content.

Sigla used in the translation:

{ }	=	later addition
< >	=	translation based on emendation
[ ]	=	words added for the sake of the translation
- - -	=	obscure

§5.7 *Translation and commentary*

1:1-2

(1) The words of Qohelet, son of David, king in Jerusalem.

(2) Utterly absurd, said Qohelet, utterly absurd. Everything is absurd.

The authorial voice introduces Qohelet and summarizes his message. The motto in 1:2 and 12:8 frames Qohelet's words.

1:1. The title (1:1) associates Qohelet with Solomon. Since this identification is assumed in 1:12–2:11, there is no reason to restrict

13. Crenshaw (1986) analyzes the functions of *mi yodeaʿ* questions in the HB and shows that Qohelet's express skepticism and deny knowability, leaving no door open for hope of knowledge.

the original title to the phrase "words of Qohelet" (thus Galling). The vast wealth and wisdom of Qohelet reflect traditions about Solomon, probably with direct dependence on 1 Kgs 3:12; 5:9-14; 1 Chron 29:25; 2 Chron 1:12; etc.

1:2. (*hăbel hăbalim 'amar qohelet hăbel hăbalim hakkol habel*): This, the book's motto, is not an "im allerhöchsten Grade missverständliche Summierung Qoheletscher Aussagen" by an editor (Ellermeier, 1967:100). In my view, the motto is the author's, who is here quoting Qohelet, his persona; see Excursus III. In any case, it is a fair encapsulation of Qohelet's thought, for he indeed implies that *everything* is *hebel* by "going around" the world and applying the term to numerous phenomena. Furthermore, the motto is rephrased in 1:14, where Qohelet calls "all the events that occur under the sun" *hebel*, a statement equivalent to *hakkol hebel*.

Ellermeier, who understands *hebel* to mean "Nichtigkeit", claims that the phrase *hăbel hăbalim* cannot express "in the highest degree", for there are no degrees to nothingness. Furthermore, he says, if we take *hăbel hăbalim* to mean "*hebel* in the highest degree", the end of the verse, "all is *hebel*", is a weakening of the opening statement, "(all) is utterly *hebel*". Ellermeier explains *hăbel hăbalim* as iterative: "immer wieder 'hebel'", but he gives no examples of bound phrases having an iterative sense, and it is doubtful that a superlative (as Ellermeier grants this phrase to be) can have an iterative meaning (except when iteration is implied by the particular phrase).

Understanding *hebel* as meaning "absurd" answers the difficulties Ellermeier raises, for there *are* degrees of absurdity. The motto says that life is absurd to the highest degree. It is true that *hakkol habel* is weaker than (*hakkol*) *hăbel hăbalim*, but this weakening serves a rhetorical purpose. The phrase *hakkol habel* provides the subject of *hăbel hăbalim* and resumes the predicate in a de-emphasized form. In this way some weight is given to the subject, *hakkol*, in a sentence that places massive emphasis on the predicate, thus: "*everything* is absurd". Consequently, the motto, which introduces Qohelet's words and (in a shorter form) closes them (12:8), reflects first the intensity of the *hebel*-judgment and then its universality.

The quoting phrase, *'amar qohelet*, functions on the aesthetic level to control the rhythm of the motto. Because of the slight caesura it provides we tend to pause and absorb the thought rather than slip over the clause as we would do if we read *hăbel hăbalim hăbel hăbalim hakkol habel.* Rhetorically, it interposes the frame narrator (see Excursus IV) between Qohelet and the reader. The frame narrator appears as an interpreter, who, by abstracting this sentence (or idea) from Qohelet's teachings and placing it at the head of the monologue, shows us by authoritative example how we are to interpret the rest of Qohelet's words.

The book's motto is a thesis that we can expect to see validated by the following monologue, and which by this expectation controls the way we read. Thus, for example, after reading 1:2 no one would take 1:4-7 as a celebration of the stability of the natural order. Instead we immediately ask: what is *hebel* about these natural processes? At the same time, we start to redefine *hebel* in accordance with what we read and will continue to do so throughout the book. Similarly, the practical counsels Qohelet offers later will not be understood as guides to achieving a mastery of life or avoiding absurdity, since such control is precluded by the universality of *hebel*.

The five-fold repetition of *hebel* sets that word reverberating, so that every recurrence of the term throughout the monologue points back to and is subsumed in this statement. This strong interpretive guidance allows the monologue to wander about (*latur*!) without going astray.

1:3-11

(3) What adequate gain does man get through all his toil at which he labors under the sun?

(4) A generation goes and a generation comes,
but the world remains forever the same.
(5) The sun rises and the sun sets,
then goes panting to its place,
whence it rises.
(6) Going to the south,
and rounding to the north,
round and round goes the wind,
and on its rounds the wind returns.
(7) All the rivers flow to the sea,
but the sea is never filled.
That place to which the rivers go,
there they go again.

(8) Words are all weary;
man is unable to speak.

The eye is not sated with seeing,
  nor the ear filled by hearing.
(9) That which happens is that which shall happen,
  and that which occurs is that which shall occur,
    and there is nothing at all new under the sun.

(10) If there is anything of which one might say, "See, this is new", it has already happened in the aeons that preceded us. (11) There is no remembrance of things past, nor of the things yet to come will there be remembrance among those who come still later.

The futility of toil

(a) Thesis (1:3)
(b) Argument by analogy (1:4-7)
(c) Reaction to observations in (b) (1:8)
(a′) Conclusion abstracted from (b) which justifies (a) (1:9)
(e) Prose appendix, reinforcing (a′) (1:10-11)

Argument: If the mighty efforts of nature can achieve nothing new, surely man's toil is futile. Since there is nothing new, man's toil can achieve nothing that would not have occurred anyway.

The generalization in v. 2 leads into the description of eternal repetition just as the same generalization in 12:8 flows out of the description of human ephemerality. While v. 2 has a certain independence as the author's encapsulation of Qohelet's teaching, the reader does not forget that verse while reading on. The following unit is naturally understood in light of the motto and will naturally be taken as demonstrative of the principle it expresses.

Verse 3 is even more closely linked with the following verses than is v. 2, for the description of nature in vv. 4-7 serves only to demonstrate the thesis about human toil. Verse 8 turns our attention back to the human realm, and v. 9 points back to v. 3 by echoing the phrase "under the sun". What the description of nature configured, we now learn, is that nothing new ever happens, and this fact validates the opening statement that toil is never adequately compensated. Verses 10-11 form a prose appendix to the preceding section, wrapping up the argument of vv. 4-9 by explaining why some people might assume the contrary.[14]

14. Good (1978) offers a careful reconstruction and analysis of the dynamic process of reading this unit and attempts to perceive the process as it unfolds.

1:3. This is a rhetorical question whose negative answer is implicit in the choice of the word *'amal* to designate human activities (see §2.111) as well as in the negativism of the preceding verse. No labors are adequately compensated. This may be learned from the observation of natural processes, which, however mighty, seem to accomplish nothing in particular.

'amal here refers not only to employment directed at gaining wealth, but to all human efforts.

Ṭaḥat haššameš. "Under the sun" ("sky" in 1:13; 2:3; 3:1) is the sphere of human life, in short, "the world"; it excludes the underworld (see 9:6) and the heavens, God's domain. There are two ways in which this phrase might be used, restrictive and expansive. In the first, the purpose of the phrase would be modestly to restrict the application of Qohelet's observations *only* to the world, so as to exclude other spheres that are beyond human knowledge. "Under the sun" then would be used to distinguish the field of observation from the non-human spheres of reality. In this case, Qohelet would be holding out the possibility of a different situation elsewhere, i.e., in the heaven or the underworld. This is the traditional understanding of the phrase; it preserves Qohelet's piety intact and suggests that he has hopes for a better life beyond the sun. The meaning of the phrase is the same in the second possible use, but its function is different. In this case, Qohelet's purpose would be to emphasize the *breadth* of his observations, claiming that such-and-such is true in the *entire* world "under the sun", not just in part of it. The second function is more likely, for if the phrase were restrictive, 1:9 would be saying that only under the sun is there nothing new, thereby implicitly conceding the possibility of something new occurring elsewhere than in the human sphere (i.e., in the realm of the divine or in Sheol), and it seems improbable that this is Qohelet's intention. Nor is Qohelet likely, however modest the scope of his vision, to concede that although toil has no adequate compensation in this life (1:3), it may have one elsewhere; and so on for the other occurrences of this phrase. Furthermore, since most of the facts that Qohelet observes "under the sun" can hardly be imagined to exist in any other sphere but human life, there is no need to exclude other spheres of reality.

1:4-7. The staticity of nature. Each of these verses makes the same point: much movement but no change. How much the less can man's toil be expected to affect the course of events.

1:4. This verse is commonly understood to contrast the permanence of the earth with the ephemerality of the generations. Yet the permanence of the physical earth has no relevance to the individual. The key to understanding this verse lies in recognizing that *ha'areṣ* here does not mean the physical earth, but humanity as a whole—"le monde" rather than "la terre" (e.g., Gen 11:1; 1 Kgs 2:2; Ps 33:8).

The movement of the generations is not an image of transience. The other images in 1:4-8 do not show the disappearance of the objects in the cycle. Qoh 1:4 represents the fact that humanity "remains always the same". (*'amad* here means "remain as is", as in Lev 13:5; Jer 32:14; Ps 33:11.) Qohelet observes that the movement of generations does not change the face of humanity—just as the rivers' incessant flow into the sea does not change *it*. No sooner does one generation depart than another arrives to fill the gap. Thus the "world" never changes in spite of any appearance to the contrary. The poem shows that the persistent movements of natural phenomena, of which mankind, taken as a whole, is one, do not really affect anything.

1:5. The sun's great, arduous journey across the sky merely brings it back to its starting point. The strain of the trek is implied by *šo'ep*, "pant". Even if *šo'ep* is to be derived etymologically from ŠWP, "to walk, proceed" (thus Rashi, Gordis, Ginsberg; similarly Targum), the reader would naturally connect *šo'ep* in this form with Š'P, "to pant".

1:6. The wind, which might well be perceived as wandering aimlessly, in Qohelet's vision follows a fixed circuit. *Sobeb sobeb* functions adverbially to *holek*.

1:7. The rivers' ceaseless flowing does not fill up the sea conclusively. The sea can always take more water, always absorb without trace more of the rivers' labor.

1:8. The *d^ebarim* that are weary are not the "things" mentioned—the world, sun, wind, and rivers. *Dabar* is nowhere used of physical entities. Nor are all the "matters" described in vv. 4-7 weary. Rather, it is words that are weary, too feeble to communicate. Consequently man cannot speak—"of these matters" is implied.

A possible, and perhaps expected reaction to the constancy of these phenomena would be exultation in the solidity and reliability of God's creation. Qohelet's reaction is frustration. Futility of effort is intrinsic to the world. Such a world is not truly graspable by human speech or perception. Sights and sounds may inundate the senses but cannot satisfy or fill them and thus do not produce understanding. Isa 6:9-10 also expresses the concept of a hearing and seeing that consists of superficial absorption of sense impressions devoid of understanding (LXX makes the distinction between sense perception and understanding explicit).

1:9. As in the natural world, so too in human life there is no true change, only dreary repetition. As Augustine observed when arguing against the theory of cyclical time, Qohelet is speaking of recurrence of *types* of beings and events:

> Even monstrous and irregular productions, though differing from one another, and though some are reported as solitary instances, yet resemble one another generally, insofar as they are miraculous and monstrous, and, in this sense, have been, and shall be, and are no new and recent things under the sun.[15]

Archetypal events (including deeds, seen as events)—birth, death, war, embracing, and so on—come to realization in specific manifestations: the birth of particular individuals, particular acts of embracing, the outbreak of particular wars, etc. But, as Mircea Eliade observed, the concept of archetypes reduces the reality of specific, nonrepetitive events:

> Hegel affirmed that in nature things repeat themselves for ever and that there is "nothing new under the sun. All that we have so far demonstrated confirms the existence of a similar conception in the man of archaic societies: for him things repeat themselves for ever and nothing new happens under the sun. But this repetition has a meaning . . . it alone confers a reality upon events; events repeat themselves because they imitate an archetype—the exemplary event. Furthermore, through this repetition, time is suspended, or at least its virulence is diminished (1954:90).

The last sentence does not apply to Qohelet, for whom the repetitiveness was a heavy burden. But the notion that repeated events alone are real, or are, we might say, more real than others, does apply. For to say that "there is nothing new under the sun" requires excluding all undeniably "new" events from the category of "everything". World War II, the book of Qohelet, the death of

15. *City of God*, XII, 13 (transl. M. Dods). Augustine also considers it possible that 1:9 speaks of predestination.

Lincoln—these had not happened prior to their recognized occurrence. But in some sense Qohelet regards their reality as inhering in their conformity to archetype: war, book, death. Only in that way can he deny their newness.

'ŚH: *na'ăśah* here may mean either "happens" or "is done". "Happens" is preferable because the rephrasing of this idea in 3:15 omits *na'ăśah*, suggesting that *na'ăśah* + *hayah* in 1:9 are adequately reformulated by *hayah* alone.

1:10-11. If anyone thinks that something is truly new, that notion is only due to poor memory. *Ri'šonim* and *'aḥăronim* refer to earlier and later events rather than to earlier and later generations, since this passage deals not with the problem of whether people are remembered but whether events are.

LXX's ὃς λαλήσει καὶ ἐρεῖ and Syr *kl dnmll wn'mr* represent *šydbr wy'mr*. MT is superior because it offers an antecedent for *hu'*.

1:12-18

(12) I am Qohelet. I have been king over Israel in Jerusalem. (13) I set my heart to investigate and to explore with wisdom all that occurs under the heavens—it is an unfortunate business that God has given people to busy themselves with. (14) When I observed all the events that occur under the sun, I realized that they are all absurdity and vexation.
(15) Nothing twisted can be straightened out, No deficiency can be <made up for>.[a]

(16) I spoke with my heart: "See, I have amassed wisdom far beyond anyone who preceded me over Jerusalem". And my heart observed much wisdom and knowledge. (17) But when I applied my heart to the appropriation of wisdom and knowledge,[b] {inanity and folly[c]}, I realized that this too is a vexation.
(18) For in much wisdom there is much irritation, and whoever increases knowledge increases pain.

[a] *l^{e}himmālôt* (MT *l^{e}himmānôt*) [b] point *wāda'at* (MT *w^{e}da'at*) [c] a gloss.

Qohelet introduces himself as king, describes his task, and gives his conclusion—everything is absurd—from which he deduces that the success of his wisdom was also its bane.

The unit is composed of two sections, with B (vv. 16-18) looking back at the inquiry described in A (vv. 12-15), reflecting on it and reacting to its results.

Argument:
A. Presentation of inquiry

- a. Self-presentation (1:12)
- b. Undertaking of inquiry: to use wisdom to gain an understanding of the world (1:13)
- c. Finding: everything is absurd and perverse (1:14-15)

B. Narration and evaluation of inquiry

- a. Method and process of inquiry (1:16-17a)
- b. Reflection on the inquiry: a miserable task (1:17b-18) (anticipated in v. 13b)

As is widely recognized, the royal fiction does not extend beyond chapter 2 (see, for example, Gordis). This means that neither Qohelet nor the epilogist has further need to invoke this fiction, but not that either repudiates any of the conclusions reached or the experiences known under this guise. On the contrary, the guise is meant to strengthen these conclusions and validate the experiences, for Solomon had the wealth to grant himself the maximum of pleasures, and thus to carry through the experiment most thoroughly, as well as the wisdom to evaluate his experiences—and to judge wisdom itself.

1:12. This verse can be rendered either "I, Qohelet, have been king, etc." or "I am Qohelet. I have been king, etc." The latter translation seems the more appropriate, since the speaker has not yet introduced himself and can be expected to do so before stating his office (1:1 is the title, not Qohelet's words; 1:2 is the author's summary of what Qohelet said). "I am Qohelet" resembles the opening of various royal inscriptions, e.g., "I am Kilamuwa, the son of Hayya" (Gibson, 1982:III, 34); "I am Azitawadda, blessed by Baal, servant of Baal, whom Awarku, king of the Danunians, made powerful" (ibid., 47); "I am Yehaumilk, king of Byblos, etc." (ibid., 95). These introductory self-identifications, like Qohelet's, precede autobiographical statements in which the speaker relates his virtues and achievements.

1:13. "The heavens": The reading "sun" is not necessary, but it does have a good claim to authenticity, being attested by Syr, Jerome, Targum, and the bulk of the LXX tradition, as well as several Hebrew MSS. The interchange between the pragmatic synonyms *šemeš* and *šamayim* may have occurred either in the transmission of texts or in the process of translation.

ʿŚH (*maʿăśeh* and *naʿăśah*). Qohelet designates the object of his investigation as (a) *kol ʾăšer naʿăśah taḥat haššamayim* (v. 13) and (b) *kol hammaʿăśim šennaʿăśu taḥat haššameš* (v. 14). Is he saying that he will examine all that is *done* on earth (sc., by mankind) or all that *happens* in life? The likelihood of the second interpretation is shown by the following considerations. First, Qohelet's investigation comprehends much more than people's deeds. He also, in fact primarily, observes things that *happen* to people, such as undeserved gain, the unfair allocation of lifespans, the obliteration of distinctions by death, and death and oblivion themselves. Second, in 8:17, when Qohelet looks back to the programmatic statement of 1:13-14, he identifies (c) *hammaʿăśeh ʾăšer naʿăśah taḥat haššameš* with (d) *kol maʿăśeh haʾĕlohim* by using (d) to resume (c) (on the syntax, see ad loc.). Phrase (d) is certainly not restricted to human actions, so it is unlikely that (c) is. Phrase (c) in turn is indistinguishable from (a) and (b) (see above), both of which Qohelet uses to designate the object of examination in this passage.

ʿinyan: The antecedent of *huʾ* (*ʿinyan raʿ*) in v. 13 is not *kol ʾăšer naʿăśah taḥat haššameš*, for neither events nor human deeds (if *naʿăśah* be taken that way) are "given" to man by God. The "unfortunate business" mentioned in 1:14 is the attempt to understand what occurs on earth. This activity Qohelet considers imposed on man by God (see further 3:10, as emended). It is a hopeless task, for even if pursued day and night (8:16b) by the most competent persons (8:17b), its goal cannot be attained (8:17). One cannot make sense out of something that lacks it (1:14).

Hertzberg and Ellermeier (1967:177-86) take the object of *lidroš* and *latur* to be "wisdom" rather than "all that happens under the sun", arguing that TWR elsewhere governs a direct object and that the hiphil of TWR once governs *b-* (Judg 1:23). Nevertheless, "wisdom" is best understood (with most commentators) as the *means* (Delitzsch: *organon*) by which Qohelet investigates life. It is doubtful that *ʿal* can indicate "dasjenige, in Hinsicht worauf oder vielleicht noch besser: weswegen Qohelet die Weisheit unter die Lupe nehmen that" (Ellermeier, p. 179; he gives no examples of that usage elsewhere). In any case, wisdom is only one of the objects of Qohelet's study; his field of investigation, as 1:2 and 12:8 show, is "everything", i.e., "all that happens" under the sun.

1:15. "What is twisted [*m*ᵉ*ʿuwwat*]" and "what is lacking [*ḥesron*]" do not refer to human actions, as if to say that no one can right wrongs that others have committed. Qohelet never speaks of attempts to right injustices. The distortions and the lacks he refers to are God's doing and thus irremediable. Qoh 7:13 says explicitly that this is so. Qoh 1:15 is thus a reprise of the *hebel*-judgment of v. 14.

The emendation of *lhmnwt* to *lhmlwt* (*l^ehimmalot*), a mishnaic-type spelling of a III-' verb (first suggested by Ewald; see also Levy), commends itself by the context, though it lacks support in the Versions.[16] The interchange of *nun/lamed* is an attested scribal error; see Perles (1895:53) and Kennedy (1928:89).[17] MT means "that which is lacking cannot be numbered", but this is a pointless truism, not a complaint about the unchangeability of the world, as is the parallel phrase (15a). MT cannot mean "an untold number of things are lacking" (Barton)—also a pointless remark.

As a first step in his investigation of what happens on earth, Qohelet seeks to amass wisdom and knowledge. He succeeds in this venture, but finds that his success brings with it deep discomfort.

1:16. As well as acquiring wisdom, Qohelet *observed* it. *Lir'ot ḥokmah* means to observe wisdom and to consider its consequences, as in 2:12; the idiom does not occur elsewhere. (The words *ra'iti ḥokmah* in 9:13, if MT be maintained, means to see something *as* [an example of] wisdom.)

1:17. The phrase *holelot w^eśiklut* is probably secondary. In this passage Qohelet is describing the consequences of wisdom alone. The conclusion, "I knew that this too is a vexation", has a singular pronoun as its subject, showing that Qohelet is judging one thing not two, and furthermore v. 18 gives the reason only for an evaluation of *ḥokmah* and *da'at*. The phrase *holelot w^eśiklut* is probably an

16. The evidence Levy brings does not actually witness to the suggested reading. Sym translates not by ἀναπληῶσαι but by ἀναπληῶσαι ἀριθμὸν, a contextual translation of *lhmnwt*. Also Rabbi Bar Hehe's remark *h'y lhymnwt lhml'wt myb'y*, meaning "this *lhymnwt* should be *lhml'wt*" (*b. Hag.* 9*b*) is not (contrary to Levy) evidence for *lhmlwt* but rather for MT. Bar Hehe is remarking on *lhmnwt* as a peculiarity requiring a special interpretation. The suggested emendation is thus conjectural.

17. Good examples are Job 15:35 (LXX testifies to *tkyl* for *tkyn*); Neh 3:30; 12:44; 13:7 (*nškh* for *lškh* in these three verses); 1 Sam 6:18 (*'bl* for *'bn*; cf. v. 14 and LXX).

addition based on 2:12a or 7:25, made by a scribe seeking to provide a more acceptable target for the *hebel*-judgment.

MT places the pause after *w^eda'at*, thus making this verb govern "inanity and folly" as direct objects. We should point (*ḥokmah*) *wāda'at* (an understanding implied by LXX). The same hendiadys appears in v. 16 and is distributed in a parallelism in v. 18.

The phrases *yada' ḥokmah* and *yada' da'at* mean to gain or appropriate wisdom for oneself; compare *yada' ḥokmah* in Prov 1:2 and 24:14, *yada' da'at* in Prov 17:27 and Dan 1:4, and similar phrases with synonyms (*hebin*, *binah*) in Prov 4:1; 17:24; 19:25; Job 38:4; etc. Thus, strictly speaking, it is not wisdom as such that Qohelet is judging absurd, but rather the "knowing" of wisdom", which is to say, its acquisition. Similarly, it is becoming "so very wise" that he deplores in 2:15 and becoming "exceedingly wise" that he warns against in 7:16.

1:18. Whatever wisdom's advantages, too much of it makes one miserable, as Qohelet knows from his own experience. Much wisdom is a source of pain and chagrin, for it enables—in fact, forces—its possessor to perceive the absurdities that take place under the sun.

Yosip is a finite verb functioning nominally. On this usage see Grossberg, 1979:31-33.

2:1-26. Chapter 2 is a single unit composed of three major sections. Because of the length of the unit, the three sections will be translated and discussed separately. This unit continues the narration of the inquiry begun in the preceding unit (note the "too" in 2:1b).

A. 2:1-11, pleasure and toil
B. 2:12-17, wisdom and folly
C. 2:18-26, toil and pleasure, wisdom and folly.

A. **2:1-11**

> (1) I said in my heart, "Come, let me make you experience pleasure and have enjoyment". But I realized that it too is an absurdity.
> (2) Of amusement I said, "Inane!" and of pleasure, "What does this accomplish?"
>
> (3) I went about in my heart to ply my body with wine (my heart behaving in wisdom and <not seized>[a] by folly), so that I might see what is good for people to do under the heavens during the few days of their lives.

(4) I did great things: I built myself houses, planted myself vineyards, (5) made myself gardens and orchards and planted in them fruit trees of all kinds. (6) I made myself pools of water from which to irrigate a wood growing with trees. (7) I acquired male and female slaves, and I had home-born servants as well. I also had many herds of cattle and flocks, more than all who were before me in Jerusalem. (8) I also amassed for myself silver and gold and treasures of kings and provinces. I got myself singers and songstresses and the pleasures of men—a fair number of concubines. (9) I grew far greater than anyone before me in Jerusalem, and still my wisdom remained with me. (10) Whatever my eyes saw I did not withhold from them. I did not restrain my heart from any type of pleasure, so my heart received pleasure through all my toil, and this was my portion from all my toil.

(11) But when I turned [to consider] all the things my hands had done and the toil I had laboriously performed, I realized that it was all an absurdity and a vexation, and that there is no adequate gain [to be had] under the sun.

[a] *w^elō' 'ōḥēz* (MT *w^ele'ĕḥōz*)

Argument:

A. Pleasure and toil

- (a) Undertaking of inquiry to examine pleasure (2:1a)
- (b) Finding: pleasure is absurd (2:1b-2)
- (c) Narration of process of inquiry (2:3-9) v. 3: general; vv. 4-9: specifics
- (d) Summary finding: pleasure was his portion (2:10)
- (e) Reflection on this finding: his toil was absurd (2:11)

In terms of literary structure, the subdivisions are to be grouped somewhat differently. (a) and (b) together form the introduction to the unit, (c) and (d) describe the experiment—its procedure and outcome—and (e), separated from the foregoing by the phrase "I turned", reflects upon the finding and its implications.

Qohelet tells how he undertook to amass wealth and to immerse himself in pleasures of all sorts in order to discover what is good to do. The answer was pleasure, though he realized that this too is absurd, because it "does", or "produces" nothing. The feeling of pleasure is not considered enough of a "something" to give meaning to pleasurable actions. Thus the toil that produced the means of pleasure was absurd and vexatious. Both 1:12-18 and 2:1-11 tell of undertaking an inquiry (of the world/of pleasure), immediately state a finding (all events are absurd/pleasure is absurd), report more expansively on the method of the undertaking (amassing wisdom/amassing wealth and pleasures), then reflect on the value of the efforts of the undertaking (amassing wisdom/toiling for wealth).

On the considerations weighing against Tur-Sinai's striking emendation (he transfers the words *bayyayin 'et b^{e}šari w^{e}libbi noheg* from v. 3 to v. 1 after *'nskh*), see Gordis, ad loc. On NSH piel = "experience", "give experience" see Greenberg, 1960:276.

2:1. Literally, "...Come and let me give you experience [cohortative] of pleasure. And see [imperative] good!" In 11:9 too an imperative and jussive are parallel.

Hinneh at the start of a sentence usually indicates participant perspective (in this case, Qohelet "himself" rather than his heart) together with a sense of discovery (Andersen, 1974:94f.). It has a focusing effect that tends to subordinate a preceding verb of perception (or intention, or the like) and to make it a virtual circumstantial clause. The translation "When... and I realized" attempts to reflect this subordination.

There is a jump between the intention, expressed as an invitation to his heart to try pleasure, and the realization that pleasure is absurd, introduced by *hinneh*. The subsequent narrative will supply the intervening events. We are to understand this *hebel*-judgment not as something Qohelet knew before he started, but as something he discovered by experiment and meditation.

2:1-2. The only possible antecedent for "it" in the *hebel*-judgment (v. 1b) is experiencing pleasure (*ṭob* = *śimḥah* = "pleasure", not "happiness"; see §§2.121, 2.122).

2:3. *Tarti b^{e}libbi*: TWR + inf. here seems to be the equivalent of SBB + inf. (2:20), showing the beginning or the next stage in a series of actions. ŠWB functions similarly (4:1, 7; 9:11). TWR does not mean "explore" or "search" here, because the actions designated by the infinitives are certainly not the goals of his search.

The idiom *limšok bayyayin 'et b^{e}śari* has no parallel and is an interpretive crux, but its general sense—to enjoy wine—is clear; it is translated above as "ply" in accordance with context.

The question Qohelet puts before himself is what is good for man to do (*'ey zeh* = "what", as often in MH, not "which [sc., of two things]"). To ascertain this, Qohelet tries various pleasurable diversions.

Qohelet reports at one and the same time how he acquired property and sources of enjoyment. He amassed silver and gold (2:8) and other valuables, and he spent his wealth and efforts on acquiring pleasurable things. This unit, then, speaks of both pleasure and toil, and he will judge both.

To become wealthy requires wisdom. Qohelet speaks of one "whose wealth was gained by toiling in wisdom and knowledge and skill" (2:21), thinking of his own example (cf. v. 20c). And, as Qohelet stresses, his wisdom remained with him throughout his labors and his pleasures. Nevertheless, as we will learn, toil is absurd (2:11), and the one who does *not* toil must be reckoned wiser than the toiler (2:26).

For MT's *wl'ḥz* we should read *w^e^lo' 'oḥez b^e^siklut* (BHS), lit., "and not seizing folly". This emendation resolves the awkward parenthesis, "my heart behaving in wisdom", that stands between two coordinated purpose clauses in MT. The emended phrase, "and not seizing folly", is restated in 2:9, "and still my wisdom stayed with me". If we maintain MT, we must interpret this phrase as referring to pleasure in general, which has been judged foolish (2:2), rather than to a particular type of pleasure that is more foolish than others.

The idiom "(my heart) not seizing folly" is equivalent to English "folly not seizing my heart"; compare "my flesh seized horror" = "horror seized my flesh" (Job 21:6) and "the ancients seized trembling" = "trembling seized the ancients" (Job 18:20); similarly Isa 13:8.

Qohelet seeks to discover "what is good for people to do under the heavens during the few days of their lives". He gives the answer in 2:10—to take pleasure in what one's toil produces. He will repeat this answer, using language reminiscent of 2:3, in his recurring recommendation that people "see good" and "do good" (i.e., do pleasurable things) during the few days of their lives.

2:4-8. 'ŚH: *ma'ăśay* in v. 4 may mean either "actions" or "property" (translated for convenience as "things" in 2:4, 11). *'aśah* in vv. 5, 6, 8 means "acquire". It is synonymous with *qaniti* in v. 7.

Isaksson (1987:55f.) says that the series of Suffix Conjugation (SC) forms (*qaṭal*) give the "autobiographical thread" the character of a "resumé-type narration". Qohelet is not telling a story (for which Prefix Conjugation forms would be used), but rather is *characterizing* himself: he is a person of the sort who has built houses, who has planted vineyards, etc., and he may still be doing this. That is not to say that the verbs are present tense. Qohelet is still drawing a distinction between present and past. He is interested not in present acts of aggrandizement but in the aggrandizement he undertook in the past. Qohelet *is* looking backwards, not to repudiate past actions or conclusions but to evaluate them.

2:8. On *šiddah* = "concubine" see Gordis. Ibn Ezra explained *šiddah w*^e^*šiddot* to mean "women", for he sensed that the phrase *ta'ănugot b*^e^*ney ha'adam*, defined by apposition, alludes to women, and noted that women (as objects of sexual pleasure) are not mentioned elsewhere in this narration.

Most, perhaps all, commentators understand the singular-plural idiom as showing multiplicity. That interpretation is reasonable in context, but Judg 5:30, which is mentioned as a grammatical parallel (thus Ibn Ezra), differs both morphologically, using singular-dual, and semantically, for it does not indicate a large quantity, but rather "a damsel or two". *Šiddah w*^e^*šiddot* may be expressing multiplicity by hendiadys of singular-plural as *dor dorim* does by a bound phrase (or asyndectic parataxis) (Ps 72:5).

2:10. *Kol* sometimes means "all types of"; e.g., Cant 3:6; see GKC §127b.

'amal (twice) is ambiguous in both occurrences. It may refer to the immediate source of pleasure, i.e., Qohelet's wealth, or to the farther source, i.e., his toil. The unusual use of *min* with *śamaḥ* may mark the *indirect* source of benefit (thus Delitzsch). The predicate complement with *mem* in 2 Chr 20:27, following the piel, accords with this explanation, but Prov 5:18, the only other place the idiom occurs, does not (there, however, there is some manuscript and versional evidence for reading *bet*).

Lys (p. 221) takes *'amal* to mean "besogne" and sees a deliberate paradox here: "pour connaître la joie il faut prendre de la peine, et la prendre soi-même". But the point of such a paradox would be to urge people to work harder, and that is certainly not one of Qohelet's lessons.

2:11. On the ambiguity of *ma'ăśim* and *'amal* in this important verse see §2.111. What essentially troubles Qohelet throughout 2:1-26, especially in 2:18-26, is not that wealth itself is trivial, but that human *efforts* are robbed of their significance by death and chance.

In §1.12 (1a) and §2.22 I discuss the reasons for this judgment: first the inanity of pleasure (2:1-2) and second, the unjust allocation of the toiler's wealth, the second reason reinforcing the first.

Context restricts the application of the statement, "there is no *yitron* under the sun", to the particular form of activity under observation, toil. The phrase "in toil" is implicit in this statement. It is explicit in the parallel verses, 1:3 and 3:9, and it is unlikely that 2:11 alone, despite a context dealing specifically with toil, would have a universal scope. For a clear case of implicit restriction of a *yitron*-statement see 6:11.

B. **2:12-17**

> (12) And I turned to observe wisdom and inane folly, for what will the man be like who will succeed <me and rule>[a] over what [others] will have earned earlier? (13) And I saw that wisdom has an advantage over folly as great as the advantage of light over darkness:
>
> (14) The wise man has his eyes in his head, while the fool goes about in darkness.
>
> But I also realized that the very same fate befalls them both. (15) So I said in my heart, "What happens to the fool will happen to me too, so to what purpose, then, have I become so very wise? And I said in my heart that this too is an absurdity. (16) For the wise man, just like the fool, is never remembered, inasmuch as in the days to come both are soon forgotten. Oh, how the wise man dies just like the fool!
>
> (17) So I became disgusted with life, for I was distressed by what happens under the sun, as it is all absurdity and vexation.

[a] point *'aḥăray hammōlēk* (MT *'aḥărêy hammelek*).

Argument:
B. Wisdom and Folly

a. Undertaking of inquiry (v. 12a [+b?])
b. Finding of inquiry: the superiority of wisdom (vv. 13-14a)
c. Reflection on this finding: the injustice done to the wise man (vv. 14b-16)
d. Reaction to the reflection (v. 17)

Note the similarity of this procedure to that of 1:12-18 and 2:1-11: Qohelet tells how he undertook an investigation, reports the finding, tells how he reflected on the finding, and reports his reaction.

Qohelet sees two components in his labors: wisdom and toil (2:9, 10, 19). Having concluded his examination of pleasure and having judged the toil that produced it to be absurd, he turns to consider wisdom (he mentions folly in 2:12a only incidentally to evaluating wisdom).

2:12a. Qohelet says he will examine two things: wisdom and folly. The words *holelot w^{e}siklut* are correctly grouped together by the Massoretic accentuation and form a hendiadys meaning "inane folly", "senseless folly", or the like. Qohelet will evaluate both "wisdom" and "inane folly" by considering the effects of these qualities.

Galling places v. 12a after 12b because 12b seems to intrude between intention (12a) and result (13), and 12b, for all its obscurity, seems to motivate the judgment in 11. There may, however, be an alternating structure here: 12b explaining 11, 13 explaining 12a. (For other possible examples see Gordis, pp. 246, 268, 321.)

Qoh 2:12b makes no sense as it stands. The least implausible treatment of this obscure sentence is that of Ginsberg, who reads *ki meh ha'adam šeyabo' 'aḥăray, hammolek 'et 'ăšer k^{e}bar 'aśuhu*, lit., "for what is [the quality of] the man who will come after me, [the man] who will control what [others] have already accumulated". For *mah* meaning "what is the quality of?" see Num 13:18. *Hammolek 'et* is admittedly an awkward construction, in spite of Ginsberg's comparison to Arabic *malaka*, which governs a direct object. Moreover, *malak* is not used of controlling or possessing property in BH (Ginsberg brings only this obscure half-verse as an example of that usage). Still, the construction does seem to be equivalent to *yišlaṭ b-* in v. 19. *'aśuhu* is an impersonal 3rd pl. equivalent to a passive. The complaint implied in this question is rephrased in vv. 18f: what kind of person will enjoy the wise man's earnings? Ehrlich points *'aḥărey himmalek*, sc., "nach Änderung der Gesinnung", and calls the rest of the verse "heillos verderbt". But perhaps that is true of the entire sentence.

2:14. The wise man has knowledge while the fool lives in ignorance. On the relation between 2:13-14a and 14b see §§3.31-3.32. Qoh 2:13-14a is a superlative affirmation of the advantage of wisdom over folly. Light and darkness are polar opposites.

Gordis considers vv. 13-14 a quotation that Qohelet rejects in v. 15. Gordis expresses this relation by supplying before v. 13: "I have heard it said". But the Hebrew, *w^e ra'iti 'ani še-* is as clear a way as possible of introducing one's *own* knowledge. At any rate, it is arbitrary to assign this statement to another viewpoint while leaving other affirmations of wisdom's value (such as 7:11f.) to Qohelet.

Miqreh = "fate" in the sense of what happens to someone, as opposed to what he does to himself (not in the sense of what is predetermined).

2:15. In spite of wisdom's superiority, fool and wise man suffer the same fate. This inequity makes it senseless to grow very wise, but does not, in Qohelet's mind, eliminate wisdom's advantage. A lesser degree of wisdom might have practical advantages without the pains of consciousness that accompany great wisdom (1:18).

Ginsberg says that taking *yoter* as adverbial ("why then have I become greatly wise") produces a banality, because if the wise man dies like the fool, it is not worthwhile to grow wise *at all*. But in 1:18 and 7:16 Qohelet warns against *much* wisdom, for it opens one's eyes to painful realities. Some wisdom, like some labor, is necessary and valuable, but too much hurts. In any case, Qohelet did grow "very wise", and it is natural for him to describe himself in those terms.

The antecedent of this *hebel*-judgment may be the situation as a whole: the fool and the wise man (namely, Qohelet) sharing the same fate. More likely, the antecedent of "this" is "my becoming very wise", an action implicit in the immediately preceding phrase. Whatever the formal antecedent, the reason for the *hebel*-judgment is essentially the same: the fact that wise and fool end alike in nothingness.

2:16. Qohelet does not accept the promise that "the memory of the righteous is for a blessing, while the name of the wicked will rot" (Prov 10:7). He believes that both wise man and fool are quickly forgotten. *Hayyamim habba'im* is an adverbial accusative, which, as the modifier "already" shows, refers to the near future.

2:17. 'ŚH (*hamma'ăśeh šenna'ăśah*): This verse caps off the preceding unit (2:12-16), which speaks of the equalization of wise and fool at death. The *ma'ăśeh* here is an event, formulated without reference to agency.

C. **2:18-26**

(18) And I became disgusted with my wealth for which I had toiled under the sun, since I would be leaving it to a man who succeeds me (19) (and who knows whether he will be wise or foolish?), and he will control all my wealth for which I had toiled in wisdom under the sun. This too is an absurdity.

(20) So I turned to rid my heart of illusions concerning all the toil at which I had labored under the sun. (21) For sometimes a man whose wealth was [gained by toiling] in wisdom, knowledge, and skill ends up giving it as a portion to someone who did not toil for it. This too is an absurdity and a great evil. (22) For what does a man get out of his toil and his heart's pursuit at which he toils under the sun, (23) since all his days his business is but pain and irritation, and his heart finds no rest at night? This too is an absurdity.

(24) There is nothing better for a man <than>[a] to eat and drink and give himself enjoyment through his toil. I saw that this too is from the hand of God, (25) for who will eat, or who will fret, except as <he>[b] determines? (26) For to the one whom God likes he gives wisdom and knowledge and pleasure, while to the one who is offensive he gives the business of gathering and amassing in order to give [the earnings] to that one whom God likes. This too is an absurdity and a vexation.

[a] *miššeyō'kal* (MT *šeyyō'kal*) [b] *mimmennû* (MT *mimmennî*)

Section C progresses by a sequence of statements and motivations, with levels of subordination as shown by indentation in the following outline. This section, reversing the procedure of A and B, proceeds from Qohelet's reaction ("I became disgusted") rather than to it, and this reaction is then explained by reporting the observations that led to it. Qohelet identifies a single situation—one man toils and another gets his wealth—and broods on it, reiterating it in several ways, judging it absurd, and motivating the judgment. He chains his reasons and evaluations in such a way as to give the appearance of developing an extended, reinforced argument.

Argument:

C. Toil and pleasure, wisdom and folly

a. Reflection on the absurdity of toil (18-23)
Reaction (disgust) (18a)

Reason (the injustice to the toiler) (18b-19a)
Evaluation of this fact: absurd (19b)
Reaction (decides to disabuse himself) (20)
Reason (the injustice to the toiler) (21abα)
Evaluation of this fact: absurd and evil (21bβ)
Reason for this evaluation (the misery of the toiler) (22-23a)
Evaluation of this fact: absurd (23b)

b. Affirmation and practical conclusion: nothing is better than enjoyment of pleasures (24)

c. Limitation on affirmation: God determines who will be allowed enjoyment and who will be forced to toil (25-26abα).
Evaluation: this is absurd (26bβ)

Toil is not adequately compensated, even if it brings wealth, because it happens that one man toils (in wisdom) and another (who may be a fool!) receives the earnings. This is unjust, an absurdity for which God's inexplicable will is responsible. Enjoyment of what you have while you have it is the only reasonable recourse. This advice is here incidental to the complaint, and his praise of pleasure as God's gift easily slides back into that complaint, now stated theologically: God (rather than human effort) determines the possibility of enjoying life.

The two senses of *'amal* are almost inextricably intertwined in this passage. Yet we can inquire into which sense fits best in each occurrence: the toilsome labor itself, or earnings, the material fruits of toil.

In 2:18, the *'amal* (noun) that Qohelet hates seems to be his earnings, since the suffix of *'anniḥennu* can apply only to property, for that alone is what Qohelet can (and must) turn over to his successor. (The verb means "gained through toil".) Although Qohelet is not truly disgusted with wealth in itself, if he can say that he became disgusted with life (2:17), he can lash out at his property as well. He holds both in contempt, at least temporarily, because they have failed to live up to his earlier expectations. But at root Qohelet believes that possession of wealth is a blessing and its loss grievous. Wealth makes pleasure possible, and God gives it to the one he favors.

In 2:19, *'ămali* means "earnings", for that, and not the toil, is what the successor will get. The verb correspondingly means "gained through toil".

In 2:20, *he'amal še'amalti* could refer to either the toil he undertook or the earnings he gained. "Toil" seems more appropriate (for both noun and verb) since Qohelet spoke of his disillusionment with his wealth in v. 18. He now proceeds to speak of the failure of toil to secure its goals.

In 2:21a, *'amal* again refers to earnings, as that is what is "given" to the successor. Yet the adverbial phrases "in wisdom, in knowledge, and in skill", modify the activity of toiling. Here the noun binds the two ideas most closely, as the above translation tries to reflect.

In v. 21b, however, the verb *'amal* means "toiled" (as even Ginsberg concedes) not "earned", because it governs *bo*, "for it", not the accusative as in v. 19b. Furthermore, it cannot be said that the fortunate man did not "gain" this wealth, but rather that he did not invest toil in it.

In 2:22, *'amal* (twice) means "toil", for it is coordinated with *ra'yon libbo*, "his heart's pursuit"—an activity, not a material possession. Note that *'amel* in v. 22b seems to indicate any difficult activity, for one of its direct objects in 22b is "his heart's pursuit". The "heart's pursuit" is something that one can *'amel*, "do laboriously", just as one can "*'amel*", toil.

In 2:24, *'amal* is ambiguous. If it means "toil", *bᵉ'ămalo* indicates the indirect source (or possibly the temporal context) of his pleasure.

2:18. *La'adam*, whether or not the *lamed* is pointed correctly, is generic (cf. *la'adam* in v. 22), referring to whichever man it is who receives Qohelet's wealth.

2:19. This verse is parenthetical. Even if the person who gets Qohelet's wealth happens to be wise, the basic injustice remains: Qohelet did the work and the other person gets the wealth. The injustice is, of course, more severe if the toiler was wise and the recipient a fool.

2:20. In 2:10, Qohelet "turned" to disabuse his heart of any hopes he might have about toil. This verse resumes and rephrases the "turn" in the development of his thought marked in v. 11, and the entire section C elaborates the reasons for the *hebel*-judgment in that verse.

Lᵉya'eš means "to disillusion (oneself)", "to give up hope", as in MH. The illusion that Qohelet had, judging from the reasons he gives for surrendering it, was that wealth is the result of toil alone.

2:21. "Sometimes, etc.": lit., "there is a man, etc.".

2:23. restates v. 22, with *'inyano* resuming *kol 'ămalo* and *lo' šakab libbo* resuming *ra'yon libbo*. His business "is" pain and irritation insofar as it produces them.

2:24f. The emendation of *b'dm šy'kl* to *b'dm mšy'kl*, with a comparative *mem* as in 3:22, seems hardly disputable. (Syr, LXX [S^c,V], and Tar read "except", but this may be due to translation needs rather than to a different *Vorlage*). *Yaḥuš* means "worry", "fret" (a sense clearly attested in Job 20:2); see the thoroughgoing study of this verb by Ellermeier (1963a). The one who "frets" is the "sinner"; the one who "eats" is the recipient of God's favor (2:26). *Mimmenni* should be emended to *mimmennu* (thus LXX, Syr, Syh, 8 MSS K-R). MT has Qohelet saying that no one will eat or drink except for him, which is neither relevant nor true. Verses 21 and 26 indicate that someone else will indeed do so. Verse 25 as emended is paralleled by 3:13 and 5:18, which state that whether one will "eat and drink" is dependent on God's will. The thought of God's all-determining will brings Qohelet back to his main complaint, which he now formulates theologically.

2:26. Qohelet calls the toiler a *ḥoṭe'*, sc., "one who is offensive", "offender" (usually translated "sinner"), and the recipient of the toiler's wealth "God's favorite" (lit., "one good before God"). It might seem that for an offensive man to toil only for the benefit of a God-favored man is an instance of divine justice. But that situation would not be *hebel* by any definition. Furthermore, Qohelet has just said that the fortunate recipient may be a fool (2:19), while the unfortunate man may toil in wisdom (v. 21). Certainly the *ḥoṭe'* and "God's favorite" are not simply sinner and saint.

Gordis (pp. 94, 217-18) takes *ḥoṭe'* here to mean both "fool", in a non-moral sense, and "sinner", in the sense of one who violates God's will by failing to "work for the advancement of his own happiness" (*ibid*., pp. 91f.). But in this very verse we learn that the *ḥote'* is very much at work—presumably intending to increase his own means of pleasure—while the man who pleases God gets all good things without working for them. Moreover, this verse itself shows that the enjoyment of life is dependent on God's favor and not the other way around.

Many interpreters recognize that the *ḥote'* here is not a sinner, but one who has incurred God's disfavor (thus Hertzberg, Galling).

Ginsberg says it means "unfortunate". To be sure, one burdened with toil is indeed unfortunate, but ḤṬʾ always denotes an additional component, namely offensiveness to someone. Since the offense is usually of a moral nature (even in Qohelet: 7:20; 8:12; 9:2), the translation "sinner" is usually correct, but not always so. In Qoh 10:4, the *ḥăṭa'im* that enrage a ruler cannot be presumed to be moral sins; they are any actions that offend him. (Note that the ruler too shows inexplicable, erroneous favor toward some people; 10:5-6.) Occasionally elsewhere in the Bible—but only where ḤṬʾ refers to offenses against humans—the term lacks moral implications. In 1 Kgs 1:21, Bathsheba says that she and her son will be *ḥaṭṭa'im* if Adonijah succeeds, meaning that they will be offensive to him, treated as offenders, not that they will actually be guilty of moral infraction. Similarly, *w^eḥaṭa't 'ammeka* in Exod 5:16 means "and the offense is your people's". The people are not admitting to any moral guilt, but are saying that Moses' meddling, offensive to the king, will be reckoned as their own. In 1 Kgs 8:31 the person in question may not have *sinned* (the case is not yet adjudicated) but he is offensive to his fellow. See also 1 Kgs 18:9 (Obadiah asks Elijah how he has offended him, not what sin has brought misfortune upon him); Gen 40:1 (there is no implication of a moral failing on the part of the butler and baker); and Prov 20:2 (the person who angers a king in effect offends not only the king but himself). In Qoh 2:26 and 7:26 the *ḥote'* is someone who is offensive to God. While most sages take it for granted that God is offended only by sin or moral folly, Qohelet believes that God (like a human ruler) may treat a person as offensive for inexplicable reasons and not necessarily because of actual sin or folly.

Verse 26 gives a twist to Qohelet's observations in this section. He concludes that the fortunate non-toiler has been granted wisdom, for it is surely wise to enjoy life. The wisdom God bestows upon those he favors is not the content of knowledge (see the distinction drawn in§3.1). Such knowledge might well increase his misery, as it did for Qohelet. Rather, God has given him *reason* (*da'at* = *ḥokmah*), the savvy to do what is beneficial, which in context means avoiding toil and enjoying what comes to one's hand. This is what Qohelet recommends doing, and he naturally considers this behavior wise.

Still, the unfortunate man has toiled for naught, the fortunate man received benefits without effort. The former may have turned out to be foolish, and the latter was certainly smart not to toil. But for all that, there was a disjunction of effort and result, and this is an absurdity. This offends Qohelet's sense of justice. He may also be pained at the thought that he, as one who toiled only to pass his wealth on to someone else, is somehow offensive to God.

3:1-15

(1) For everything there is a moment,
  and a time for every matter under the heavens:
(2) a time for being born,
  and a time for dying;
 a time for planting,
  and a time for uprooting what is planted;
(3) a time for killing,
  and a time for healing;
 a time for breaking through,
  and a time for building up;
(4) a time for weeping,
  and a time for laughing;
 a time of mourning,
  and a time of dancing;
(5) a time for throwing stones away,
  and a time of gathering stones;
 a time for embracing,
  and a time for shunning embracing;
(6) a time for seeking,
  and a time for losing;
 a time for keeping,
  and a time for throwing away;
(7) a time for rending,
  and a time for sewing;
 a time for keeping silent,
  and a time for speaking;
(8) a time for loving,
  and a time for hating;
 a time of war,
  and a time of peace.

(9) What adequate gain does one who does anything get from toiling?

(10) I have seen the business that God has given man to occupy himself with: (11) he makes everything happen appropriately in its

time, but he also places <toil>[a] in their hearts, without man being able to apprehend in any way whatsoever that which God has brought to pass.

(12) I realized that there is nothing good for <man>[b] but to have pleasure and to pursue enjoyment during his lifetime. (13) And for any man to eat and drink and experience pleasure through all his toil, this is the gift of God.

(14) I know that whatever God makes happen will always occur. It is impossible to add to it, and impossible to take away from it. And God has done [this] so that people will fear him. (15) Whatever happens already has happened, and what is to happen already has happened. Thus God seeks what is pursued [?].

[a] *'āmāl* (MT *'ôlām*) [b] *bā'ādām* (MT *bām*)

Argument: All events have a time when they will occur, and God determines when this is. Thus man cannot change the course of events, and his arduous efforts are not appropriately rewarded.

A. The Catalogue of Times (3:1-9)

- a. The principle: everything has a time (v. 1)
- b. Restatement of the principle by specific examples (vv. 2-8)
- c. Conclusion: there is no adequate return in toil (vv. 9)

B. The implications of the above principle (3:10-15)

- a. With respect to the task of seeking knowledge: man cannot understand the events of life (vv. 10-11)
- b. With respect to practical behavior: enjoy life (vv. 12-13)
- c. With respect to power: man does not control the course of events (vv. 14-15; the theme is foreshadowed in 13b)

Verse 9 undoubtedly continues the movement of thought begun in v. 1, for vv. 1-8 require a conclusion applying their theme to human life. The connection of vv. 10-15 with the earlier verses is seen in v. 11a, *'et hakkol 'aśah yapeh b*^{e}*'itto*, which restates theologically the theme introduced in 3:1. Likewise, v. 15, which reaffirms that there is nothing new under the sun, recapitulates v. 1, since for everything to have a time (vv. 1ff.) entails the eternal recurrence of the same classes of events (v. 15).

The lesson of the Catalogue of Times (3:1-9) is not that everything has an *opportune* time, a time one should discover and choose for action. It is hard to say that birth, death, and losing have an "opportune" time, and in any case such occurrences are not directed at producing any particular benefit for the person undergoing them. The "rightness" or "opportuneness" of a particular time is not at issue here.

The teaching of 3:1-9 is rather that the occurrence of all events is beyond human control, for God makes everything happen in its proper time (proper, that is, from his viewpoint). Therefore strenuous labor does not pay off in proportion to its unpleasantness.

Subsequent verses confirm that the Catalogue of Times shows divine control of events. In 3:11 Qohelet reiterates the point of the Catalogue by stating that God makes everything happen appropriately in its time, and again in 3:14 he restates the idea that God is the cause of all that happens. The meaning of the sentence, "for everything there is a moment/time", is clarified also by 3:17. Having observed injustices in v. 16, Qohelet comforts himself, at least momentarily, with the thought that "God will judge the righteous and the wicked, for there is a time for every matter". This sentence cannot mean that everything has an *opportune* time (as if there were a specific moment that God *should* choose for judgment). The point is that God *will* judge the wicked at the appropriate moment, because judgment too has a time. The events listed in the Catalogue are typical not specific. Every *type* of event has a time in which it will occur. "For everything there is a time" in 3:1 rephrases 1:9 and is in turn rephrased by 3:15 at the end of the unit: "Whatever happens already has happened, and what is to happen already has happened...". And it is clear that 1:9 and 3:15 speak of *types* of events, not of specific events (in other words, a certain person's death does not recur; see the comment on 1:9).

3:2. The pairing of *laledet* with "for dying" shows that the qal infinitive here has an intransitive sense, "being born"; cf. *liṭboaḥ* in Jer 25:34 (Ginsburg, Delitzsch, Zimmerli, et al.).

3:5a. The interpretation suggested above makes the ordinariness of some of the acts mentioned more understandable. They need not be explained as metaphors or symbols. "Throwing stones away" and "gathering stones" means just that. There are various reasons why one might cast stones, such as to clear a field or to remove a stone house, and there are various reasons why one might gather stones, such as to collect materials for a house or to make a grave heap. When the time comes for these things to be done, they will be done; so relax.

3:9. *'amal*, 'ŚH (*mah yitron ha'ośeh ba'ăšer hu' 'amel*): This verse forms the climax of the Catalogue of Times; the application of the words *'amel* and *'ośeh* is defined in relation to this Catalogue. Qoh 3:9 does not (contrary to Ginsberg) mean "What is the profit of one who earns (something) in what he gains?" for vv. 1-9 do not speak of a person's earnings, and vv. 10-11 do not give a reason why wealth holds no profit. Furthermore, the "times" encompass the entire range of acts and events in life, with "gainful employment" mentioned only incidentally (planting and building). 'ŚH refers to any deed one may undertake, while 'ML refers to laborious, strained activity.

Distinguishing between *'amal* and *'aśah* explains the syntax of v. 9. "Toiling", arduous labor, is a sort of "doing". A "doer" has no compensation in "toiling", which is overdoing. Toil, even if it does produce a profit, achieves no more than mere "doing", because human efforts can push only so far.

3:11. The first part of this verse does not (contrary to almost all interpreters) refer to God's original act of creation. "Everything" in v. 11 resumes "everything" in v. 1, and that, as the merismic pairs in vv. 2-8 show, refers to all that happens in human life rather than to the entirety of the created world. The pairs of events in 3:2-8 did not come into being in the act of creation. The point of v. 11 is that God makes everything, even events that occur through human agency, happen in its proper time. Sir 39:33 (cf. v. 16), which seems to be dependent on Qoh 3:11 as well as on Pss 104:27 and 145:15, uses similar language in speaking of God's providence, not his acts of creation: "The works of God [*ma'ăśey 'el*] are all good, and he supplies every need in its time [*'itto*]".

Yapeh is not an aesthetic evaluation—most of the events listed in the Catalogue are not beautiful—but an affirmation of the appropriateness of the times God chooses. *Yapeh* frequently means "appropriate", "proper" in MH; see Jastrow, *Dict*.

'ŚH: *'aśah* in v. 11a, as argued above, means "make happen" (Ginsberg) and is applied to God's ongoing control of events. Similarly, *hamma'ăśeh 'ăšer 'aśah ha'ĕlohim* in v. 11b means "the events that God has brought [or 'brings'] to pass". It is this that man cannot "find out" or "apprehend" (*yimṣa'*).

'amal: The crux in MT's *gam 'et ha'olam natan b^{e}libbam* has lent itself to interesting speculations about "eternity" in the human heart. But it is more in line with Qohelet's thought to read *'ml* for *'lm*, a very minor emendation (MacDonald, 1899). In 8:17, which strongly resembles 3:11 in phraseology, Qohelet uses 'ML to designate man's toiling to apprehend (*limṣo'*) that which God has brought to pass. This is toil of the heart, a mental labor, similar to "heart's pursuit" mentioned in 2:22.

The laborious task that God has placed in man's heart is defined by the rest of the verse—namely, the attempt to understand "what God has brought to pass". Thus *'et* (*he'amal*) *natan b^{e}libbam* in v. 11bα resumes *ha'inyan 'ăšer natan 'ĕlohim libney ha'adam* in v. 10 and is equivalent to the *'inyan ra' natan 'ĕlohim libney ha'adam la'ănot bo* in 1:13.

The phrase *mero'š w^{e}'ad sop* in v. 11bβ, lit., "from beginning to end", emphasizes negation of existence ("not any") rather than negation of universality ("not all"). The usual translation, "without man being able to find out the work that God has done from beginning to end" (or the like), has Qohelet complaining about the impossibility of knowing the entirety of God's work. Such a complaint is trivial, because it would be senseless to hope for absolute knowledge of everything. Rather, Qohelet is saying that man can *in no way* apprehend *ma'ăśeh ha'ĕlohim*. To be sure, Qohelet does have things to say about divine activity, but he does not define that knowledge as "apprehending" or "understanding" (MṢ', YD') all that God does or makes happen.

3:12f. There is nothing better (*ṭob*) than to experience pleasure (*ṭob*) in life. But this enjoyment depends entirely on God's will (v. 14). As in 2:24f., the advice to enjoy life comes in the context of God's control of all that happens.

Bam: The conjectural emendation *b'dm* for *bm* (BHS) is attractive though not essential; but cf. *ba'adam* in the parallel 2:24. The emendation supplies a masc. sg. antecedent for *ḥayyayw*.

3:14. *L^{e}'olam* does not indicate duration, as if Qohelet were asserting the eternality of everything God creates or makes happen; that is a notion both untrue and irrelevant. Nor does it mean "unchanging" (contrary to Jenni, 1953:22); *l^{e}'olam* never has that sense elsewhere. Rather, it is a sentence modifier placed as an afterthought (compare the positioning of *mero'š w^{e}'ad sop* at the end of the sentence in 3:11). In other words, it is always the case that what happens is only what God has made happen.

The usual translation of 3:14b is, "and God caused people to fear him" (lit., "God caused that [people] fear him"). But this translation produces a short sentence unrelated to the preceding statement (v. 14a) and lacking motivation. Moreover, all Qohelet's statements about human wickedness, in particular 8:13b, show that Qohelet does not believe that God has caused mankind in general to fear him. Rather, God intends for people to fear him (thus *še-* introduces a purpose clause), but he does not impose that fear. By enforcing human ignorance and helplessness, God *occasions* fear but does not directly cause it. *'aśah* in v. 14b means "did" or "brought about", the implied object being the immutability of divinely caused events. *'aśah* is used absolutely, with the direct object implicit in the immediate context; cf. Prov 31:13; Ezra 10:4; 1 Chron 28:10; Ezek 20:44; 1 Sam 14:45; etc.

Whoever has the wisdom to recognize God's control of times (3:11), which is to say, his control of events (3:14f.), will fear God and share the attitude epitomized in the humble confession of the psalmist: "My times (*'ittotay*) are in your hand" (Ps 31:16).

Ben Sira interprets Qoh 3:14 by paraphrase: "One cannot take away and one cannot add, and one should not investigate God's wonders" (18:6; retroverting οὐκ ἔστιν ἐξιχνιάσαι as *'eyn laḥqor*, which has monitory force). The first stich stays close to Qohelet's wording. The second is more interpretive but conveys essentially the same idea as Qoh 3:14b, inasmuch as the acceptance of one's limitations is tantamount to fearing God.

3:15a. As Ibn Ezra observes, *mah šehayah* is equivalent to *ma'aśeh ha'ĕlohim*; that which has happened (or, happens) is the same as the events that God brings to pass. Thus v. 15a uses the phraseology of 1:9a to restate 3:14. The events God brings to pass steamroller over whatever man can do, so nothing new can interrupt the awesome cycles of events that God has ordained.

3:15b. A crux. For the early interpretations, see Salters, 1976. *Radap* is a near synonym of *biqqeš* (Levy; see Ps 34:15, and compare Zeph 2:3 with Deut 16:20), so the sentence means, approximately, "God seeks what has already been sought". Of the ancient Versions, only Vul understands the sentence in this way: "et Deus instaurat quod abiit", sc., "and God repeats what has passed away"; Levy: "und Gott strebt wieder nach dem (schon einmal) Erstrebten". It is not clear what "seeking" or "pursuing" has to do with divine causation of events, but the gist of the sentence seems to be that God seeks to do things he has already done.

3:16-22

> (16) I further saw that under the sun, in the place of justice, wickedness is there, and in the place of righteousness, wickedness is there. (17) I said in my heart, "God will judge the righteous and the wicked, for there is a time for every matter, and upon all that is done[a] there [?]".
>
> (18) I said in my heart with regard to mankind, "---[b] and to <show>[c] that they are but beasts".[d] (19) For what happens to men and what happens to the beast is one and the same thing: as the one dies so dies the other, and both have the same life-breath. So man has no advantage over the beast, for both are absurd. (20) Both go to the same place. Both are from the dust, and both to the dust return. (21) And who knows <whether man's> life-spirit goes upward[e] while the beast's life-spirit goes down[f] to the ground?
>
> (22) And I saw that there is nothing better than that a man get pleasure through his activities, for that is his portion, for who can enable him to see what will happen afterwards?

[a] *hanna'ăśāh* (MT *hamma'ăśeh*) [b] word missing? [c] point *w*^{e}*lar'ôt* (MT *w*^{e}*lir'ôt*) [d] omit *lāhem* [e] point *hă'ôlāh* (MT *hā'ôlāh*) [f] point *hăyōredet* (MT *hayyōredet*)

Injustice pervades the world and death prevents adequate recompense. Argument:

a. Observation of injustice (3:16)
b. Affirmation of judgment (3:17)
c. Reflection: death wipes out differences (3:18-21)
d. Conclusion: pleasure is the only recourse (3:22)

Qohelet observes the perversions of justice that pervade the world. "Where justice/righteousness should be" probably refers specifically to courts of law. Seeing this injustice, Qohelet tells himself that God will judge the wicked. Inasmuch as *everything* has a time, Qohelet reasons, divine judgment too must come to pass. But this thought is small comfort, because if the sentence is death, the universality of death makes that sentence meaningless as punishment.

Observation of injustice—like others of Qohelet's unhappy observations—brings him to thoughts of death. Individual existence is absurd, because all distinctions in life, even the difference between humans and other creatures, are obliterated by death.

According to the belief most clearly attested in the HB, death means loss of the life-breath and descent to Sheol, a fate shared by all creatures. When God "takes back" (*'osep*) the spirit (that is, the life-spirit common to all creatures, not the "soul"), the creature dies (Ps 104:29; Job 34:14-15). This "taking back" of the life-spirit does not imply an afterlife, but merely the dissolution of the components of the living being. The likely source of this idea is a belief common in popular hellenistic religion that the human soul is made of a spark of ether and will return to the heavenly ethereal sphere upon death (see Hengel, 1974:I, 124). Although Qohelet is aware of such a notion, he refuses to draw comfort from mere speculation.

Nevertheless, Qohelet has taken a step toward the idea of the afterlife. Death, according to the possibility Qohelet raises and dismisses, would not mean merely that God withdrew the life-breath that makes life possible for man and beast. It would mean that the human soul attained a higher state than eternal somnolence in the underworld. If the human soul did have an elevated fate, then (Qohelet virtually grants) human life would not be pointless. But we cannot know whether this is the case. Since man cannot know the future, nothing remains but to enjoy the present.

3:16. *M^{e}qom hammišpaṭ//m^{e}qom haṣṣedeq*. This "place" is not the place where justice and righteousness reside (for, as Qohelet insists, they do *not* do so), but rather a place that can be *called* by these names even when the virtues are absent, namely the court, the place where righteous judgment (*mišpaṭ ṣedeq*) properly should reside. In English we can speak of a "Court of Justice" in the same way, even if the particular court is corrupt. The phrases *m^{e}qom hammišpaṭ* and *m^{e}qom haṣṣedeq* form a hendiadys equivalent to *m^{e}qom mišpaṭ-ṣedeq*, the place of righteous judgment.

3:17. *Šam*, "there", at the end of v. 17 is difficult. It is hardly an allusion, facetious or otherwise, to an afterlife (as Gordis holds), for Qohelet does not have enough of a belief in judgment after death to say, even ironically, that justice will come in the afterlife; and if he did believe that, his problem would be solved. Barton, Ginsberg, et al., emend to *śam*, "set", but that places the verb awkwardly late in the clause. As it stands, *šam* is best taken as a reference to the place where just judgment should be, i.e., the court (v. 16). There will be judgment for everything done there. This idea would be better conveyed by *hanna'ăśah* rather than *hamma'ăśeh*, and perhaps we should read the former word here. Orthographically the difference is small.

Podechard's attractive conjecture, restoring *mišpaṭ* (of which *šm* would be a remnant), produces a meaningful, well-structured sentence. *'et // mišpaṭ* here would be a split word pair, which appears as a hendiadys in 8:6. In 12:14 as well, *mišpaṭ* is complemented by *'al* + the deed judged. But the emendation is too extensive to be accepted in the absence of other evidence. Even without this emendation, however, the sentence affirms a time of judgment for all deeds. We may explain the choice of the preposition *'al* as a reflex of the noun *mišpaṭ* implicit in the verb *yišpoṭ*. This sentence repeats the idea of 3:1, except that the context is here limited to the time of judgment upon injustices.

'ŚH: *hamma'ăśeh* (or *hanna'ăśah*, if we so emend in v. 17b) refers to deeds, for it is these (and not events) that can be objects of judgment.

3:18. A crux. *L^ebaram* is probably a by-form of BRR, which means "to sift, single out" in MH. A finite verb or a substantive seems to be missing (this is so even if we read *lo' baram* with Ehrlich, for that leaves *w^elir'ot* stranded). Further, in the absence of a preceding finite verb, *ha'ĕlohim* as the subject of the infinitive after an inf. + dir. obj. is harsh.

In spite of some insoluble difficulties, we can approach the general sense of the verse. We should read *lar'ot* (apocopated hiphil; thus LXX, Syr, Vul) for *lir'ot*. The function of *lahem* is unclear; in the absence of a preceding verb it is not an ethical dative. *Lahem* cannot mean "per se, in themselves" (contrary to Gordis), and in any case that translation is no more meaningful than MT. The word is probably a partial dittograph of *hemmah*. The point of the verse seems to be that God made humans mortal to show them that they are but beasts so as to distance them from divine powers. In Genesis 3 God feels threatened by the possibility that if the humans are left in Eden, they might wrest eternal life by eating from the second tree denied them.

3:19. *Hebel* is predicated of *hakkol*, which probably means "both" (as it clearly does three times in v. 20), sc., "man and beast".

3:22. *'aḥărayw* has been understood in three ways: (1) "after him", with reference to what will happen to the individual after death, (2) "after him", with reference to what will happen on earth after his life, and (3) "afterwards", with reference to what will happen on earth in the lifetime of the individual. Podechard (pp. 317-19) examines the question carefully and concludes, contrary to most commentators, that the word refers to the future within the individual's lifetime. Against interpretation (1), Podechard points out that "after him" would not be a natural way to refer to what happens to the individual in Sheol (for what happens to one does not happen "after" him). Furthermore, in 6:12, a restatement of this verse, Qohelet says that no one knows what will happen *'aḥărayw* under the sun, i.e., on earth. Against interpretation (2), Podechard argues that what happens on earth after one's death is of no interest; it certainly provides no motivation to enjoy life in the present. *'aḥărayw* means "afterwards", "in the future", a sense it clearly has in Qoh 9:3 and Jer 51:46.

Nevertheless, the present verse does seem to speak of ignorance of what happens after death, with the rhetorical question in v. 22b rephrasing the one in v. 21. In view of the considerations raised by Podechard, it is best to understand *'aḥărayw* as having the lexical meaning of "afterwards", although in the present context the word is specifically applied to the time after death. Elsewhere the reference is to the future more generally.

Qoh 4:1-16 is a loose thematic cluster of five passages dealing with human relations. The linking theme is expressed in various ways:

A. 4:1-3 The lack of sympathetic fellowship for the oppressed
B. 4:4-6 Jealousy as the fuel for toil
C. 4:7-8 The lone man's pointless labor
D. 4:9-12 The value of companionship
E. 4:13-16 The conflict among successive rulers, showing an injustice suffered by wisdom

A. Qoh 4:1-3 takes up the theme of social oppression raised in 3:16, but it is best taken as a new unit because 3:16-22 comes to a decisive conclusion in the generalization of v. 22, and 4:1 introduces a "turning" and a new observation. Section A connects to the following by the theme of fellowship. Section B is linked to C by the theme of toil, which is in turn connected to D by the theme of the lone man, and that passage introduces the theme of the "companion" (*šeni*), which becomes important in E. Such chaining is not a product of artificial "Stichwort" redaction, for the significant links among the passages are themes rather than specific words. Rather, this chaining reveals the movement of an individual mind from one topic to a related one. In spite of these linkages, the handling of the theme is sufficiently varied that the sections are best considered separately.

A. **4:1-3**

> (1) Turning and observing all the oppressions that occur under the sun, I saw the tears of the oppressed—and they have no comforter. Their oppressors possess[a] power—but *they* have no comforter. (2) So I reckoned the deceased, who have already died, more fortunate than the living, who are still alive. (3) But better than either is the one who never existed, who has not observed the evil events that occur under the sun.

[a] *b-* (MT *m-*)

In the few verses in which Qohelet points out wrongs committed by one person against another (3:16; 4:1-3; 8:9, 10), he does not demand a change of behavior. The possibility that human character could be modified does not seem to cross his mind. Social injustice is just one of many distortions in an unchanging and unchangeable world. The only significant area of freedom is in the individual's reactions to such evils. In general, Qohelet is less concerned with actions than with internal responses—in emotion or attitude—to the facts of life.

Qohelet's observation here has as its focal point (marked by *hinneh*) not the oppression itself, which is a given and not a discovery, but the tears of the oppressed. While observing oppressions (*w*[e]*šabti 'ăni wa'er'eh*), Qohelet beholds (*w*[e]*hinneh*) the uncomforted weeping of the persecuted. The repetition of the clause, "and they have no comforter", shows that what troubles Qohelet in these tears is less the misery of the oppressed than the lack of a humane response to their suffering. Here then is the hope he found frustrated: not that oppression disappear (such a possibility does not occur to him, even as a far-fetched eventuality), not that the oppressed refrain from weeping (how could they?), but that other people respond with sympathy to their anguish. Loyal companionship is, after all, truly good (cf. 4:9-12; 9:9), but the oppressed are denied it. The absurdity of social oppression is thus unnecessarily exacerbated.

Qohelet does not see himself as the needed source of consolation. He feels sorry for the pain of the downtrodden and regrets that no one will offer them solace, yet he seems more concerned with the disturbed equanimity of himself and the reader, whom he never envisions as a victim. He grasps the problem entirely from the perspective of an onlooker: How unfortunate is he who must behold such evils! When he recognizes a wrong—in this case, the lack of human sympathy—he bemoans it but resigns himself to it. He does not even urge us to comfort the afflicted (which is something that *could* be done, even in a world that offers little scope to human effectiveness). He is just sorry that we must see these things. (According to Ogden [1984a:449], Qohelet considers the pain of the wise man observing the human scene to be more intense than the pain of the oppressed. It would be more precise to say that Qohelet is more sensitive to, and more bothered by the wise man's pain; but he does not compare the two forms of suffering.) Elsewhere he advises us to ease life's discomforts by the balm of pleasure. But this also is a way of easing the discomfort of the observer, not of the sufferer.

4:1. In *w^{e}šabti 'ăni wa'er'eh* (4:1, 7; similarly 9:11) the verb *šub* serves as an adverb to the following verb. It does not mean "again"—before 4:1 Qohelet did not "see" oppressions, and before 9:11 he did not "see" that "the race is not to the wise, etc". Here, as in 2 Chr 19:4; Isa 6:10, 13; Jer 18:4; etc., *šub* points to another in a series of actions or events and means "afterwards", "next", or the like. The verbs *paniti* (Qoh 2:11, 12), *sabboti* (2:20), and *tarti* (2:3) function similarly. *W^{e}hinneh* indicates perception or recognition (from the participant's perspective) and marks the preceding clause as subordinate.

Miyyad should be emended to *b^{e}yad* (*b*/*m* is a frequent graphic interchange), since the oppressed do not get strength from the hand of their oppressors (*koaḥ* never means "oppression", or even "the effects of the exercise of power"). As emended, the clause literally means: "And in their oppressors' hand is power".

'ŚH (*na'ăšim*): "Oppressions" may equally well be said to "occur" (thus LXX γινομένας) or "be done" (sc., by people).

4:3. *Hamma'ăśeh hara' 'ăšer na'ăśah*: It is unclear whether this refers to oppressive actions, to the fact that people suffer oppression yet have no one to comfort them (which fact might be called an "occurrence"), or to all the unfortunate events that occur in life. I translate "events" because it is not the evil deeds alone that trouble Qohelet but rather the combination of these deeds with comfortless suffering.

Although Qohelet is burdened and grieved by the thought of death in this passage, his despair leads him to declare that death is better than life and not to have been born is better than ever having seen life's evils.

B. **4:4-6**

> (4) And I saw that all toil and all skilled work are [merely] one man's envy of another. This too is an absurdity and a vexation. (5) The fool clasps his hands together and eats his flesh. (6) Yet better is one handful earned calmly than two fistfuls of wealth with vexation.

4:4. *'amal*, 'ŚH: *Ma'ăśeh* means "activity" or, more specifically, "work", and is nearly synonymous with *'amal*, here meaning "toil". It is work, not wealth, that is driven by envy.

Kišron hamma'ăśeh means "skill of work", rather than "success of work" (contrary to Ginsberg), since the context (vv. 5-6) deals with the reasonableness of efforts rather than with their outcome. Skilled work is motivated by envy, which (as Prov 14:30 observes) is a "rotting of the bones"). Accompanied by this sick motivation, toil and ambition are necessarily self-destructive and self-defeating.

4:5-6. Two complementary—not contradictory—proverbs, the first condemning indolence, the second excessive work.

"Clasping the hands together" means to be idle (cf. Prov 6:10; 24:33). "Eat one's flesh" is a strikingly crass image of self-destruction: the impoverished fool is forced to cannibalize himself. Verse 5 may well be a conventional proverb, which Qohelet answers by one of his own in v. 6 (thus Gordis), but the second proverb does not invalidate the first. A fool destroys himself through laziness—therefore Qohelet never counsels indolence—while the toiler destroys himself through his strivings and the attendant vexation. The *naḥat* commended in v. 6 is not the same as the fool's inactivity, deprecated in v. 5.

4:6. Lit., “Better one handful of repose than two fistfuls of toil and vexation”. *‘amal* here means “earnings gained through toil”, not the activity of toiling, for it would be trite to observe that a certain amount of repose is better than twice as much toil, when any amount of repose is better than any amount of toil. The conjunction before *r*^{e}*‘ut ruaḥ* is a *waw-concomitantiae* signifying “together with”, “accompanied by” (for the phenomenon see GKC §154a, note 1 (b)).

Naḥat is not mere idleness, the “clasping of hands”, but rather behavior characterized by inner repose, without a flurry of activity. In 9:17 *naḥat* is applied to calm delivery of words. In 6:5 it must mean something besides simple absence of activity, because the stillbirth self-evidently has “more” non-activity than the living, and because it is not the non-activity that gives it an advantage over the living. Isa 30:15 also clearly uses the word with reference to an inner state, composure. In Qoh 4:6, *naḥat* is best understood as a metonym for property gained through calm, unagitated activity, just as *‘amal* is a metonym for property gained through toil, its contrary.

Qoh 4:6 teaches that a little property gained without toil is better than much wealth gained by toil and vexation. Prov 15:16 expresses a similar idea, except that the preferred term in the comparison is a religious attitude rather than a psychological state: “Better a little in the fear of the Lord than a great treasure with disturbance in it (*me’oṣar rab um*^{e}*humah bo*)”. *R*^{e}*‘ut ruaḥ* means much the same thing as *m*^{e}*humah*.

C. 4:7-8

> (7) I observed another absurdity under the sun: (8) the case of a man all alone who has no companion, neither son nor brother, and nevertheless his toil is endless and his eye is never sated with wealth. (So for whom am *I* toiling and depriving myself of pleasure?) This too is an absurdity and an unfortunate business.

Qohelet finds it absurd that someone without an heir should continue toiling.

4:8. “. . . the case of”: lit., “there is a . . .”. *‘amal* in v. 8a and 8b may mean either wealth or toil. In 8a the latter is less hyperbolic, for no one’s wealth is “endless” or “limitless”, but one’s work may be, insofar as it persists through life. In v. 8b *‘amel* is coordinated with self-deprivation and probably means “toil”.

In v. 8aβ *gam* is a coordinating conjunction (see Ellermeier, 1967:234). In other words, there are two factors in this man's behavior: external—he never ceases working—and internal—he is never satisfied with what he has. And yet there is no one to enjoy what he gains. Such behavior is obviously absurd.

In v. 8bα Qohelet switches to the first person. Gordis supplies "*He never asks himself*" before the sentence, which he explains as an unmarked quotation of the hypothetical argument the lone man should have used. But even if there are unmarked quotations in the HB (on the subject, see Excursus I), I do not see how the reader could be expected to recognize an unmarked quotation of something never said, in fact, of something the man never even *thought* of saying. Rather, the interjection in the middle of v. 8 shows that Qohelet is speaking out of his own experience. In 2:18-19 as well Qohelet shows that he sees himself as the unfortunate toiler.

D. **4:9-12**

> (9) Better two than one, for *they* have a good reward in their toil. (10) For if they fall, one can help the other up, but woe to one who falls and has no companion to help him up. (11) Also, if two lie down, they will keep warm, but how can the lone man keep warm? (12) And if someone attacks either of them, the two can stand against him. And the three-fold rope will not quickly snap.

Qohelet believes that benefits inhere in friendship, but they are rather cheerless ones: companions can aid each other in difficulties—after a fall, when one is attacked, in the cold. He does not mention the emotional value of fellowship.

4:9. *'amal* does not mean "wealth", for the passage does not mention the benefits of property. *'amal* here means "toil" and refers not only to efforts directed at gaining wealth, but to life's activities in general.

4:10. Since it is not generally difficult to get up after a fall, and since if both companions fall they cannot actually offer each other much help in getting up, we should probably understand the main point of the saying as alluding to any trouble or difficulty in life.

4:12. *yitᵉpo*: LXX (ἐπικραταιωθῇ) and Syr (*ne'šan*) do not seem to reflect the awkward *waw* on *ytqpw*. It is, however, explicable as an objective suffix followed by a noun in apposition (Ellermeier, 1967:175). The subject of *yitqᵉpo* is indefinite. *Ha'eḥad* is one of the two companions, as in v. 10, not an indefinite "someone", which would not have the article. *Negdo*: i.e., against the attacker.

"The three-ply rope will not quickly snap": This statement is not completely apposite in this passage, which speaks of *two* companions. It is an ancient proverb found in Gilgamesh (Schaffer, 1967, 1969). Menahem Haran (private communication) suggests that Qohelet is splitting a graded numerical proverb—originally "Two are better than one, and the three-ply cord will not quickly snap"—and inserting comments of his own between the halves. This sentence heightens the earlier praise of companionship: if the companionship of two is fortunate, how much the more so is the companionship of three!

E. **4:13-16**

> (13) Better a poor but wise young man than an old but foolish king who no longer knows how to be wary, (14) for from prison he came forth to rule, and this though he was born poor in his reign. (15) I saw all the living, those who go about under the sun, on the side of the *next* young man who would arise in his place. (16) There was no end to all the people, all those whom he led. Nor would those who would come still later take pleasure in him. This too is surely an absurdity and a vexation.

Argument:

13-14 What wisdom can accomplish

13	A "better than"-saying praising wisdom (2 stichs)
14	A story that proves the saying (2 stichs)
15-16a	The ephemerality of such accomplishments
15	Qohelet's observation (or prediction) of the outcome: the masses go with whoever arises next (2 stichs)
16a	The exacerbation of the outcome: the latter ruler's following is massive, while the wise youth is forgotten (2 stichs)

16b: Such an occurrence is absurd (1 stich)

The following exposition is especially indebted to Ellermeier (1967:216-32) in several important particulars.

The ambiguity in almost all the pronouns and in the subjects of the verbs causes great difficulties in the interpretation of this passage. There are syntactical ambiguities as well, especially in vv. 15-16. Also uncertain is whether the tale speaks of two persons—an old king and his successor (who is called *haššeni*)—or three—an old king, a youth that succeeds him, and that youth's successor ("the second young man"). The variety of ways of resolving the ambiguities has given rise to a great diversity of interpretations (see Ellermeier, 1967:217, for a summary). In spite of these difficulties, most commentators agree that the point of the story is to teach that wisdom's value is limited.

Many attempts have been made to identify the persons in this tale with biblical characters, such as Nimrod and Abraham, Saul and David, Pharaoh and Joseph, Nebuchadnezzar and Daniel, or with later historical characters, such as Antiochus III and Ptolemy Philopator, Antiochus Epiphanes and Alexander Balas, Ptolemy IV and Ptolemy V. None of these personages, however, quite fits the description, and some are much too late to be mentioned in Qohelet. The elliptical character of the narration does give the impression that Qohelet is relating an event that was actual to his audience (though perhaps dimly remembered), and that he expects them to recognize the event and flesh it out. The audience must be able to grant the plausibility of the event described in vv. 13-14 in order for the twist in vv. 15-16 to be effective. Furthermore, the fact that the young man came forth from prison (v. 14b) does not belong to the typical features of the event and does not bear directly on the message; thus it seems to be an authentic historical recollection. Qohelet's thesis, as Ogden (1980a:315) observes, requires "documentation", some sort of rooting in the real world. Whether or not the event is actual, it is presented as historical. Yet Qohelet's interest lies not in the details but in its typical and recurrent features, above all in the fact that political power, even if obtained through wisdom, will be passed on to someone else. Qohelet says the same thing about the pursuit of power and popularity as he said about the pursuit of wealth: it is absurd that those efforts, which are exerted in wisdom, must yield their fruits to another who did not work for them (2:18-26). The old king's loss of rule was not absurd, since it was the expected result of folly. The youth who succeeded him gained his power through his wisdom (otherwise the mention of his wisdom would be pointless), and he passed it on to another who had not worked for it. As Qohelet will remind us, "favor does not belong to the knowledgeable" (9:11). The first change of rule demonstrates the power of wisdom, the second its frailty. As in 9:13-15, wisdom is seen to fail in achieving appropriate rewards.

What Qohelet regards as valuable (and vulnerable) in rulership is esteem and favor, the possibility that innumerable people will follow a leader and "take pleasure" in him. This popularity is the large-scale counterpart of the companionship that Qohelet values in 4:9-12. It is this, rather than the loss of power, that Qohelet finds disturbing.

4:13. The king's age is not to be understood as the cause of his folly, but as a strength that folly overwhelms, just as the young man's wisdom overcomes the defect of poverty and youth. Considering that the king's folly consisted in a lack of caution, and further that the young man rose from prison, we may surmise that the latter had been imprisoned because he was thought to present a danger to the old king, and then came forth to seize power.

4:14. The subject of *yaṣa'* is the young man, not the king. There would be no point in describing the old king's past. Verse 14 motivates v. 13 by stating that the young man's wisdom enabled him to attain the throne from a position of extreme lowliness. *Ki gam* is concessive to *yaṣa' limlok*. *Malkuto* refers to the reign of the old king and emphasizes the contrast between the two men: the old king was reigning at the time his unknown successor was born into poverty.

4:15. The structure of this sentence is "I saw all the living (namely, those who go about under the sun) with the next young man . . ." (thus the accents), not "I saw all the people who go about under the sun with the next young man". The phrase *ham^{e}hall^{e}kim taḥat haššameš* is a relative clause modifying *haḥayyim* (Ellermeier, 1967:231f.); it is equivalent to *ro'ey haššameš* (7:11; C. D. Ginsburg). Being "with" (*'im*) indicates alliance and support (e.g., Gen 28:20; 26:3; 1 Kgs 8:57; and with the synonymous *'et*: 2 Kgs 6:16; 9:32, with reference to political support). The modifier "under the sun" is a generalization, not an exaggeration. The point is that *everyone's* loyalties go with whatever ruler comes along next. The phrase also emphasizes that these people are alive, in contrast to the previous ruler (the wise youth), who will then be dead.

Hayyeled haššeni is not the youth mentioned in v. 13. *Haššeni* does not mean "the youth, the second one", i.e., the old man's successor (thus Gordis), for *šeni* never means "successor". Nor would the wise youth be called "second" in the sense of second in rank—"Stellvertreter" (Hertzberg)—since if he arose from prison merely to be deputy, that would not demonstrate the old king's folly. *Haššeni* is best rendered "the next" (Ellermeier; cf. Exod 2:13; Judg 20:24f.), since translating it as "the second (youth)" gives the impression that he has already been mentioned. *Hayyeled haššeni* is not a specific person, but whoever comes next in the succession of rulers. The switch to *yiqtol* (*ya'ămod*) in v. 15 also points to the appearance of another person in the story, since it implies that the "arising in his place" occurred after the events of v. 14, i.e., after the coming forth from prison to rule. (Qohelet never uses *yiqtol* for simple past tense.) The change in tense also suggests that Qohelet's temporal perspective is contemporaneous with the reign of the first young man, who is the center of this story. From that perspective, the ascendancy of the next young man is yet to come.

Qohelet "sees"—i.e., foresees—that all the living would be with (on the side of) whoever comes to power next. Qohelet calls the supplanter a "young man", thus implying that the people's loyalty is so unstable that they will flock after anyone, *even* a mere stripling.

4:16. The phrase *l^{e}kol 'ăšer hayah lipneyhem* does not mean "all who existed before them" (sc., the king and the wise young man), for it is irrelevant how many people lived before the events of this anecdote. Rather, the phrase means "all those before whom he (sc., the next young man) was"; in other words: all those whose leader he was (thus Targum, Ginsburg, Delitzsch, Podechard). This clause refers to the same group as "all the living" (v. 15a).

"Take pleasure in him". Subjects who are happy with their king are said to "take pleasure in" or "have joy from" (*śamaḥ b-*) him (Judg 9:19). The antecedent of *bo* is the wise youth rather than the "next young man". If the point of the sentence were that even the successor to the wise youth will have a successor, we would expect mention of the successor's death or loss of rule, and furthermore, the prepositional phrase would probably be placed in emphatic (frontal) position, i.e., *gam bo lo' yiśm^{e}ḥu ha'aḥăronim . . .*

Hebel: The antecedent of "this" in the *hebel*-judgment is a situation: a wise man losing his power to another and being forgotten. There is no activity in the immediate context that might be called *hebel*. The *ki* introducing the *hebel*-judgment is not causal; the clause in no way motivates the preceding statement, either as cause or as evidence. It may have asseverative force.

This unit has so many ambiguities that I append the paraphrase immediately:

> (13) A poor youth who is shrewd is better off than an old king who is puerile and no longer has the sense to take precautions. (14) For it happened that one such youth, in spite of having been born in poverty in the old king's kingdom, went from prison to power. (15) Nevertheless, I could foresee that all the living, who go about on earth, would join the following of whatever young man would take over next. (16) Limitless masses would follow the successor, and, what's more, even later generations would not appreciate that first shrewd youth. Surely this injustice is a vexatious absurdity.

4:17–5:6

> (17) Tread carefully when you go to the House of God, for to obey is more acceptable than for fools to offer sacrifice, since they do not know how to do wrong. (5:1) Do not be hasty with your mouth, and let not your heart rush to utter a word to God, for God is in heaven and you are on the earth. Therefore let your words be few. (2) For as a dream comes accompanied by much busyness, so does a fool's voice come accompanied by much talk.
>
> (3) When you make a vow to God do not delay in paying it, for there is no pleasure in fools. What you vow—pay! (4) Better that you not vow than that you vow and not pay. (5) Do not let your mouth bring punishment upon your flesh, and do not say to <God>[a]: "It was a mistake"—lest God grow angry at your voice and destroy the work of your hands; (6) for a lot of talk[b] is <like> a lot[c] of dreams and absurdities. Rather, fear God!

[a] *hā'ělōhîm* (MT *hammal'āk*) [b] *dᵉbārîm* (MT *ûdᵉbārîm*) [c] *kᵉrōb* (MT *bᵉrōb*)

An admonition to behave properly toward God opens (4:17) and closes (5:6b) this unit. The theme of the unit is vows, warning of the folly of excessive and rash vows (5:1f.) and the dangers of delaying their payment (5:3). The theme of vows subsumes remarks about sacrifices and speech. Qohelet advises circumspection in making vows, then says that if they are made, they must be paid, warning that God will get angry and punish you if you default. This unit is remarkable for the conventionality of its content. But Qohelet's concerns about the working of divine justice do not lead him to abandon moral or religious principles or to reject belief in divine punishment, as a probability if not a certainty.

4:17. Although the difficult and probably corrupt second half of this verse has not been satisfactorily explained, the basic message is discernible: behave carefully in the Temple, for obedience is better than the sacrifices fools bring. To be sure, obedience is better than *anyone's* sacrifice. Qohelet is warning against wrong forms of behavior in the cult, and is only incidentally associating such behavior with fools. A similar superfluous addition of "fools" appears in 7:5.

The idiom *šᵉmor ragleyka* (qere: *rglk*), lit. "guard your feet", means behaving carefully in all your ways (Tur-Sinai); thus: "tread carefully", "be careful what you do". Compare Ps 119:101 and especially Ps 26:12, where "my foot stands on level ground" is equivalent to "and I walk in my innocence" (v. 11); see further Job 23:11; 31:5; Prov 4:27 ("remove your foot from evil"). Qoh 4:17 urges prudence in the Temple generally and introduces the following section, which warns against precipitant vows. The basic idea of *šᵉmor ragleyka* is rephrased at the end of this unit by *'et ha'ĕlohim yᵉra'*, "fear God".

Qarob apparently means "near to God's favor", i.e., "acceptable". The adjective/noun *qarob* is used of one who has an intimate relationship, both of God (Ps 34:19; 85:10; 119:151) and of humans (Ps 148:14 [Israel]; Ezek 43:19 [Zadokites]; Lev 10:3 [priests]). Though it is not elsewhere used of actions, in 1 Kgs 8:59 it is used of words of prayer and means "acceptable".

The end of 4:17 is a crux. All the Versions support MT, which can only mean, "for they do not know how to do evil", as if ignorance of how to do evil were a bad quality. All attempts to explain the present text are forced, and even so do not produce an appropriate meaning. A recent defense of MT is Lohfink's (1983), who argues that the ignorant are not fully conscious, as they themselves testify by making a *šᵉgagah*-offering (5:5). Without full awareness, they cannot have true fear of God, which alone allows for freedom, and they therefore lack the moral responsibility that makes it possible truly to do evil. But Lohfink's interpretation attributes to Qohelet an intricate psychological-ethical theory that has no anchoring in the text or the language. (Would not an evil act performed by a person who lacks full moral responsibility, a child for instance, be referred to as "doing *ra'*"?) Moreover, this interpretation makes Qohelet imply that if fools did possess the intellectual requisites for genuine moral responsibility, their sacrifices would indeed be better than obedience.

An emendation would be in order if that would solve the problem, but none proposed so far is persuasive. The emendation to *milla'ăśot* (haplography), accepted by McNeile, Barton, Podechard, BHS, and others, is graphically minor, but there is no evidence that *min* can mean "except for". Ginsberg suggests (uncertainly) *'od*; but the resulting clause, "for they do not know how to do anything else", does not motivate the advice of v. 17a. Reading *ki 'im* (Renan) makes sense but is graphically too distant from MT to be justified without versional evidence. Since MT is clear and grammatically feasible, I translate the sentence without understanding its point in context.

Qohelet is in no way repudiating the cult. On the contrary, he must assume that offering sacrifices is essentially commendable, or the comparison he draws would not praise obedience.

5:1. As the phrase "to God" shows, the topic of this verse is circumspection in uttering vows rather than caution in speech generally, although Qohelet would undoubtedly affirm the latter as well (cf. 6:11; 10:14). To speak "before" God (thus, literally, in 5:1, 5b [in LXX's *Vorlage*]) looks like an Aramaism, for (*'ămar/'anpeq 'imra'*) *qŏdam*, meaning "speak to".

5:2. A parenthetical remark of proverbial character, motivating the advice in 5:1. The main point of this verse comes in the second part, for the context is a caution against excessive speech. The first part of the verse is generally understood as a warning that too much work during the day causes disturbing dreams at night. However, dreams are not bad in themselves, and Qohelet does not indicate that he is referring to nightmares. This sentence probably means that the dreams give rise to activity (*'inyan*), rather than activity giving rise to dreams. The phrase *ba' b^e-* here means "come with", "come bringing", i.e., "accompanied by", a sense it has in Lev 16:3; Ps 66:13; etc. (BDB p. 98b; GKC §119n). Just as the voice of the fool is accompanied by a lot of talk (rather than deriving from it), so too the dream comes *bringing* much activity. *'inyan* therefore refers to the meaningless, busy swirl of thought that takes place in dreams (thus Tyler) rather than to daytime tasks that might cause dreams.

5:3. The impersonal locution, "There is no pleasure in fools", may be motivated by a hesitation (that recalls a targumic characteristic) to speak of God's emotions directly.

5:5. The second prohibition explicates the first. Declaring that one's vow is a mistake is the way that one's mouth may bring punishment upon his flesh.

Lahăḥti' means "bring punishment upon", as in Isa 29:21; Deut 24:4.

Instead of the much discussed "angel", LXX, followed by Syr, read "God". There was no reason for those highly literalistic versions to change "angel" to "God", but neither was there any particular theological need to change "God" to "angel". The two readings must be granted equal textual claim to validity. From the literary perspective, however, "to God" seems the preferable reading, for it is the expression used in 5:1, and its repetition gives a tighter structure to the passage: Do not make rash vows to God (*lipney ha'ĕlohim*) so that you do not have to say to God (*lipney ha'ĕlohim*) that your vow was a mistake.

'ŚH: *ma'ăśeh-yad* must refer to earnings. Note that the punishment will take the form of material loss. Qohelet does not deny the intrinsic value of wealth.

5:6. A summary conclusion. To make sense of v. 6a it is necessary to remove the *waw* of *d^ebarim*. *D^ebarim harbeh* is the subject of the sentence. But although the sentence thus emended is grammatical, it says the converse of what is required, which is that a plethora of talk entails a lot of dreams and absurdities (and not the other way around). It would not disparage dreams and absurdities (absurd thoughts) to say that there are many words in them, and in any case dreams and vapors are not a topic of interest in this unit. We should therefore also emend *brb* to *krb*, making the sentence comparative. The *ki* at the beginning of 6b would then be adversative to the negative imperatives in 5a ("Do not let your mouth . . ., and do not say . . .".) (on the phenomenon see GKC §133a). Fearing God is the opposite of making thoughtless vows and excuses. The intervening sentences (5b-6a) are parenthetical strengthenings of the warnings in v. 5a.

5:7-8

> (7) If you see oppression of the poor and robbery of justice and right in the state, do not be surprised at the matter, since every highly placed person has a higher one looking out for him, and there are higher ones over them. (8) And the advantage of a land - - - - tilled field.

5:7-8 seems to be an isolated sentence on the ubiquity of social oppression and greed. It may be loosely connected by theme with the following unit, especially 5:10a.

5:7. It is usually assumed that the cause of oppression described here is the existence of a hierarchy in the bureaucracy. But the idea that bureaucratic hierarchy is a source of trouble seems too modern, and in any case a superior's *watching* his subordinates would not cause oppression and injustice. The point of the verse is rather that people with power *look out* for one another, making it impossible to root out corruption. (For *šamar* in the sense of "watch over, protect" see 1 Sam 26:16 and Prov 6:22.)

5:8 remains obscure, but it is possible to surmise something of its theme. The verse speaks of the advantage (*yitron*) a land possesses, suggesting a comparison, and the object of comparison may be the unfortunate province described in the preceding verse. ("Land" in v. 8 is the land as a polity, not the physical land.) In 10:16-17 as well Qohelet contrasts an unfortunate land, suffering from dissolute rulers, with a fortunate land, benefitted by responsible rulers. In 5:7-8, the unfortunate land suffers from self-serving officials. The present text suggests that the advantage of the land mentioned in 5:8 consists in having its fields worked. ("Worked", i.e., tilled, is the only meaning testified for 'BD-niphal—Deut 21:4; Ezek 36:9, 34.) The text is almost certainly corrupt, particulary the middle of the verse, *bkl hy'* [qere *hw'*] *mlk l-*. The end of the verse may derive from *'im kl śdh n'bd*, allowing for the translation: "And there is an advantage to the land in all [regards] if every field is tilled."

The next unit, 5:9-6:12, comprises five loosely related sections on the themes of greed, satisfaction, and dissatisfaction. The sections will be discussed separately because of the length of the unit.

A.	5:9-11. Introductory observations on satisfaction and dissatisfaction
B.	5:12-16. The bad case (a *ra'ah ḥolah*): a man hoards his wealth and loses it.
C.	5:17-19. The good case (a *ṭob*): a man is allowed to enjoy his wealth.
B′.	6:1-6. The bad case made worse (it is a *ra'ah* and a *hebel woḥŏli ra'*): a man is not allowed to enjoy his wealth; rather, another gets to consume it.
A′.	6:7-9. Dissatisfaction
D.	6:10-12. Conclusion: human ignorance

A. **5:9-11**

> (9) He who loves silver will not be sated with silver, nor whoever loves wealth[a] with produce. This too is an absurdity. (10) As property increases, so do those who would consume it, so the only benefit [in it] for its owner is the sight of his eyes. (11) Sweet is the sleep of the <slave>,[b] whether he eats little or much, whereas the rich man's surfeit does not allow him to sleep.

[a] *hāmôn* (MT *behāmôn*) [b] point *hā'ebed* (MT *hā'ōbēd*)

One reason people do not derive satisfaction from their wealth is that others take it away. It is therefore imperative to enjoy what you have before you (10), even if that is only a little (11).

5:9. *Mi* = "whoever" (Exod 24:14; 32:26; etc.). Read *hmwn* for *bhmwn* (dittography; BHS and most). *Lo' t^{e}bu'ah* is elliptical for *lo' yiśba' t^{e}bu'ah*, the force of the verb carrying into the parallel stich. *Zeh* of the *hebel*-judgment can only refer to the situation or fact described in the verse as a whole: the person who loves wealth being perpetually dissatisfied with what he has.

Money should be a means, not an end in itself, for if one aims at wealth he will never be satisfied with what he has. Rather, one should seek to "get satisfaction from the wealth" (6:3; cf. 4:8), i.e., the wealth he already has.

5:10. *Kišron* here, as commonly recognized, means "benefit", "success" (Ibn Ezra, Delitzsch, Ginsberg, Hertzberg, et al.; cf. 11:6). *Mah* is sometimes equivalent to *'eyn* or *lo'* (e.g., Job 16:6; 1 Kgs 12:16; compare Cant 8:4 with 2:7; and see König, 1897:II, §§352β-δ). Thus *mah* X *ki 'im* Y (like MH *'eyn* X *'ella'* Y) means "X is only Y". The point of this verse is not that one who possesses something is soon left with only a mere vision (Gordis). Rather, "the sight of his eyes" *is* the benefit. *R^{e}'ut* (qere) *'eynayim* (like *mar'ey 'eynayim* in 11:9 and 6:9) is something desirable. Wealth is in constant danger of disappearing because it attracts others who will try to take it for themselves; therefore the only benefit (*kišron*) wealth can offer is the immediate experience of pleasure.

5:11. Better the untroubled sleep of the slave than the insomnia induced by worry over one's possessions.

Almost all MSS of the LXX have τοῦ δούλου, i.e., they read the consonantal text as *ha'ebed*, "the slave", a vocalization to be preferred to MT's *ha'obed*. The contrast MT presents between the rich man and the worker is not meaningful, because the rich man too works hard; in fact it is his toil that keeps him awake. The contrast hinges on whether one has possessions to worry about. In BH *ha'obed* is not used to designate the common laborer, the worker in contrast to other classes. (In Ezek 48:18f. *'obdey ha'ir* refers to those who work in the city in contradistinction to those who work outside the city, not to the social class of workers as opposed to a leisure class.) The term that designates a physical laborer in contrast to a man who earns his living through trade, possession of properties, and the like, is *śakir*.

Haśśaba' does not mean the satiety or satisfaction felt by the rich man, but rather the surfeit of property he possesses (for *śaba'* in the sense of "surfeit", "abundance", see Gen 41:29, 30, 31; Prov 3:10; etc.). Qohelet does not elsewhere demean satisfaction. He considers it desirable (4:8; 6:3), while he regards satiety as unobtainable (6:7). The contrast between the rich man and the slave is not that the former brought on indigestion by overeating, since a slave too may have eaten much (v. 11aβ). The rich man cannot sleep because he must worry about his wealth (Ibn Ezra, Rashbam, Podechard, Ginsberg; cf. 2:23 and Sir 31:1; Avot 2:8). After all, the more he earns the more he must worry about others seeking to consume it (5:10). The reason the slave can sleep is, by contrast, that he has no property to worry about losing.

B. 5:12-16

> (12) There is a sick misfortune that I have seen under the sun: wealth is stored up by its owner to his harm, (13) and then that wealth is lost in an unfortunate business, so when he begets a son he has nothing whatsoever. (14) Just as he came forth naked from his mother's womb, so shall he return—just as he came—and he will carry away nothing of his toil that he might take in his possession.
>
> (15) This too is a sick misfortune: just as[a] he came so shall he go, so how can he be adequately compensated for toiling for the wind? (16) Moreover, all his days he eats in darkness and great irritation[b] and sickness[c] and wrath.

[a] point *kil'ummat* (MT *kol 'ummat*) [b] point *w^eka'as* (MT *w^ekā'as*) [c] *woḥŏli* (MT *w^eḥolyô*)

An unfortunate situation. Qohelet describes two aspects of the situation, calling each a "sick misfortune" (*ra'ah ḥolah*). First (5:12), a man hoards money, harming himself by worry and self-deprivation to do so, then suddenly he loses it all (v. 16 reiterates the self-imposed misery); second (5:15), he leaves the world as poor as he came into it.

This passage, which describes the miser who eats in darkness rather than spending money on oil for his lamp (5:16), is linked to the preceding section by the theme of the rich man who frets. That theme, of incidental importance in the preceding section, becomes central here. "To his harm" (v. 12) refers to the agitation and self-deprivation he undergoes while toiling and hoarding (cf. 2:23). The tragedy of this man is that he makes himself suffer to amass his wealth, then suddenly loses it in an unfortunate incident. His lack of an heir exacerbates his tragedy but is not the heart of the problem. The problem is that no one got any enjoyment out of this wealth, *not even* an heir.

It is not clear whether the reason that the son's birth heightens the tragedy is that the toiler will have nothing to bequeath him, or that during his lifetime, following the misfortune, he has nothing to give his son. In 4:8 the absurdity of the lone man's toil is worsened by his lacking a relative to benefit from his present labor.

5:14. Verses 14a and 15a probably speak of the father, the toiler, as vv. 14b and 15b clearly do. For the problem is not that some people (such as the son) die poor, but that some people (like the father) waste their lives toiling for naught.

'amal here refers to wealth—what one would like to take with him but cannot.

5:15. *Ruaḥ* in *ya'ămol laruaḥ* designates something that is ephemeral, not something that is unattainable or that lacks value. The toiler had wealth but it evaporated. Qohelet is bothered by the thought of the loss of wealth, not by its triviality.

5:16. LXX's καὶ πένθει, "and mourns", reflects *w'bl*; but "mourning" is not an appropriate term to describe the agitation of the miser. (In Syr, *wb'bl'* has been inserted under the influence of LXX and *wbḥmt'* has been erroneously repeated [Schoors 1985b:351, et al.].) We should, however, follow LXX in reading *woḥŏli* for MT *wḥlyw*. None of the Versions reflects the suffix, which is awkward here. Even if we follow Gordis in taking *w^{e}ḥolyo* as an independent sentence ("and he has illness"), *waqaṣep* is left hanging. LXX correctly takes *wk‘s* as one of three nouns coordinated with *ḥošek* and governed by its *bet* (Euringer, Barton, Podechard). A single preposition can govern a series of related nouns; see König 1897:II, §319l.

C. **5:17-19**

> (17) Here is what I[a] have seen to be good: it is appropriate to eat and drink and experience enjoyment in all one's toil at which he labors under the sun during the few days of his life that God has given him, for that is his portion. (18) Furthermore, if God gives anyone wealth and property and enables him to partake of it and to take his portion and to get pleasure through his toil—that is a gift of God. (19) For then he will not much call to mind the days of his life, since God is keeping <him> occupied[b] with his heart's pleasures.

[a] point *’ăni* (MT *’āni*) [b] *ma‘ănehu* (MT *ma‘ăneh*)

The fortunate situation. It is good, Qohelet concludes (v. 17), to take pleasure in what one possesses. To be sure, man cannot determine whether he will be able to do this (v. 18). One may gain wealth by his own efforts, but God decides if man will be allowed to keep it. The possibility of enjoyment is God's great gift—the gift of oblivion; God "keeps him occupied", distracts him with pleasures. Pleasure dulls the pain of consciousness, the same pain that wisdom exacerbates (1:18).

The Egyptian phrase for entertainment means literally "diverting the heart". Pictures of banqueting scenes, which show man and wife eating, drinking, and listening to music in the company of friends and relatives, are labeled "diverting the heart". The poet of the "Antef Song" (Pap. Harris 500, 6,2-7,3; see Fox, 1977b:203-207), despairing of the efficacy of mortuary rites to guarantee immortality, urges his listeners to enjoy themselves in the present: "Be hale, while your heart is intent on self-forgetfulness . . . Follow your heart while you live".

5:17. Qohelet here observes a "good" to match the "bad" (i.e., the misfortune) that he saw in v. 12 (Yaḥyeh). The words *ṭob ’ăšer yapeh* have given the interpreters difficulty. In fact, these words do not constitute a phrase. *Ṭob* (which should have a disjunctive accent) is the dir. obj. of *ra'iti*, while *'ăšer* nominalizes the following clause, setting it in apposition to *ṭob*. *'ăšer* in this use is best translated "namely" or represented by a colon (Podechard: "Voici: ce que j'ai reconnu bon, (c'est) qu'il est convenable . . . de manger, etc."). A clear example of this usage is 8:14aα (second *'ăšer*); see also 8:11a (if 10b is taken with 11) and 9:1aβ. Here is what he has seen to be good: the fact that it is appropriate to eat and drink, etc. In this verse it is not, to be precise, the enjoyment of life that is called good, but the fact that it is appropriate or pleasant (*yapeh*) to enjoy life. This is almost the only fact about life that seems to please Qohelet.

5:17-18. *'amal*: probably "life's toils"; see §2.111.

5:18. A more literal translation is, "Furthermore, every man to whom God has given wealth and property and enabled him to partake of it and to take his portion and to have pleasure in his toil—that is a gift of God".

"To partake of it" or "to consume some of it" (*le'ĕkol mimmennu*): *mimmennu* is partitive, a nuance ignored by most translations. In Qohelet's view you need not consume all you own. If someone else gets part of your wealth without toiling for it, that is, to be sure, unfair (2:21-26), but that injustice need not spoil the pleasure *you* receive from your earnings. Yet it seems to do just that for Qohelet.

5:19. The verb *zakar* means "call to mind" and may refer to thinking about present facts or about future matters that are already known; e.g., Ps 8:5; Isa 47:7; and especially Lam 1:9: *lo' zak^{e}rah 'aḥăritah*, "she did not call to mind her future". The man blessed with pleasure, Qohelet says, will not often call to mind the days of his life, i.e., think about their brevity. For *ma'ăneh* point *ma'ănehu*, following LXX and Syr (thus most commentators). 'NH hiphil corresponds to Syriac *'a'niy*, "busy one (with)"; thus Syr can translate exactly: *ma'ne' leh*. Gordis, arguing that Qohelet does not regard joy as a narcotic, derives *ma'ănehu* from 'NH-I ("answer") and assigns it the meaning of "provide". But it is doubtful that 'NH means "provide". In any case, the notion that pleasure might distract one from unhappy thoughts is present in the first part of the verse. It is true, however, that this idea is isolated in the book of Qohelet.

B′. **6:1-6**

> (1) There is an evil I have seen under the sun, and it weighs heavy on man: (2) [It happens that] God gives a man wealth and property and prestige, so that he does not lack for his appetite anything he might desire, yet God does not allow him to consume any of it, but rather a stranger consumes it. This is an absurdity and an evil sickness. (3) Even if a man begets a hundred children and lives many years, however many the years he may live, if his appetite does not receive satisfaction from property, and furthermore he does not have a proper burial—I say that the stillbirth is better off than he. (4) For he comes into absurdity and goes into darkness, and in darkness his name is covered. (5) Even the one who neither saw nor knew the sun has more repose than he. (6) And even if a man should live a thousand years twice over, if he did not experience enjoyment . . . Do not all go to the same place?

6:1-6. The unfortunate situation exacerbated.

In 5:12-16 Qohelet spoke of the "sick misfortune" of a man who derived no pleasure from his wealth while he toiled and hoarded his earnings, then lost it all anyway. In 6:1-6 Qohelet speaks of an "evil sickness", a case similar to the first, except that God turns the wealth over to a stranger. The second case doubles the absurdity: one who did not toil for the wealth receives it. The blame is placed squarely on God, with no moralizing terminology. But the transfer of the wealth to a stranger—an obvious misfortune—is not the heart of the problem here. However many children a man has for heirs and however long he may live, his life is wasted if he himself has not known pleasure.

The absurdity described in this passage and in 5:12-16 is worse than that of 2:18-26. There we heard of the injustice done to the toiler whose earnings God gave to another. Here we learn that even the apparently fortunate man, upon whom God bestows wealth and prestige, may suffer the vagaries of the divine will, for God may take away that man's fortune before he dies, before he derives benefit from it. Such a man, and not only the unfortunate toiler, is worse off than a stillbirth, who was at least spared the misery of seeing life's evils (cf. 4:3).

6:2. On the syntax of this sentence, see Ellermeier, 1967:292-95 and Isaksson 1987:120-22. The latter observes that 5:18, using *qaṭal* forms, describes the general rule while 6:2, using the *yiqṭol*, describes an exception, an anomaly: the possibility that God may give a man wealth then deprive him of it.

Kabod here is the prestige attendant upon wealth (thus too in 2 Chr 1:11); this prestige will be transferred with the wealth to the fortunate recipient.

6:3. The clause, "and furthermore he does not have a proper burial (*qᵉburah*)", has perplexed the commentators, for it seems strange that Qohelet would place so much importance on the form of burial, as if that could somehow compensate for a life of joyless toil. One exegetical expedient is to change the negative *lo'* into a conditional *lu'*, "even if" (Gordis); but if this were a concessive clause it should have to come with the other concessive clauses, i.e., before *wᵉnapšo lo' tiśba'*. Another expedient, transferring the clause to v. 5a (Ginsberg, following Hitzig), is a major conjectural emendation that would be justified only *in extremis*. MT is satisfactory in both the pointing and placement of the clause. For elsewhere too Qohelet reveals his concern for burial and for the remembrance that a proper burial helps preserve. This concern is shown also by his anger at seeing the wicked receiving an honorable burial while the righteous are neglected (8:10), and by his chagrin at the thought that everyone's name will perish in darkness (6:4). While Qohelet probably did not consider a stately burial sufficient to bestow meaning on a pleasureless life, he does seem to have believed that the lack of a burial worsens life's tragedy and absurdity.

6:4. The subject of this sentence is the toiler not the stillbirth, because the latter does not have a name.

For MT *ylk*, the Qumran fragment has *hlk*, a confirmation of LXX πορεύεται = *holek* (most MSS; the future in 147-157-159, 253, 299 and Syh is hexaplaric). The participle seems to be an attempt to put the verb into an apparently more suitable tense.

6:5. For *naḥat*, Qumran has *nwḥt*, a *quṭl* form, on which see Kutscher, 1974:502ff. *Naḥat* means "rest, repose" in Qohelet (4:6; 9:17), as elsewhere in the HB. This sentence is not a conclusion but another reason why the stillbirth is better off: it at least has rest and quiet—in contrast to the toiler, who not only lives in darkness analogous to that of the stillbirth (6:4; 5:16a), but also suffers continual agitation (5:16b).

6:6. Qohelet starts to insist once again that length of life is not enough to redeem it, but he breaks off in mid-sentence and exclaims in despair upon the universality of death's power.

A′. **6:7-9**

> (7) All a man's toil is for his mouth, and yet the appetite is never filled. (8) (What advantage has the wise man over the fool? What good does it do the poor man to know how to get along with the living?) (9) Better the sight of the eyes than the wandering of the appetite. This too is an absurdity and a vexation.

The importance of getting satisfaction out of one's wealth (6:2-6) leads into thoughts on the voraciousness of the appetite.

> 6:7 // 5:9: man toils to fill an insatiable appetite.
> 6:9 // 5:10b-11a: the possibility of getting some satisfaction from one's possessions.

It is possible to get satisfaction from one's property without sating the appetite for wealth. Therefore, instead of striving for everything you want, enjoy what you now have. The wealth one sees before him (*mar'eh 'eynayim* = *r*^{e}*'ut 'eynayw*; 5:10) is better than the object of one's longing. Yet even actual satisfactions are absurd (6:9).

6:7. A concessive sentence; see Ellermeier, 1967:249-53. Man toils to satisfy his appetite, though, like the sea, it can never be sated to the full. "Mouth" and "appetite" (*nepeš*; possibly "throat"; *ibid.*) do not, of course, refer to the hunger for food alone (5:11), but rather to a diffuse yet painful yearning for possessions of all sorts. Such a desire, never appeased by actual possessions, is really a longing for *possession* in and of itself.

'amal may mean either "wealth" (one can consume all his wealth yet not be sated) or "toil" (although one's toil is aimed at consumption, he is never sated, even when he does consume what he earns).

6:8 breaks the connection between v. 7 and v. 9 and may be displaced. It might, however, be taken as a parenthesis, a proverb on satisfying the appetite through toil, as if to say: in this regard, the wise man, however much his skill and energy allow him to earn, has no advantage over the incompetent and lazy fool.

Ki mah yoter leḥakam min hakk^{e}*sil*. Since the appetite is insatiable, the wise man, who has the ability to earn wealth, has no advantage over the fool, who can be expected to be incompetent in his occupation. In this context (namely, the question of satisfaction, vv. 7, 9) the statement of v. 8a should be understood not as a categorical denial that the wise man has any advantage (which would be quite contrary to Qohelet's other statements about the wise and the fool), but as a denial of advantage with respect to achieving satisfaction.

Mah le'ani yodea' lahălok neged haḥayyim is a crux. Ehrlich says that this phrase as it stands must mean "was hat der Arme zu verstehen?" But finding this "widersinnig", he emends to *mah hayyodea'*—hardly an improvement, since he still finds the verse unclear. In his comment on Judg 18:23, Ehrlich mentions Jon 1:6; m. *Ker*. 5:2; m. *Middot* 2:2; and Mekilta VII, 135ff. as examples of the construction *mah l-* with undefined participle. The construction means "why should X do Y?". The question expresses surprise and usually disapproval as well. This is indeed the construction of 6:8b, and Ehrlich is wrong in thinking the sentence produced by his analysis to be meaningless. The point of the proverb is: since the wise man has no advantage over the fool, there is no reason for a poor man to know how to get along with the living. For, as Qohelet will say later, "the wisdom of the poor man is held in contempt, and his words are not heard" (9:16).

Lahălok neged haḥayyim: The closest parallel to the phrase *lahălok neged* is Prov 14:7: *lek minneged l^e('iš k^{e}sil)*, etc., "go with [lit., "opposite"] a foolish man, and you will not know knowledgeable lips", i.e., if you consort with fools, you will hear only folly. "Go around with" is the notion required by Qoh 6:8 as well. *Minneged l-* may bear the same sense as *neged*, in line with the series of near-equivalences *mittaḥat l-* = *taḥat*; *me'al l-* = *'al*; *miqqedem l-* = *qedem*; etc. *Neged* is nearly synonymous with *lipney*, so we can compare the phrase *halak/hithallek lipney*, "go before", usually used of loyalty to God (there is no discernible difference between the qal and the hitpael in this phrase). It is also used of a leader vis-à-vis the people (1 Sam 12:2), and of a priest vis-à-vis the king (1 Sam 2:35). Thus the phrase can be applied to a variety of relationships. The common denominator seems to be the idea of "living in the presence of", thus "getting along well with" (whence "be loyal to God" as opposed to departing from [SWR *min*] his presence). Comparison with Prov 14:7 suggests that *lahălok neged* is something one does with people. Thus *haḥayyim* probably means "the living" (Podechard, Barton) rather than "life" (Gordis).

Qoh 6:8b casts doubt on the value a poor man derives from knowing how to get along well with people, perhaps with the implication that wealth counts for more than behavior in human relations.

6:9. It is difficult to identify the antecedent of "this" in the *hebel*-judgment. It might be "the wandering of the appetite [*nepeš*]" (i.e., yearning), though the absurdity of that is self-evident. Furthermore, a negative judgment beginning "this too is" is more meaningfully directed at the *preferred* term of a comparison. Hence Qohelet is probably saying: granted that pleasure is better than hopeless yearning (that being obviously irrational), nevertheless pleasure too is absurd; cf. 2:1-2.

D. **6:10-12**

> (10) Whatever has happened was previously called by name, and its nature was known.[a] <And man cannot>[a] dispute with the one who is stronger than he. (11) For there are many words that only increase absurdity, and what advantage is there [in them] for man? (12) For who knows what is good for man in life during the few days of his absurd life (which he passes like a shadow), for who can tell man what will happen afterwards under the sun?

[a] *w*^{e}*lō' yûkal 'ādām* (MT *'ādām, w*^{e}*lō' yûkal*)

As at 3:22 and 7:14, Qohelet concludes a series of observations by throwing up his hands, as it were, in despair of attaining an understanding of life and a knowledge of the future. This section also introduces the theme of 7:1-12: what is good.

Life is unchangeable; therefore it is pointless to argue with God. And the future is hidden. The questions in vv. 11b, 12a, and 12b are equivalent to negations.

The phraseology of v. 12b echoes that of v. 10a: *mah šehayah* and *mah yihyeh* (these concepts were identified with each other in 1:9 and 3:15); *k*^{e}*bar* and *'aḥărayw*; *noda'* and *mi yodea'*; *'adam* and *'adam*. Together vv. 12b and 10a form a frame that contrasts God's knowledge (v. 10a) with man's ignorance (v. 12b) of events before they happen. In the context of that frame, the topic of this unit is seen to be speech about the events of life. It is absurd to waste words (as Job did) in arguing with God about what happens in the world. Whatever God makes happen will come to pass, and man cannot change it. What is more, man cannot even *know* what will happen (except in terms of the general pattern of recurrent events), and thus cannot formulate rules of behavior based on observation of consequences. Therefore he cannot say what is good to do.

Mah šehayah and *mah yihyeh* are events present and future. 7:24 shows that *mah šehayah* is present rather than past tense, for that verse speaks of the incomprehensibility of life in general, rather than only of the hiddenness of history. Again, *hayah* is better translated "happen" than "be", since Qohelet is not speaking of the simple existence of things. *Mah yihyeh* (v. 12b) does not refer to the future *existence* of things, as if it were important to know that a certain person or a certain building, for example, will exist in the future. The knowledge that could bear on the decision about what is good for man (v. 12a) is knowledge of future occurrence, not future existence.

6:10. *Mah šehayah k^e^bar niqra' š^e^mo* is a way of saying that whatever happens has already been known, for that which can be named is known. In other words, there is nothing new under the sun.

W^e^noda' 'ăšer hu', literally "and what it is was known". As Gordis observes, MT's *w^e^noda' 'ăšer hu' 'adam* cannot mean "it is known what man is", which would have been expressed by *w^e^noda' mah hu' ha'adam* (the nominalizing *'ăšer* indicates identity or category, not quality). But he is wrong in explaining v. 10aβbα as "anticipation" (prolepsis). As his own examples show, in syntactic anticipation a noun or noun phrase that is the semantic subject of an object clause is treated as the direct object of the main verb, and that is not the case here. The best way to make sense of this verse is to place *'adam* after *yukal* (*'adam* may have been omitted, then restored interlinearly, and finally misplaced at the next copying [Ginsberg]). The clause *w^e^noda' 'ăšer hu'* is equivalent to *niqra' š^e^mo*, "its name was given [lit., "called"]". The "already" of v. 10aα applies to *noda'* as well. The knowledge in question is foreknowledge. The implicit subject of *noda'* can only be God, the one who knows what happens before it occurs (this is most clearly asserted in Sir 23:20). God's exclusive knowledge makes it a hopeless task to dispute with him (v. 10b).

6:11. Ginsberg explains *yeš* as emphatic. Elsewhere, however, the construction with *yeš* as predicate emphasizer occurs only in interrogative or conditional sentences, and the subject is always a pronoun (Gen 24:42, 49; 43:4; Deut 13:4b; and Judg 6:36; see

Muraoka, 1985:77-81). Furthermore the type of emphasis required in this verse is not quite what this construction usually expresses, namely "the fact that a state of things or behavior of a certain man or men is *actually* as one wants or expects it to be, or as one thinks it should be" (*ibid.*, pp. 77f.). The literal translation, "there are many words that increase absurdity", is accurate, though not entirely clear in context. It implies that only some words increase absurdity. This means that Qohelet is not simply condemning excess speech in this verse (though he undoubtedly disapproves of it); rather he asserts the meaninglessness of a certain kind of speech: argumentation with God.

The scope of denial is implicitly restricted by the immediate context, in this case the futility of disputation with God. *Mah yitron la'adam* does not mean that no *yitron* whatsoever exists in the world, but that there is no *yitron* in many words, specifically those expended in disputation with God, who is stronger than man (6:10).

6:12. The words *wayya'ăśem kaṣṣel* are a parenthetical remark describing how quickly man's life passes. *'ăšer* motivates the negation implicit in the rhetorical question of v. 12aα.

'ŚH in this verse means "spend (time)", as in Ruth 2:19 and MH (Gordis). This occurrence of the verb may be classified with 'ŚH ii ("do", etc.).

'aḥărayw means "afterwards", "in the future" (see note on 3:22), here with reference to future events in one's lifetime. Knowledge of what happens after death would not enable one to say what is good to do in life (unless the knowledge had to do with recompense in the afterlife, a concept totally outside the purview of Wisdom Literature prior to the Wisdom of Solomon). Moreover, in 7:14b, which reiterates 6:12b, the future in question is clearly within this life.

7:1-12 + 19, 13-14

(1) A name is better than good oil,
  and the day of death than the day of one's birth.
(2) It is better to go to a house of mourning
  than to go to a house of feasting,
inasmuch as that is the end of every man,
  and the living should take it to heart.
(3) Irritation is better than merriment,
  for a heart is improved by a scowl.

(4) The heart of wise men is in the house of mourning,
and the heart of fools is in the house of merrymaking.
(5) It is better to hear the rebuke of a wise man
than <to> hear[a] the singing of fools,
(6) for as the sound of thorns under the pot
so is the merriment of the fool.
And this too is absurdity.
(7) For extorted wealth makes the wise man inane,
and a gift corrupts the mind.
(8) Better the conclusion of a matter than its beginning;
better a patient spirit than a haughty spirit.
(9) Do not let your spirit hastily become irritated,
for irritation rests in the breast of fools.
(10) Do not say, "How has it happened that the earlier days were better than these?"
for not <in> wisdom[b] do you ask about this.
(11) Wisdom is as good as an inheritance,
an advantage for those who see the sun.
(12) for to be in the shelter of wisdom is to be in the shelter of silver,
but the advantage of knowledge is that wisdom keeps its possessor alive.
(19) Wisdom helps the wise man
more than the <wealth>[c] of the rulers who are in a city.

(13) Observe what God has brought to pass: no one can straighten what (God) has twisted. (14) In a day of good fortune, enjoy the good, and in a day of misfortune, observe: God has made the one to happen next to the other, so that man should not be able to apprehend anything [that might happen] afterwards.

[a] *miššĕmōaʿ* (MT *mēʾîš šōmēaʿ*) [b] *b^ehokmāh* (MT *mēḥokmāh*) [c] *mēʿōšer haššallîṭîm* (MT *mēʿăśārāh šallîṭîm*)

A. 7:1-12 + 19	Some things that are better than others
B. 7:13-14	Man's ignorance (v. 14bβ) and impotence (vv. 13-14a) before God, and how to live in such a state

Section A is a series of proverbs on "good things", including a series of "better than" proverbs. Since he has just declared that no one can say what is "good" for man to do (6:12), he now may be speaking somewhat tongue-in-cheek, but he is still serious about the advice itself. Qohelet's skepticism about the certainty of knowledge does not keep him from offering ordinary counsel and observations. At the same time, he does not place great stock in his own sagacity, and he deliberately weakens the force of his advice by skeptical remarks (e.g., 7:6b) and by self-directed irony. These qualities moderate the assertive confidence of section A, as does the bracketing of the counsels of this section between reminders of human limitations, particularly with regard to knowledge of the future (6:12b//7:14b).

The proverbs of 7:1-6 are united by words belonging to two semantic fields: words associated with pleasure—*mišteh*, *śeḥoq*, *śimḥah*, *šir*—and their antonyms, words associated with displeasure—*'ebel*, *ka'as*, *ro'a panim*, *'ebel*, *ga'ărah*. Verses 2-6a proceed by alternation, with v. 4 elaborating v. 2 and vv. 5-6a elaborating v. 3. Verses 8-12 append five maxims on the value of wisdom.

7:1. *Šem* by itself can imply a good, or at least a desired, reputation (Prov 22:1; Gen 6:4). The point of the verse lies in the second stich (preference of the day of death) rather than in the first (praise of reputation), because the second stich introduces a topic—death—that is of concern in the succeeding verses (2-4). Just as a good reputation is preferable to good oil, so is the day of death preferable to the day of birth.

"Oil" (v. 1) is echoed by "house of feasting" (v. 2), and that by "house of merrymaking" (v. 4), for oil for anointing was one of the luxuries offered at banquets. Similarly "day of death" (v. 1) is echoed by "house of mourning" (v. 2), and that by "house of mourning" in v. 4.

7:2 + 4. Qohelet, unlike the other sages, believes that wisdom brings melancholy (1:18). This idea is in accord with LXX Prov 14:10, which says that the mien of the wise man is generally somber: "As for the heart of a perceptive (αἰσθητική) man—his soul is sad. And when he rejoices, it is not mixed with pride". Such sadness is not, of course, a reason to avoid wisdom, but rather to accept solemnity. Qohelet is not advocating sadness for its own sake; he advocates awareness of the facts of life, and this makes for melancholy. Since death is inevitable, "the living should take it to heart" (v. 2b)—and this is what the wise man does (v. 4). Qohelet is not wholehearted in his recommendation, for in 5:19 he praises *śimḥah* for providing distraction from the painful consciousness of finitude.

Beyt mišteh (v. 2) = *beyt śimḥah* (v. 4). In v. 4, *śimḥah* means "merrymaking", "feasting", as in Neh 8:17f., where it is said that the people went to "make" (*la'ăśot*) a great *śimḥah*, meaning the feast of Tabernacles. See also Est 9:17, 18, 19, 22, where *mišteh* and *śimḥah* are collocated in a way that suggests their synonymy. The Qumran fragment to Qoh 7:2 has a synonymous reading, *śimḥah* for *mišteh*.

7:3 + 5-6a. The value of reproof. Verse 3b presents a paradox: how can a "bad face" (which usually implies sadness; cf. Gen 40:7; Neh 2:2f.) make the heart "good" (this usually means cheerful; e.g., Prov 15:13)? Paradox invites resolution by the reinterpretation of its terms. The first part of the saying suggests that we revise our understanding by associating *roa' panim* with *ka'as* and taking the sentence to mean that the anger and "bad" face, i.e., the scowl, of someone else may improve the heart, i.e., the mind, of the person at whom this facial expression is directed. A rebuke (often praised in the book of Proverbs) is instructive; it "improves the mind", while the sounds of merriment are hollow. (This is true not only of a fool's merriment, but, as 7:3 shows, of anyone's. Qohelet is thinking of the folly of merriment and so adds "fool"; cf. the superfluous "fools" in 4:17.) Verse 5 reinforces the lesson: better to hear the wise man's rebuke than the sounds of foolish merriment.[18]

Ka'as refers to a range of emotions from anxiety (e.g., 5:16) to anger (e.g., 7:3), and it is frequently uncertain which English word is the most precise translation in context. I translate "irritation" throughout for consistency, and because it too can refer both to anger directed at someone and to an unfocused discomfort.

In v. 5 MT has an unbalanced comparison between an action ("to hear") and a person ("than a man hearing"). Delitzsch's explanation, that the two-fold act of hearing is distributed between two subjects, is unsatisfactory, for to convey that notion the first term of comparison would have to be a person (e.g., *ṭob šomea'* . . .). We should emend *m'yš šm'* to *mšm'*. (The error resulted from dittography of *š*, followed by adjustments seeking to make sense of the separated letters.)

Šir refers to the music that accompanies merrymaking (cf. Isa 24:9, where *šir* is the background for drinking; also Sir 35:5; m. *Sotah* (8:11). Here it may be a synecdoche for all the sounds of merrymaking. As in v. 3, the antonymic pair represents rebuke versus merrymaking, not rebuke versus praise. (Although G'R may denote

18. NJV translates, "Vexation is better than revelry, for though the face be sad, the heart may be glad." But the fact that a sad face *may* hide a happy heart says nothing on behalf of vexation.

originally a physical expression of anger [MacIntosh, 1969], the wise man's expression of anger is a rebuke and naturally connotes moral censure.) *Śᵉḥoq*, which in v. 6 resumes *šir*, likewise implies merry-making, again perhaps as synecdoche (§2.123).

7:6b. *Hebel.* It is very difficult to determine the antecedent of this *hebel*-judgment. It could be the merriment of the fool, which is undoubtedly *hebel* in almost any sense we might ascribe to the word; but to call the fool's merriment absurd is to restate the obvious. Gordis suggests that this *hebel*-judgment refers to the "general theme of the passage", in other words to the proposition that the wise man's rebuke is better than the fool's merriment (or praise, as Gordis understands *šir*). But nowhere is *hebel* used to invalidate a proposition, as if meaning "false" or (in Gordis' limp paraphrase) "to be taken with a grain of salt". A possible antecedent is "the rebuke of a wise man" in v. 5a. Verse 6 is parenthetical, probably a proverb cited to strengthen the observation made in v. 5. The motivation of the *hebel*-judgment might be seen in v. 7, if vv. 5-7 form a "Zwar-Aber Aussage": granted that the rebuke of the wise is better than the merry noise of the fool, yet even that rebuke is absurd, meaningless, for the truth of a wise man's words can be undermined by lust for wealth (on the vulnerability of wisdom see 9:18). The idea that the purpose of a gift is to avert reproof appears in Sir 20:29: "Gifts and presents can blind the eyes of wise men and avert reproofs like a muzzle on the mouth". It may be, however, that the motivation of the *hebel*-judgment is now missing (see below).

7:7. The Qumran fragment has space for 15-20 letters between 7:6 and 7:7 (Muilenberg, 1954:26f.). Although these letters are lost in a lacuna, the arrangement of the lines on the fragment indicates that something once stood before 7:7—perhaps only a long erasure, but perhaps a sentence. In fact, Delitzsch already surmised that something was lost before 7:7. He suggested supplying a saying along the lines of Prov 16:8, which, it turns out, would fit well in the lacuna of the Qumran Qohelet.

7:7 is a variant of a maxim found in Exod 23:8 and Deut 16:19. Sir 8:2b has similar warning about the corruptibility of princes (*rabbim*, *nᵉdibim*).

'ošeq here refers to the wealth gained through acts of oppression (cf. Lev 5:23; Ps 62:11) rather than the acts of oppression themselves.

wiy'abbed: The Qumran fragment (Muilenberg, 1954:27) has

wy'wh, "perverts", "makes iniquitous", which appears to be a functional synonym used for the sake of greater specificity.

7:8. The first stich restates v. 1: the end of a matter is better than its beginning. Therefore one should wait patiently to see how things turn out, for only then will the oppressive uncertainty about the future be resolved. "Patience" can serve as an antonym of "haughtiness" because it is prideful to imagine that one can know the future.

7:9. The context, in which Qohelet lauds patience (v. 8) and rejects the notion that the present is worse than the past (v. 10), narrows down the nature of the anger in v. 9 to grief over present misfortunes and injustices.

Verse 9b contains a striking image: anger rests in the fool's arms. Delitzsch thinks of a demon making itself at home in the fool's bosom. More to the point is the image of a baby snuggling in its father's arms. The fool coddles his vexation, nurtures it, lets it grow, while all along, of course, it is gnawing at him.

7:9 disparages *ka'as* (irritation, anger), while 7:3 praises it. Gordis says the word has different meanings in the two verses: in v. 3 it means "serious of disposition", in v. 9 "uncontrolled bad temper". Other commentators similarly distinguish two meanings. The distinction, however, lies less in the meaning of the word than in its application. *Ka'as* in both verses means "irritation", "anger", but in v. 3 the word is applied to the anger of reproof, in v. 9 to the anger one feels at unfortunate events that befall him. Neither verse is a statement about anger in all circumstances.

7:10. The reading *b^{e}ḥokmah*, reflected in LXX (ἐν σοφίᾳ and Syr (*bḥekmta'*), is grammatically preferable to MT's *meḥokmah*. *B^{e}ḥokmah* indicates the manner of the asking—"(not) wisely"—while MT's *meḥokmah* indicates the source or motive of the question, which is less relevant here. The Septuagintal reading is not, contrary to Gordis, merely a matter of Greek idiom. LXX-Qoh has few compunctions about violating Greek idiom, and in any case ἐκ σοφίας (for *meḥokmah*) would be good Greek.

This verse is usually understood as a rejection of the notion that the past was the "good old days". But if that were Qohelet's intent, we would expect him to *deny* that "the earlier days were better than these", not simply to declare that it is unwise to ask about this, as if conceding the validity of the assumption behind the question.

Yaḥyah aptly compares the question to Job's complaints. Some misfortunes occur "without cause", Job's being an example.

> Therefore Qohelet said that one should not speak and utter words of complaint about one's troubles or inquire of God about their reason, 'for not from wisdom do you ask about this,' for you are obligated to put your hand on your mouth and to justify the judgment of Heaven, even if it is true that the earlier times were better, before the wealth was lost.

The issue is a change of fortunes in someone's life. The proper attitude toward a downturn in one's fortunes is inculcated in 7:14, which also speaks of the right response to the ups and downs of life: in good times, enjoy the good fortune, and when bad times come upon you, do not ask why the past was better. Inexplicable fluctuations of fortunes are God's way of keeping man in fear of him.

7:11. Wisdom is as good as a monetary inheritance (v. 11a); indeed, wisdom is even more advantageous (*yoter*) than an inheritance (v. 11b) to its possessor. Both v. 11 and v. 12 say that wisdom is as good as wealth (11a//12a) and, in fact, has an advantage over it (11b//12b). For the comparative use of *ʿim* see 2:16 and Job 9:26; 37:18 (Podechard, Ginsberg [on 2:16]; etc.).

To say that wisdom "is" an advantage (*yoter*) (sc., for someone) is equivalent to saying that wisdom "has" an advantage (sc., for someone) (as in 2:13; possession is implicit in the construction in 7:12b). *Ḥokmah* appears in nominal predication with *yitron* in 10:10 as well. Wisdom's advantage is spelled out in v. 12b—it keeps its possessors alive. That is why Qohelet refers to people in this verse as "those who see the sun", i.e., the living.

7:12. "Shelter", lit., "shade", a metaphor for shelter and protection (Num 14:9; Isa 30:2, 3; Jer 48:45; etc.). Sym's ὅτι ὡς . . . ὁμοίως) apparently represents *k*^{e}*ṣel* . . . *k*^{e}*ṣel*; LXX and Syh testify to the second *kaph*. The meaning of the proverb in that form ("The shade of wisdom is like the shade of silver") is essentially the same, but MT is stronger: Wisdom brings with it the protective value of wealth (Prov 3:16; 8:18; 24:3f.), but its protection is not merely "like" that of silver. Wisdom (*daʿat*) has an advantage, insofar as it keeps its possessor alive (*daʿat* is resumed by its synonym *ḥokmah*). Wealth, on the other hand, does not help its possessor escape death (cf. 8:8b, reading *ʿšr* for *ršʿ*; Prov 11:28).

7:19. This saying is irrelevant in its current place and interrupts the connection between v. 18 and v. 20. It does not (contrary to Galling, 2nd ed.) constitute an example for the precept of v. 16, from which it is in any case too far removed to serve that function. Such dislocations can occur accidentally, as when a scribe omits a verse, then writes it in the margin, and a later scribe copies it into the wrong place. They can also occur intentionally. A comparison of Pap. Prisse (the oldest MS of the Wisdom of Ptahhotep) with three later copies shows frequent relocations of sentences as well as of groups of sentences too large to have been dislocated accidentally. Sometimes the relocations seem to have ideological or exegetical reasons. Qoh 7:19 may have been moved to its present place to remind the reader that, although Qohelet advised against too much wisdom, wisdom is nevertheless of immense value. The original location of the verse is uncertain. I follow Ginsberg in placing it after 7:12, where it continues the teaching of wisdom's advantage over wealth.

Ta'oz. Qum reads *t'zr*; LXX βοηθήσει probably represents *t'zr* (βοηθέω usually renders 'ZR; it once represents 'WZ [Isa 30:2], not 'ZZ). The variants are a synonym interchange, and both words mean "help" (on the synonymity of 'ZR and 'ZZ see Brin, 1960). The Qum-LXX reading seems to be a substitution of a more familiar expression, *'azar l-*.

m'śrh šlyṭym: This reading is peculiar, for ten rulers are an unlikely source of help (or power) for a wise man, nor would we expect to find ten in one city. We should follow Perles (1895:42) in relocating the word division and reading *m'šr hšlyṭym*, "the wealth of the rulers". These "rulers" are local officers and administrators of the sort whose ranks Qohelet mentions in 5:7. Here, as in 7:11f., Qohelet is calling wisdom more valuable than wealth. By this reading, 7:19 is even more closely aligned thematically with 7:11-12.

7:13-14, section B, continues the theme of patient acceptance of turns of fortune. Recognition of human inability to change things can help one accept difficulties while waiting patiently for their outcome.

7:13. The *ma'aśeh 'ĕlohim* is the fact described in v. 13b; thus NJV: "Observe God's doing! Who can straighten out what he has twisted?"

7:14. "Enjoy the good": lit., "be in good" (cf. the similar expressions in Ps 25:13; Job 21:13).

'ŚH. *'aśah ha'ĕlohim* refers to good and bad fortune (the *ṭob* and the *ra'ah*) that God causes to occur in a person's life; thus translate, "brought to pass". *Yom* here, like *'et* in *'et ra'ah* (9:12), means "time" (and not precisely "day"), in the sense of a complex of circumstances that occur together. By making different types of "times", God keeps man off balance. One never knows what will happen next.

7:15-18, 20-22

> (15) I have seen both in my absurd life: there is a righteous man who perishes in his righteousness and a wicked man who lives long in his wickedness. (16) Do not be very righteous nor become exceedingly wise, lest you be dumbfounded. (17) Do not be very wicked nor act the fool, lest you die before your time. (18) Better that you take hold of the one, while not letting go of the other. For he who fears God fulfills them both. (. . . [a])
> (20) For there is no man on earth so righteous that he does only good and never sins.
> (21) Furthermore, you should pay no heed to all the things people say, so that you do not hear your slave reviling you. (22) For you know in your heart that many times you too have reviled others.

[a] 7:19 is placed after 7:12 and discussed there.

Divine injustice and human ignorance

There are two main ways of interpreting the peculiar advice Qohelet offers in this section:

(1) Do not *be* very righteous and wise or very wicked and foolish. But why would Qohelet object to a high degree of righteousness? (His objection to excessive wisdom is more understandable.)

Even if this interpretation is correct, the passage does not counsel the Peripatetic ideal of the Golden Mean (contrary to Delitzsch, Hertzberg, Gordis, etc.). According to that principle, wisdom is not one of the extremes to be avoided, but is rather the mid-point between two extremes—too much and too little of any quality—both of which are folly.

(2) Do not be *self-righteous*, and do not make great pretensions to wisdom (for this view see particularly Whybray, 1978). But while *titḥakkam* can mean "pretend to wisdom", it is doubtful that *tĕhi ṣaddiq* can mean "claim to be righteous". Moreover, this interpretation creates an awkward imbalance between a warning not to *pretend* to be something (v. 16a) and a warning not to *be* something (v. 17a).

A difficulty that arises in both interpretations is that Qohelet seems to be advising the reader to be *somewhat* wicked in v. 17aα; see below.

The first interpretation seems to me the more adequate. Qohelet is teaching the avoidance of an extreme of wisdom (such as he himself acquired) because (we may deduce from the context) it makes one aware of inequities such as those described in 7:15, and this awareness will leave one shocked (v. 16b). As he said in 1:18, "in much wisdom there is much irritation, and whoever increases knowledge increases pain". Qohelet does not say why one should not be very righteous, but again v. 15 suggests that it is the failure of righteousness to produce its just reward that inspires this advice.

A high degree of righteousness may also be a form of hybris. Since, as v. 20 says, no one can be entirely righteous, living on too high a level of righteousness (e.g., giving away most of one's wealth to the poor) gives the appearance of striving to go beyond human limitations. Qohelet teaches us to accept in ourselves a mixture of good and bad, just as we should accept that same mixture in the events of our days (v. 14). Only in this way can we show true fear of God. Pushing too hard in either direction displays a presumptuous confidence in one's own powers. In Hertzberg's words:

> Der tiefste Grund für die hier empfohlene Ablehnung der Extreme ist das instinktive Gefühl, jene Wege seien nur-menschlich und damit anti-göttlich—ὕβρις! (p. 154)

Such advice has precedent in Wisdom Literature. Ptahhotep says, "Follow your heart as long as you live. Do no more than is required. Do not shorten the time of following the heart" (l. 186f.; cf. *AEL* I, 66). Kagemeni cautions: "Do not go beyond what is set down [sc., in this book]" (Pap. Prisse 2,6; *AEL* I, 60).

Qohelet's advice is not, however, only a humble expression of the acceptance of human limitations. It also holds a note of bitterness, occasioned by the observation of injustice in 7:14. If neither wise, righteous behavior nor wicked, foolish behavior produces the appropriate consequences, one should avoid too much of either. Statements like this and 2:17 express feelings that welled up in Qohelet in the course of his meditations but that should not be given the weight of a philosophical proposition in determining the character of his thought as a whole.

7:15. The *bet* of *b^{e}ṣidqo* and *b^{e}ra'ato* means "in the state of" (*b*-) and not "because of" (contrary to Hertzberg). Even if wickedness does not inevitably cause early death, it certainly does not cause long life. The point is that someone may die young in spite of being in a state of righteousness and another live long in spite of being in a state of wickedness. "In (the state of)" may mean "although", when there is a tension between the subject and the condition it is in (Ginsberg renders "although", comparing Num 14:11; Lev 26:27; Ps 27:3; etc.). It is because Qohelet had expected to see retribution that he is shocked when the rule is violated.

7:16. *Titḥakkam*: the hitpael of ḤKM does not necessarily connote slyness or a pretense of wisdom. (In Exod 1:10, *l^{e}hitḥakkem* refers to *genuine* wisdom, for Pharaoh is speaking of his own plan.) *Hitḥakkem* seems to mean "to act wise" or "make a show of wisdom" in Sir 10:26; 35:4, but it means "become (genuinely) wise" in Sir 6:32; 38:24, 25. In Qoh 7:16, the conjunction of *titḥakkam* with "be righteous" and its contrast with "be wicked" and "act the fool" shows that it refers to genuine wisdom. The hitpael in this case seems to indicate *becoming* wise rather than manifesting wisdom, since the impression one's wisdom makes on others is not at issue.

'al t^{e}hi ṣaddiq harbeh: Whybray (1978:192-196) argues that this means "do not claim to be a *ṣaddiq*". But Qohelet's words as they stand do not refer merely to a pretense of righteousness. He could have expressed that idea by a prohibition such as *'al to'mar ṣaddiq 'ani*. Moreover, the syntactically and structurally parallel *'al t^{e}hi sakal* clearly refers to reality not pretense.

Tiššomem is a hitpael of ŠMM with assimilation of the *taw* (GKC §54c). ŠMM-hitpael means "be shocked, dumbfounded", e.g., Isa 59:16; 63:5; Ps 143:4; Dan 8:27; Sir 43:24; and that is its meaning here (thus LXX, Syr, Vul), not "be destroyed". Qohelet does regard wisdom as a source of emotional disturbance (1:18), but not of physical destruction.

7:17. By warning against acting *very* wickedly, Qohelet seems to be recommending a *little* wickedness. Some interpreters eliminate the implications of such advice by interpreting the "wickedness" as something other than moral evil, such as transgression of the letter of the law (Delitzsch), or belonging to a party less rigorously attentive to divine precepts (Ehrlich). But the term *raša'*, "wicked", would not be applied to either type of behavior in BH or MH; it always denotes truly immoral behavior. More likely, the word *harbeh* is simply a concession to human weakness, a recognition that man cannot be entirely blameless but can avoid great wickedness (cf. v. 20; thus Whybray, 1978:197).

7:18. "The one" and "the other" (*zeh . . . zeh*) refer to the two counsels given in vv. 16-17, since there is nothing else in the context that one should "take hold of" and "not let go of".

Yeṣe' 'et kullam probably means "do his duty by both", sc., by the two counsels in vv. 16-17 (Targum, Rashi, Delitzsch, et al.). This explanation, it must be admitted, requires the assumption that the idiom *yaṣa' y*^{e}*dey ḥobah*, first attested in the Mishna, had by Qohelet's time already been shortened to *yaṣa'*. Others take *yeṣe'* here to mean "leave", "escape" (e.g., Hertzberg, Zimmerli; thus LXX, Sym, Syr [emending *nqp* to *npq*]). But "escape" does not work as a translation of *yeṣe'*, since the dir. obj., "both of them" (*kullam*), has its antecedent in the immediately preceding pronouns ("this . . . this"), which refer to desirable behaviors.

7:19. See after 7:12.

7:20. To be human is to be flawed, so one should not expect too great a degree of righteousness in anyone.

7:21-22. To the phrase *kol hadd*^{e}*barim 'ăšer y*^{e}*dabberu* LXX (B, S), Syr, and Tar add "the wicked". This is a gloss restricting the scope of the warning to words spoken by evildoers, lest one think that it refers to the reproof of the wise as well.

The teaching of these verses is incidental to v. 20: Do not pay attention to the conversations of others, lest you hear people—even your own slave—reviling you. You know that people may be demeaning you, since you yourself have often done just that to others. Verse 22 does not give a reason for ignoring insults; rather it explains why you are likely to hear insults if you listen too carefully. The purpose of this advice is not to encourage tolerance for others' flaws but to reduce the chances of causing oneself unpleasantness.

7:23–8:1a

(23) All this I tested with wisdom. I said, "I will understand <it>",[a] but it was remote from me. (24) Remote indeed is that which happens, and very deep. Who can apprehend it?

(25) I turned, together with my heart, to understand and to explore and to seek out wisdom and calculation, and to understand

wickedness, stupidity, [b]and folly <and> madness.[b] (26) And I found woman more bitter than death, for she is nets, and her heart is snares, her hands bonds. He whom God likes will escape her, but he who is offensive will be caught by her. (27) See, that is what I have found, said <the> Qohelet,[c] [as I added] one to one to find a solution. (28) <A [good] woman>[d] I continually sought but did not find. One [good] person in a thousand I did find, but a [good] woman in all these I did not find. (29) Only, see, this I did find: God makes people straight, but they seek out great solutions.

(8:1a) Who is <so>[e] wise, and who knows the meaning of anything?

[a] point *'eḥkāmehā* (MT *'eḥkāmāh*) [b–b] *w^eśiklut w^ehôlēlôt* (MT *w^ehaśśiklut hôlēlôt*) [c] *'āmar haqqōhelet* (MT *'ām^{e}rāh qōhelet*) [d] *'iššāh* (MT *'ăšer*) [e] *kōh ḥākām* (MT *k^eheḥākām*)

Most commentators (including Delitzsch, Barton, Podechard, Gordis, and Zimmerli) close this unit at v. 29, others at 8:1 (Hertzberg, Galling, Lauha, Ellermeier [1967:138], et al.). Some divide this passage into two units, either at v. 25 (Zimmerli, Lauha) or at v. 26 (Gordis). In fact, the unit beginning at 7:23 closes in 8:1a (Fox-Porten, 1979; Lohfink, 1979), which is a general statement that recapitulates 7:23f. Qoh 8:1a and 7:23f. form an inclusio by the repetition of ḤKM (twice in 7:23f., once in 8:1a) and by the recurrence of rhetorical questions beginning with "who" (once in 7:23f., twice in 8:1a). The unit does not include 8:1b, which introduces a topic (ingratiation) that relates to the advice in 8:2-6 (behavior before the king) rather than to the matters treated in 7:23-8:1a.

Verses 23-24 summarize Qohelet's investigation so far, while vv. 25-29 focus on a particular undertaking, his "search" for a woman. Although "I turned" in v. 25 marks a new observation, the passage that begins there is linked to the preceding by the theme-words *biqqeš* and *maṣa'* and by the inclusio that 8:1a forms with 7:23.

A. Inaccessibility of knowledge: A. 7:23-24, A′. 8:1a
Theme words: ḤKM (*baḥokmah* / *ḥakam*); rhetorical questions with "who can . . .?" (*mi yimṣa'ennu* / *mi koh ḥakam umi yode'a . . .*)

B. The discovery: woman's danger and man's circuitousness: 7:25-29
Theme words: BQŠ (*baqqeš* / *biqšah*; *biqšu*); *ḥešbon* (*ḥešbon* / *ḥešbon*; *ḥišbonot*); MṢ' (*moṣe'* / *maṣa'ti*; *limṣo'*; *maṣa'ti*)

Despite the efforts of some exegetes, this passage remains irreparably misogynistic. Qoh 9:9, where woman is listed alongside other things from which a man can derive pleasure, does not ameliorate the sourness of this passage. Lohfink (1979) effectively argues against other attempts to soften its acidity, but his own attempt is no more persuasive. According to Lohfink, in 7:26 Qohelet cites a traditional saying in order to argue (in vv. 27f.) with traditional wisdom. But Lohfink fails to show either that Qohelet is attributing the remark in v. 26 to someone else or that he in any way rejects that opinion. *Moṣe' 'ăni* can only introduce Qohelet's own conclusion, not an opinion he repudiates. Moreover, the sentiments of those verses are far from the attitudes of traditional Wisdom. (Only Ben Sira makes genuinely misogynistic remarks [25:24; 42:13f.]. But even he reserves most of his spleen for the evil or loose woman [esp. 9:3-9; 25:13-26], while expressing appreciation for the benefits a good wife brings [esp. 26:1-18; 36:22-25].) According to Lohfink's tortuous analysis, Qohelet is quoting a claim that woman is "stronger" (*mar*) than death (but who would claim that?), then replying that the people he observed were, after a while, not to be found (in other words, they had died), and all women had proved mortal (p. 283). But this interpretation has Qohelet contrasting the woman's mortality with the occasional immortality of men—a strange notion that would occur to no one. In any case, Qohelet's answer, thus understood, hardly contradicts or even softens 7:26. Qohelet remains a misogynist.

While Qohelet does not contradict the sentiments of 7:26-28, he may not intend his dyspeptic words to be taken too seriously. There are signs of a somewhat wry, ironic tone in this unit, suggesting that Qohelet does not intend to give all his remarks the weight of philosophical statements. Griping about the dangers of the opposite sex is a commonplace of ordinary banter, folk songs, and even serious literature throughout the world. As a continuation of 7:23-24, this section, with its ironic self-undermining calculations, serves to demonstrate the remoteness of wisdom.

7:23-24. These verses summarize Qohelet's investigation so far by reformulating 1:13 and stating his conclusion. In 1:13 he decided "to investigate and to explore with wisdom all that occurs under the heavens". *Lidroš w^{e}latur* in 1:13 is functionally synonymous with *nissiti* in 7:23; *baḥokmah* appears in both verses; and *kol 'ăšer na'ăśah* *taḥat haššamayim* in 1:13 is equivalent to *mah šehayyah* in 7:24; which refers to the same thing as *zoh* in 7:23, namely, all that happens in life.

By the usual understanding of this verse, Qohelet says that he decided to become wise but found it impossible. The problem with this interpretation is that Qohelet insists throughout that he succeeded quite well in becoming wise, and he never denies that his knowledge, whatever its limitations, was truly wisdom (and the epilogist agrees: 12:9). In fact, in 7:23 itself he says that he availed himself of wisdom in his search. Most commentators understand the *ḥokmah* implied by *'eḥkamah* as different in degree or kind from the wisdom that Qohelet does claim to have. Delitzsch, for example, takes *'eḥkamah* as expressing a wish "sie [Weisheit] voll und ganz zu besitzen d.h. doch wol: nicht blos gründliche Beobachtungen verzeichnen und probehaltige Rathschläge ertheilen, sondern die Widersprüche des Lebens ausgleichen, die Räthsel des Diesseits und Jenseits lösen und überhaupt die den Menschen peinigenden wichtigsten und höchsten Fragen beantworten zu können". But can we really extract all that from the verb *ḥakam*? And would the inability to obtain this degree of knowledge be considered a failure to become wise? At any rate, Qohelet is not so arrogant as to demand a degree of wisdom no sage ever claimed, wisdom of a breadth obviously reserved for God. Furthermore, Qohelet does not draw a quantitative distinction between accessible and inaccessible degrees of *ḥokmah*. Wisdom is attainable; Qohelet's complaint is not that he lacked a certain degree of wisdom, but that human wisdom itself does not reach as far as he would like.

Gordis too understands *'eḥkamah* to refer to a special kind of wisdom, namely "*ḥokmah* par excellence", the "fundamental" or "speculative" wisdom, as distinct from the "lower" or "practical" wisdom. This distinction (which the Israelite sages would not have drawn) is of no help here, because the type of wisdom claimed by Qohelet includes not only "practical" wisdom but also "speculative" wisdom, the "organon" (see Gordis, p. 199) whereby he explored "all that occurs under the heavens" (1:13).

One solution to the problem is to maintain *'eḥkamah* but to identify the antecedent of *w^{e}hi'* (in the clause "but it [*w^{e}hi'*] was far from me") as *zoh* rather than "wisdom", a notion implicit in *'eḥkamah*. On behalf of this identification we may note that *w^{e}hi'* *r^{e}ḥoqah mimmenni* is immediately rephrased as *raḥoq mah šehayah*, suggesting that *w^{e}hi'* is equivalent to *mah šehayah*, i.e., all that occurs. By this interpretation, Qohelet is saying: "I determined to become wise (and succeeded in this); nevertheless the events of life were beyond my comprehension". The problem is that "I said" expresses intention but not necessarily fulfillment.

A better alternative is to vocalize *'ḥkmh* as *'eḥkameha*, "I will understand it", an Aramaism equivalent to *'eda'eha* (Ginsberg). As Ginsberg observes, the sentence *'amarti 'ḥkmh ... mi yimṣa'ennu* is rephrased (and generalized) in 8:17b as *w^{e}gam 'im yo'mar heḥakam lada'at lo' yukal limṣo'*. This interpretation too takes the antecedent of *hi'* as *zoh*. Qohelet is saying: "I examined by wisdom all that occurs in the world; I determined to understand it, but it [sc., all that occurs] was beyond my grasp".

7:24. *Mah šehayah* signifies "that which happens", as in 1:9; 3:15; and 6:10; it is virtually synonymous with *ma'ăśeh ha'ĕlohim*, "what God brings to pass". This is what Qohelet's wisdom did not suffice to grasp. Qoh 7:24a thus rephrases v. 23b, while v. 24b generalizes with a categorical denial: *no one* can understand what happens in life.

Syr and LXX (+ Syh) read *mšhyh*, "more than it was". MT is preferable, because Qohelet nowhere suggests that his investigation brought him *farther* away from the understanding he sought.

Maṣa' is a near-synonym of *yada'*, as is clear in 8:17, where *lada'at* is resumed by *limṣo'* in the last clause of the verse.

7:25. Qohelet, in a way reminiscent of Egyptian usage, thinks of his heart as an entity distinct from his ego, the "I"; see §3.211.

The syntax of MT v. 25b is difficult. Treating *reša' kesel w^{e}haśśiklut holelot* as two sets of double accusatives and translating "wickedness is foolishness, and folly is madness" (Gordis, Barton, Delitzsch, et al.) produces a banality and leaves the last clause without relation to context. LXX (καὶ τοῦ γνῶναι ἀσεβοῦς ἀφροσύνην καὶ σκληρίαν καὶ περιφοράν) can be retroverted to *wld't rs' ksl wsklwt whwllwt*, according to which all four nouns are direct objects of *lada'at*. Minimally we should read *whwllwt* with LXX and Syr (as Euringer observes, LXX would probably have rendered *wsklwt hwllwt* with a genitive construction, as it did for the first two nouns). In 1:17 and 2:12 as well, "folly" and "madness" are coordinated. We should probably follow LXX also in reading *w^{e}śiklut* without an article.

Qohelet sets out to understand all sorts of human capabilities and dispositions. *Ḥešbon* refers to both the process of reckoning and the solution reached. Its semantic range is well reflected by LXX's λογισμός (v. 29), which designates both the calculation and the solution.

7:26. The "wickedness, stupidity, and folly and madness" that Qohelet now observes turn out to be ensnarement by a woman. There is bathos in these words: the result of his search in the lofty realms of intellect is just this: a woman is dangerous. The irony is heightened by the play on "heart": Qohelet's heart, which accompanies him on his investigation (7:25), leads him to an awareness of the woman's "heart". The unusual phrase, *'ănî wᵉlibbî* in v. 25 (confirmed by LXX and Syr) both focuses attention on the word "heart" and presents Qohelet's heart as an independent entity ready to meet—and be caught by—the woman's heart.

Mar means "bitter", not "strong". Pardee (1978:257-66) throws doubt on the existence of an independent root MRR "strong" in BH. With regard to this verse he points out that death is associated with bitterness elsewhere (see esp. 1 Sam 15:32—certainly the *strength* of death has not departed from Agag), and the evil woman is associated with death in Prov 5:4.

'ašer may be a causal conjunction or a relative adjective. If it is a relative adjective, the clause is not restrictive, as if Qohelet were condemning only those women who fit the description. 7:28 shows that he is directing his remarks against womankind as a whole.

Ṭob lipney ha'ĕlohim and *ḥote'*: As in 2:26 (*q.v.*), "he whom God likes" and "he who is offensive" [sc., to God] may be no more or less virtuous than others. In 2:26, and probably here as well, Qohelet calls a man pleasing or offensive to God in accordance with his fate rather than his deeds. This verse is probably a play on Prov 18:22, "He who finds a woman finds something good, and receives favor from the Lord". *Ṭob lipney ha'ĕlohim* is synonymous with "receives favor" (*mepiq raṣon*). Qohelet's comments on women in general resemble what is said about the "strange" woman (i.e., the woman who is not yours) in Proverbs; note especially Prov 22:14: "A deep pit is the mouth of strange women; he who is cursed by the Lord will fall therein"; similarly Prov 23:27.

7:27. MT's *'mrh qhlt* should be redivided to read *'mr hqhlt*, as in 12:8. "Qohelet" is here treated as a common noun.

The pronoun *zeh* is not prospective, because nothing mentioned in the following verse may be said to have been "found" except for "one person in a thousand", but that is not the result of the (fruitless) search described in v. 27b. The pronoun apparently refers to the statement in the preceding verse (thus the translation "that"), which presents the conclusion Qohelet has just arrived at (Hertzberg). Qohelet is saying, "See where my painstaking search led me: to the knowledge that woman is a menace!"

Qohelet emphasizes the arithmetical nature of the *ḥešbon* he is making. He added one to one—a painstaking process—to arrive at a sum total, a *ḥešbon*. He may be hinting rather wryly that he scrutinized the field of womanhood no less carefully than the other pleasures he finds absurd and mad.

7:28. This verse rephrases the conclusion stated in v. 26. The syntax of MT is difficult. As a relative clause, *'ăšer 'od biqša napši w^elo' maṣa'ti* lacks a relevant antecedent. *Ḥešbon* does not provide a meaningful antecedent because in v. 28b Qohelet goes on to specify precisely what *ḥešbon* he found. As a nominal clause *'ăšer . . . maṣa'ti* would be hanging in the air. *'ăšer* cannot resume *zeh* of v. 27, which refers to what he found, because the clause *'ăšer . . . w^elo' maṣa'ti* speaks of something he did *not* find. Therefore it is best to follow Ehrlich's conjectural emendation of *'šr* to *'šh*. Orthographically the change is very slight (see the qere-ketiv variants in 1 Kgs 22:49; for other possible examples see Delitzsch, 1920:§§116c, 123b), and it produces a simple and meaningful construction: "A woman I sought continually but did not find". *'od* = "continually", as in Gen 46:29; Ruth 1:14; Ps 84:5. The rest of the verse emphasizes the validity of this conclusion by pointing out the broad statistical base of the survey.

'adam, here as elsewhere in Qohelet and almost always in the HB, means *homo*, not *vir*. *'iššah* is a subset of *'adam*; in other words: "Out of a thousand people I found one (good) one, but even within this thousandth part of the population ['all these'] I could not find a single (good) woman".

Virtually all commentators take *'adam* and *'iššah* as elliptical for "a good person" and "a good woman" or the like (Hertzberg: "das Weib, im rechten und höchsten Sinne"; Lauha: "eine echte, tadellose Frau"; similarly Delitzsch, Barton, Podechard, Gordis, et al.). It is unclear how much one should read into these terms, but certainly in this context both imply approbation. (He could not say that he found only one *male* in a thousand.) Such an ellipsis does not appear elsewhere with *'iššah* or *'adam*. (It does occur with *'iš* in 1 Sam 4:9b; 26:15; 1 Kgs 2:2; and most clearly in Avot 2:5. These cases are not, however, quite comparable, because in them the context refers to masculinity and the associated virtues, and these allow *'iš* to connote excellence.) The unusual elliptical terminology in Qoh 7:28 may be intended to allow for a double entendre with the phrase *maṣa' 'iššah*, which also means to find a wife. (Ehrlich takes *'iššah* in v. 28 to mean "wife", but the rest of his exegesis of this passage is forced and based on an arbitrary emendation.) *Maṣa' 'iššah* means "find a wife" in Prov 18:22 (this is the only sense in which one could legitimately "find a woman"). *'iššah*, undefined and not in a bound construction, means "wife" in Prov 19:14b as well (a man would receive a woman "from the Lord" only as a wife). Qohelet may be hinting that for all his searching and calculating, he did not succeed in finding a wife (9:9 does not show that he did).

7:29. The use of *l^{e}bad* to introduce a main clause is unparalleled in BH. It is probably a calque on Aramaic *l^{e}ḥud*, commonly used at the beginning of sentences (Ginsberg explains *l^{e}bad* as a translation of it). *L^{e}ḥud* translates introductory *raq* in the Targumim to Gen 19:8; Exod 8:24, 25; Num 20:19; Deut 12:15; and often.

'ŚH: Here alone in Qohelet does *'aśah* mean "create", "make", when predicated of God.

In this verse too *'adam* means *homo*, its usual sense. In the lack of a contrast to "woman", *'adam* refers to the broader category.

Yašar, "straight" or "straightforward" here refers not to moral integrity but to intellectual directness or simplicity, as is indicated by the contrast between it and "seeking solutions".

Rabbim = "great" (Ginsberg; cf. 10:6). It is not so much the quantity of the sought-for solutions that bothers Qohelet as their qualitative "greatness".

What Qohelet finally found as a result of all his *ḥešbon*-seeking is simply this: man(kind) seeks great *ḥišš^{e}bonot*. This is clearly self-directed irony. Qohelet is the one who sought a *ḥešbon* and got himself all tangled up in his calculations (v. 25). The entire book of Qohelet, in fact, tells of his search for *ḥišš^{e}bonot*. Such cogitation, he says here, is contrary to the way man was created. Yet elsewhere he tells us that God himself placed this desire in man's heart (1:13; 3:11).

8:1a. Interrogative "who?", occurs 15 times in the book, each time in a rhetorical question where it means "no one". Here, as in 2:16b, Qohelet recapitulates an earlier generalization (2:14b; 7:23f.) by a rhetorical question.

MT's *my khḥkm* should be divided *my kh ḥkm* (Aq, Sym, and probably LXX, in which τίς οἶδεν σοφούς is derived from ΤΙΣ ΩΔΕ ΣΟΦΟΣ—see Euringer). The Massoretic word division in v. 1aα produces a sentence that evaluates the wise man positively: no one (else) is like the wise man. But since v. 1aβ can only mean that no one knows the meaning of a matter, we require a negative evaluation also in v. 1aα, i.e., a statement of the limits of the wise man's capacity for understanding. A declaration of the incomparability of the wiseman would require a sentence like *umi kamohu yodea' pešer dabar*. *Dabar* (unlike *haddabar*) need not refer to any specific word or thing but may mean "something, anything" (BDB 183b).

Verse 1aβ restates v. 1aα. We may paraphrase the half-verse by putting 8:1a in the indicative and combining the two parts: No one is so wise as to understand the meaning of anything. This statement is hyperbolic but understandable, since Qohelet has defined the kind of knowledge that no one can have. Together these rhetorical questions reiterate *mi yimṣa'ennu*, "no one can apprehend it" (7:24). The question *mi koh ḥakam*, "who is so wise?", echoes *'amarti 'ḥkmh* (in either pointing). In 7:23 and 8:1aα (as in 2:18-20 + 21-23), Qohelet makes a statement about himself and then reformulates it as a general rule.

8:1b-9

(1b) A man's wisdom illuminates his face,
while the impudence of his face [a]changes <it>.[a]

(2) Obey the king's orders, and with regard to the oath of God (3) be not hasty. Leave his presence; do not tarry in a bad situation. For he can do whatever he wishes, (4) inasmuch as king's word is authority, and who dare say to him, "What are you doing?"

(5) He who keeps a command will experience no misfortune, and the wise man's heart should be aware of the time of judgment (6) (for every matter has a time < . . . >[b], for man's evil weighs heavy upon him. (7) For he does not know *what* will happen, for none can tell him *when* it will happen.

(8) No man has authority over the life-spirit so as to imprison the life-spirit, and there is no authority in the day of death, and there is no release in war, and wickedness will not let its possessor escape.
(9) All this I observed as I gave thought to all that happens under the sun when one man has authority over another to his harm.

[a]—[a] *yešann'ennû* (MT *yešunne' 'ănî*) [b] omit *ûmišpāṭ*

Observations on the theme of authority. Warnings about behavior in the presence of a king, whose command must be obeyed, lead to the theme of keeping a command, then to the question of the time of judgment. Verse 5 is the pivotal verse, where the subject changes from royal commands to the time set for judgment. In both form and in content v. 5 has the appearance of a conventional proverb, and we may surmise that Qohelet quotes it in order to cap off his counsels on how to behave in the king's presence, after which he continues with the theme introduced in the second stich of the proverb. Verses 5b-7 digress from the topic of human authority. Verse 8 returns to this topic, emphasizing the limitations inherent in human powers. Although vv. 8-9 do not directly continue the thought of the foregoing verses, they are part of the same unit as 8:1-7, since the conclusion in v. 9, which speaks of "all this", must apply to all that has been said about authority, not only to v. 8.

The argument develops in 8:2-7 much the same as in 3:16-17. Qohelet observes injustices people commit, takes comfort in his belief that judgment will eventually be executed, then finds that comfort undermined—in 3:18-21 by the universality of death, in 8:7 by human ignorance of the time of judgment. See further §§4.2, 4.4.

8:1b-2. MT's "and the impudence of his face is changed" is awkward, as is *'ănî* at the beginning of v. 2. Also, one who possessed wisdom to start with would not have impudence that required changing. Verse 2 is hardly a solution to a riddle supposedly asked in v. 1; nothing has been asked to which Qohelet could volunteer an answer. Nor is *'ănî* likely to be short for "I say" (Gordis); such a usage is unparalleled in BH and only vaguely paralleled in the Gemarah. The problems of vv. 1b-2a are solved by reading *yešann'ennu*, "changes it" (sc. his face). The consonantal change is minor, from *yšn' 'ny* to *yšn'nw*. MT's *'ny* is not represented in LXX, Syr, or Targum.

"Change one's face" means to change the facial expression, making it cheerful or sullen. This is clearly the meaning of the idiom in Sir 12:18 and 13:25,[19] where the unusual spelling *yšn'* shows that Sira is probably influenced by the usage in Qoh 8:1. (When verbs III-' and III-H coalesce in MH, they take the form of III-H, so this verb is not simply an expected protomishnaic development.) A man's wisdom will not make him actually happy in the presence of a despot, but it does teach him to put on a cheerful guise and to ingratiate himself with whoever is in power. Impudence, on the other hand, makes a man dare to change his look to a scowl, and this may well put him in a "bad situation" with the ruler.

8:2-3. The syntax of vv. 2b-3a in MT does not support the meaning commonly derived from these words. *w^e'al dibrat* does not mean "and that, because of" (Gordis; similarly Barton, Hertzberg). The *waw* is intrusive; it does not "emphasize the reason" (Gordis) but separates it from the foregoing. (GKC §154a, note 1(b) does not apply here; none of the examples listed there have a *waw* before a causal or motive clause or phrase.) And while *'al tibbahel mippanayw telek* could mean "do not hasten to go from his presence" (in accordance with GKC §120g), this advice does not accord with the next sentence, "do not tarry [lit., stand] in a bad situation". An adversative particle (at least a *waw*) would be required to mark an adversative relation between v. 3aα and v. 3aβ.

The verse division belongs after *tibbahel* (thus LXX and Syr; Ginsberg). By this division, 8:2b counsels circumspection in swearing oaths, and v. 3 advises leaving the king's presence when he is angry. MT makes obedience to the king a moral issue based on an oath sworn in God's name rather than just a matter of prudence, as it clearly is in vv. 3f. Ahiqar 101-104, quoted by Ginsberg in this context, is a striking parallel that validates the interpretation favored here. The suggested division does, however, leave the sentence *w^e'al . . . tibbahel* without close connection to the context. Perhaps

19. The Greek to Sir 25:17 has "changes her face" where the Hebrew has "darkens his face." In spite of the different pronoun, the Greek shows the meaning of "changes the face" by using that phrase to translate "darkens the face", which means to cause a surly countenance.

the sentence implies: do not be hasty to swear innocence when the ruler is angry at you; just leave his presence.

8:5. Instead of taking v. 5a as a radical reversal of Qohelet's awareness that righteous people may indeed suffer "something bad" (a fact known to even the most conventional sages), we should understand the scope of this statement to be restricted by context. Verse 5a points back to vv. 2-4, with *šomer miṣwah* echoing *pi melek šᵉmor*. The command one must obey is the king's, not (in this context) God's (Delitzsch, Gordis, Hertzberg, Ginsberg, et al.). (God's commands are not mentioned in didactic Wisdom Literature prior to Ben Sira.) The *dabar ra'* of v. 5 echoes the *dabar ra'* of v. 3, though there it refers to an action that angers the king, here to something the king may do when angry.

8:5-6. *'et umišpaṭ* (v. 5) is a hendiadys equivalent to *'et mišpaṭ* (Ginsburg, Delitzsch, Ginsberg, et al.). The latter form may in fact be the correct reading; it is reflected in LXX's καιρὸν κρίσεως in v. 5 (LXX represents the *waw* in v. 6). Qohelet elsewhere says that God "makes everything happen appropriately in its time" (3:11a and 8:6a), but man cannot know when that will come (3:11b and 8:7).

The phrase *'et umišpaṭ* alone might mean "the appropriate time and manner of procedure" (Gordis), but in this sentence that idea would lack connection to context and would not lead into the complaint of v. 6b, that "man's evil weighs heavy upon him". Rather, the phrase probably means "time of judgment" (Ginsberg, Hertzberg cf. LXX). Qoh 3:16-17 follows the same sequence of thought: observation of human evil (3:16; cf. 8:1b-4) leads to the thought that God will *judge* everyone, because every *matter* (*ḥepeṣ*), including judgment, has a *time* (3:17; cf. 8:6a). The statement about the enormity of human evil (8:6) suggests that the *mišpaṭ* in v. 5 concerns evildoing.

Verse 5b asserts that the wise man will know (perhaps "should know") the "time of judgment" (*'et umišpaṭ*). This seems to contradict vv. 6b-7—and other statements in Qohelet (e.g., 6:12; 7:14b)—which assert that man cannot know the time of an occurrence. Verse 5b is best construed to mean that the wise man knows that there *is* a time of judgment. *Yeda'*, then, means being aware of, knowing about, rather than knowing the details. Awareness that the despot will face judgment may provide some comfort to his suffering subjects and allow the wise man to maintain composure in the despot's presence. Outward behavior ("keeping a commandment") is contrasted with inner knowledge (thus the formulation, "the wise man's heart"; see Levy). Knowing the "time of judgment" means being able to say to oneself, as Qohelet does in 3:17, "God will judge the righteous and the wicked, for there is a time for every matter . . .". But this is slim comfort, for the despot may be a "wicked man who lives long in his wickedness".

8:6. We should probably omit *umišpaṭ* in v. 6a. It may have arisen under the influence of the word in the preceding line (Ginsberg). While it is true that every *deed* has a time of judgment, and that everything, including judgment, has a time, it is not true that everything has a time of *judgment*.

Awareness of human evil weighs heavily on man, on the wise man in particular; thus he should remember that a day of reckoning for the despot will come. In v. 6b, the antecedent of "(weighs heavy upon) him" may be the wise man of v. 5 or the "man" of v. 6b. In the latter case, this verse resembles 1:13 and 3:10 in ascribing to mankind in general a task or burden that is actually the wise man's in particular, for it is he who seeks understanding and who is most aware of life's evils.

8:7 explains why man's evil weighs heavily upon him. If one knew when the reckoning will come, he might not be so oppressed by awareness of social injustice.

8:8. This verse points back to the theme of "control" in v. 4 and reminds us that, however powerful the authority (*šilṭon*, v. 4) that one man may wield over others, no one has control (*šilṭon*) over his life-spirit in the day of death. Death, if nothing else, frees man from human tyranny (Job 3:17-19).

Weʾeyn mišlaḥat bammilḥamah: Although we expect another reference to the inescapability of death, there is no evidence that dying itself was viewed as a battle, a "Todeskampf" (Ehrlich). Ginsberg (p. 41) hypothesizes that *milḥamah* translates *bqrbʾ*, a corruption of an original *bqbrʾ*, "in the grave". "Grave" undoubtedly fits the context better than "war". The Aramaic translation theory is attractive here, but even if we accept this retroversion we are left with the question of the meaning of "war" for the presumptive translator. The meaning of *mišlaḥat* is likewise unclear, but "release" is the most likely meaning, since this verse denies the possibility of *escape*. But the meaning of this sentence has not yet been satisfactorily explained.

8:9 shows that the particular form of evil (*reša'*) Qohelet has in mind is the wickedness of the ruler. The clause "will not let its possessor escape" may be a litotes for "will keep him from escaping" (sc., an early death).

8:9. 'ŚH (*kol hamma'ăśeh 'ăšer na'ăśah taḥat haššameš*): Qohelet is not observing what people *do* when they have authority so much as what *happens* as a result of this authority.

8:10-15

> (10a) And then I saw the wicked [a]<brought to>[a] burial, and they proceeded from the holy place[b], while those who had acted honestly were neglected in the city.
>
> (10b) This too is an absurdity: (11) the sentence for a wicked deed is not carried out quickly; for which reason peoples' hearts are intent on doing evil. (12) For an offender may do evil <for years>[c] but live long, although I know too that it will go well with God-fearing people, because they are afraid of him, (13) and that it will not go well with the wicked man, and, like a shadow, he will not last long, because he is not afraid of God. (14) There is an absurdity that happens on the earth: there are righteous people who receive what is appropriate to the deeds of the wicked, and there are wicked people who receive what is appropriate to the deeds of the righteous. I said that this too is an absurdity.
>
> (15) So I praised pleasure, because there is nothing good for man under the sun but to eat, drink, and experience enjoyment, and this will accompany him in his toil throughout the days of his life which God has given him under the sun.

[a]—[a] *qᵉbārîm mūbā'îm* (MT *qᵉbûrîm wābā'û*)
[b] point *ûmimmāqôm* (MT *ûmimmᵉqôm*) [c] *mē'āz* (MT *mᵉ'at*)

Inequities in the ways society (v. 10a) and God (vv. 11-14) treat the wicked and the righteous. In 8:11-14, as in 2:18-26, Qohelet describes a situation in several ways, calling it repeatedly an absurdity. The absurdity described here is that an offender (= a sinner) may live a long life, while a righteous person may die young. Since the punishment that Qohelet has in mind in this passage is a divinely imposed death sentence, delaying punishment is tantamount to failure to carry it out. *Hebel* throughout this unit is predicated of a situation or event rather than of an act.

8:10a. Instead of MT's meaningless *qbrym wb'w wmmqwm*, LXX (εἰς τάφους εἰσαχθέντας καὶ ἐκ τόπου ἁγίου) reflects *qbrym mwb'ym*[20] *wmmqwm*, definitely the preferable reading. Syr too treats *qbrym* as a passive participle, but it agrees with MT otherwise. The plural *qbrym*, attested by all Versions and supported by the use of the plural (*q^e barot*) in Job 21:32, may be a plural of abstraction ("burial"; cf. Job 17:1) or a plural of composition referring to a sepulcher compounded of many individual graves (2 Chr 35:24; cf. also 2 Chr 16:14; 2 Kgs 22:20; Neh 3:16).

Job complains of the very injustice Qohelet describes: "But he [sc., the wicked man] is brought [*yubal*—passive, like the proposed *muba'im*] to burial . . . and everyone proceeds after him, and before him people without number" (Job 21:32f.).

The "holy place" is either the temple (the "holy place" of Matt 24:15) or the synagogue—certainly not the cemetery, which was ritually unclean, not holy. The lack of the article favors the identification of the "holy place" with the synagogue, and this is supported by an inscription from 'Ain Dak, which refers to the synagogue as *'tr' qdyšh* (Montgomery, 1924:243). By this interpretation, the verse presupposes a custom of honoring a dead person by beginning the funeral procession at the synagogue. A custom of eulogizing the dead (*hesped*) in the synagogue is attested in the Talmud (b. *Meg.* 28b; b. *Rosh Hashanah* 25a; b. *Moed Q.* 21b). We should probably point *maqom* as absolute, as in Lev 6:9, 19, 20; etc.; see GKC §128w, n. 1 (MT may be understanding *qadoš* as an epithet of God).

Verse 10aβ is generally thought to mean that the remembrance of honest people is lost soon after their death. But that fate would not distinguish them from the wicked, since "in the days to come both [the fool and the wise man] are soon forgotten" (2:16), and furthermore the phrase "in the city" is superfluous if *w^e yištakk^e ḥu*

20. The retroversion of εἰσαχθέντας to *muba'im* is not certain, since εἰσάγω-passive twice represents BW'-qal (Num 27:17 [though there it is used in a free rendering of a fixed idiom] and 1 Kgs 7:14 [LXX 7:2]). Of the 23 times that BW'-hophal occurs in the Bible, it is represented by εἰσάγω-passive only three times; it is, however, represented by other compounds of ἄγω in the passive five times. In Aq, εἰσάγω (only active) always represents BW'-hiphil, so this verb in the passive is an expected rendering of the hophal.

means that the memory of them is lost, for they are forgotten everywhere. Rather, we are to understand the last sentence (*w^eyištakk^eḥu* ... *'aśu*) to mean that the bodies of honest people lie neglected at the time of their death. The wicked, in unfair contrast, are taken from the city in procession to the cemetery. This is not to say that the bodies of the dead are left within the city forever, but rather that immediately after their death, the wicked are treated with honor and the righteous neglected. ŠKḤ can imply actual neglect rather than a failure of memory; e.g., Ps 9:19 (of neglecting a poor person, not caring for him); Ps 102:5 (of neglecting to eat one's food); Isa 49:15 (of a woman neglecting her baby); Deut 24:19 (of leaving a sheaf lying in the field). (The reading *wyštbḥw*, "were praised" [LXX, Aq, and some MSS], requires taking *ken* to mean "thus", but the verse does not mention anything that the wicked "did" which "thus" could resume.)

8:10b. I take the *hebel*-judgment in 8:10b as introducing a new passage (thus Wildeboer, Ginsberg). If "this too is hebel" is taken as retrospective, in accordance with the Massoretic verse-division, *'ăšer* in v. 11 lacks a discernible function. Causality would be inappropriate, since v. 11 does not motivate v. 10, and *'ăšer* as a causal conjunction is never prospective. *'ăšer* is here the nominalizing particle (best translated "namely" or represented by a colon), just as in v. 14a, where the same case is reformulated (cf. also 9:1aβ). To be sure, the exact phrase *gam zeh hebel* does not elsewhere introduce a description, but Qohelet does label a phenomenon *hebel* before describing it in 8:14 (and cf. 4:7). Furthermore, the introductory phase in 5:15, *w^egam zoh ra'ah ḥolah*, which introduces the description of a misfortune, is syntactically identical to *gam zeh hebel* in 8:10b, except for the additional *waw*, which should perhaps be read in this verse as well (haplography; thus Ginsberg). This arrangement is, of course, far from certain. But whether the phrase is applied to 8:10a or to 8:11-13, the meaning of *hebel* is the same, because both passages describe an unjust, absurd situation.

8:11-12a. Verse 12a motivates v. 11 by explaining in what way the sentence may be delayed. In v. 11 Qohelet is not denying the working of divine retribution in all cases, but rather observing that there are cases where God postpones the punishment, in other words, lets the guilty man live long. *Ma'ărik lo* = *ma'ărik lo yamim*. The subject of *ma'ărik* may be the man (as in v. 13a) or God (as in 1 Kgs 3:14).

'ăšer functions as a noun-substitute (Ginsberg) and allows the following sentence to stand in apposition to a preceding noun or noun-clause (in this case, *hebel*); similarly in 8:14 (second *'ăšer*) and 9:1.

'ŚH: *ma'ăśeh hara'ah*, lit., "the deed of evil", refers to human actions.

". . . people dare to do evil"; lit., "the heart of people is full in them to do evil". Most commentators understand this expression to mean "dare" (Ginsberg, Delitzsch, Gordis, Hertzberg, Lauha, et al.) rather than "be inclined", "desire" (Podechard). The parallel commonly mentioned, *'ăšer mĕla'o libbo la'ăśot*, "whose heart has filled him to do" (Esth 7:5), is itself ambiguous, and, in any case, the expression "(his) heart filled him" may imply something quite different from "(their) heart is full". The heart being "full" of something is a conceptual extension of having something "in" one's heart (see the two phrasings in 9:3bα), and the latter idiom implies desire or intention (Isa 63:4; Jer 20:9; Ps 84:6; Prov 2:10a [note the parallel "be pleasant to your soul" in 10b]; it can also imply knowledge; e.g., Isa 51:7). The notion "desire", "be inclined" fits better than "dare" in Qoh 9:3 as well, for there the phrase *leb . . . male' ra'* is not followed by an infinitive that might indicate what they dare to do.

8:12-13. Here the "offender" is a sinner, as usually in the Bible, for were he not immoral, his long life would not disturb Qohelet's sense of justice.

MT's *m^{e}'at* (requiring the translation "does evil one hundred") is awkward, if not impossible. LXX's ἀπὸ τότε (Syh *mn hydyn*) reflects *me'az*, "from of old", "for years" (ἀπὸ τότε renders *me'az* in Exod 4:10 [Aq]; Pss 76:8; 93:2 [LXX, Sym]; Prov 8:22 [Aq, Theod]); and Isa 16:13 (Theod). LXX's reading hardly comes about from misunderstanding *m't* as a meaningless *me'et* (contrary to Euringer, Gordis), which would have been translated ἀπὸ καιροῦ (as it is in five of its six occurrences). *Me'az* is precisely what is required by the context, to emphasize that the punishment is delayed.

Kaṣṣel is an adverbial modifier to the preceding negative clause, *lo' ya'ărik yamim*.

Ki gam (v. 12b), like *gam ki*, means "although" (Gordis). Verse 12 says: "It is a fact that . . . although I also know that . . .". Although Qohelet "knows" the principle of retribution and nowhere denies it, he *also* knows there are cases that violate the rule. It is because

Qohelet generally maintains the axioms of Wisdom that he is shocked by their violation and finds the aberrations absurd.

Gordis takes 8:12b-13 as a quotation of a conventional idea that Qohelet then rejects in his own words, but nothing indicates that some of these words are the opinion of another person; see Excursus I.

8:14. Qohelet restates vv. 10b-13. In context, the complaint in this verse probably refers specifically to undeserved brevity or length of life rather than to any undeserved fortune or misfortune whatsoever.

'ŚH: *ma'ăśeh haṣṣaddiqim* and *ma'ăśeh harešaʿim* are probably human deeds. It is also possible that the phrases refer to what *happens to* the righteous and the wicked. *Ma'ăśeh* is a collective term.

8:15. *'amal* here seems to refer to toil in a broad sense, for pleasure should accompany a person through all life's activities and efforts.

8:16–9:6

> (16) When I set my heart to gain wisdom and to observe the business that is done on the earth ([a]<my> eyes seeing[a] sleep neither by day nor by night), (17) I saw that man cannot apprehend anything that God brings to pass, that is, the events that occur under the sun, for even if a man seeks arduously, he will not apprehend it. And even if the wise man intends to understand it, he is not able to apprehend it.
>
> (9:1) Now I considered all this carefully, and <my heart saw>[b] all this: the righteous and the wise and their deeds are in the hand of God, but man has no knowledge of love or hate. Everything one sees is (2) <absurd>,[c] inasmuch as all have the same fate: the righteous and the wicked, the good <and the bad>,[d] and the pure and the impure, and he who gives sacrifice and he who does not give sacrifice; the good person just as the offender, the one who swears oaths just as the one who fears to swear oaths. (3) This is the <worst>[e] of all that happens under the sun: everyone has the same fate. Moreover, the human heart is full of evil, and inanity is in their hearts while they live. And afterwards—they join the dead!
>
> (4) Now whoever is still linked to all the living has something that can be relied on (for a live dog is better off than a dead lion), (5) for the living know that they will die, while the dead know nothing and no longer have any recompense, for their memory is forgotten. (6) Even their love, their hatred, and their jealousy have already

perished, and they no longer have a portion in all that happens under the sun.

[a] *b[e]ʿêynay ʾêynennî* (MT *b[e]ʿêynāyw ʾêynennû*)
[b] *w[e]libbî rāʾāh* (MT *w[e]lābûr*) [c] *hebel* (MT *hakkōl*, joined to v. 2). [d] add *w[e]lāraʿ*
[e] *zeh hārāʿ* (MT *zeh rāʿ*)

Argument:

a.	8:16-17 The search for understanding life fails,
b.	9:1 and man cannot know even whether God loves or hates him,
c.	9:2-3 for the universality of death obscures the ways of God's favor.
d.	9:4-6 Still, life is better than non-existence.

8:16–9:6 constitutes a single unit in which two related topics are joined sequentially. 9:1 rephrases and explains the observation of 8:16-17 that people cannot understand what happens in life: they cannot even understand the ways of God's favor, because everything they see is absurd (9:1-2), inasmuch as all people, whatever their merits, suffer the same fate. 9:2 (*kaʾăšer* . . .) is the pivot, linked syntactically to v. 1 while introducing a new topic—death, the ultimate absurdity.

8:16-17. One cannot understand what happens on earth; therefore wisdom, which alone one might think could attain this understanding, can only lead to frustration. These verses echo 1:13-18, where Qohelet set forth his task and told the results.

Ladaʿat ḥokmah in 8:16 means "to attain (or possess) wisdom", as in 1:17, *q.v.* In 1:18, Qohelet said that wisdom leads to misery; in 8:17 he says it leads nowhere, for it cannot achieve its goal of understanding life. Qoh 8:16-17 (a single complex sentence) generalizes the statement of 7:23-24, where Qohelet says that he failed to gain understanding (*mi yimṣaʾennu* in 7:24) of "that which happens", in other words, of "what God brings to pass".

In 8:16a, the "business" (*haʿinyan*) that is done on earth is, as in 1:13, the ceaseless examination, with wisdom, of *maʿăśeh haʾĕlohim*; this business is, in fact, wisdom itself. As in 1:16, Qohelet says that he both gained wisdom (8:16aα) and observed it (v. 16aβ). In 8:17 Qohelet rephrases *maʿăśeh haʾĕlohim* (17a) as *hammaʿăśeh ʾăšer na'ăśah taḥat haššemeš* (17b) (see Ginsberg, Gordis, Ellermeier [1967:299]); these two phrases are equivalent to *hamma'ăśeh 'ăšer 'aśah ha'ĕlohim* in 3:11. All three phrases refer to events. What Qohelet examined and found incomprehensible was nothing less than all that happens on earth.

8:16. *'inyan*: In the precursors of this verse, 1:13 and 3:10, *'inyan* refers to the wise-man's task (epitomized by Qohelet's own). *Ha'inyan 'ašer na'ăśah 'al ha'areṣ* in 8:16aβγ is equivalent to *ḥokmah* in v. 16bα. Wisdom is the activity that is performed day and night without rest.

8:16b requires emendation to the first person. The *waw-yod* confusion this emendation presupposes is less unlikely than the unmotivated switch to the third person.

8:17a. On the syntax see Ellermeier, 1967:295-300. The syntax of 8:17a has a precise parallel in Jon 3:10, where *ki* introduces epexegesis of the dir. obj. of *wayyar'*: "God saw what they had done, namely, that they had repented of their evil ways".

"... cannot apprehend anything": Since *kol ... ha'ĕlohim* is the proleptic direct object of *lo yukal limṣo'*, the *kol* is negatived, and a negatived *kol* may mean "not any" as well as "not all". In this verse, "not any" is to be preferred, rather than imputing to Qohelet the ludicrous complaint that he was unable to understand the totality of the events that God makes happen (similarly in 3:11). On the other hand, "cannot apprehend anything" must be understood in a modified sense, since Qohelet nowhere insists that absolute and utter ignorance is inevitable, and he himself "apprehends" or "finds" (MṢ') many things. Qohelet is asserting that no one can understand the cause and rationale of events in life. Even so, "cannot apprehend anything" is hyperbolic, but it is less unreasonable than the desire, implied by the other translation, to understand *all* of God's activity in human events.

8:17b. *B^ešel 'ăšer* is an Aramaism, from *b^edil d^e-*; a development of this idiom, *b^ešel š^e-*, appears in 4QMMT B 12, C 32 and in a letter of Bar Kokhba (*DJD* II, 165f.) meaning "so that" (Qimron, 1986:89). In this verse, the idiom seems to introduce a causal clause (as the Aramaic idiom can do) rather than a final or result clause.

W^egam 'im yo'mar heḥakam lada'at: This clause is usually understood to refer to the wise man's *claim* to have this knowledge. This understanding is reflected in most translations, for example,

Zimmerli's: "Und auch wenn der Weise behauptet es zu erkennen, er kann es nicht herausfinden". Barton, on the basis of inadequate parallels, translates: "Even if the wise man thinks he is about to know . . .". Delitzsch correctly interprets this phrase in accordance with *'amarti 'ḥkmh* in 7:23, where *'amar* undoubtedly means "intended" rather than "claimed". *'amar* often expresses intention (BDB p. 56a). We may further note that *w^{e}gam 'im yo'mar heḥakam lada'at* rephrases Qohelet's description of his own activity in 8:16: *ka'ăšer natatti 'et libbi lada'at ḥokmah*, with *yo'mar* corresponding to *natatti 'et libbi*, "I determined", lit., "gave my heart", *not* "claimed". The point of the verse is: *even* a wise man—one best equipped to gain knowledge—who undertakes to attain this understanding will fail in the quest.

9:1-2. The opening *ki* is a loose causal particle that explains why the above is said rather than why it is true. (On the "evidential" function of *ki* see Claasen, 1983:37-44.) It is often impossible to render this relation in English without overloading the sentence ("I say all this because . . .").

LXX's καὶ καρδία μου σὺν πᾶν εἶδεν τοῦτο (followed by Syh) shows an inner Greek transposition—literal retroversion would produce an impossible word order in Hebrew. Nevertheless, the Greek does witness to *wlby r'h 't kl* in its *Vorlage*, a reading preferable to MT's syntactically impossible *wlbwr 't*. The only consonantal changes assumed are *w/y*, a very common one, and a loss of *heh* through parablepsis.

'ăbādêyhem (distinguished by the vocalizers from *'abdeyhem*, "their slaves") is an Aramaism equivalent to Hebrew *ma'ăśeyhem* (LXX: ἐργασίαι). This is one of the points where the theory of an Aramaic origin is most persuasive. It is difficult to understand why an author composing in Hebrew would use a common word, *ma'ăśeh*, numerous times, then once choose a unique Aramaism (unattested, as far as I can ascertain, in Hebrew literature before or after Qohelet) that expresses no more than the Hebrew equivalent does. It seems more likely that a translator would understand *'bd'* correctly most of the time but misread it in one occurrence, being misled by seeing that word (*'bdyhwn*) appearing in conjunction with two nouns that refer to classes of people.

Bĕyad ha'ĕlohim, "in the hand of God" means "in God's possession, control"; see Ehrlich's comment on Ezra 7:14. Of course, all people are under God's control. But the righteous and the wise might be thought to have greater power over their fate than most, because (conventional Wisdom teaches) the behavior of the righteous brings the expected blessings, whereas the fate of the wicked is (to them) a surprise. Qohelet insists that the lives and deeds *even* of the wise and righteous are subject to God's free and unpredictable exercise of power.

9:1aβ reformulates 8:16-17, which says that no one can understand *ma'ăśeh ha'ĕlohim*, "God's doing", i.e., all that he brings to pass. To understand "God's doing" means to understand the workings of his favor. "Love" and "hate" in 9:1 are not human emotions in the abstract, as if to say that human psychology is incomprehensible—a point not relevant to the immediate context or to the book as a whole. Rather, "love" and "hate" are God's favor and disfavor toward individuals. It is the *divine* psychology that is obscure. You cannot know whom or what God loves and hates—until you see the effects of his attitude.

Hakkol lipneyhem, lit., "all that is before them", i.e., "all that they see" or (since the 3rd pl. is indefinite) "everything one sees"; cf. the use of *lipney* in *ṭob lipney ha'ĕlohim* (2:26). The verse division should fall before *ka'ăšer*, and *hkl* should be emended to *hbl*. LXX (Syh), Sym, Vul, and Syr read *hbl* at the juncture of vv. 1 and 2. (Syr has a conflate reading, *hbl' kl* = *hbl hkl*.) MT's reading ("Everything is before them. All as to all") is meaningless. The text as emended—"Everything one sees is absurd"—is an amplification of "man has no knowledge of [God's] love or hate". The absurd allocation of fates makes the ways of God's favor inscrutable.

LXX's ἐν τοῖς πᾶσιν is an early corruption of ἐν οἷς τοῖς πᾶσιν (cf. 8:16; 11:5; McNeile, p. 149), ἐν + relative pronoun reflecting *ka'ăšer* as in 4:17; 8:16; and 11:5. Both *ka'ăšer* and *ba'ăšer* can introduce motive or causal clauses.

9:2-3. In 8:11-14 Qohelet observed an injustice that befalls some people—lifespans incommensurate with what they deserve. Now he marks an injustice that is universal—death. Equal fates for unequal persons is an absurdity which not even the fortunate are spared.

Welaṭṭob lacks a pair in an otherwise paired series. We should add *welara'* with LXX (which in this book is too literalistic to have added a word for the sake of literary balance) = Syh, as well as Syr and Vul (independently?).

9:3. Observing the universality of death leads man to inane, irrational behavior. ʿŚH: The verse gives an example of something that *happens*, namely, everyone's having the same fate.

Zeh raʿ bᵉ(kol ʾăšer naʿăśah). Vul, Ibn Ezra, Ginsburg, and others understand this phrase as a superlative, and still others interpret it as a virtual (but not syntactic) superlative (Gordis: "the root of the evil"; Lauha, in comment: "das Grundübel"). A superlative does seem required here, for the universality of death is not a misfortune or evil *in* all events, but rather the worst of all that happens, for it is a fundamental and irreparable inequity. Since the anarthrous noun + *bᵉ-* does not (contrary to Ginsburg) constitute a superlative, we should read *zh hrʿ* (haplography; thus Ehrlich).

9:4. Thoughts on death lead into a meditation on the benefits of life. *Biṭṭaḥon* is not "hope" (knowing that one will die is not a "hope") or a feeling of security, but rather something that can be relied on, something that one can be certain about (cf. Isa 36:4). It is in this regard that a living dog is better off than a dead lion, because the living possess one scrap of knowledge—that they will die—while the dead do not have even this.

The *lamed* of *lᵉkeleb* is probably not emphatic (Gordis), because an emphatic particle would come before the predicate. Better: "for it [indefinite *huʾ*] is better for a live dog than (for) a dead lion" or, more idiomatically: "a live dog is better off than a dead lion". The first part of the sentence is a variant of the common expression, *ṭob lᵉ-* (e.g., 2:3; 6:12; 8:12). In the second part, *min haʾaryeh* is elliptical for *meʾăšer laʾaryeh*.

9:5. Contrary to 4:3, this verse affirms that "[c]onsciousness on any terms is preferable to nonexistence, and knowledge, however limited and melancholy in content, is better than ignorance" (Gordis).

9:6. This verse shows that man's "portion" in life includes participation in the experiences of life, among them the emotions of love, hatred, and envy, for one who has these has a "portion in all that happens under the sun". These experiences, so important in the individual's life, are not necessarily pleasant, but they do belong to the totality of life's experience, and are therefore (according to this verse, at least) better than the vacuum of death.

ʿŚH: *naʿăśah* here is ambiguous.

9:7-10

(7) Go, eat your bread in pleasure and drink your wine with a merry heart, for already God has favored what you are doing. (8) Let your garments be white at all times, and let your head not lack oil. (9) During all your absurd days that God gives you under the sun, enjoy life with a woman you love, all your absurd days, for this is your portion in life and in your toil that you labor at under the sun. (10) All that you are able to do, do <in accordance with>[a] your strength, for there is no activity or calculation or knowledge or wisdom in Sheol, where you are headed.

[a] *k^e^koḥăkā* (MT *b^e^koḥăkā*)

Qohelet affirms the value of enjoying life and participating in its activities because at least that is *something*, whereas the void of death stretches on indefinitely.

'ŚH: *ma'ăśeyka* refers to activities of the sort specified in the first part of the verse.

As always when praising pleasure, Qohelet remarks that it is God's gift. If you are given the opportunity to enjoy life, that is in itself evidence that God has approved of the pleasurable activities you undertake.

9:9. "Enjoy life": lit., "see (i.e., experience) life". Qohelet regards experience of life as a value in itself.

'amal means "toil" (in the broad sense), "not wealth", for enjoying life with one's wife is not a portion a man has in his wealth, but it is one that accompanies him during life's activities in general. Here too *'amal* is a near-synonym of *ḥayyim*.

LXX has *kol y^e^mey ḥayyeyka* only once (the repetition is supplied in various ways in some MSS; see McNeile, p. 150). But the repetition is poetically effective, sounding a note of resigned, quiet melancholy and finality similar to "And miles to go before I sleep,/ And miles to go before I sleep" at the end of Frost's "Stopping by Woods on a Snowy Evening".

9:10 'ŚH: *ma'ăśeh* here means "action" rather than "events", for the reason to be active in this life (v. 10a) is the absence of any *activity* in the netherworld (v. 10b).

Timṣa' yad: The hand "finding" or "reaching" signifies metaphorically the concept of *ability* (most clearly in Lev 12:8; 25:28; Isa 10:10). Nowhere does it mean "happen to do (something)" without also implying the *ability* to do it. Qohelet is advising us to expend effort only in accordance with our abilities, to do what we can manage to do. The disjunctive accent belongs after *la'ăśot*.

For MT's *b^{e}koḥăka*, "with your strength" (i.e., with your full strength), read *k^{e}koḥăka*, "according to your strength", with LXX (Syh) ὡς ἡ δύναμίς σου. Qohelet does not recommend all-out expenditure of effort (as would be implied by *b^{e}koḥăka*), but only moderate exertions in accordance with one's abilities.

Ibn Ezra, apparently considering the preceding context, applies 9:10a specifically to pleasurable acts. But the next sentence (v. 10b) speaks of the entire range of human activities, so the broadening of scope could begin in v. 10a.

9:11-12

> (11) I next saw that under the sun the race does not belong to the swift, nor the war to the mighty, nor bread to the wise, nor wealth to the intelligent, nor favor to the knowledgeable, for a time of accident befalls them all. (12) Nor does man know his time. Like fish caught in an evil net and birds caught in a trap, so people are ensnared by a time of misfortune, when it falls upon them suddenly.

Talents and merits do not necessarily produce their deserved and expected results, because everyone is subject to the vagaries of chance.

9:11. *Ḥăkamim*, *n^{e}bonim*, and *yod^e'im* are synonyms (cf. the series in Dan 1:4).

Lo' laqqallim hammeroṣ... does not mean that the swift never win, but that they do not possess the race, thus do not control it; in other words, they do not *necessarily* win it (Ellermeier, 1967:245: "d.h. sie haben keine Garantie dafür"). It is not the loss of a race by the swiftest runner that troubles Qohelet, nor the poverty of a wise man, but rather the evidence such inequities provide of the ineffectuality of human skills and powers.

The cause of this ineffectuality is *'et wapega'*, lit. "time and accident". The phrase is a hendiadys governing a singular verb; it means "time of accident". A *time*, as well as a misfortune, may befall someone (cf. v. 12b). Like English "accident", *pega'* can apparently be either neutral ("happening", "chance") or negative ("mishap", "disaster"). In its only other occurrence (1 Kgs 5:18), *pega'* is modified by *ra'*, "evil", and it is unclear whether *ra'* is a necessary modifier or a redundant addition for emphasis. In MH, according to Jastrow, *Dict.*, it always connotes misfortune. The verb *paga'* can mean "encounter with hostility", "harm" (e.g., Josh 2:16; Judg 8:21), or simply "meet" (e.g., 1 Sam 10:5; Gen 32:2). But even if *'et wapega'* is semantically neutral, the occurrences Qohelet has in mind in this verse are unfortunate, for they deprive people of the just rewards of their talents. Ginsberg says that *'et wapega'* refers specifically to the time of death. But the fact that everyone dies does not explain why the swift do not necessarily win the race, and so on.

9:12. Qohelet moves from discussion of misfortune in general to the time of misfortune *par excellence*, death. *'itto* here refers to the time of death, like *'itteka* in (7:17).

The "time of misfortune" (a bound construction, like the synonymous *yom ra'ah* in 7:14) that Qohelet speaks of in v. 11b "falls" upon people like a trap. The quality of suddenness is usually associated with disaster in the Hebrew Bible (Daube, 1964:5 and *passim*). The phrase "a time of misfortune" can refer to any calamitous moment or period, the day of any misfortune (*ra'ah*: 7:14; 11:2) that may occur on earth. In this verse, "time of misfortune", refers to the particular calamity that brings one's death.

9:13–10:3

> (13) This too I have seen concerning wisdom under the sun, and I regard it as significant:
> (14) There was a small city with few people in it. And a great king came and encompassed it and built great siege works against it. (15) And in it he apprehended a man who was poor but wise, and it was he who saved the city by his wisdom. Yet no one remembered that poor man. (16) I said, "Better wisdom than might"; yet the wisdom of the poor man is held in contempt, and his words are not heard.
>
> (17) The words of the wise spoken gently are heard more than the shout of a ruler among fools. (18) Better wisdom than weapons, yet one offender can destroy much of value. (10:1) A fly <dies>[a] and spoils a <chalice>[b] of precious[c] perfumer's ointment. A little folly <outweighs>[d] wisdom.
>
> (2) The wise man's heart is at his right, and the fool's heart is at his left. (3) And even when the fool walks in the road his heart is absent, and it says to everyone, "He is a fool!"

[a] *zᵉbûb yāmût* (MT *zᵉbûbêy māwet*) [b] *gᵉbîa'* (MT *yabbîa'*) [c] joining *yaqar* to 10:1a. [d] *tikbad* (MT *mikkābōd*)

A. 9:13-16. An incident demonstrating wisdom's excellence and vulnerability
B. 9:17-10:1. Proverbs continuing the theme of wisdom's excellence and vulnerability
C. 10:2-3. The fool damages himself

While wisdom's preciousness makes its vulnerability to folly all the more absurd, folly damages the fool above all. Throughout 9:13-10:20 the topics of rulers and speech, wise and foolish, recur. But there is no overall design or movement of thought, and the topical clustering seems merely associative.

9:13. *Gam zoh ra'iti ḥokmah*: As MT stands, *ḥokmah* must be a predicative accusative, which is to say, it defines the state in which the first accusative is perceived to be (e.g., Gen 7:1: "I have seen you to be a righteous man"). But the event Qohelet is about to describe is not wisdom, but an occurrence in which wisdom suffered an injustice. *Gam zoh ra'iti taḥat haššemeš* would be more in line with Qohelet's usage elsewhere (cf. 3:16; 4:7; 5:12; and 9:11; none of these uses a double accusative). Nevertheless, I am maintaining the word because it is present in all the Versions, and because I cannot think of a good reason for it to be added secondarily here.

9:15. Most commentators take *umaṣa'* as "impersonal" (Gordis, Barton, Hertzberg, et al.). But even if *maṣa'* means "one found", *someone* did the finding; *maṣa'* is not the same as the niphal "there was found", meaning "there existed". Ehrlich and Delitzsch correctly identify the subject as the foreign king mentioned in the immediately preceding sentence. The sequence of events becomes clearer when we recognize that *maṣa'* means "apprehended", "captured". (Iwry [1966] identifies this sense of the word, but not for the present passage.) The king did not merely stumble across a poor wise man: that would imply that the king was wandering about instead of forcibly besieging the city. We are rather to picture the king capturing an impoverished citizen, who proved able by persuasion or guile to get the king to spare the city.

Discussion of this verse has focused on the question of whether the poor man succeeded in saving the city and was later forgotten, or whether he *would have* saved the city but was ignored (*w*[e]*'adam lo' zakar*) (thus Hertzberg, Zimmerli). Since there is no marker of hypotheticality in v. 15, it is best to take the verb as indicative—he *did* save the city. It would be an entirely unpersuasive lesson for Qohelet to claim that this man could have saved the city but was not allowed to do so. The reader would certainly wonder how Qohelet could know that the wise man *could* have done this.

The main reason for thinking that the wise man did not actually save the city is that if he had done so and "no one remembered" him (as *lo' zakar* must be translated in that case), there would be no story for Qohelet to tell. But one can easily say "no one remembers" something meaning that no one *else* remembers it. Moreover, even if the story was remembered, the identity of that particular wise man was forgotten. In any case, *zakar* is not the appropriate verb to indicate hearkening to advice. Sometimes *zakar* does mean "pay attention to" in the sense of giving thought to facts already known (rather than recalling past events, its usual meaning); e.g., Qoh 5:19; 11:8; 12:1. But in this use too the verb implies an orientation to the past, insofar as the subject is recalling a fact already known. *Zakar* would not be used in the sense of paying attention to new information, new advice, or the like. For that reason *zakar* is not among the many verbs used in Proverbs to indicate the son's hearkening to his father's advice. "Remember" is the only sense *zakar* has that is appropriate in this context. Thus there is no justification for taking *umillaṭ hu'* as hypothetical, and there is no reason to deny that the wise man's advice succeeded in saving the city.

It is uncertain whether this story is based on an historical event or is only a typical case invented by Qohelet. What is clear is that Qohelet is not concerned with anchoring the parable in an historical event. He is not basing his message on information presumed to be known to the reader, but simply saying that such and such happened. Whether or not it did, then, is not important for the point Qohelet has to make.

The subject of *millaṭ* is displaced from its usual position and thereby emphasized, becoming the virtual predicate: it was he (of all people!) who saved the city.

9:16 is commonly thought to prove that the wise man of v. 15 *could have* but *did not* save the city. The point of the verse is, however, quite different. “Better wisdom than might” is the conclusion Qohelet draws from the fact that the poor man *did* save the city (if he had not, v. 16a would not be true). In v. 16b Qohelet complains that despite the fact (demonstrated by the anecdote) that wisdom is powerful enough to save a city, people tend to ignore a wise man if he is poor. Verse 16b does not restate what happened in the case described in vv. 13-15 any more than v. 17 or v. 18b does. Rather it takes note of another affront to wisdom which, as the story shows and v. 16a declares, deserves better treatment.

9:17. The disjunctive should be moved back to *b*^{e}*naḥat*, which describes the manner in which the words are spoken, a manner contrasting with the ruler’s shouting.

In v. 16b Qohelet quoted the discouraging thought that came to him when he considered the way the wise man was neglected after having saved his city. Verse 17 modifies that thought by stating the rule: the words of the wise, *even when* spoken quietly, though vulnerable and often contemned, are nevertheless more effective than the words of a ruler among fools, even when those words are shouted.

9:18. Qohelet returns to his complaint of v. 16b that although wisdom is more powerful than weapons of war, one offender can undo much of the benefit that wisdom can provide. Here too the word *ḥote’* does not necessarily have moral connotations, for it is not immorality but incompetence or thickheadedness that undoes the efficacy of wisdom.

10:1 reinforces 9:18 by a proverbial metaphor. The commentators agree on the point of 10:1—the power of much wisdom can be nullified by a little folly—but disagree on the details of the text and its meaning.

MT’s *z*^{e}*bubey mawet* means “deadly flies” or “doomed flies” (cf. *ben mawet* in 2 Sam 12:5) not “dead flies”. But flies are not deadly, and in any case their deadliness would not spoil the ointment; nor is it relevant that they are doomed. We should redivide *zbwby mwt* as *zbwb ymwt* (Perles [1895:43], attributed to Luzzatto). This very minor emendation commends itself, because the idea of the proverb requires setting a minimal quantity of the bad substance (just one dead fly = a little folly) over against a large quantity of the valuable substance (much ointment = wisdom). Moreover, it provides a singular subject for *yab’iš*. *Yamut yab’iš* is an asyndeton showing quick succession: no sooner does a fly die than it decays and spoils the ointment.

MT's *yabbia'* does not make sense, for though a dead fly might ruin the ointment, it will not make it bubble (or ferment, as *yabbia'* is sometimes thought to mean). Reading *gabi'a* (BHS), produces a meaningful sentence. In some forms of the square script (e.g., Qumran, as in 1Q Isa^a) the left diagonal of the *yod* extends down far enough that the letter resembles a *gimel*, a resemblance sufficient to explain the miscopying of the latter as *yod*. LXX's σκευασίαν "preparation" (supported by Syh *twqn'*) is more likely to be a rendering of *gby'* than of *yby'*, assuming that the translator took "chalice" as a metonym for its contents.[21] "Chalice" is hyperbolic: even a little dead fly can ruin a whole chalice full of perfume.

Qoh 9:13–10:1 proceeds like 8:11-14:

An injustice: 8:11-12a//9:13-16
The rule this violates: 8:12b-13//9:17-18a
Reassertion of the injustice: 8:14//9:18b-10:1

10:1b is a crux. The Versions differ radically from MT and from one another and offer no help. There is no justification for construing *mikkabod* to mean "in abundance" (thus, e.g., Gordis). The best expedient is to take *yaqar* with the preceding as a modifier of *šemen roqeaḥ* and to emend *mkbwd* to *tkbd* (John Hobbins, private communication). Thus read, the sentence explains the image of v. 1a.

10:2-3. A wise man's mind is a source of strength, the fool's of harm. Even when the fool is merely walking along the road, his folly is evident to everyone, perhaps because he gets lost (v. 15). The unusual syntax of v. 3a, with the subject of the circumstantial clause set in frontal extraposition, places emphasis on "the way" rather than on "walking". The effect seems to be an implicit contrast between the "way"—where one just trods along unthinkingly—and other places—the city gate or the market, for example, where intelligence is necessary. *Even* on the road the fool's heart betrays him. As Prov 12:23b puts it, "The heart of fools cries out, 'Folly!'"

21. The only other appearance of σκευασία in the Greek versions is in Ezek 24:10, where Sym uses it to translate *merqaḥah*, "spice pot" or "spice". Syr's *m'n'*, "vessel", seems to be based on LXX, confusing the rare σκευασία with σκεῦος (Syr would render *gabia'* by *'sqp'* or *'gn'*).

The parallel with Prov 12:23b suggests that the subject of "says" in Qoh 10:3 is the fool's heart, which is, so to speak, no longer with him. (Contrast the way that Qohelet, being wise, goes about *with* his heart; 7:25.) The lack of a conjunction before *sakal hu'* favors taking that phrase as the heart's words mocking its owner. Thus it is that the heart of the fool is "at his left": it is working against him, as are his lips (10:12). On the concept of the heart as a distinct entity, see §3.211. To the concept underlying Qoh 10:3 we may compare the words of a girl in an Egyptian love song, as she scolds her heart for deserting her and making her foolish (see Fox, 1985:53, 59). The notion of a fool's absent heart declaring its owner's stupidity also recalls the Book of the Dead, in which the heart is perceived as a potential accuser of the deceased. In Spell 28, the deceased declares: "I have my heart and control it. It shall not tell what I have done . . . Obey me, my heart, (for) I am thy lord while thou art in my body" (Allen, 1974:38).

10:4-7

> (4) If the ruler grows angry at you, do not leave your place, for the ability to soothe anger can set aside great offenses. (5) There is an evil I have seen under the sun, an error that proceeds from the ruler: (6) a fool is appointed to great heights while rich men sit in lowly places. (7) I saw slaves on horses and princes walking on the ground like slaves.

Observations on rulers and subjects

10:4. As Ibn Ezra observes, this verse reverts to the topic of 9:17: a soft-spoken wise man in contrast to a shouting ruler. *Marpe'* designates the *power* of healing or soothing as well as the *act* of healing or soothing. For the potential sense of *marpe'* see Mal 3:20, where *marpe'* clearly refers to the power to heal; Prov 14:30, where *leb marpe'* is a heart that has the ability to heal others; and Prov 15:4, where *marpe'* is a quality (soothing power) inhering in the tongue, just as deceit can be "in it" (sc., the tongue; v. 4b). *Marpe'* seems to be associated with both RPH and RP', as Gordis observes, and it is hardly possible to assign the word to one root or the other. *Marpe'* is healing (RP') in the sense of soothing (RPH). It is a near-synonym of *naḥat* (9:17). The assumption bridging 10:4a and 4b is that when the wise man stays in his place he will make use of his *marpe'*—"soothing ability"—to calm the ruler. Prov 16:14 makes a similar observation.

Even closer is Sir 20:28b, "And the man who pleases the great atones for wrongdoing".

Qohelet distinguishes behavior before a *melek* (8:2) from behavior before a *mošel*, probably meaning a local authority. When a king is angry, one should get away as soon as possible, presumably in silence and with permission. When a lesser authority is angry, one can remain in his presence and attempt to calm him down, an act that requires a certain degree of familiarity with him. On the distinction between *melek* and *mošel*, see Lohfink, 1981:541f.

10:5-7. In Qohelet's eyes it is "bad" that people are placed in inappropriate positions, as when fools are given high appointments or slaves elevated to privilege. Such things offend Qohelet's sense of propriety.

10:6. "Folly" = "fool" (abstract for concrete; thus Ibn Ezra). Qohelet, like the author of Prov 30:21-23, is indignant at disturbances of the social order. According to the latter, one of the things that makes the earth quake is a slave coming to rule (v. 22a; cf. 23b). In the eyes of both Qohelet and the sage of Prov 30:21-23, there is something ridiculous and unaesthetic in dislocations of the proper order. For Proverbs, such human failings are extraneous burdens placed upon the orderly world, and they will be shaken off it as if by an earthquake. For Qohelet, these absurdities are the substance of reality and determine the character of life.

10:8-11

> (8) He who digs a pit will fall into it, and he who breaks through a wall will be bitten by a snake. (9) He who moves stones will be hurt by them, and he who splits wood will be endangered by it. (10) If the iron is dull and he does not sharpen the edge, then he must exert more force; but the advantage of <the skilled man>[a] is wisdom. (11) If a snake bites for lack of a charm, what gain does the snake charmer have?

[a] point *hakkaššîr* (MT *hakšêyr*)

Maxims on deeds and consequences: preparing for the unexpected

10:8-9. These proverbs (whose validity Qohelet in no way denies) rephrase an idea found in similar form in Psalms (7:16, 17; 9:16), Proverbs (26:27), and Ben Sira (27:25-27): a person's deeds rebound upon him. Falling in a pit one dug for someone else is usually a figure for the peripety that the wise found so satisfying. Qoh 10:8-9, however, has a different emphasis. Here digging a pit is one of four actions of the sort that would be performed in the course of one's everyday chores. These occurrences may be simply unexpected misfortunes, and not necessarily retribution. Their point is summed up in v. 14: "Man does not know what will happen". A man works day and night in earning his living and ends up causing his own loss. He digs a pit or a cistern, or takes down a tottering wall, or moves stones, or splits firewood, and he gets hurt in carrying out these ordinary tasks. Such reversals could have been called *hebel.*

10:10. The antecedent of *hu'* is "he who splits wood" in v. 9. *Ḥăyalim* is probably not the subject of the sentence, for the non-coordination of number in a conjoined predicate would be rough. Nor is *ḥăyalim* adverbial, for the piel (the conjugation used in this sentence) is with rare exception transitive. Rather, *ḥăyalim* is the direct object of *y^{e}gabber* and the clause means: "then he must exert more force" (Yaḥyah). If one neglects to sharpen his axe, he must use greater strength. This might be the source of the danger mentioned in v. 9, because a dull axe wielded with force knocks more chips off the wood.

Verse 10b is obscure. The best expedient is to point *hakkaššîr* (= Aramaic *kaššira'*), "the skilled man". "The advantage of the skilled man is wisdom" means that wisdom (here in the sense of technical skill) gives the skilled man an advantage over the one who substitutes force for preparedness and good sense. One must use his wisdom before it becomes necessary to apply force, just as the "possessor of a tongue" must use his skill before it is too late for such skills to be of use.

10:11. "Snake charmer": lit., "possessor of a tongue" (10:11). If a snake bites because it was not charmed, it is too late for the snake charmer's skill to benefit him. This proverb too assumes the efficacy of wisdom while noting its vulnerability. Generalized, the point is that no one, *not even* the skilled man, can undo damage after the fact.

Skills, including magical knowledge, are included in *ḥokmah*. The *ḥakam* often appears in conjunction with other kinds of magicians; see, e.g., Gen 41:8; Exod 7:11; Isa 44:25; Dan 2:27, 13; Isa 3:3 (where *n^{e}bon laḥaš*, "one knowledgeable in spells", stands alongside *ḥăkam* *ḥărašim*, "one skilled in spells"). The snake charmer is called *m*^{e}*ḥukkam*, "skilled" or "learned" in Ps 58:6.

10:12-15

> (12) The words of a wise man's mouth bring him favor, while a fool's lips devour him. (13) The fool starts out speaking folly and ends up speaking evil inanity. (14) And it is the fool who speaks at length. Man does not know what will happen, for who can tell him what will happen afterwards? (15) [a]The fool's toil exhausts him,[a] for he doesn't even know how to get to town.

[a]—[a] *'ămāl hakk*^{e}*sîl m*^{e}*yagg*^{e}*'ennû* (MT *'ămāl hakk*^{e}*sîlîm t*^{e}*yagg*^{e}*'ennû*)

Wise and foolish speech (connected to the preceding by the phrase *ba'al hallašon* in v. 11)

10:12-14: A wise man's talk benefits him, the fool's harms him—yet it is the latter who talks the most.

10:12. Qoh 10:12 states more generally the theme of 8:1b; 9:17; and 10:4. The wise man's words "are" favor in the sense that they produce favor; compare the construction in 2:23aα and 12:12bβ.

10:14. Since Qohelet does not mention death in this unit, it is likely that *me'aḥărayw* means "afterwards" (including the future in this life); thus in 6:12, which this verse closely resembles (reversing the clauses); see the comment at 3:22. It is ignorance of the future in this life, rather than ignorance of what happens after death, that makes it foolish to talk a lot.

10:15 is an afterthought to vv. 12-14a. It continues the thought of v. 3 and may originally have been located there. Combined, the two verses say: even when just walking on the road the fool reveals to everyone that he is stupid (v. 3), for he wearies himself by getting lost on the way to town (v. 15).

The phrase "doesn't know how to go to town" may have meaning both literally and idiomatically. As an idiom it may refer to incompetence. Compare the Egyptian phrase, "does not reach the city", which means "does not attain its goal"; e.g., *Eloquent Peasant*, B1, 326f., where the idiom stands in antithesis to "reach land", an Egyptian cliché for succeeding. The fool's toil wearies him because he is unable to accomplish what he sets out to do.

'ml hksylym tyg'nw: the text is undoubtedly corrupt. The non-

coordination of number ("fools"—"him"), though possible, is very awkward, and the non-coordination of gender is almost certainly an error. (The fact that some nouns may have either gender does not, contrary to Delitzsch, mean that *this* noun can.) One suggested emendation is *'ml hksyl mty yyg'nw*, "The toil of the fool—when will it weary him?" (Ehrlich, Hertzberg). But this reading implies that the fool is *not* wearied by his toil, whereas the rest of the verse speaks of the fool's feebleness, not his power of endurance. Albrecht (1896:113), noting that this verse is the only example in which an abstract form (*qāṭāl*) and its gender are not coordinated, emends to *yyg'nw*. This emendation, however, leaves a non-coordination of number and does not account for the appearance of the *taw*. I suggest reading *'ml hksyl myg'nw*. LXX (S, A) shows the singular ("the fool . . . him"). We may surmise that the second *yod* of MT *hksylym* was added after the *mem* was incorrectly joined to *hksyl*. The *taw* is probably a dittograph of the *mem* of *myg'nw* (for examples of *t-/m* interchange, showing that they were at times similar enough to lead to near dittographies, see Delitzsch, 1920:§129b and Kennedy, 1928:98f.). Alternatively, the intrusive *t-* may be a near dittograph of the following *y-* (for *t-/y-* interchanges see Delitzsch, 1920:§§124a, 117 and Kennedy, 1928:81f.).

10:16-20

(16) Woe to you, O land whose king is a lackey and whose princes feast in the morning! (17) How fortunate you are, O land whose king is a nobleman and whose princes feast at the proper time, in a manly fashion and not in drunkenness!

(18) (Through sloth[a] a roof sags,
    and through slackness of hands a house leaks.)

(19) For merriment they prepare food, as well as wine, which cheers the living. And money keeps them all occupied!

(20) Even in your thoughts do not insult the king,
    and do not insult a rich man even in your bed chamber,
  for the birds of the sky will carry the sound,
    and a winged creature report the matter.

[a] *'aṣlat* or *'aṣlût* (MT *'ăṣaltayim*)

Virtues and failings in the ruling class

Does Qohelet have his own land in mind in condemning lazy aristocrats? Verse 20 seems to be an ironic warning directed against

Qohelet's own words in the opening verse of this passage, perhaps implying that he has just insulted actual people.

10:16. *Na'ar* more likely means "servant" than "youth" here, since it stands in contrast to *ben ḥorim*, sc., a member of the well-to-do classes. If so, *na'ar* refers to this person's origins rather than to his current position. Qohelet reflects class prejudice even when mocking the behavior of some members of the upper classes. He feels it is as inappropriate for a servant to rise to power as for noblemen to sit around drinking in the morning. He shares the attitude of the author of Prov 30:22, who believes that the earth shakes when a slave comes to rule (*yimlok*).

10:18. A parenthetical reinforcement of vv. 16f., perhaps a proverb.

'ăṣaltayim: Most commentators (including Delitzsch, Hertzberg, Gordis) explain the dual form as intensive. But the intensive function of the dual is not well established, and, more fundamentally, logic calls for a *non*-intensive form here. An admonition against indolence should warn us that laziness (i.e., any laziness)—and not only a double portion of laziness—brings one's house to disrepair. We should read *'aṣlat-* (Graetz) or *'aṣlut-* (Bickell); in either case the final *-ym* is a dittograph. The two hemistichs combine to make a single point: indolence causes the roof of a house to sag and leak.

10:19 describes the banquets the rich prepare for themselves daily. The subject of the verbs is found in v. 17—the princes and nobility. *'aśah leḥem* is an Aramaism, equivalent to *'ăbad lĕḥem*, "prepare food, a feast" (Dan 5:1) (Ginsberg). *Śᵉḥoq* means "merriment", "amusement", as in 2:2. *Yᵉśammaḥ ḥayyim* is a relative clause (Ibn Ezra; compare the sayings in Ps 104:15; Judg 9:13).

Ya'ăneh is commonly explained to mean "answer for", whence "provide", with reference to Hos 2:23f. But in the Hosea passage, *'anah* does not mean "provide" in the first three sentences, for God does not "provide" the heavens nor the heavens the earth. Hosea apparently envisions a cosmic conversation of the sort mentioned in Ps 19:2-3 and UT *'nt* (III:10-28), a notion inappropriate, even metaphorically, to our verse. In any case, both the idea that money provides everything or responds affirmatively to everyone is an irrelevant economic comment. *Ya'ăneh* here is best taken as a hiphil meaning "to occupy, keep busy", as in 5:19, q.v. In both verses the "busy-ness" meant is the enjoyment of pleasures, and in both the direct object of the verb is the people who occupy themselves in this fashion. Wealth provides the means of pleasure and keeps the rich amused.

This verse is not cynical towards the wealthy or even critical of them. It applies to the banqueters most recently mentioned (v. 17) as well as to the dissolute nobles of v. 16. Neither Qohelet nor the other sages objected to the preparation of food and wine for merriment ("Joy of heart and happiness of soul, is wine drunk at the proper time and temperately" [Sir 31:27, Greek text]). They censured only the failure to confine these pleasures to the proper time and measure ("Wine drunk to excess is bitterness of soul" [Sir 31:29a]). Qoh 10:19 is an incidental remark describing the good fortune of the wealthy: they have the means to keep themselves preoccupied, a state Qohelet considers a divine blessing (5:19).

10:20. This remark is perhaps called forth by the reproach against the lazy king and nobility in v. 16.

Maddaʿ means "mind", "thought" (rather than "knowledge") in 1QS 7.3 (if a man "gets angry in his *maddaʿ*") and 7.5 ("if a man commits deceit "in his *maddaʿ*"; similarly 6.9). Other suggested translations of *maddaʿ* are "intimates", "bed", and "bedroom" (some reading *maṣṣaʿăka*; thus Perles [1895:71f.], Ehrlich). But "mind", "thoughts" is a meaningful hyperbole; in other words: don't even *think* about it!

11:1-6

> (1) Release your bread upon the water, for in the course of time you will find it. (2) Give a portion to seven people, even eight, for you do not know what misfortune will occur on earth. (3) If the clouds fill up, they will empty out rain on the earth. If a tree should fall, whether in the south or the north, wherever the tree may fall, there will it be. (4) He who watches the wind will not sow, and he who scrutinizes the clouds will not reap. (5) Just as you cannot understand how the life-breath gets <into>[a] the fetus in the womb of a pregnant woman, so you cannot understand the work of God, who makes everything happen. (6) In the morning sow your seed, and in the evening let not your hand be slack, for you do not know which will prosper, this or that, or whether both will be equally good.

[a] *ba(ʿăṣāmîm)* (MT *ka-*)

Argument: In a world of uncertainties, prepare for all eventualities, because you cannot know in advance which will come to pass (vv. 1b, 2b, 4, 5, 6), and in any case you cannot affect the course of events (v. 3). What will be will be. Therefore, do not waste time pondering the future (cf. 6:12b; 10:14; etc.), but rather adapt yourself as well as you can to various possibilities. Instead of straining for wisdom, just go ahead and do what you must.

11:1-2. There are several ways of interpreting these maxims, including:

(1) Send your merchandise over the seas, but divide it among several boats for safety's sake (Delitzsch, Gordis, Zimmerli, et al.).

(2) More broadly: take chances, even long-shots, and in the far future you may benefit from them (v. 1), but protect yourself against unexpected misfortunes by spreading around the risk (v. 2) (Podechard).

(3) Do deeds of charity, distributing your wealth to people in need (Targum, Rashi, Ibn Ezra, Barton, et al.).

(4) An observation: an unreflective, improvident deed (v. 1a) may, contrary to expectations, succeed (v. 1b), while a prudent and cautious deed (v. 2a) may, contrary to expectations, fail (v. 2b). The consequences of a man's actions do not depend on him and are unpredictable (Hertzberg, Galling, Ellermeier [1967:253-61]).

Interpretation 1 is unlikely because when someone makes an investment, he hopes to "find" more than the principal (Ginsberg), and furthermore, "bread" is an unparalleled and improbable metaphor for merchandise. Interpretation 2 depends on the meaning of "releasing bread on the water". Parallels to be mentioned below suggest that it alludes to acts of charity rather than to business investments. Ginsberg's objection to interpretation 1 applies here as well. Interpretation 4 turns the advice into a statement, whereas in this unit Qohelet seeks to draw practical conclusions for human activity from consideration of the fact of human ignorance, as we see clearly in vv. 4 and 6. The imperatives in 11:1-2 also are most naturally read as true advice. Moreover, v. 2b is not " ... *das Gegenteil des Erwarteten darstellende Folge*" (Hertzberg; italics in original), as it would have to be if this interpretation were right; rather, this statement is an abstraction of the principle.

Interpretation 3 is best, in view of the parallels mentioned below, but the element of surprise (from interpretation 2) should be given greater emphasis. In other words: wager on charitable and gracious deeds, even if this seems like a long-shot, because the unexpected may happen and your deeds pay off. As Rashbam puts it: "do a favour to a man whom you reckon you would never benefit from, for after many days he too will do you a favour" (Japhet-Salters, 1985:200). To this advice we may compare the strikingly similar counsel in the Instruction of Onchsheshonqy, an Egyptian wisdom book from about the same period as Qohelet: "Do a good deed and throw it in the water; when it dries you will find it" (19,10; transl. Lichtheim, *AEL* III, 174). If this translation is correct,[22] this maxim is teaching that one should do a good deed and forget about it; then in hard times it will return to benefit him. Ben Sira offers similar advice: "Lose your money for the sake of a brother or friend" (29:10). As the context in Sira shows, this means that you should give charity (v. 9) without expecting repayment, but you may anticipate some future reward from God (vv. 11-13); cf. also Sir 3:31 and Ps 112:9. The Instruction of Ptahhotep too gives advice to this effect:

(339) Satisfy your acquaintances with what has accrued to you,
(340) as is possible for the one whom god favors.
(341) As for him who neglects to satisfy his acquaintances,
(342) it will be said, "This is a selfish soul [Ka]!"
(343) One does not know what will happen, such that he might understand the morrow.
[(345) There is no one who knows (the outcome of) his plans, so that he might plan for the morrow.[23]]

22. Stricker (1958:72) renders the saying similarly. Glanville (1955:45) translates "Do a good deed (only) to throw it into mid-river, and it is extinguished when you find it". I am not able to judge the accuracy of translations from Demotic, but the proverb is more meaningful in Lichtheim's and Stricker's translation than in Glanville's. The metaphor of "extinguishing" a good deed is obscure, and in any case one would not wish to find an "extinguished" deed.

23. Or: "... who knows his fortune" [*sḫrw*]. Line 345, which appears in two later MSS (L1, L2) is a variant of l. 343, which appears only in the oldest MS, Pap. Prisse. In L1 (where "knows" is omitted) and L2, the variant follows 344.

(344) A (true) soul is an honest soul, in which one can find repose [?].
(346) If misfortunes[24] occur,
(347) it is (one's) acquaintances who say, "Welcome!"
(348) One does not receive relief from one's town.[25]
(349) When there is misfortune, one receives (aid) [from] one's acquaintances.

Ptahhotep teaches that it is prudent to give of your wealth to others because you do not know what the future will bring. In the time of disaster, you will receive help only from people you have treated kindly. In other words, do unto others *that* they may do unto you.

Šallaḥ: ŠLḤ-piel usually means "to release", occasionally "to send". It nowhere means "to throw" (sc., an object). It can be applied to expulsion (of a people), as in Jer 28:16; Lev 18:24; and 20:23. But this last usage need not derive metaphorically from "throw"; it may be a stronger form of "sending". ŠLḤ-piel is once used of shooting an arrow (1 Sam 20:20; dir. obj. implicit), but an arrow may be said to be "released" as well as to be "thrown". Thus the image 11:1 suggests is that of a person placing his bread on the water and letting it float off, rather than casting it in the water. We are to think of a hard, rounded "pita", which can float briefly, instead of a loaf. The image of letting something go rather than throwing it accords better with the preposition *'al pᵉney*, lit., "on the surface of" (rather than *b-* or *'el tok*). Taylor observes that this phrase is used of objects floating on the water in the Mishna (*Ohalot* 8:5; *Parah* 9:6; *Betsah* 5:2).

Mah yihyeh ra'ah = *mah ra'ah tihyeh* (Ginsberg); cf Est 6:3.

11:3. "South" and "north" constitute a merism signifying "anywhere".

11:4. A farmer who constantly frets about the weather will never

24. *Spw n ḥsswt*, on which see Volten (1955:362f.), who translates "Widerwärtigkeit, Missgeschick". *Ḥsswt*, which usually means "praised things" or the like, is clearly a euphemism for misfortune. Lichtheim (*AEL* I, p. 69) translates: "If praiseworthy deeds are done . . ."; but "praiseworthy deeds" does not accord with the verb *ḫpr*, "occur" or with its variant *iw*, "come to pass".

25. In other words, you cannot take your neighbors' help for granted, so you must prepare the ground for receiving aid in time of trouble. L2 creates a simpler, though rather banal, concept by substituting "enemies" for "town".

get around to his tasks. If he puts off sowing until the western wind, the harbinger of rain, blows, he may end up not sowing, and if he scrutinizes the clouds, postponing harvesting until he is absolutely certain of dry weather (for rain immediately upon harvesting could spoil the grain), he may fail to harvest. Generalized, the maxim teaches that the attempt to plan too precisely for the future can prevent action. Better to plunge into your work without too much thought. Generalized further, it teaches the uselessness of speculative thought about *ma'ăśeh ha'ĕlohim*, a point made explicit in v. 5b.

11:5 MT's *k'ṣmym*, "like the fetus", brings in the comparison too soon. We should read *b'ṣmym* with BHS and many commentators, in accordance with many MSS K-R and Targum (where, however, *bgwp 'wlym' šlyl'*, "in the body of an embryo", may be interpretive). The preposition *b*ᵉ- often means "into". The unknown is not what the spirit does in the body of the fetus, but how the spirit gets there.

The animation of a fetus is given as the epitome of an *unknowable* event rather than a mysterious one. The entrance of life into the fetus is, to be sure, profoundly mysterious, but the other occurrences mentioned in this unit are not mysterious so much as simply unpredictable.

'ŚH (*ma'ăśeh ha'ĕlohim 'ăšer ya'ăśeh 'et hakkol*): Not "... who does everything", for God does not "do" everything; nor is the *creation* of everything relevant here. Rather, the phrase refers to God's ongoing governance of the world. Exigencies of translation prevent rendering *ma'ăśeh ha'ĕlohim* in this verse as "what God brings to pass", but the phrase still refers to a particular aspect of God's work—the causation of events. *Ma'ăśeh ha'ĕlohim* refers to events such as a misfortune happening on the earth (v. 2b), the clouds emptying (v. 3aα), a tree falling (v. 3aβb), a particular planting succeeding (v. 6b), and the life-spirit finding its way into the fetus (v. 5a).

11:6. *La'ereb* = "in the evening" (see 1 Chron 23:30; Ps 30:6; Brockelmann, 1956:§107b), not "until evening", or "toward evening", because two distinct times are spoken of ("the one" and "the other"). The phrase is a merism meaning "at all times". This is not to say that Qohelet is advocating work without pause. The message is rather that one should sow (more generally: work) whenever the opportunity or need arises, rather than attempting to determine the best moment, "for you do not know" which of the possibilities will succeed. The structure and the message of 11:6 are the same as in vv. 1-2, and thus this verse rounds out the unit with its central teaching: compensate for your ignorance by preparing for multiple eventualities.

11:7–12:8 is a single unit, organized as a series of imperatives advising enjoyment of life when young. Because of its length and complexity, its two parts, A (11:7-10) and B (12:1-8) will be discussed separately.

Argument:
A. 11:7-10 (*Carpe diem*)

1. 11:7-8 Enjoy all of life (for what follows is absurd),
2. 11:9-10 especially the time of youth (for it is fleeting).

B. 12:1-8 (*Memento mori*)

1. 12:1aα And remember your grave (?)
2. 12:1aβb before the miseries of old age,
3. 12:2-5 before your death and funeral,
4. 12:6-7 before your death and burial.
5. 12:8 Everything is absurd.

The two major sections are linked syntactically in 12:1. The advice of section A continues in 12:1a. Then 12:1b begins a series of temporal clauses that describe aging and death (section B), all of which goes to motivate the advice of section A. *Hebel*-judgments in 11:8 and 10 demarcate the two segments of section A, and the phrase *‘ad ’ăšer lo’* subdivides B. Qoh 12:8 is both the culmination of the poem and a summary of the book, and it reintroduces the voice of the frame narrator.

Although the theme of the unit is *carpe diem*, the imperative to enjoy life when the opportunity is given, far more emphasis is placed on the negative—the somber limits on this opportunity—than on the positive enjoyment itself. One must partake of life's pleasures while young (11:9-12:1a), before old age restricts (12:1b) and death eliminates (12:2-8) this possibility.

Witzenrath (1979:5-27) shows how this unit achieves cohesiveness of texture by repetition of certain lexemes (*harbeh*, ŚMḤ, ZKR, *hebel*, *yaldut*, *yamim*, *qol*, *ŚWB*) and by the clustering of words belonging to the same semantic fields (light, ages of life, time, house, voice, plants, valuables, vessels, wells).

A. **11:7-10**

(7) Sweet is the light,
  and the eyes enjoy seeing the sun.
(8) Now even if a man live many years,
  he should take pleasure in them all,
 and remember that the days of darkness are many.
  All that comes is absurdity.

(9) Rejoice, young man, in your youth,
  and let your heart give you cheer in the days of your prime.
 And follow your heart
  and the sight of your eyes.
 And know that for all these things
  God will bring you to judgment.
(10) And remove anger from your heart,
  and banish unpleasantness from your flesh,
 for youth and life's prime are fleeting.

Being alive is sweet, even if one's experiences of life are not.

Qohelet does not say "it is good to see the sun", but (literally), "it is good for the eyes to see the sun"—a statement of a subjective value. Whatever one may discover about the absurdity and bitterness of all that happens under the sun, it is a fact that people enjoy living. Therefore they should treasure every minute of it, because the days of darkness stretch on forever.

Ellermeier (1967:303-306) argues that 11:7-8 is not advice but only an observation of the fact that people consider life good. He takes v. 8abα as the reason for this observation: even someone who lives a long life never considers the years excessive but takes pleasure in them all. Yet while 11:7 is indeed an observation, it is the basis for advice, which v. 8 gives explicitly (in the jussive: *yiśmaḥ*, *yizkor*). The *ki* in v. 8a is an evidential connective motivating the sequence of thought ("I say this because") rather than introducing the cause of a fact ("this is so because") (on this usage see Claasen, 1983:37-40). In other words, Qohelet reminds the reader of the desirability of living in order to motivate him to enjoy himself during all the time allotted him.

11:8. Death is absurd and guarantees life's absurdity as well. But absurd or not, the light of life is sweet. See also the discussion in §1.12 (3).

In 11:8 Qohelet says that people should think of death so as to appreciate life more. In 5:19 he praises pleasure for diverting the mind from the brevity of life. This dual attitude toward death is inherent in the *carpe diem*. The Antef Song, for example, first describes the gloom of death, then advocates pleasure as diversion (see on 5:19). We are told to remember death so that we will pursue the pleasures that will divert our thoughts from death. People often think most about what they most fear.

11:9a. The "ways of your heart" are the ways in which your heart goes; we might translate: "Go where your heart goes". Underlying this idiom is the notion that one who desires something moves in imagination into the desired situation. In this sense, the heart goes ahead of a person, who may then decide whether to follow or not. Similarly, to "go in (= according to) the sight of your eyes" means to go toward whatever your eyes desire.

11:9b. Though commentators often remove this sentence as a gloss (thus Zimmerli, Galling, Ginsberg, and many), the belief of man's accountability for his deeds is not foreign to Qohelet (cf. 3:17 and 8:6a [note that the latter is rarely considered a gloss]).

11:10. The advice to follow the ways of one's heart caused discomfort to later readers. LXX adds ἄμωμος, "innocently" after v. 10a (in Syh with an obelus; B and 68 omit, erroneously, καρδίας σου). In the same vein, several LXX witnesses simply prefix a negative (μή) to the next phrase, reading, "and (go) not in the sight of your eyes" (B, S*, and several minuscules). This same tendency is manifest in Ben Sira's cautionary reversal of Qohelet's advice: "Do not go after your heart and your eyes, to go in evil delights" (5:2, MS A).[26] The apparently hedonistic advice in vv. 9-10a was worrisome enough to provoke dispute about the book's canonicity (*Qoh Rab* to 1:3).

Hebel here denotes ephemerality, for that is the only quality of youth that makes pleasure-seeking urgent. At the same time, it connotes absurdity, for it is unreasonable that the best part of life is

26. The Greek lacks the additional moralizing element, reading, "Do not follow your soul and your strength, going in the desires of your heart". The fact that the following line is almost certainly influenced by Qohelet strengthens the probability that Sir 5:2 is a response to him. Verse 3 uses the peculiar phase *m*ᵉ*baqqeš nirdapim*, which is derived from *y*ᵉ*baqqeš 'et nirdap* in Qoh 3:15.

so brief; see §1.12 (3). LXX (similarly Syr) moralizes, translating *šaḥărut* as ἄνοια, “ignorance”.

12:1-8

(1) And remember your Creator[a] in the days of your youth—
before the days of unpleasantness come,
and years arrive of which you will say:
“I take no pleasure in them”;
(2) before the sun grows dark—
with the light and the moon and the stars—
and the clouds return after the rain;
(3) in the day when the keepers of the house tremble,
and the powerful men writhe,
and the grinding-maids are idle, for their numbers have dwindled,
and the ladies looking through the lattices grow gloomy,[27]
(4) and the doors in the street are closed,
as the sound of the mill fades low;
and the bird begins to sing,
and all the songstresses are bowed low
(5) and are also afraid of a height,
and [scenes] of fright are along the way,
while the almond tree blossoms,
and the <squill>[b] becomes laden,
and the caperberry <buds>[c]—
for a man is going to his eternal home,
and the mourners are walking about in the street;
(6) before the silver cord snaps,[d]
and the golden bowl is smashed,[e]
and the jug breaks at the well,
and the jar is smashed into the pit,
(7) and the soil returns to the earth as it was before,
and the life-spirit returns to God, who gave it.

(8) Absurdity of absurdities, says the Qohelet,
All is absurdity.

[a] *bôr'*^{e}*kā* (MT *bôr*^{e}*'eykā*) [b] *ḥāṣāb* (MT *ḥāgāb*) [c] *w*^{e}*tipraḥ* (MT *w*^{e}*tāpēr*) [d] *yinnātēq* (MT *yrḥq* ketiv, *yērātēq* qere) [e] point *tērōṣ* (MT *tārūṣ*)

27. Literally, “grow dark”.

EXCURSUS II
AGING AND DEATH IN QOHELET 12

Qoh 12:1-8 is the most difficult passage in a difficult book. Continuing the *carpe diem* theme begun in 11:7, Qohelet urges the reader to enjoy life before it is too late. The nature of 12:2-5 in particular has been debated at length. These verses have almost always been read as an allegory representing the physical deterioration of aging, an interpretation in part valid but in general inadequate. Even if this poem is an allegory entirely or in part, it communicates in other ways as well, and these have been largely ignored.

This study will explore the interplay among literal, symbolic, and figurative dimensions of the poem's meaning, seeking to bring out scenes, connotations and implications that are accessible to the reader independently of the poem's possible allegorical significance.

(1) *Earlier approaches to interpretation*

The allegorical interpretation of this poem, first found in *Qohelet Rabbah* and b. *Shabbat* 131b-132a, is still the dominant one. In this reading, each object mentioned in the poem is decoded as a part of the body, and the whole is taken as a description of the physical degeneration of aging. Allegorical decoding does (I will argue) have some validity in the explication of individual images, but the text as a whole largely resists this reading, and even in the interpretation of details the basis for an allegorical reading is not secure. It is mainly out of exegetical habit that we see the watchmen, for example, as the legs (or the arms), and the doors in the street as the lips (or the orifices, or the ears), and the stars as the pupils of the eyes (or the cheeks, or the five senses). The procrustean character of the allegorical interpretation may make it seem more effective than it really is. It is not difficult to connect almost any image[28] with

28. "Image" refers to any depiction of a sensory object (in this case, verbal) and to the mental replication of this depiction. Images may, but need not, function in metaphors (as vehicle *or* as referent), similes, symbols, or allegories.

something within the multifarious physical and psychological process of aging, and when this cannot be done, the interpreter is free to treat the image as literal or as a metaphor outside the allegorical frame. Difficulties in accommodating the text to the interpretation can be met by invoking the author's "Oriental richness of imagination and carelessness in exact use of metaphor" (Barton, p. 187). Yet even with all this hermeneutic flexibility, the allegorical interpretations leave much unexplained.[29]

Some of the images of the poem may well be figurative representations of aging and death. But the poem as a whole is not an allegory. And it is certainly not *only* that. The "allegorical approach" has commonly treated the imagery as if it were a disguise covering the "true" meaning of the poem. The interpreter's task then becomes to strip off this disguise and triumphantly to reveal what lies hidden behind it. Once removed, the guise itself ceases to be of interest. The allegorical interpretation has invariably failed to recognize that the imagery, the surface of the poem, is what the author chooses to show us first and most clearly. Rather than thinking of imagery as an expendable outer garb, we should compare it to the visible surface of a painting. The imagery *is* the painting. We can discuss the painting's symbolism, emotive overtones, ideological message, and so on, but only as projections of the surface imagery, not as substitutes for it. To understand the poem we must first look carefully at the surface the author shows us.

Various forms of a literal interpretation have been suggested. According to M. Gilbert (1981), vv. 3-4 describe the actual experience of the old: shaking, bending, blindness, obscurity, and isolation. But doors in the street would not actually close as one grows old, nor would milling cease as aged people became too few, for there would be others in the house. Moreover, the phrasing of these verses implies that all this happens at once, whereas everyone in a town would not grow old simultaneously. O. Loretz (1964:189-93) understands 12:2-5a as an essentially literal description of a winter's day, which serves as a metaphor of old age. This is followed by the coming of spring (v. 5b), teaching that although plants may revive, man cannot.

29. Taylor (1874:51-63) summarizes various forms of the "anatomical" interpretation and shows that it can be maintained only by an exegesis too convoluted to be persuasive. His arguments are, I believe, basically valid. However, his insistence on "all or nothing", as if any variance from *consistent* anatomical figuration excludes the presence of any such figuration, seems extreme.

Although Loretz's understanding of v. 5b is, I believe, essentially correct, the events described earlier have nothing to do with winter. Winter, especially in Palestine, would not make men twist and tremble unless they were extraordinary cowards, nor would it cause the maids to halt their grinding, because preparation of bread is an endless chore. For similar reasons, I cannot accept C. D. Ginsburg's reading of the poem as a description of a gathering storm serving as a metaphor for the approach of death, or Leahy's interpretation of the poem as a depiction of fearful reactions to a thunderstorm, thereby representing the emotions in a household when someone dies (Leahy, 1952). The rain has stopped (v. 2b), and anyway a rainstorm is not *that* frightening. Moreover, the sun, moon, and stars would not be darkened all at once by a rainstorm.

J. F. A. Sawyer (1976) has offered a radical reinterpretation of 12:2-5. He accepts the presence of an allegory on aging in the *Massoretic* text of 12:2-5, but argues that the allegorizing elements are secondary accretions deriving from a very ancient interpretation of the text as allegorical. When these accretions are removed, he says, we find the figure of a ruined house representing the failure of human efforts. The poem envisages three situations that may interrupt the young man's progress towards achieving success and fulfillment (p. 523).

Sawyer's procedure is, however, circular, for the presumed accretions betray themselves only by their supposedly allegorical nature.[30] Various other emendations[31] and strained translations[32] are proposed for the sake of the presumed parable, not for independent textual-philological reasons. The reconstructed parable says: "Just as

30. E.g., "*ḥšk* is perhaps more appropriate to the allegory than to the present interpretation" (*ibid*., p. 526); *ki mi'eṭu* in v. 3 "makes good sense only for the allegorizers" (and therefore should perhaps be omitted; p. 526).

31. Including: *bayyom* to *kayyom* (3a) in order to "bring the parable into line with [various] quasi-proverbial allusions to Israel's history" (p. 529); *w*^{e}*ḥaš*^{e}*ku* to *w*^{e}*ḥaš*^{e}*ku* (3b), understood to mean "are held back", i.e., "appear [at the windows] no more" (pp. 526, 530); *w*^{e}*yiššaḥu* to *w*^{e}*yaśiḥu* (4b), translated "chattering" (mockingly) (p. 527); *ki* to *ken* (5bα) (p. 530).

32. Including: "move", whence "leave" (sc., the house) for *yazu'u* (3a) (*ibid*., p. 525); "to be ruined in a court of law" for *hit'aww*^{e}*tu* (3a) (p. 525); "so when a man goes" for *ken* [thus he reads] *holek ha'adam* (5bβ) (p. 530).

when an estate falls into disrepair (vv. 3a-4a), nature is indifferent (vv. 4a-5a), so too when a man dies (v. 5bα), life in his city goes on unchanged (v. 5bβ)" (my paraphrase). Even this tenuously reconstructed parable does not warn about unexpected disasters, but rather complains of nature's indifference. (In Sawyer's view, the parable also shows society's indifference.) Certainly the mourners going about their business does not demonstrate indifference; on the contrary, they are displaying at least a formalized concern for the dead man and doing what he presumably wanted. Furthermore, nature's and society's indifference to disaster would not be a reason to enjoy life while young.

H. Witzenrath (1979:46-50) interprets 12:3-4a as depicting the decay (*Verfall*) of a house, this process representing human ephemerality and death. She says that the images of these sentences (like the others in 12:2, 4-5aα, 6) describe the movement from a positive state (strength / activity / brightness / openness) to a negative one (weakness / inactivity / darkness / closure). As I will later argue, these images do indeed relate primarily to death, but not by depicting the dilapidation of a house, and not merely by suggesting a movement toward the "negative". First of all, only one of the images (the doors closed to the street) pertains to the house as such, whereas the house-body metaphor in the verses upon which Witzenrath bases her interpretation, Job 4:19 and Isa 38:12, takes as its vehicle the image of a house or a tent, not a town or estate. Second, the images in Qoh 12:3-4a do not suggest decay and dilapidation so much as pain and cessation of normal activity. The scene does not represent the experience of dying and death but rather other people's *response* to a death.

No interpretation of this poem is entirely satisfactory; none (including the one I will offer) solves all the difficulties. The poem's obscurities are due in part to a number of philological-textual problems, in part to the fragmentary state of our knowledge of Israelite mourning customs and symbols, and in part to the poem's enigmatic character, which the abundance of unique or rare symbols suggests may be deliberate.

(2) *Three types of meaning*

In spite of these difficulties, we can go a considerable way toward grasping the poem's significance. The poem retains its power even over those who do not understand it completely—and no one does. It is important to take stock of just how much the poem does communicate, even as it withholds the meaning of many details. We begin by looking at literal description. The powerful men are, first of all, but not exclusively, powerful men; the women at the windows who "grow dark" are just that, and we should ask who they are and why they are bowing down and "growing dark". Then we ask what the imagery conveys apart from description. Imagery conveys moods as well as paraphrasable meanings, and these moods can often be described even where the meaning remains obscure.

This essay asks about three types of meaning in Qoh 12:1-7: (a) the literal, (b) the symbolic, and (c) the figurative/allegorical. These meaning-types are not mutually exclusive. On the contrary, the figurative and the symbolic require a literal base line from which both types of the extended meaning may proceed.

(a) *Literal meaning*

The literal meaning is the one given by a reading that attends to the things, actions, and events that the images depict. It is the meaning most adequately captured by paraphrase. A literal reading thinks of the images as phenomena we could actually see, were we present at the scene depicted. A movie showing the literal meaning of Jotham's allegory (Judg 9:7-15), for example, would show trees discussing who will rule over them. Looking at Qoh 12:1-7 that way, we ask: if we came into a village and saw the things this poem describes, what would we be observing?

Literal meaning may be conveyed in part by metaphor (vv. 2 and 7 are undoubtedly metaphorical). But in a literal reading, the metaphors aid in communicating the first level of meaning and are strictly subordinated to it.[33] A literal reading does not assume the presence of a governing metaphor or look for a meaning conveyed by the images independently of the literal content.

33. For example, the lamentation for the prince of Tyre in Ezekiel 28 calls him a beautiful "seal" (read *ḥotam*) in the garden of Eden (v. 12). This is a trope for beauty and contributes to the description of the first man in Eden. It remains within the bounds of the literal meaning of the allegory, which is the depiction of the first man in Eden as resplendent in wealth and beauty before being corrupted. Similarly, within a literal reading of Jotham's allegory, "shade" (Judg 9:15) may be recognized as a metaphor for "protection" as well as a reference to actual blockage of sunlight.

Of the various literal interpretations that have been attempted, I find most convincing that of C. Taylor, *The Dirge of Coheleth*. He argues vigorously that 12:2-5 is a "dirge describing the state of a household or community on an occasion of death and mourning" (pp. iii-iv). Although Taylor calls the poem a dirge, he seems to mean that it is a dirge-like description of a funeral. M. Anat (1970) goes further, maintaining that the poem is based on an actual dirge (*qinah*), which he attempts to reconstruct by stripping away whatever does not fit his metrical scheme. In spite of his arbitrary methods and far-fetched interpretations, Anat does show that some of the statements in this passage pertain to mourning. But the poem itself is not a dirge, for the purpose of a dirge is to bewail the loss of the deceased and to praise his virtues, and these themes are lacking in Qohelet 12.

We know very little about funerary laments in ancient Israel, but it is quite possible that some of the lines (e.g. vv. 3, 5aβb) are taken from actual dirges. Except for 2 Sam 1:17-27 and 3:33f., all we know of dirges is at one remove.[34] The prophets almost certainly draw on existing *qinot* either to create mocking laments (e.g. Isa 14:4-20; Ezek 26:17f.; 27:3b-10; 28:12-19), or to dramatize an impending national disaster by bewailing it or by quoting those destined to suffer it (e.g. Mic 2:4). Lamentations 1, 2, and 4 are communal laments (i.e., laments for a communal disaster). Lamentations 3 and several psalms are communal entreaties that include passages of lamentation (e.g. Pss 44, 60, 74, 79, 80, 85). References to communal mourning include Amos 5:16; 2 Sam 1:12; 1 Macc 1:27; 9:41. But Qoh 12:1-7 is not a dirge, for a dirge mourns the deceased rather than describing the funeral.

On behalf of the interpretation of 12:2-5 as depicting a funeral, we may consider that although Qohelet does urge enjoyment of life during one's youth, he does not show an obsession with physical decrepitude that would make him likely to conclude his teachings with a long threnody on the ailments of aging. He does, on the other hand, reveal an obsession with death, and his gaze most naturally returns to that subject as he brings his teachings to a close.

The syntax of the passage supports the idea that 12:2-5 describes the time of death and mourning rather than the process of aging. Qoh

34. Laments are quoted in rabbinic sources, e.g., *Sem*. 1:9; b. *B. Bat*. 91 a-b; b. *Meg*. 6a; 28b; b. *Ber*. 6b; b. *Mo'ed Q*. 25b.

12:3-5 is an extended temporal clause depicting the events that occur at the same time as "a man is going to his eternal home, and mourners are walking about in the street" (v. 5b). A man's going to his "eternal home" (v. 5bα) might be thought to mean that he is aging and heading to death, but the mourners' procession (v. 5bβ) can only signify the funeral, and thus v. 5bα as well speaks of the procession to the grave. Therefore all the events of vv. 3-5 happen at the time of an individual's death, not during the slow decline to death (though the blossoming, v. 5aβγ, continues beyond the funeral). Moreover, the darkening of the luminaries (v. 2) occurs "in the day when" (i.e., in the proximate time when) the events of the long temporal clause (vv. 3-5) take place, not long before them.[35]

During the funeral, doors are closed and the mill grows silent (thus Anat, 1970:379). While Qohelet's description of the gloom a funeral casts on a village may be exaggerated, there is evidence to show that a passing cortege could bring activities temporarily to a halt. Josephus says that "all who pass by when a corpse is being buried must accompany the funeral and join in the lamentations" (*Contra Apionem*, 2.205). B. *Mo'ed Q.* 27b and j. *Bik.* 65c (cf. *Shulḥan Arukh*, Y. D. 361, 4) speak of the obligation to rise and accompany a cortege for at least a symbolic four paces. From a time closer to Qohelet, Sira (7:34; 38:16-17) shows that participation in a funeral was considered an important communal obligation.

The strength of Taylor's case lies in his attempt to grasp what is happening on the literal plane rather than jumping quickly, as most commentators do, to figurative meanings. He is, however, wrong in his insistent exclusion of all meaning other than the literal in vv. 3-5, for the literal meaning may well have a symbolic or figurative function. The funerary interpretation can, I believe, account for the passage as a whole better than can the figurative approach. Nevertheless, many gaps remain, and not all details accommodate themselves to the funeral-scene interpretation.

35. *Bayyom še-* connects the events of v. 2 with those of vv. 3-5. The long temporal clause that it introduces must modify "the sun grows dark, etc." (and not "remember, etc." [1a]—for the remembering must take place before, not when, the events of vv. 3-5 occur). All of vv. 3-5 speaks of the same time (whether *yom* means "day" or a less definite "time", the events are pictured as concurrent). That "day", as v. 5b shows, is the time of death, when the mourners go about in the streets and the village falls silent. Although the events described are concurrent, the processes they symbolize may not be.

The scene is one of communal mourning. The image of the mourners going about the streets is explicitly funerary, and several other images are probably taken from the same situation. On the first level, then, the scene describes what happens when one dies. The unit 11:7-12:7 as a whole says: enjoy yourself before your funeral; but it says this dramatically and memorably, while conveying the finality, bitterness, and absurdity of mortality. It does not matter if some details do not contribute directly to constructing the funeral scene, because there are unambiguous signs, above all the framework of temporal clauses, that indicate that the poem speaks of dying and death.

Qohelet leads us through a village, building the scene step by step but leaving many puzzles. What village is this? We may wonder if this is in some sense the place, the state, we will come to when we grow old or when we die. We see sturdy men writhing. What nameless dread terrifies them so? The grinding-maids, whatever else they represent, are in the first instance grinding-maids. When they leave off from their work, one of the background sounds of everyday life stops, and the unwonted silence makes us aware of their earlier presence. Milling was a never-ending task, and in normal times its sound would drone on unabated. Hence its silencing would leave a disturbing void. The gloom of the ladies at the lattices darkens the mood of the village. In the past their half-hidden presence, scarcely noticed, signaled human contact. They observed, noted, and registered the busy movements of everyday life. Now their faces grow dark, an idiom that elsewhere implies grief. What grieves them? Doors are shut—against what?—and the sounds of daily life cease. Suddenly we realize that the background hum of human activity was reassuring, a constant reminder that we belong to the land of the living. Now it is gone, and all we hear is the indifferent chirp of the bird and the keening of the mourners; they alone are going about their business. Mourning women bow low. Fear is all around. Then: the budding, growing, blooming of plants. But this rebirth is without cheer, because it mocks the finality of *our* end. For humans there is the snapping of a cord, the plunge into the pit, the smashing of the vessel at the bottom.

Still leaving aside the symbolic significances—though these soon begin to intrude themselves into a literal reading—we may ask about the connotations of the imagery. The imagery of the poem, prior to any symbolic or figurative decoding, creates an atmosphere of pain, contortion, and constriction. It draws us into a world of decay, abandonment, dreary silence, and speechless grief, and makes us associate this atmosphere with aging and death—whose pain is heightened by contrast with the rejuvenation of nature.

The imagery is unsettling in an almost surrealistic way. The luminaries and light itself are extinguished. Clouds hang overhead. All is murky. Then we encounter a succession of images of distortion and despair: trembling, writhing, cessation of activity, darkening, shutting, silence, bowing, fear. What do all these people see that so disconcerts them? For whom are they mourning so intensely? The answer is inevitable (and now we move from literal to symbolic): they mourn for *you*, you to whom Qohelet addressed his advice and warnings; the "you" of v. 1. It is *your* fate that appalls them, for this, Qohelet says, is what awaits *you*. Your death is eclipsing their world, and you are present at the terrible scene.

(b) *Symbolism*

Already we have seen that some features of the picture—still taken quite literally—disturb the mental construction of the funeral scene. These features show that this is no ordinary funeral. By diverting our attention from the mundane, they provoke a reading on another level, a symbolic reading.[36]

The distinction between symbolism and allegory (or figuration) is not an absolute one, but the terms are useful in discussing two perspectives on this poem. For present purposes, we can use Samuel Taylor Coleridge's classic definition of symbolism:

> ... a symbol [in contrast to an allegory] ... is characterized by a translucence of the Special in the Individual or of the General in the Especial or of the Universal in the General. Above all by the translucence of the Eternal through and in the Temporal. It always partakes of the Reality which it renders intelligible; and while it enunciates the whole, abides itself as a living part in that Unity, of which it is the representative. (1832:40)

Coleridge is defining a particular type of symbolism, which we may

36. The following discussion of symbolism draws especially on Kurz, 1982:65-83.

designate "inherent symbolism",[37] in which conception and embodiment are simultaneous and interpenetrating. Such symbols are characterized by an "immediate presentation of something not immediate", thus evoking an ineffable, "total organic response" (Mischel, 1952:72). Since the symbol carries with it an indefinite penumbra of connotations, paraphrase cannot exhaust its meaning, nor can a symbolic image be directly translated into an entity in another domain, as an allegorical-type figure can (e.g. grinding maids = teeth; thornbush = Abimelech). Rather, in a symbol we observe a reality thickened and clarified (e.g. Esther both *is* a Jew in the diaspora and symbolically *embodies* the experience of the Jewish people in the diaspora; Abel's murder *is* brotherly conflict and also *represents* all human strife). By this understanding of symbolism, how does the poem in Qoh 12:1-7 communicate symbolically?

The poem makes the reader see his death from another perspective, that of an outside observer. From this vantage point, he sees more than an ordinary death and burial. The poem depicts a community at mourning, but also something beyond that. (It is in this regard that Taylor's determined "literal rendering" of the poem as an ordinary funeral falls short.) After all, rarely does an individual's death cause communal grief so extreme and so pervasive. The sun, moon, and stars do not truly go dark when someone dies, and light itself, the primal light of creation, does not disappear. Nor does the return of actual clouds (a welcome phenomenon in Israel) cause consternation.

While the poem describes the death and funeral of an individual, some of its imagery concurrently suggests a disaster of cosmic magnitude. The universality of the darkness and the silence—encompassing everything from the stars to the mills, from the powerful men to the menials, from the rich women to the maids—is reminiscent of prophetic depictions of the national and universal desolation awaiting humanity and nature at the end of this age.

37. Following Levin, 1956:15. "Symbolism" commonly refers to more kinds of signification than Coleridge's definition allows. Symbols may also be related to their referents by convention, prescription, or extrinsic association. Allegory, for its part, is a symbolic mode; see further Fletcher, 1964:14. In this discussion I am using "symbol" to refer to what Levin calls "inherent" or "natural" symbols.

Normal sounds are silenced and the land is blanketed in darkness and terror.[38]

> I will eliminate from them
> the voice of gladness and the voice of happiness,
> the voice of the groom and the voice of the bride,
> the sound of the millstones and the light of the candle.
> And all this land will become a desolate destruction. (Jer 25:10-11a)
>
> And I will cover . . . the heavens,
> and I will make their stars go dark.
> I will cover the sun with a cloud,
> and the moon will not shine its light.
> All the luminaries in the heavens
> I will blacken above you;
> and I will set darkness upon your land,
> says the Lord God. (Ezek 32:7-8)

The day of the Lord is

> a day of darkness and gloom,
> a day of cloud and mist . . .
> Before it peoples writhe,
> and all faces gather blackness . . .
> The sun and the moon go dark,
> and the stars withdraw their radiance. (Joel 2:2a, 6, 10b)

The cruel and wrathful day of the Lord will

> make the earth a desolation,
> and destroy sinners from upon it.
> For the stars of the heavens and their constellations
> will not shine their light:
> The sun will go dark when it arises,
> and the moon will not radiate its light. (Isa 13:9b-10)

Threat of darkness is a frequent prophetic topos; e.g. Isa 5:30; 8:22; Amos 5:18-20; Zeph 1:15. The extinguishing of light symbolizes the undoing of creation, the return to primeval darkness. The prophetic eschatology does not regard the day of the Lord as the actual

38. The patristic commentator Gregory Thaumaturgus, in his *Metaphrasis*, apparently interprets Qoh 12:1-6 as describing "that great and terrible day of God" (quoted in Plumptre, 1881:90f.).

annihilation of the universe,[39] but it does use hyperbolic, end-of-the-world imagery to suggest the extremity of that day's horror.

The prophets' eschatological symbolism draws upon imagery and possibly phraseology familiar from mourning practices, while applying the images and phrases to a personified city, land, or world: "The field is robbed, the land mourns" (Joel 1:10); "Shall the earth not quake for this, and all its inhabitants mourn?" (Amos 8:8); "The earth mourns and is withered; miserable, withered, is the land" (Isa 24:4); "Her doors moan and mourn; wiped out, she sits on the ground" (Isa 3:26); "For this the earth mourns, the heavens grow dark above" (Jer 4:28); and many more like these.

The cessation of the daily chore of milling, restated in v. 4, epitomizes the disruption of ordinary activities. What has happened to the maids? In terms of the scene depicted, their numbers around the mill may simply have dwindled as they stopped their chores in order to join the mourning. But eschatological overtones call to mind the inactivity that follows depopulation; compare, for example, Isa 13:12: "I will make man scarcer than fine gold, people than gold of Ophir". Depopulation will silence the millstones (Jer 25:10, quoted above; cf. Rev 18:22f.).

The emotional reaction of the denizens of the village in Qoh 12 is heightened beyond the formalized expressions of grief at a funeral. Everyone in this village seems not only to have joined in the formalized expressions of mourning, but to be smitten with terror and grief. Again their behavior recalls the horrified quaking and writhing common in eschatological scenes. The men in 12:3 tremble and twist just as people will do on the day of the Lord, when

> .. . . all hands will grow slack,
> and every human heart melt,
> and they will be terrified.
> Pangs and pains will seize them,
> they will writhe like a woman in labor. (Isa 13:7f.)

Their agony recalls that of the prophet, who says:

> Therefore my loins are full of trembling.
> I am seized with pangs,

39. See the definition and discussion of "eschatology" in Lindblom 1952. Eschatology refers to visions of a new age in which the relations of history or the world are altered and conditions in general are radically changed (p. 81).

> like the pangs of a woman in labor.
> I am too twisted [*na'ăweyti*] to hear,
> too terrified to look. (Isa 21:3)

The shaking and writhing of males is considered especially shocking (Jer 30:6). The terror or grief—we cannot tell which—of the men in Qohelet's village suggests they have seen a disaster of high magnitude. And, in a sense, that is the case, because every individual is a microcosm and every death is a catastrophe; it is, in fact, the end of a world.

The light that is extinguished in 12:2 is the light that is called sweet in 11:7, namely the light of life. Likewise the darkening of the light is the onset of the eternal darkness mentioned in 11:8. In one sense this is the extinction of an individual life; in another, the extinction of a universe. For the person who dies, the stars blink out, the sun goes dark (only the living "see the sun"), activities cease, and the world grows silent.

Both Qohelet and the prophets draw upon images of mourning and universal cataclysm. For the prophets, these images depict the disaster to a nation or the world at large. For Qohelet they represent the demise of the individual. Qohelet is shaping symbolism in a way contrary to its usual direction of signification. Symbolism usually views the general through the particular (Daniel representing the Jewish people in exile; a woman's mourning representing Jerusalem's; Jerusalem's mourning representing Israel's misery). Qohelet views the particular through the general, the small writ large.[40] He audaciously invokes images of general disaster to symbolize every death; more precisely—the death of you, the reader, to whom Qohelet is speaking when he addresses the youth, his ostensive audience.

The eschatological symbolism is manifest but restrained. Qohelet avoids heaping up pictures of natural upheaval and universal panic, slaughter, and destruction. Such extremes would prevent the association of the imagery with the individual death. Still, Qohelet

40. Many of John Donne's metaphors are of this sort, such as his description of his beloved as "my America, my new-found land", or his declaration: "She is all States, and all Princes, I" ("The Sun Rising"). For Donne and his contemporaries, such images were a deliberate expression of the concept of man as microcosm. "I am a little world made cunningly of elements", Donne wrote in *Holy Sonnets*, V.

does choose to depict a vast catastrophe to evoke a vision of death, that most ordinary of tragedies; and the angst he thereby reveals is not restricted to this poem. Throughout the book, Qohelet reveals an obsession with death unparalleled in biblical literature. There may be no explanation for this outside the author's personality; not every literary phenomenon has social or historical causes. But Qohelet's obsession with death intersects another of his peculiarities: he reveals no consciousness of himself as part of a nation or a community. All his values are solitary, measured by benefit or harm to the individual. This individualism imposes itself on his attitude toward death. Every death is an unmitigated loss, for its shock cannot be buffered by communal continuity.

(c) *Allegory and figuration*

It is doubtful that this poem, even as understood by the commentators who take the images as anatomical figures, would properly be classified as an allegory, as this term is commonly used in other areas of literary study. An allegory is an extended and complex image composed of an organized set of figures or tokens representing certain concepts, events, or entities in an extra-textual domain. A succession of interrelated figures (related usually within a narrative structure) is subordinated to concepts or entities existing in a distinct domain of reality. An allegory should embrace an entire text or a relatively independent segment thereof, for the literal meaning must stand on its own (see Kurz, 1982:32f.). The interpretation of Qohelet 12 as an allegory of old age does not establish any cohesiveness among the figures themselves. Rather it treats them as independent figures drawn from disparate domains (houses, flora, fauna, people, luminaries, and more), each figure representing something in the external world. Some images are often left outside the "allegory" (see, for example, Gordis, p. 329). Qoh 12:1-8 lacks the degree of internal consistency necessary to give meaning and cogency to an allegory, especially one lacking an explanatory introduction or conclusion or other interpretive guides, such as a narrative context.[41]

However, my concern here is not with the misapplication of a term but with the question of whether the poem is what its interpreters

41. Crenshaw (1986b:10) says that because of the switches to and from literal imagery we should avoid the allegorical interpretation, but he does take most of the images as symbols of the aging process.

think it is. It is no refutation of an interpretation to claim that it is using a term in an eccentric fashion. Still, it is more accurate to refer to this approach as the "figurative interpretation" when it takes the poem as in the main a loose succession of figures, each representing a different symptom of aging. The attempt to explain the totality as a series of anatomical figures will be called the "allegorical interpretation".

Whereas the symbolic meaning of an image extends the literal, the figurative meaning of an image replaces it through a series of equations: the thornbush = Abimelech, the vineyard = Israel (Isa 5:1-6), (Orwell's) pigs = Bolsheviks, etc. As such, the contours of figurative meaning are more defined than the symbolic, the signifier (farm animals, etc.) and the signified (political parties, etc.) being kept in two distinct domains. A figurative reading calls for a decoding or a translation between these two domains. A figurative reading of Qohelet 12 translates the grinding maids into teeth, the women at the windows into eyes, and so on. Once the image is translated into referent, the figure is depleted of meaning, and interpretation can proceed without further reference to it.

There is, nevertheless, a certain rhetorical gain in figurative imagery, one inhering in the process of reading rather than in the results. That process, whatever answers it arrives at, requires the reader to scrutinize the individual images while simultaneously calling to mind the unhappy facts of aging and death. We discover for ourselves the truth of Qohelet's warning that misery lies ahead.

The possibility that Qohelet's poem includes several figures for aging mixed with literal statements is established by a Sumerian saying that does just that:

> My grain roasting fails,
> Now my youthful vigor, strength and personal god have left my
> loins like an exhausted ass.
> My black mountain has produced white gypsum.
> My mother has brought in a man from the forest;
> he gave me captivity.
> My mongoose which used to eat strong smelling things
> does not stretch its neck towards beer and butter.
> My urine used to flow in a strong torrent,
> but now you flee from my wind.
> My child whom I used to feed with butter and milk,
> I can no more support it.

And I have had to sell my little slave girl;
an evil demon makes me sick. (Alster, 1975:93)

This text has two interpretive guides Qohelet's poem lacks: the first-person possessive, which directs us away from the literal plane (e.g. black mountains producing white gypsum) to something the speaker possesses (white hair); and a consistency in the domain of the signified—the difficulties of aging. Nevertheless, it does show that the objection occasionally made against the allegorical interpretation, namely that the figures are not coordinated and thus the poem is not allegorical,[42] has validity only as a comment on the term "allegorical". It does not preclude the possibility that some of the images are figures of aging.

A few of the images in Qoh 12:2-8 lend themselves naturally to interpretation as figures for the infirmities of aging, though only two do so with much clarity. The women looking through the windows seem to represent eyes, because they are said to "look", and because *ḥašak* is used elsewhere of eyes but not of people. The grinding-maids seem to represent the teeth, because milling is an obvious analogy to chewing, and because the maids are said to "grow few", a process more usual with teeth than with maids. Moreover, the Hebrew terms used for both sets of women, literally "the lookers" (*haro'ot*) and "the grinders" (*haṭṭoḥănot*), do not explicitly designate humans. Another pair of images, the keepers of the house and the powerful men, accommodate themselves easily to a figurative interpretation as the arms and legs, though it is uncertain which is which.

Some of the images in Qoh 12:2-6 are figures not of aging but of death. In v. 6 the smashing of the jug and jar into the cistern is undoubtedly figurative, though it is unclear whether the components of the image each have a specific referent, and also whether the images represent death or burial or both. Likewise, the darkening of the luminaries in v. 2 represents death figuratively. In any case, the images of vv. 2 and 6 are outside the description of aging, which is usually thought to be the point of the poem.

If the poem draws imagery from actual dirges, it may well have borrowed cryptic figures from them. Some biblical dirges are called

42. E.g. Taylor claims that it is "scarcely possible to harmonize the various details on any rational plan. But assuredly, unless a consistent whole can be made out, there is but slight reason for granting the details of the interpretation" (1874:53).

mᵉšalim or speak of the dead figuratively: Isaiah 14, called a *mašal* in v. 4 (LXX θρῆνον) speaks allegorically of Babylon as a divinity, Helel son of Dawn. Ezekiel's dirge (*qinah*) over Tyre speaks of the prince of Tyre as the first man, who is in turn described figuratively as a precious seal (Ezek 28:12-19). Num 21:27-30 is a dirge over Moab spoken by *hammošᵉlim*, "the mashal makers", and *mᵉšalim* are said to require interpretation (Prov 1:6). Some of the dirges recorded in the Talmud use images, some of them cryptic; e.g. "Our brothers are merchants, whose goods are examined at the customs house" (b. *Mo'ed Q*. 28b); "I have many coins, but no money changer to accept them" (b. *San*. 68a); "Borrow a Milesian robe for a free man who left no provision" (b. *Mo'ed Q*. 28b).[43] Some of the strange images in Qohelet's poem, such as the voice of the bird, the fear of the height (?), the terrors (obstacles?) in the path, and the almond, locust, and caperberry, may be figures whose meaning cannot be inferred from the passage itself.

The more images that can be identified with events in the process of aging, the closer the poem approaches allegory, but all the images besides those in v. 3 and 6 resist such identification. The only way to establish further linkages is to ferret out analogous features, sometimes quite far-fetched ones, between images and referents, and this immediately leads into interpretive tangles. In v. 4a, for example, the "mill" is most naturally taken as something used by the grinding-maids mentioned in the preceding sentence. But if the latter are the teeth, the mill itself cannot be. And it is no help to take the "mill" as the mouth, because (1) the mouth does not grow silent in old age; and (2) if the "mill" is the mouth, the "doors" must be the lips ("doors" seems to represent lips in Job 41:6). But in what sense is the silencing of the mouth the *circumstance* of the lips' closing? And if the doors are figurative, what is the "street" they are on? Is that street different from the literal street in the next verse? The attempt to translate the other images in vv. 2, 4b, and 5 leads to similar blind alleys. The images that do work as figures do not add up to an allegory.

Information of the sort conveyed by allegorical-type figures (the eyes dim, the legs shake, the teeth fall out, and the like) is of marginal importance in this poem. First of all, the reader must *start* with the knowledge the presumed figures communicate. We can know that the

43. Talmudic laments are collected, translated, and analyzed by Feldman, 1977:109-37.

strong men's quaking represents the legs' shaking (if this is indeed so) only if we know that legs grow shaky with age. It cannot be the poem's goal to inform us of this. At any rate, how great would our gain be if we knew for certain that Qohelet intended the powerful men to represent legs or the almond blossoms white hair? Not even the young need a sage to tell them that aging weakens the legs and grays the hair. But the poem's purpose is not to convey information; it is to create an attitude toward aging and (more important) death. A reader, especially a young one like the youth ostensibly addressed in this unit, may not be aware of the fear, loneliness, and nostalgia for an earlier reality irretrievably lost, which are the lot of many (and to some extent, perhaps all) of the aged, Qohelet undoubtedly among them. They might not know of the prospective mourning for a vanished existence. This awareness is engendered by the interaction of the literal and symbolic types of meaning.

I do not present this three-fold interpretation as a "new reading" and certainly not as a novel decoding of hitherto hidden messages. This interpretation claims to give explicit (though not complete) formulation to the primary effects the poem is intended to have on the reader. An imaginative reading will, I believe, convey some inkling of the pain and fear that hover over the scene and will connect that sense with thoughts of one's own death. Furthermore, because the entire scene is syntactically circumstantial to a main clause in the second person (12:1a), the scene must represent the fate of the ostensive audience, and through him, the reader. After all, Qohelet says quite clearly that this is what lies ahead for *you*. Moreover, the ancient reader would, I believe, discern a funeral scene in the description. Beyond that, the familiar eschatological symbolism associated with the scene would evoke a sense of death as the undoing of a world, one's own very personal world. All these figures, symbols, allusions, and overtones are controlled by the culmination of the poem, with its unveiled, literal language (12:7-8), where we are reminded that all these images finally pertain to the individual's death, and that this event in itself means that "everything is absurd".

* * *

Structure and movement

Qoh 12:1a is introductory to 12:1-7, the second section of the carpe diem begun in 11:7. Qoh 12:8 is the climax of the poem and the summary of the book's theme. The body of the poem, 12:1b-7, divides into three parts, unequal in length but unmistakably marked by the conjunction *'ad 'ăšer lo'*: (a) 12:1b, (b) 12:2-5, and (c) 12:6-7. All of this section is, in fact, one long sentence consisting of an imperative (*z^ekor*, v. 1a) and three complex temporal ("before") clauses describing the time prior to which one must perform the action advised in v. 1a (probably, to think of one's death so as to seize life's pleasures). Qoh 12:2-5 itself includes a long temporal clause (vv. 3-5b), which describes "the day when" the luminaries go dark (v. 2). The sentence seems to conclude formally with v. 5b, but v. 6 resumes the series of "before" clauses and must itself be dependent on the imperative in v. 1a. The effect of this convoluted syntax is to pull the reader without pause forward to the declaration of universal absurdity in 12:8.

The phrase *'ad 'ăšer lo'* does not mark a caesura so much as give renewed momentum to the scenic development. Without this impetus, such an intricate series of dependent clauses would peter out in vagueness. With it, the poetic movement toward the climactic smashing of the jar in the pit is suggestive of man's relentless approach to the grave. The three sections of 12:1b-7 differ in focus:

(A) 12:1b-2:	the process of dying, first old age (described literally), then the cessation of life (described figuratively)
(B) 12:3-5:	the reactions to death—the funeral (described mostly in literal terms)
(C) 12:6-7:	the process of dying, suggestive of burial (described figuratively, then literally)

Exegetical notes

12:1a. *Bwr'k* (i.e., *bôr'ekā*) without *yod* is a Massoretic reading and at least as authoritative as the one common in printed Bibles (see Baer [1886:68f.] and Euringer [1890:124-26]). The *yod* of *bwr'yk* is not an error but a fuller representation of the *e*-vowel. Both readings are singular nouns and show alternative treatments of verbs III-H with consonantal suffixes.[44] Both writings are pointed on analogy to verbs III-H (Gordis).

44. Examples of infixed *y* with singular nouns: *mḥnyk*, Deut 23:15; *mštyhm*, Isa 5:12; *mqnyk*, Isa 30:23; *nwtyhm*, Isa 42:5. The other examples in GKC §93ss may be plurals. All examples are at disjunctive accents.

Bor'eyka: Many commentators have found the reference to the Creator inappropriate here, for 12:1a requires a reference to a thought that will encourage one to enjoy life *prior* to old age and death, and a vague religious exhortation would not do that. Verse 1a cannot, however, be removed as a gloss (contrary to McNeile, Barton, et al.), because 12:1b cannot follow directly on 11:10b as a temporal clause, and if we begin a sentence with 12:1b, as Barton does, all of 12:1b-7 lacks a main clause. Various emendations have been suggested, but they are made unnecessary by the observation of Gilbert (1981:100) that in this context to think on one's creator is to think of death, for, as 12:7 says, the life-spirit must go back to the one who gave it. Gilbert believes that the sentence also implies a warning not to sin, but that does not seem relevant to context. The only counsels that would be meaningful in 12:1a are advice to enjoy life (found in five other forms in 11:9-10) and advice to keep death in mind (as in 11:8bα), and the latter is what is intended by the call to remember one's Creator.

12:1b. The "days of unpleasantness" are the years of old age, contrasting with the time of youth. They are not (contrary to Ogden, 1984b:34) the eternity of death. Once in Sheol, one would probably be unable to evaluate his current situation (that would be a *ḥešbon*, of which there are none in Sheol; 9:10). In any case, "I take no pleasure in them" would be a limp complaint when directed against one's eternity in the underworld.

12:2. "The light and the moon and the stars". Gordis says that this is a hendiadys meaning "the light of the moon and the stars". But three nouns do not elsewhere combine in that way. According to Gen 1:3-5, there is a primordial light independent of the luminaries, and that is the *'or* that Qohelet says will go dark.

The light that is extinguished in 12:2 is the light that is sweet in 11:7, namely the light of life. Likewise the darkening of the light is the onset of the eternal darkness mentioned in 11:8. The day the lights go out is "the day when" all that is described in 12:3-7 happens, and that is the time of death and the funeral.

The significance of the rain and of the clouds' returning after them is unclear. ŠWB *'ăḥar* may mean "follow" (e.g., Ruth 1:15, where *'aḥărey* is spatial) (John Hobbins, private communication). In that case, the rain has not necessarily ended. Clouds symbolize misery in Joel 2:2 and Zeph 1:15. The cloud covering the sun is an eschatological image in Ezek 32:7. But if the darkening in 12:2a refers to death, as comparison with 11:7 suggests, then the clouds may serve the depiction of the scene of gloom and despair rather than function as a figure for misery.

12:3. *Bayyom še-* connects the events of v. 2 with those of vv. 3-5. The long temporal clause that it introduces must modify "the sun grows dark, etc." (and not "remember, etc." [1a]—for the remembering must take place before, not when, the events of vv. 3-5 occur). All of vv. 3-5 speaks of the same time (whether *yom* means "day" or, less specifically, "time", the events are pictured as concurrent). That "day", as v. 5b shows, is the time of death, when the mourners go about in the streets and the village falls silent. Although the events described are concurrent, the processes they symbolize may not be.

"The keepers of the house" are servants, not watchmen. Taylor (pp. 8f.) notes that the term "keeper" is applied to various kinds of servants, not only to guards (2 Sam 20:3 refers to ten concubines David left "to keep the house"). Taylor also suggests that *'anšey heḥayil*, the "powerful men", are men of influence and position, in contrast to the servants or keepers of the house (*ibid.*). *Ḥayil*, of course, often means wealth (e.g., Isa 30:6; 60:5; Jer 17:3; Job 5:5). *'anšey/bᵉney ḥayil* sometimes refers to skillful, worthy men (e.g., Gen 47:6; Exod 18:21; 2 Kgs 2:16). In some places *'iš/ben/gibbor ḥayil* may indicate social status, e.g., Ruth 2:1 (Boaz's military prowess is irrelevant). In 1 Chron 9:13, *gibborey ḥeyl-* seems to mean "in charge of", thus to be a designation of position. In Ps 76:6, LXX (75:6) translates *'anšey ḥayil* as οἱ ἄνδρες τοῦ πλούτου, and, although this translation is not appropriate in that context, it does show an early understanding of the phrase as referring to wealth or social status. Nowhere, however, is the reference to possession of wealth or high social status unequivocal.

Wᵉyazu'u: The only other occurrence of ZW'-qal in BH is Esth 5:9, where it means to tremble in fear of someone, the sense the Aramaic cognate clearly has in Dan 5:19; 6:27.

Wᵉhit'awwᵉtu: In context the term seems to refer to a gesture of mourning, but it is not a usual term for bowing down.[45]

45. Prostration in grief is expressed by *napal* (*'al panayw*) (*'arṣah*) (Josh 7:6; Ezek 9:8; 11:13), *hištaḥăweh* (Job 1:20), and ŠḤḤ-qal (Pss 35:14; 38:7 [together with *na'ăweyti*]; 44:26; 107:39; Isa 5:15) (on *napal 'arṣah* and *na'ăweyti* see Gruber, 1980:463-79). The derivatives of 'WT never mean simply "to bow/make bow down", but indicate twisting or distortion,

The "grinding-maids", lit., "grinders" (fem.), are the maidservants, the counterparts of the men who keep the house. The "ladies looking through the lattices" are the well-to do women, women of leisure, the counterparts of the "powerful men". If Taylor is right that *'anšey ḥayil* refers to influential, well-to-do men, the four types of people mentioned form an ABA′B′ pattern and together embrace the range of social classes in the village. A similar all-encompassing grouping appears in Isa 24:2: "(Layman shall be like priest,) servant like his master, maid servant like her mistress".

Qoh 12:3bα is the phrase most amenable to the anatomical interpretation, for "grinders" (*ṭoḥănot*) is a natural trope for teeth, which do "grow few". It is, however, uncertain that *mi'eṭu* does have that meaning.

Crenshaw (1986:9) observes that a decrease in the number of grinding women would force them to work all the harder, not to cease their toils. He therefore suggests that the subject is impersonal and as such refers to the inhabitants (similarly Gilbert, 1981:104). As the old die out, the maids have less grinding to do. But this does not improve the logic of the sentence, since young people would always be taking their place.

Jenni (1968:52) explains *mi'eṭu* as elliptical for "(ihre Zahl) verringern", though it seems like an unnecessary fiction to assume an ellipsis, as he does, when the fuller phrase (**mi'ăṭu misparam?*) does not occur. More helpful is his claim that whereas the root in the qal, a conjugation frequently intransitive (*ma'ăṭu*), denotes the process *in actu*, the piel intransitive is resultative: "weil ihrer wenig geworden sind" (*ibid.*). Ibn Ezra takes the verb as elliptical for *mi'ăṭu haṭṭeḥinah* (or *mi'ăṭu ṭaḥon*), "they do little grinding". But the verb he supplies is not clearly implicit in the preceding clause. Also the

always—except in the present verse—connoting moral deviance. While moral connotations are not appropriate here, the term does seem to indicate more than merely bowing down. The men are twisted and distorted out of their normal form; i.e., they writhe. The by-form 'WH has nearly the same semantic range as 'WT. Like Qoh 12:2f., Ps 38:7 joins the motifs of writhing ('WH-niphal), bowing low, and gloominess: *na'ăweyti šaḥoti 'ad m*e*od, kol hayyom qoder hillakti*, "I writhe and am bowed exceedingly low; every day I go about in gloom". The three actions in Ps 38:7 display violent grief (in the psalm, the grief is due to feelings of guilt). In Isa 21:3 (quoted above), writhing ('WH-niphal) and terror (BHL-niphal) are the reactions to a frightening vision.

grinding-maids would not cease their grinding, or even slack off from it, because of "grinding a little". On the other hand, the diminution of their ranks might well bring the work at least to a partial halt because several people might need to work together on the mill. The reason for the thinning of their numbers may be that they have gone to join the mourning. *Baṭel* (a hapax in BH; common in MH) means "be idle", "cease" from work.

"The ladies looking through", lit., "the lookers" (fem. pl.) grow dark: *ḥašᵉku* here means "grow dark" in the sense of growing gloomy. ḤŠK alone is not elsewhere used in this sense, but the phrase *ḥašᵉku ʿeyneynu*, lit., "our eyes grew dark", means to become despondent, virtually blind with grief (Lam 5:17). (In Ps 69:24 the phrase *teḥšaknah ʿeyneyhem* refers to literal blindness.) The metaphorical transfer from "dark" to "gloomy" is a natural one. This transfer is lexicalized in the synonymous QDR, which denotes the gloom of mourning; e.g., Jer 8:21; 14:2; Job 5:11; and Ps 38:7. In the last verse, emotional darkness (QDR) appears in conjunction with bowing (ŠḤḤ) and writhing (ʿWH); see above. On the literal level, then, the sentence means that the women of the village will grieve. If this image is also a figure for the eyes, it means that one loses eyesight with age. But the choice of ḤŠK instead of KHH implies that this is not merely a physiological process, but also an emotional one, namely the loss of joy. So whether the women's "darkening" is read literally or figuratively, it connotes grief.

12:4. From this point the allegorical interpretation has hard going. The doors have been identified as the legs (Targum), the bodily apertures (Rashi), and the lips (Ibn Ezra). Gordis takes the closing of the doors to depict the continued decay of the mansion. But there is no reason to continue the physiological interpretation, even if we regard the earlier images as metaphors for aging. In any case, the funeral scene continues. During the funeral, doors are closed and the mill grows silent (thus Anat, 1970:379).

Wᵉyaqum lᵉqol haṣṣippor: This sentence has not been satisfactorily explained. The usual translation, "He rises to the voice of the bird", is awkward because the presumed subject, the old man, has not been mentioned previously, and also because it is not a great affliction to be awakened by the birds, especially when the usual time of rising is dawn. At any rate, the discomfort a bird might cause at dawn would be *waking* one up (from sleep) rather than making one *rise up* (from bed), and QWM means "rise up", not "awaken", which is expressed by QWṢ and 'WR.[46] Furthermore, a sudden jump from the figurative plane of an elaborate allegory to a literal statement (without the subject of the sentence being specified) then back again would be abrasive and hard to follow. Anat (1970:379) reads *weyiqmal qol* (suggested earlier by Zapletal), "the voice of the birds withers"; this he interprets to mean that even the birds participate in the general mourning. QML is, however, correctly used only of plants or of matter that can decay. Taylor (1874:19f.) translates, "and the bird rises to voice", in the sense of "starts to sing" (cf. *qum lammišpaṭ*, Pss 76:10; 132:8; etc.). He understands this to refer to birds of ill omen. In particular, the owl is thought to make mournful sounds, as in Mic 1:8: "I will make lamentation like jackals, mourning like ostriches [or owls]"; see also Job 30:28-31. A reference to the hooting of desert birds would indeed add to the dreary atmosphere our passage seeks to create, but the generic term *ṣippor* alone would not call to mind specifically an owl or another bird of ill-omen. Still, Taylor's translation fits MT and requires no emendations (the non-coordination of gender between the verb and the non-adjacent subject [*ṣippor* is fem.] is not a major drawback; GKC §145o). The singing bird stands in harsh contrast to the "songstresses", i.e., the wailing women, bowing in lament. Verse 5aβ draws a similar contrast.

Weyiššaḥu kol benot haššir: Taylor (1874:25-27) understands this sentence to mean that singing girls become silent; but why, then, are they said to be "bowed low"? In accordance with a well-known use of *ben/bat* as a noun of relation (BDB, p. 121b, §8), *benot haššir* can indeed mean "songstresses"; cf. Ugaritic *bnt hll*, lit., "the daughters of praise (sc., songs)", which refers to the *kṯrt*, the female singers.[47] *Benot haššir*, the songstresses, are probably mourning women, perhaps professionals, who sing their laments (note that in Amos 8:3, the songs of the palace have a mourning tone). In 2 Chron 35:25, the "singers" (*šarim*) and the "songstresses" (*šarot*) speak "laments" (*qinot*). The songstresses in Qoh 12:4 are bowed down in the traditional posture of lamentation. Bowing low, sitting on the

46. *Taqum* [*miššenateka*] in Prov 6:9b means "rise up" [for work]; it is the antonym of *tiškab* (9a).

47. Dahood, 1952:215. The *krt* are called *bnt hll snnt*, lit., "the daughters of song, swallows". This does not mean that they *are* swallows or that swallows are called *bnt hll* or (in Hebrew) *benot haššir*.

ground, and falling to the ground are expressions of mourning (see Gruber, 1980:460-79). Note in particular: "I went about as in mourning for a mother, I was bowed down (*šaḥoti*) in gloom" (Ps 35:14; see further Ps 38:7; 107:39; Isa 2:9; 5:15).

12:5aα. *Gam miggaboah yira'u*: Most commentators suppose this to mean that old people are afraid of heights, either because they develop acrophobia (is that true?) or because they do not like walking up hills (though then the object of their "fear" would be "heights" [*m*e*romim*] or "hills", "rough ground", or the like). Moreover, these interpretations produce a sudden switch from a description of an old man to a description of old people, and from figurative to literal statement. Also, *m*e*romim*, not *gaboah*, designates heights in the abstract. *Gaboah* is an adjective applied to tall or lofty entities; *gobah* (to which MT might easily be emended) refers to the height of a person or thing, not to heights or high places. Anat (1970:379; similarly Yaḥyah) explains *gaboah* as the "High One", sc., God. By this interpretation, fear of God fills the mourners as they accompany the dead. But the anarthrous *gaboah* alone, meaning "tall one", is not a recognizable epithet for God. Taylor supposes the clause, "When also they fear from on high and terrors are on the path", to be a merism equivalent to "terrors are on all sides" (1874:28), but "high" and "path" are not opposites.

The subject of *yira'u* is "the songstresses". The *gam* suggests that *miggaboah* [or *miggobah*] *yira'u* is an action belonging to the same semantic field as *yiššaḥu*—signs of mourning—as does the complementary relationship of height and lowness (the latter implicit in ŠḤḤ). This phrase and the next may refer to the emotions (at once ritual and genuine) of the mourners. Certainly they refer to fear, but the context and cause of this emotion cannot be determined.

*W*e*ḥatḥattim badderek*: literally, "And terrors are along the way". This probably refers to the emotions of those who observe the cortege passing (thus Anat, 1970:379). In other words, scenes of dismay accompany the procession.

12:5aβ. These phrases have most often been interpreted symbolically, usually as sexual allusions (it is easy to see sexual implications in the most diverse images, even caperberries and locusts). They are more likely descriptions of nature which stand in *contrast* to man. Nature, but not man, is reborn in the spring (Hertzberg; Loretz, 1964: 191-92). This thought is expressed in Job 14:7-10: "A tree has hope: if it is cut off, it may be renewed . . . But man dies and is helpless. A human expires and disappears".

W^e^yane'ṣ is correctly pointed as NṢṢ-hiphil.

W^e^yistabbel heḥagab is obscure. Since it occurs between and parallel to two sentences describing the blossoming of trees, this phrase also probably refers to a kind of plant. *Ḥagab* might be the name of a tree; in English "locust" is, interestingly, also the name of a kind of tree, so called from its locust-shaped pods. But since such a usage is unknown elsewhere in Hebrew, it is better to follow Ginsberg (p. 137) in emending *ḥagab* to *ḥaṣab* (the latter word is known from MH). The *ḥaṣab*, sc., "sea onion", "squill", gives the appearance of dying in May, when it contracts into its bulb. With the increase of moisture in August, the bulb becomes loaded (thus, *w^e^yistabbel*) and quickly bursts into life again. The hitpael of SBL can mean "be laden" in the sense of "be fecund", like the pual of that root in Ps 144:14. It is certainly less far-fetched to hypothesize that *ḥagab* refers to something other than the insect (such as a tree) or should be emended to *ḥaṣab* than to conjecture that the locust is an otherwise unknown, and rather weird, figure for the penis (Rashi, Ibn Ezra, b. *Shab*. 152a), the ankles (Targum), or the back of the pelvic cavity (Delitzsch; on the basis of a dubious Arabic etymology).

For *wtpr* read *w^e^tipraḥ* (*ḥ/h* haplography) = "will blossom" (Perles, 1895:30); PRḤ is parallel to NṢṢ in Cant 7:13 as well.

Ha'ăbiyyonah: LXX has, correctly, ἡ κάππαρις, "the caper", the sense the term bears in MH.

Ki holek ha'adam 'el beyt 'olamo (v. 5bα): The coordinate clause, "and the mourners walk about in the street" (v. 5bβ shows that v. 5bα refers not to the long process of aging but to an event occurring within a short period, the time it takes the mourners to go on their rounds. In other words, the clause signifies the dead man's procession to the grave. *Halak* is used of going from life to the underworld or to the grave in Qoh 3:20; 9:10; Ps 39:14; 1 Chron 17:11; etc. The *ki* at the beginning of v. 5b may be understood as giving the reason for the entire complex of occurrences of vv. 3-5a, not specifically for the events of v. 5a.

12:6. Here we undoubtedly do have figurative images. Their general significance is clear: death or burial, or both together. The individual application of the images is, however, obscure.

The verse seems to picture three vessels suspended by a cord over a well. The cord snaps, and the vessels fall and shatter. The image of a vessel falling into a spring at the bottom of a pit, a *bor*, is especially appropriate because the grave is called *bor* (Prov 28:17; Isa 14:15; 38:18; etc.). The smashing of an earthen vessel represents the destruction of life in Jer 18:6; Isa 30:14; and Ps 2:9. A man is called a "precious vessel" (*k*ᵉ*li ḥemdah*) in a dirge in b. *Meg*. 6a. Qohelet heightens the vessel-human metaphor by depicting the vessel three ways and describing the details of its smashing. The three-fold image might be a way of emphasizing that *everyone* dies. Ginsberg applies the three images variously: the gold bowl (*gullat hazzahab*) is the nobleman, the jug (*kad*) is the common man, and the jar (*galgal*) is the poor man. But there is no gradation evident in the last two items.

Yrtq (qere), *yrḥq* (ketiv): LXX has ἀνατραπῇ, probably a corruption of ἀναρραγῇ or ἀπορραγῇ (McNeile, p. 168); ἀπορρήγνυμι is used for *yinnateq* in 4:12. Symmachus has κοπῆναι in 12:6. The Syriac uses *ntpsq* in both places. The versional evidence is ambiguous, since the translation "break", "snap", is necessitated by context and is probably an ad hoc rendering of the same text as MT. RTQ is rare (the verb occurs elsewhere only in Nah 3:10 [in the pual], where it means "bind"). We should probably emend the qere to *yinnateq*, which is used of a cord's snapping in Qoh 4:12 (thus McNeile, Barton, Podechard, et al.). (On *nun/resh* interchanges see Delitzsch, 1920:§111, and Kennedy, 1928:100f.) Some *nun/resh* interchanges may be phonetic in origin (as in Nebuchadnezzar/Nebuchadrezzar), but graphic factors may explain others. *Yerateq* is unlikely to be a "privative niphal" (a dubious category) from *rattoq*, "chain" (Gordis).

Taruṣ as pointed could be understood as a by-form of *teroṣ*, on the analogy of the hollow verbs (Gordis), but we should probably point *teroṣ*. MT's pointing likely reflects an interpretation of *trwṣ* as "run", though RWṢ is not used elsewhere of a fall.

Galgal probably means "bowl" or the like, rather than "wheel". It is unlikely that a wheel would be dislodged by the snapping of a rope, but if it were, it would not be smashed (*naroṣ*) by the fall, but, at most, cracked—not a very strong image. Moreover, "wheel" is not a good parallel to "jug" (*kad*), nor (if one understands the sentences as sequential) would the breaking of the wheel be the last step in the destruction of a well. Furthermore, wells in ancient Palestine do not seem to have used pulleys, but simply ropes drawn along the side of the well, leaving grooves recognizable on the well-walls. (An eighth century BCE well-wheel was found at Calneh, but this may be unique.) Dahood (1952:216f.) explains *galgal* to mean "pot" or the like, deriving this sense from the root-meaning, GLL = "round". He refers to a vase on which *galgal* is inscribed in Punic characters, and to Akkadian *gulgullu*, which in addition to "skull" also means "water pitcher" (or "cooking pot").

This verse probably gives three similar metaphors for the same compound event—death and burial. The function of the image is to convey the sense that death, like the smashing of a pitcher, is irremediable, and that man descends into the pit like a pitcher plunging into a well.

12:7. The first sentence, "and the soil returns to the earth as it was before", applies both to the earthen vessel, lying broken in the well, and to the human body, lying buried in the ground, bereft of life-breath.

In 3:20-21, Qohelet said that man has no advantage over the beast because no one knows whether man's life-spirit goes upward at death. In 12:7 he states that man's life-spirit goes back to God, and this must be upwards. There is indeed a contradiction here, but it is not between a belief in an afterlife and a rejection of that belief. The return of the life-spirit to God simply means death. Neither verse affirms an afterlife. Schoors (1985b) examined the passages that refer to death and concluded that Qohelet views death as extinction.

At death, whether of man or beast, the elements of life—body and breath—separate, and God takes back his gift of life. Ps 104:29, in describing the death of all creatures, says: "You gather in their life-spirit and they expire, and they return to their dirt"; see also Job 34:14f. and Sir 40:11 (Hebrew). In the ancient Hebrew anthropology, the person *is* the body, no less than the animal's body *is* the animal. The life-spirit or breath (*ruaḥ*) is an addition that vivifies the person. This concept is evident in Ezek 37:8-10 and Gen 2:7. The creature God forms is a man *before* he gets the *ruaḥ*, at which time he becomes a *nepeš ḥayyah*, a living being. (The notion that man *is* a soul who *has* a body is Greek in origin; the only glimmer of this concept in the HB is in Qoh 3:21.) When the spirit is removed, *the person*, and not only the body, is said to go to the earth, or to Sheol, or to darkness (Ps 104:29; Qoh 6:4; 9:10; and often). Thus 12:7 does not imply continued existence of the sort that would overcome death and compensate for the miseries of life. The verse says that at death a person's body returns to the dirt and his life-spirit is withdrawn, in other words, he is deprived of breath, without which he is a helpless, weary semi-being.

The contradiction between 12:7 and 3:21 lies in the significance they attribute to the spirit's ascent. In 3:20-21 Qohelet expresses doubt that the life-spirit rises at death but implicitly grants that this event would distinguish man's demise from mere animal death, and moreover that this ascension would save man from being *hebel*. In 12:7, on the other hand, Qohelet assumes that the spirit returns to God but takes this event to mean death and nothing more, and this assumption does not prevent a *hebel*-judgment in the next verse. If the return of the spirit did mean something more than the extinguishing of life, some form of salvation for the individual, Qohelet would be reversing the entire pessimistic, worldly thrust of the book in one sentence without context or preparation. Moreover, the very next sentence, the declaration of universal absurdity, would be undermined, for if the essential part of man, the soul (as *ruaḥ* would mean in that case), were to survive with God, man would not be *hebel*, however that word is defined.

Since 12:7 does not imply afterlife, it is actually *more* pessimistic than 3:21. In the earlier verse, Qohelet at least allows that the life-spirit's ascent to God would redeem humanity from absurdity, whereas in the later verse he affirms such an ascent and yet sees no escape from death's obliterating power or life's universal absurdity.

The contradiction in the assumptions behind these two verses cannot be reconciled logically, but it does not have major implications for the book's meaning. In 3:21 Qohelet is countering an idea that was probably appearing in Jewish thought for the first time: the ascent of the soul to eternal life. Having discounted that possibility as unknowable and thus irrelevant, Qohelet leaves it aside. When, at the climax of his grim description of death in chapter 12, he speaks of the departure of the life-breath, he perceives it in the ancient way as signifying God's repossession of the life force.

12:8. In the most prominent and powerful inclusio in the Bible, the book of Qohelet returns to its opening declaration. Qoh 12:1-8 reverses the structure of 1:2-8. There the declaration of universal absurdity is demonstrated by examples of futile circularity in nature.

Here a description of the futility of human life—futile in the sense that it ends up back where it started (*k*^{e}*šehayah*; v. 7)—leads to and justifies the declaration that all is absurd.

12:9-14

> (9) Furthermore, Qohelet was a sage—he constantly taught the people knowledge; and he listened, and investigated, <and> composed[a] many sayings. (10) Qohelet sought to find pleasing words and he wrote[b] the most honest words of truth.
>
> (11) The words of the sages are like goads, and the
> [words of] masters of collections are like implanted nails set by a shepherd.
>
> (12) At the same time, my son, of these things be wary: Making many books is pointless, and <studying>[c] too much wearies the flesh.
>
> (13) The last thing to be said, when everything has been heard, is: Fear God and keep his commandments; for this
> [concerns] every man. (14) For God will bring every deed into judgment, [judging even] every secret deed, as to whether it is good or evil.

[a] *w*^{e}*tiqqēn* (MT *tiqqēn*). [b] point *w*^{e}*kātōb* (MT *w*^{e}*kātûb*)
[c] *lahăgôt* (MT *lahag*)

The book's motto (12:8) both concludes the poem on death and introduces the epilogue. The continuation of the epilogue teaches four points:

(a) Qohelet was a sage and a writer of meshalim who sought pleasing and true words (vv. 9-10).

(b) The words of sages prod one (to thought or action) by stinging him, so it is best to avoid excessive intellectual activity (vv. 11-12).

(c) One's main concern should be to fear God and obey him, for he will judge all deeds (vv. 13-14).

EXCURSUS III
AUTHOR AND SPEAKER; THE EPILOGUE

The voice that comes into prominence in the epilogue speaks in a pronouncedly didactic tone. The speaker marks off the points to be learned: "Furthermore, . . . At the same time . . . The last thing to be said . . .". He praises the sage Qohelet, generalizes about the words of sages, cautions the listener against excess in writing and speaking, and sums up with an exhortation to fear God and obey him, since judgment is certain. He addresses these words to *b^e^ni*, "my son", in the customary Wisdom fashion, thus creating a setting of discourse well known from didactic Wisdom Literature, in which the father teaches his son wisdom. The epilogist, i.e., the frame narrator, thereby represents himself as a sage, a teacher of Wisdom.

Traditional commentators assumed that because the epilogue is attached to the book of Qohelet, it was composed by Qohelet. Modern commentators have assumed that because the epilogue looks back at Qohelet and speaks *about* him, it is to be attributed to a later editor. I have argued elsewhere (1977a) that the words of Qohelet (1:3-12:7), the motto (1:2; 12:8), and the epilogue (12:9-14) are all the creation of the same person, the author of the book, who is not to be identified with Qohelet, his persona. In other words, the speaker we hear referring to Qohelet in the third person in 1:1-2; 7:27 (*'amar haqqohelet*); and 12:8, who comes to the fore in the epilogue (12:9-14), and whose "I" we hear just once in the suffix of *b^e^ni* in 12:12—this speaker is the "teller of the tale", the frame narrator of the "tale" of Qohelet. This narrator looks back and, using the common stance of wisdom teacher, tells his son about the sage Qohelet, transmitting to him Qohelet's teachings, then appreciatively but cautiously evaluating the work of Qohelet and other sages. The body of the book is formally a long quotation of Qohelet' words.

The frame-narrator presents himself not as the creator of Qohelet's teachings but as their transmitter. He keeps himself well in the background, but he does not disappear. Insofar as the frame-narrator presents himself as having selected certain of Qohelet's teachings to transmit, he is indeed analogous to an editor, though that may be a guise. The activity of the epilogist goes deeper than just gathering and (loosely) arranging Qohelet's sayings. In 7:27 in particular, the authorial voice (saying "Qohelet said") imposes itself into the middle of a sentence, though there is no necessity for doing anything other than joining the sayings, as elsewhere. In other words, the frame-narrator is composing the sayings, not merely gathering them. Furthermore, the vocative *bᵉni* is appropriate not to an editor but to someone who presents himself as speaking to his son. If another person besides Qohelet gathered and edited Qohelet's sayings, this activity went so deep as to make the redactor, for all practical interpretive purposes, the *author* of the book (see my discussion of types of editorship in Fox, 1977a:84-91).

The book of Qohelet, then, is built on successive levels of perspective, each one with its own time-frame and each encompassed in the next:

(1) The frame-narrator, who tells about
(2) Qohelet, whose voice encompasses
(2a) Qohelet-the-reporter, the narrating "I", who speaks from the vantage point of old age and looks back on
(2b) Qohelet-the-observer, the experiencing "I", who undertook the investigation that the book reports.

Levels 1 and 2 are different persons (different, that is, within the text; the distinction may, however, be fictional). Levels 2a and 2b are different perspectives of one person. The time-frame of level 1 is the present tense of the speaker in the epilogue; it is the temporal context in relation to which the phrase "Qohelet said" is past tense. The time-frame of the frame-narrator is supposed to be some time after Qohelet lived. The time-frame of level 2a is the one in which "all is absurdity" is spoken. It is the time in which Qohelet looks back on his experiences and reports them, thus it is the present to which the past tense of certain verbs of observation, cognition, and speaking is relative ("I saw", "I realized", "I said", and the like). The time-frame of level 2b is the context in which the exploring, experiencing, and cognition took place.

There are several parallels in ancient Wisdom Literature, particularly in Egypt, but also in Mesopotamia and Israel, to the use of an anonymous third-person, retrospective frame-narrative encompassing the monologue of the teacher. We find this technique in Kagemeni,[48] Ptahhotep,[49] Neferti,[50] Ipuwer,[51] Duachety, Onchsheshonqy,[52]

48. In the body of the Instruction for Kagemeni the old vizier, the father of Kagemeni, speaks to his children words of advice and writes them in a book. The epilogue speaks about the vizier in retrospect and tells how his son benefited from his father's counsels and became vizier himself. The narrative frame, which surrounds and presents the words of the main character, thus looks back upon him as a figure in the past and praises his work.

49. Ptahhotep opens with an introduction speaking about Ptahhotep and describing the circumstances in which he delivered his teaching to his son.

50. Neferti, written in the reign of Amenemhet I (12th dynasty), begins with a frame-narrative cast in the reign of Snefru (4th dynasty). The frame-narrative looks back on the ancient sage Neferti and introduces his words in an attitude of esteem. From the point of view of the speaker of the frame-narrative, Neferti and his words lie well in the past. The work is of course fictional, a prophecy *ex eventu* of the "future" triumph of Amenemhet I.

51. The introduction of the prophecy of Ipuwer is lost, but it must have given the setting implied by the ending of the work, which refers to Ipuwer in retrospect: "What Ipuwer said when he answered the Majesty of the All-Lord" (15,5). The introduction must have told how Ipuwer (like Neferti) was called to address the king. The body of the work contains Ipuwer's words of lament about the breakdown of the social order, though his "I" occurs only occasionally (6,5; 6,8; 12,6). The speech of Ipuwer, which comprises the main part of the book, is thus presented within the framework of an anonymous narrator who looks back on the sage, quotes him, and speaks about him.

52. Onchsheshonqy opens with a frame-narrative explaining how the vizier Onchsheshonqy came to write his instruction on potsherds while in prison. His words—the body of the book—are a long quotation (see the extended quoting-phrases in 4,17-21; 5, 14, 19). After the introduction, his advice to his son is transmitted. The introductory story is almost certainly fictional. Whether or not the vizier Onchsheshonqy ever existed, what we now have in the book as a whole is an anonymous frame-narrator telling the story of that sage—what he did and what he said.

Shuruppak,[53] and Ahiqar,[54] as well as in Deuteronomy[55] and Tobit.[56,57] Most of these frames, especially the shorter notices, could

53. Sumerian fragment; Lambert 1960, 92.

54. The introductory narrative tells a complex story about the betrayal of the childless vizier Ahiqar by his nephew Nadin, whom he has adopted and instructed in wisdom. In the Aramaic text, the transition between the story and the proverbs is lost, as is the end of the text, which probably returned to the frame narrative. In other versions, the proverbs are Ahiqar's instruction to Nadin, and are followed by the story of the betrayal and Nadin's undoing.

55. On Deuteronomy's affinities with Wisdom Literature see Weinfeld, 1972:part III. In its present state, but excluding the additions in 4:41-43; 32:48-52; and 34:1-12, Deuteronomy is an extended first-person monologue of Moses set within a sparse third-person framework, which is indicated by a number of quoting phrases. Deut 1:1-5 is an extended quoting-introduction; 28:69 is a retrospective summary. Briefer quoting-phrases are more numerous, e.g., 5:1; 27:19, 11; 29:1. Deut 31:14-25, whose relation to D is problematic, is a short narrative about Moses. Thus in Deuteronomy too there is a voice telling *about* the chief character, looking back on him from an indefinite distance, while remaining itself well in the background. Polzin (1980) has carefully examined the relation between the narrator's voice and Moses'.

56. Immediately after the title and brief identification, which is itself not part of the frame-narrative, Tobit begins presenting himself by a personal retrospect similar to Qohelet's. Both sages look back from the vantage-point of old age upon their earlier experiences: "I, Tobit, walked all the days of my life in ways of truth . . .". Then follows a monologue of typical wisdom counsels and observations. But the book taken as a whole is a third-person narrative. In 3:7ff. the author begins to speak *about* Tobit, with Tobit quoted at length throughout the book. Tobit 14:15 is an authorial retrospect taking us down to a time after the destruction of Nineveh, when Tobit's son dies at age 127. (Even if chapters 13 and 14 are later additions as Zimmermann argues [1958:24], the essential narrative structure of the book is as described here, though in that case the distance of the frame-narrative's retrospect would be less pronounced.) Although the emphasis here is quite different from that of Qohelet, with the frame-narrator's voice much more prominent in Tobit, the essential narrative design is the same: a frame-narrator who looks back on Tobit who looks back on himself. What is of special interest is that the first-person speaker (Tobit) can appear right after the title without a frame-narrator's introduction, even in a work where the voice of the frame-narrator does not hesitate to make itself heard throughout the work.

have been written by the authors of the instructions or an "editor", but they all testify to an ancient convention of presenting the teacher's words through a retrospective frame. It seems likely that adherence to this convention in Qohelet belongs to the original creative stage of the work.

Since there is an implied author mediating Qohelet's words, we cannot simply identify Qohelet with the author. Qohelet is a persona, a character created in the work who may be a close expression of the author's attitudes, but whose words cannot be assumed to be inseparable from the ideas of his creator. Delitzsch makes the acute observation that "In dem Buch [viz., 1:2-12:8] redet Koheleth-Salomo, dessen Maske der Verf. angenommen . . ." (p. 414). ("Persona" originally referred to the mask through which an actor speaks; it now means a character through whom an author speaks.) Loretz makes a similar point, approaching the question from an inquiry into the genre of Qohelet's monologue (1963). Loretz points to the formulaic, traditional usages in Qohelet's self-presentation and casts doubt upon the simple identification of speaker with author:

> Es gilt zu überprüfen, ob die übliche Gleichsetzung des "Ich" des Buches mit dem persönlichen "Ich" des Verfassers Ausgangspunkt einer Interpretation des Buches sein kann. Es muß also untersucht werden, ob Qohelet als historische Person oder als "poetica personalità" (Croce) zu uns spricht" (1963:48).

Qohelet may be recognized as a persona even if one regards him as based on an historical character.

The thesis summarized above has only limited implications for interpretation of Qohelet's teachings, because the author does not undermine the persona's ethos or subvert his teachings (we may easily imagine Qohelet himself urging circumspection about the teachings of the sages). The caution the epilogue expresses is a public, protective stance, intended to ease acceptance of Qohelet's pungent words. The distance the epilogist sets between himself and Qohelet is protective rather than polemical (see below). Qohelet, for his part, is not made into an unreliable persona; he does not self-

57. In Anii, the epilogue speaks about the sage but reports a discussion that followed the teaching rather than referring to the setting in which the instructions were given. The beginning of Phebhor is lost, so we do not know if this technique was used there.

destruct. Qohelet is a persona: it is the author's voice we hear speaking through the mask. To be sure, Qohelet shows an awareness of the uncertain basis of his knowledge, but this awareness is part of *his* message and does not undermine his reliability. There is little doubt that the author means us to take Qohelet's words seriously—his pessimistic, querulous reflections as well as his affirmations of ethical-religious values. In any case, there is no ideological conflict between Qohelet's teachings and the epilogue. Both express the author's views, but with different tones and emphases.[58]

The essential function of the epilogue is to mediate Qohelet's words to the reader in a way that makes them more plausible and more tolerable.

(1) The epilogue implicitly testifies to the reality of Qohelet, simply by talking about him as having lived and speaking about him in the matter-of-fact, reliable voice of a sage. Qohelet, with his puzzling name and his claims of royalty and vast wealth, is at first meeting not an entirely plausible character. The epilogist indicates that we are to react to Qohelet as a real person. The reader's acceptance of the reality of literary figures is important to certain authors even when writing the most outlandish tales. The fictitious editor became a common device of eighteenth century English novels. Swift, for instance, created a fictitious editor for *Gulliver's Travels* who does not *say* that Gulliver existed, but simply talks about his own relationship with that character, where exactly he lived, how his memoirs came to the editor, how he edited them. Also like the epilogist of Qohelet, the "editor" of *Gulliver* affirms the authenticity of the persona's memoirs by asserting that there is more material than he has included. What Swift seeks is not necessarily genuine belief in his characters' existence (though that may be the intention in the case of Qohelet) but *suspension of disbelief* for the purposes of

58. Tyler (pp. 79-85) argues that the epilogue is by the author, but on quite different grounds. He regards "Qohelet" as a "representation of Philosophy as a personified assembly". The *author's* point is supposedly that "Philosophy" shows itself vain and dissatisfying by arriving at contradictory conclusions from the same facts, after which the epilogue sets forth the positive conclusion. But contrary to Tyler, the epilogue in no way dismisses or repudiates Qohelet. Moreover, as one of Tyler's early reviewers noted (*ibid.*, p. 82f.), the religious exhortation of the epilogue is too short to be a refutation of the "philosophic" doctrines that make up most of the book.

the fiction.[59] In a similar manner Raymond Chandler Harris succeeded in making many people accept the reality of Uncle Remus, even to the point of writing letters to this literary creation, and the objective, "normal" voice of the frame-narrator that introduces and tells about Uncle Remus contributed to the character's credibility. The epilogist of Qohelet succeeded in convincing many readers that he was intimately familiar with Qohelet.[60]

The frame-narrative sets a certain protective buffer between the author and the views expressed in his work simply by distinguishing between the two. The author may be attempting to soften resistance to the book by presenting it as a report of what Qohelet said.[61] The more conservative reader may align himself with the voice heard in the epilogue and so be less inclined to reject the *book*.

(2) The epilogue projects—and thus teaches the reader to hold—an attitude of respect toward Qohelet. The epilogist's stance as Wisdom teacher helps to establish his own reliability and to show the attitude the reader is to take toward Qohelet's words. The epilogist, speaking in a voice that is reassuringly conventional, testifies that Qohelet was indeed a sage with praiseworthy goals who spoke honest words of truth. The epilogue praises Qohelet's diligence in studying Wisdom and teaching it to the people. He was, we are told, a public figure, dedicated to the people, an author of quantity as well as quality. He listened to and examined the wisdom of the past—for a sage is a link in the chain of tradition—and created many sayings of his own. He sought fine words—for the sages placed great emphasis on excellent speech—and wrote the truth. This testimony is especially important in the case of a thinker such as Qohelet whose thought may appear bizarre and even dangerous. The reader is assured that Qohelet's teachings are within the limits of tolerability, for they could be

59. See the analysis of the rhetorical function of *Gulliver's* fictitious editor and others by Romberg [1962:69-72].

60. E.g., Ellermeier (1967:100): "1,2 zeigt somit dieselbe Vertrautheit mit dem Manne Qohelet wie man es für 12, 9-11 herauszustellen hat. Wir sehen hier dieselbe Hand am Werke. Es ist der erste Epilogist, der Qohelet—vielleicht als Schüler, sicher als Anhänger—persönlich gekannt hat".

61. Romberg (1962:77ff.) discusses the comparable case where an author detaches himself from his creation by concealing himself behind an editorial fiction. On disguise of authorship as a literary device see also Matthes, 1928:33-113.

accepted and praised even by someone as pious as the narrator finally proves to be.

(3) The epilogue—especially when seen as part of an encompassing frame—identifies the book as a whole with an indisputably orthodox religious attitude. This it does, as all commentators have recognized, in 12:13-14, where the speaker places fear of God and obedience to his commands as the highest value (they are a single value, as the singular "this" in v. 13b suggests). The epilogue undoubtedly succeeded in this purpose. The book's conclusion helped its acceptance as sacred scripture, for it "ends with words of Torah" (b. *Shab* 30b). Since it is the last word in the book, the familiar piety of the conclusion could outweigh the uncomfortable observations of the preceding twelve chapters. Jerome (in his commentary to 12:13) says:

> The Hebrews say that, among other writings of Solomon which are obsolete and forgotten, this book ought to be obliterated, because it asserts that all the creatures of God are vain, and regards the whole as nothing, and prefers eating and drinking and transient pleasures before all things. From this one paragraph [12:13f.] it deserves the dignity that it should be placed among the number of the divine volumes, in which it condenses the whole of its discussion, summing up the whole enumeration, as it were, and says that the end of its discourse is very easily heard, having nothing difficult in it, namely, that we should fear God and keep his commandments (trans. Ginsburg, p. 15).

The particular belief that the book's conclusion manifests is "Gesetzesfrömmigkeit", an attitude that regards piety as residing in obedience to God's revealed Law. This belief is not attested in Wisdom Literature prior to Ben Sira. For that reason many commentators have taken the presence of this belief as proof not only that the author of the attitude is different from Qohelet, but that his attitudes are irreconcilable with those of the body of the book. Zimmerli says:

> Wenn der Epilogist dann allerdings diese Furcht Gottes als Halten der Gebote und Glauben an das göttliche Gericht über Gute und Böse beschreibt, dann interpretiert er Kohelet nach einem diesem fremden Maßstab der rechtgläubigen Gesetzesfrömmigkeit, die glaubt, daß im geoffenbarten Gebot Gottes die Weisheit, die auch den rechten Lebenserfolg bringt, geoffenbart sei (pp. 250f.).

In fact, however, the idea expressed in vv. 13-14 is not contrary to Qohelet's thought. "Orthodox legal piety" is indeed foreign to Qohelet insofar as he, like Proverbs, does not speak of specific divinely revealed commandments. Yet Qohelet does not *contradict* "Gesetzesfrömmigkeit"; he (like Proverbs) just does not advocate it explicitly. The epilogist, however, does so—in part to establish his own ethos, which he uses on behalf of the persona. Qohelet is presented as a sage conducting his discourse within the stylistic and conceptual framework of traditional Wisdom (though straining that framework to the limits). The epilogist allows Qohelet the freedom of movement necessary for his inquiries by propounding a piety that overrides Wisdom in case of conflict.

(4) While showing respect and appreciation for Qohelet, the epilogist sets a certain distance between himself and the words of Qohelet—and of other sages as well. The epilogist is somewhat chary of all the sages. Their words are like goads, so they can sting. More significantly, in the final two verses the epilogist relegates all the words of the sages—Qohelet's among them, but not more so than the others'—to a place of secondary importance by summing up the essence of human wisdom: fear God and keep his commandments, for his judgment is thorough and ineluctable. But this must be stressed: the epilogue's circumspection is directed not toward Qohelet's words in particular, but toward Wisdom as such, of which Qohelet's teaching is a part.

The epilogist's caution is in no way a polemic against Qohelet or against Wisdom in general. On the contrary, placing Wisdom in the second rank constitutes a call for tolerance of expressions of opinion. It allows everything to be heard and considered as long as everything is finally subordinated to the proper fundamental belief. By circumscribing the significance of Wisdom, the epilogist suggests that Qohelet's probing and complaining are not truly dangerous, for his conclusions are not determinative for the fundamentals of action and belief. In a similar way the rabbis affirmed the value of midrash as a means of revealing unknown truths and teaching known ones—so long as its conclusions accord with the Torah and the essentials of belief.

(5) Finally, the frame sets Qohelet's words in a broader literary and religious context. The epilogue includes Qohelet's teachings among the "words of sages". What does this classification show

about the epilogist's concept of the organization of literature and Qohelet's place in the emerging canon'?

Sheppard (1977) seeks to draw from the epilogue an understanding of editorial attitudes toward the emerging canon. He asks about the extent to which Wisdom books, in the view of the epilogue, are a fixed collection, and how the epilogue situates Qohelet in that category. Sheppard's answers to these important questions are perceptive, but in some ways they go beyond what the epilogue can tell us.

Sheppard (p. 185) points to some well-recognized correspondences between 12:13-14 and the body of the book: the admonition to fear *'ĕlohim* and keep his commandments and the affirmation that at the appointed time God will judge. These correspondences show a "thematizing" of Qohelet's words in the epilogue (p. 186; Jerome, more clearly, calls the final two verses a condensation and summary of the book). Sheppard says that this thematizing, which bears affinities above all to Ben Sira, provides an interpretation of the relationship between biblical Wisdom and the commandments of God in the Torah. Qohelet "has been thematized by the epilogue in order to include it fully within a 'canon conscious' definition of sacred wisdom" (1977:188).

I do not agree that Ben Sira has "exactly the same ideology as Qoh 12:13-14" (p. 187). Unlike Ben Sira, the epilogist does not bring wisdom (or Wisdom Literature) into the circumference of "Gesetzes-frömmigkeit". He does not say that obedience to God's commandments *produces* wisdom (as Sir 1:26 claims), nor does he identify wisdom with Torah, as Sirach 24 does. I do agree, however, that the epilogue sets Qohelet in the domain of Wisdom thought, and that Wisdom has become "a developed theological construct' (p. 187). (I understand this to refer to a concept of a type of thought with a set of beliefs to which texts so labeled are supposed to conform.) But 12:13f. does not show that the Wisdom sayings in Qohelet (or any other words of sages) are "associated explicitly with *God's* commandments" (p. 185). On the contrary, those verses imply a distinction between words of sages on the one hand—these are commendable so far as they go—and fear of God and obedience to his commandments on the other—these together constitute the essential virtue of man; this is all that really counts.

Moreover, this "construct" reveals no more "canon-consciousness" than Proverbs 1:1-7. Both passages simply recognize that there are "words of sages" worthy of respect. It is fair to say that both passages reveal an inchoate concept of "Wisdom Literature" (see Excursus IV), but this concept is "canon-conscious" only in the vaguest sense. Neither passage shows awareness of a broader *collection* of which Proverbs or Qohelet was a part. Qoh 12:11 does, however, show the concept of a genre of writings associated with *ḥăkamim*. Sheppard infers from the reference to "these" (v. 12a)—understood as "these collections"—that the writer has some specific set of Wisdom books in mind. That would be so if *w^eyoter mehemmah* etc. did indeed mean that one should avoid books other than the "collections" mentioned in v. 11. But v. 12a does not say to beware "*of* books other than these" (that would be *miyyoter*, see ad loc.). Rather, it is the aforementioned Wisdom teachings that we must be wary of.

G. Wilson (1984) argues for a variant of Sheppard's theory. Wilson understands the "words of the wise" in 12:11 as referring not to the sayings of the wise in general, but specifically to the book of Proverbs. He argues that correspondences between the prologue to Proverbs and the epilogue to Qohelet bind the two books and imply a hermeneutical principle—that fearing Yahweh and keeping his commandments constitute "the proper context within which to understand and evaluate the wisdom endeavor" (p. 192). I agree that this principle is implied by the epilogue, but see no evidence that the epilogist has specifically Proverbs + Qohelet in mind. Wilson does not bridge the gap between his assertion that "it is not impossible that the epilogist has purposely cast his description of Qohelet in light of the exhortation of Proberbs" (p. 181) (which we may grant) and his assumption that the epilogist *has* done so.

Wilson says that a canonical editor of Qohelet sought to make explicit the connection, implicit in Prov 1-9, between "fearing God" and "keeping his commandments" (p. 189). But no such connection is implied in Proverbs, which never identifies the *miṣwot* of the sage with those of God, not even implicitly. To be sure, Deuteronomy does, as Wilson points out, use Wisdom terminology in speaking about divine commandments, but there is no evidence for Deuteronomic influence on Wisdom (prior to Ben Sira, at least). (If Prov 1-9 did borrow Deuteronomic concepts, its consistent identification of *miṣwot* with the sage's instructions would be a deliberate desacralization, quite contrary to the development that Wilson argues for.) In any case, Deuteronomy's application of Wisdom rhetoric to divine law does not show an *identification* of the commandments of the wise with God's commandments.

* * *

12:9. The meaning of *yoter še-* cannot be derived from MH *yoter mišše-* meaning "beyond the fact that", as is commonly done (Podechard, Barton, Gordis; so most), because the phrase in Qohelet lacks a *mem* before the first member to mark the lesser term of the comparison. The clause *w^{e}yoter šehayah qohelet ḥakam*, translated mechanically, means: "and a remainder [= an additional thing] (is the fact) that Qohelet was a sage"; thus, "Furthermore . . .". (Hertzberg, Ginsberg; the disjunctive *zaqeph gadol* reflects a similar interpretation). (LXX περισσὸν is probably to be taken adverbially, "exceedingly . . ."). The additional information (the "*yoter*") is not the fact that Qohelet was wise—that was asserted clearly enough in 1:16—but that he was a sage and a diligent teacher of the public.

'od means either "constantly" (Ibn Ezra, Galling, Hertzberg; cf. Qoh 7:28; Gen 46:29; Ruth 1:14; Ps 84:5; etc.) or (less likely) "additionally", i.e., in addition to the Wisdom quoted thus far (Ginsberg). In either case the sentence implies that Qohelet's teaching extended beyond the Wisdom quoted in this book.

Gordis says that this verse draws a distinction between a professional Wisdom-teacher for the rich (a *ḥakam*) and a teacher of knowledge to the common people, both of which Qohelet was. But the authors of Wisdom Literature would not have distinguished teachers of the upper class from teachers of the general populace. The Wisdom writers never saw their task of instruction as limited to certain social classes (though they do reveal an unconscious class orientation). The knowledge and virtues of wisdom are accessible to all (Prov 8-9). Nor does *ḥakam* ever refer to a professional teacher of the well-to-do as opposed to a teacher of the general populace. On the contrary, this verse regards public instruction as an aspect of being a *ḥakam*. That term here appears to mean "sage" in the sense defined in §0.41, a producer of Wisdom; see Excursus IV.

W^e'izzen w^{e}ḥiqqer tiqqen m^{e}šalim harbeh: Ginsburg makes the interesting suggestion that the asyndeton in the series of verbs shows that the first two are adverbial modifiers of the third. GKC §120g-h brings several examples in which one verb serves to modify another with which it is coordinated (e.g., *mihăru šakĕḥu ma'ăśayw*, "they quickly forgot his deeds"; Ps 106:13), but it mentions no examples of two verbs modifying a third. The three verbs probably represent a sequence. Syr, 10 MSS K-R, and, more significantly, Aq have a conjunction before *tiqqen*, and a restoration of that *waw* seems preferable to an ad hoc syntactical explanation.

'izzen probably does not mean "weigh" (Delitzsch, Hertzberg, Podechard, and most)—the word for that is *šaqal*. Also, it is unlikely that a prefixed noun-form would be the source for a denominative. That process would require the extraction of the root 'ZN from *mo'znayim*, though the *'aleph* is quiescent (the root is in fact WZN [as in Arabic] or YZN), before turning it into a verb. *'izzen* might be direct verbal derivation of WZN/YZN, though that root is not attested in NW Semitic except in *mo'znayim* and cognates. Rather, 'ZN-piel is probably a denominative from *'ozen*, "ear", equivalent to 'ZN-hiphil. *'izzen* is understood to mean "listen" by Syr, Aq, Targum, Rashbam, and Ginsberg.

The sage listens to others' wisdom—see Prov 1:5-6; Sir 3:29; 6:33-35—so that he can compose proverbs of his own. As Ben Sira teaches: "When a man of understanding hears a wise word, he praises it and adds to it" (21:15).

Fishbane (1985:30-32) compares the epilogue's description of Qohelet's activities with Assyrian and Babylonian colophons. Both mention writing and (possibly) composing, but they hardly show the "striking similarity" claimed for them (*ibid*., 30). In colophons the scribe speaks in the first person of his activity in writing, composing, and collating the text. The epilogue to Qohelet does not speak in praise of scribes, but of sages. Even if there was a considerable overlap between the two groups (something commonly assumed but not demonstrated),[62] the activity of the sages praised here is not the inscription, editing, or preservation of documents, but the formulation of their own wise teachings. Of the technical terminology in Qoh 12:9-12, only the verb "write" and the root of "make" (*'ăśot*) are paralleled in the Babylonian and Assyrian colophons that Fishbane mentions. (The cognate to ʿŚH appears in a different stem, see below.) Qohelet's own activity undoubtedly bears certain similarities with those of scribes, since he composed his *m*^e^*šalim* in writing, but he is not being portrayed as a scribe.

12:10. *wktwb*: LXX's γεγραμμένον agrees with MT's consonants and pointing, but the pass. ptp. is very awkward here. Aq, Sym, Syr,

62. D. Orton discusses evidence of this in his forthcoming book, *The Understanding Scribe. Matthew and the Apocalyptic Ideal* (JSNT Supp.).

and Vul use a finite verb ("and wrote") but may have the same consonants and be interpreting the inf. abs. as a finite verb, and this expedient commends itself as agreeing with Qohelet's usage (4:2 and 8:9).

Yošer dibrey 'ĕmet: An Aramaizing equivalent of this phrase appears in Prov 22:21, *qošṭ 'imrey '^{e}met*. *Qošṭ*, which corresponds to *yošer*, is the bound form (of *qošeṭ*; see Ps 60:6), suggesting that in Qoh 12:10 *yošer* too is a bound form. In that case, *yošer dibrey 'ĕmet* is a superlative, like *qomat 'ărazayw* (// *mibḥar b^{e}rošayw*), "his tallest cedars" (Isa 37:24) and *ḥakmot śaroteyha* "her wisest princesses" (Judg 5:29). Thus: "the most honest words of truth".

12:11. *Ba'ăley 'ăsuppot*, a hapax, is difficult. *'ăsuppot* probably refers to collections of sapiential sayings; thus LXX συναγμάτων. *Ba'ăley-* has been taken to mean "members of" (Delitzsch, Barton, Gordis, Hertzberg, who compare *ba'al* meaning "participant" [in a covenant or vow]) in Gen 14:13 and Neh 6:18. But the meaning in those verses is not quite the same, because participants in a covenant may be said to be *b^e'alim* in the sense that they "possess" it. It is better to take *ba'ăley 'ăsuppot* as the "masters of (mashal) collections" (// *ḥăkamim*) and to supply *dibrey* from v. 11aα (thus Ginsburg, who notes the very same ellipsis in 10:12 and 13). MH uses *b^e'alim* to refer to men *expert* in different types of literature: *ba'ăley miqra'* = experts in Scripture; *ba'ăley 'aggadah* = experts in Aggadah, and so on. Those who are expert in collections are themselves the wise, in the more restricted sense of those wise men who study and produce mashal collections; in other words they are "sages" as I am using the term (see Excursus IV).

Dar^{e}bonot are the nails on the end of ox goads, thus parallel to *maśm^{e}rot* in v. 11aβ. Commentators have invariably thought the point of comparison between goads and words of sages to be that both spur a person on to better actions. The similarity between *ba'ăley 'ăsuppot* (however that is taken) and implanted nails is thought to be that the latter are difficult to move or remove. We would not, however, expect the parallel comparisons to refer to completely different qualities: to the ability to encourage thought or better behavior in others on the one hand, and to being in themselves unchanging and permanent on the other. I suggest that the "nails" share a metaphoric function with the "goads", which are "implanted" either in the sense that they are stuck in the flesh or in the sense that they are fixed in the end of the staff. In either case the *tertium comparationis* of the words of the sages and goads/nails is not that they are immovable but that they both sting. The goad prods one on to thought and better behavior, but it also hurts; as Ibn Ezra recognized, goads "afflict and open the mind (*m^{e}yass^{e}rim umĕpaqq^{e}ḥim hannepeš*)". The words of the sages, in other words, are a bit dangerous. Compare the far more emphatic warning of R. Eliezer b. Hyrkanus to beware of the words of *ḥăkamim*, for "they burn like fiery coals, bite like jackals, sting like scorpions" (Avot 2:15).

Nitt^{e}nu mero'eh 'eḥad: All exegetes have tried to identify the shepherd. He is generally considered to be God. But in the HB, God is called "shepherd" in his capacity as keeper and protector, which is not relevant here, and the epithet "shepherd" is never used by itself to refer to him (see Galling). Nor are the words of the wise ever considered to be "given" by God. Wisdom as a personified entity and as a personal mental quality is given by God, and perhaps the essential, abstract content of Wisdom is also a divine gift. But the specific teachings of the sages do not come from him. Similar reasons militate against identifying the shepherd as Solomon (contrary to Delitzsch and McNeile). Qohelet is clearly not identified with Solomon in the epilogue, nor could it be said that Solomon "gave" the words of the sages.

Another difficulty in the identification of the shepherd as God (or Solomon) is the modifier *'eḥad*. If the point is that there is only one divine shepherd who gives the words of the wise, rather than several, the "one" becomes very emphatic. The weight of the verse would rest there rather than in the similes of v. 11a, and the verse would become a theological declaration of monotheism divorced from context.

Whatever "shepherd" may represent metaphorically, the sentence must first make sense literally. The fact that "shepherd" and "goads" belong to one domain shows that the vehicle of the simile is continuing and the clause *nitt^{e}nu mero'eh 'eḥad* has meaning as something an actual shepherd can do. The usual interpretation has an irrelevant comparison sandwiched between subject and verb. It is better to take as the subject of *nitt^{e}nu* not the distant "words of the sages", but the immediately preceding nouns, *dar^{e}bonot/maśm^{e}rot n^{e}ṭu'im*, the goads/nails that a shepherd "gives" or "puts" in the sense that he prods his herd with them. Within the simile, it is not the words but the goads that are "given", and they are "given"—i.e., set or stuck— not by "God" or "Solomon" but by a *shepherd*, any shepherd. NTN means "to stick" (an awl) in Deut 15:17. *'eḥad* functions as an indefinite article.[63] *Within* the simile, "shepherd" is meant literally, just as goads are.[64] "Shepherd" does have a metaphoric function, one created and controlled by the ratio that the simile sets up: words are to the sage as goads to the shepherd. Goads and shepherds are not figures for words and sages. Rather, the *relation* between the two elements of the image, shepherd and goads, is a configuration of the relation between the sage and his words. Words and goads are tools to guide people on the right path, though making them uncomfortable in doing so.

12:12. *W^eyoter mehemmah b^eni hizzaher*: not "And besides these...", as if the listener were to beware of words other than those of the wise, for that sense would require *miyyoter*. Moreover, by that translation the sentence would be warning against words/collections other than those of the wise. What could those be—some sort of secular literature? If so, this warning comes entirely without preparation, and the ancient reader, no less than the modern, would need a clearer identification of the words/books of the non-wise. Otherwise how could the reader know what to avoid? A mere "other than these", would be an inadequate definition of the dangerous category of literature, especially when "these" is itself not a well-defined category.

We must set the pause at *w^eyoter* (against MT, which takes *yoter mehemmah* as an accentual unit) and translate (literally) "and an

63. As in 1 Sam 24:14; 26:20; 1 Kgs 19:4, 5; Ezek 8:8; 17:7 (see GKC §125b, BDB *'eḥad*); similarly Aramaic *ḥăda'*: Ezr 4:8; Dan 2:31; 6:18. In all these cases enumeration is not the point, since there is no need to show unity as opposed to plurality. The modifier could be removed with little effect on the sense of the sentence.

64. The words "literal" and "metaphorical" intersect in discussion of the functioning of metaphor. In a common metaphor, "lion" *literally* means brave warrior. Yet it is the "literal", feline creature that is a "metaphor for" the human warrior. We commonly apply "literal" in this context to the metaphor prior to translation to another domain, but we also apply the term to the tenor of the metaphor, its sense *after* translation. Both uses are correct, for a metaphor takes us from one "literal" domain (e.g., animals) to another (humans).

additional thing (is)" (Ginsberg), or "there's something else to be said". An addition that stands in partial contrast to the preceding is partly adversative; thus we may translate: "At the same time". The antecedent of *mehemmah* must be the subject of the preceding sentence, the words of the sages and their proverb collections (the two concepts are functionally synonymous). The "son" is to be wary of these. The next sentence (12:12b) shows that the author is suspicious of the effects of much writing and studying, the very activities attributed to Qohelet (12:9).

'ăśot s^e^parim harbeh 'eyn qeṣ does not mean "Of making many books there is no end" (AV, Gordis, Barton, and most); there is no "of" (that sense would require *beth* or *lamed* before *'ăśot*; cf. 4:8). If the predicate is understood as an assertion of non-existence, the clause *'ăśot s^e^parim harbeh* is left unrelated to *'eyn qeṣ*, lit., "the making of many books there is no end". Rather, v. 12bα, like bβ, is an affirmative sentence of classification with two nominal members; the predication puts *'ăśot s^e^parim harbeh* in the category of *'eyn qeṣ*. *Qeṣ* here means "purpose, profit" (Tur-Sinai). If it meant "end" in the sense of "conclusion, finish", then "many" in v. 12bα would be superfluous ("making many books is something that never ends"). More significantly, to say that book production never ends does not explain why one should be wary of the words of sages. As for the syntax of the predicate, *'eyn* cannot negate the predicate nexus in a nominal sentence (i.e., "X *'eyn* Y" would not mean "X is not Y"). Rather, *'eyn qeṣ* is a noun phrase, literally, "a nothingness of purpose" or "an absence of purpose", thus: "a thing of no purpose". *'ayin* is a noun, and the nominal use of *'eyn* (+ noun) is clear in prepositional phrases such as *b^e^'eyn musar*, "because of lack of instruction" (Prov 5:23); *me'eyn mayim*, "because of lack of water" (// *baṣṣama'*; Isa 50:2); *l^e^'eyn 'onim*, "to the one-of-no-strength" (// *layya'ep*; Isa 40:29); and often. Note also the strict parallelism in Prov 26:20 between *'eyn* and *'epes*, whose nominal character is clear. Qoh 12:12bα means literally "Making many books is a thing of no purpose". Writing is praiseworthy, but there is no point in overdoing it.

Fishbane (1985:31) translates *'ăśot* as "compose" or "compile", comparing Akkadian *uppušu* (D stem of *epēšu*, the equivalent of Hebrew *'aśah*), used in scribal colophons. But whether *ăśot s^e^parim* means to compile or to write books, the epilogist does not mean to ascribe the original composition of the proverbs to someone other than Qohelet. The equivalent Aramaic phrase, *'bd spr'*, occurs in a fifth century BCE papyrus (*spr' znh zy 'nh 'bdt*; Kraeling, 1953:9,22), where *'bd* means "write", not "collect". 'ŚH is used of scribal activity in Jer 8:8, but we cannot know just what these scribes are doing—writing, writing down, or compiling. The term is too broad to pin down the precise nature of Qohelet's activity.

Lahag is a crux, usually explained by reference to Arabic *lahija*, "apply oneself assiduously", a root that does not otherwise appear in Hebrew. *Qoh. Rab.* on this verse interprets *lhg* as *lahăgot*, and we should probably emend to that, adding a final *taw* (Perles, 1895:29; this is a near-haplography; on *h/t* confusions see Delitzsch, 1920:§105). The repetition of *harbeh* suggests that the parallelism is strict here and supports the reading of an infinitive. HGH means "meditate, study" (see especially Josh 1:8 and Ps 1:2). It also (and originally) means "utter, speak" and is used of teaching wisdom in Ps 37:30a: "The mouth of the righteous utters (*yehgeh*) wisdom". Either "study" or "utter" would make sense here, because study in the ancient world was essentially oral recitation. The "uttering" probably refers to studying rather than to teaching, since the infinitive with *lamed* seems to express an action that the pupil does, not one done to him. By this interpretation, the verse warns against excess in the two aspects of the sage's activity attributed to Qohelet: studying others' meshalim (*hgh* corresponding to *'izzen*, *ḥiqqer*) and writing one's own (*'ăśot sᵉparim* corresponding to *tiqqen*, *katob*). The sentence, "and to study much is a weariness of flesh", means that much study is tantamount to, or produces, this discomfort. (For this type of predication compare 2:23.)

12:13. In context, the "everything" that has been heard refers to the words of sages, Qohelet's among them. The author puts Wisdom in perspective: Wisdom is all very fine, he says, but once we have heard what the sages have to say, we must remember that what really counts is fear of God and obedience to him. The words of sages steer us in this direction, but in fact knowledge of this principle is accessible to everyone from the start. The attitude expressed here is close to the traditional Wisdom epistemology, except insofar as it assumes a revelation of God's commandments.

Ben Sira uses the phraseology of this verse for different purposes in 43:27, *'wd k'lh l' nwsp, wqṣ dbr hw' hkl*, a difficult line that is probably to be translated, "More things such as these we shall not add, and the end of the matter is: He [sc., God] is everything". "The end of the matter" means "the last thing to be said in this regard". That is the meaning of *sop dabar* as well.

Kol ha'adam: The Aramaic translation hypothesis explains this difficult phrase as deriving from Aramaic *ky dyn* [i.e., *dāyēn*] *kl 'nš'*, sc., "For he [sc., God] judges every man". *Dyn* was misread as *dēn* = "this" (Zimmermann, 1973:163; followed by Ginsberg). The Aramaic would, however, have had a subject (*hu'*) that would have left no ambiguity. Throughout the HB, *kol ha'adam* means "all men" or "every man" (see Qoh 7:2; 3:13; 5:18), not "the whole man" or "the entirety of man". The phrase in Qohelet is elliptical, but it is not clear how the ellipsis is to be completed. The similar elliptical predications in Pss 109:4 (*'ăni t^epillah*); 110:3 (*'amm^eka n^edabot*); 120:7 (*'ăni šalom*); and Job 8:9 (*t^emol 'ănaḥnu*)[65] attest to the validity of the syntax of the phrase, but they do not show exactly what the nature of the predication is in such constructions. AV (similarly Gordis) supplies "duty". Delitzsch takes the phrase as equivalent to a genitive: "for this is every man's". Context sets up a contrast between the statements and admonitions in 12:9-12 (which have to do with the sages and their pupils), and *this*, the demand stated in 12:13bα (which applies to everyone). *Zeh* is thus emphatic and contrastive. Verse 14 provides a logical motivation for v. 13bβ: this rule concerns everyone, because (*ki*) God will bring every deed into judgment. (NJV translates ". . . for this applies to all mankind" but understands "this" as prospective.)

12:14 *'al kol ne'lam*: as in 11:9, *'al* introduces the deed for which one is judged. Here *'al* is governed by the verbal notion implicit in *mišpaṭ*. God will judge a person for everything, even secret deeds (Delitzsch).

65. Contrary to Delitzsch and Barton, Qoh 3:19aα is not a predication of this sort, but is rather a bound construction serving as the proleptic subject of the sentence in 3:19aβ.

EXCURSUS IV
ḤAKAM AS "SAGE"

Whybray (1974, *passim*) argues that throughout the HB *ḥakam* refers to any person possessing the virtue of wisdom, not to a member of a professional class or to one who subscribes to a particular school of thought. When, for example, the scribes are quoted as saying "we are wise" in Jer 8:8, they are boasting of their intellectual prowess, not identifying their professional affiliation, and Jeremiah responds by using that term sarcastically. (This application of the word may, however, be seen as a forerunner of the application of the term *ḥăkamim* to the "Schriftgelehrten"; see below.) When the book of Proverbs promises to teach wisdom, it is not claiming to teach professional skills, nor does it do so.

Whybray's observation is essentially correct but pushed too far. In Jer 18:18, *ḥakam* is a group designation standing alongside priest and prophet, but not necessarily a professional title. The degree of specificity of this word might, in some contexts, be compared with that of English "intellectual", which is a both a qualitative modifier and a group designation but not so specific an occupational label as "professor". (We might carry the analogy further: someone might chide a professor for priding himself on being an "intellectual" even if he did not call himself that). *Ḥakam* is a professional designation when applied to diviners (Gen 41:8; Exod 7:11; Jer 51:57; etc.—always foreign). Most significant for our purposes, in a few verses from the latest stages of biblical Wisdom Literature *ḥăkamim* refers to a specific group, one I have designated "the sages". Even if *ḥakam* means "counsellor" or the like (and it is not clear that it ever does), the use of *ḥakam* to denote specifically producers of Wisdom Literature is not paralleled outside Wisdom Literature.

Ḥăkamim means "sages" (i.e., authors and teachers of Wisdom) in Qoh 12:11a, where the term is rephrased in parallelism as "masters of collections". Clearly the term is being applied to a specific group—Wisdom authors—rather than to anyone who is blessed with the quality of wisdom. In 12:9 Qohelet himself is called a *ḥakam* in the sense of "sage", for the plural in v. 11a designates the group to which he belonged. One of the components of his *ḥokmah*, as defined in 12:9-10, was the composition (TQN) of meshalim and the writing (KTB) of "words of truth".

Ḥăkamim means "sages" in the headings to proverb collections: Prov 22:17 (according to LXX, which apparently had *dibrey ḥăkamim* at the head of the verse); 24:23a (*gam 'elleh laḥăkamim*); and possibly 1:6b (*dibrey ḥăkamim w^{e}ḥidotam*).

Prov 22:17 (as emended above) and Prov 24:23 seem to attribute authorship of the collections they head to a specific group. Whybray (1974:50) argues that *ḥăkamim* is undetermined in meaning as well as in morphology (*laḥăkamim* may be taken as anarthrous by analogy to 22:17). But if Whybray were right, we would have to translate 24:23a as "these too are by wise men" (i.e., men who are wise). This is contrary to the use of the *lamed auctoris*, which always introduces specific designations of persons, not evaluative descriptions. Furthermore, no other headings of Wisdom texts introduce their authors by evaluative descriptions alone (though these may be conjoined to a proper name). *Ḥăkamim* in these verses has apparently come to designate a specific group; if so, the word could be semantically determined even without the article (likewise in Qoh 12:11).

In Prov 1:6 as well, *ḥăkamim* seems to designate a recognized group rather than just "men who are wise". The wise men mentioned so frequently in Proverbs are all those who possess ethical-religious wisdom and the skills for successful living, not specifically authors of proverbs and enigmatic sayings (*ḥidot*). The preface to Proverbs (1:1-6) reveals an attitude close to Ben Sira's: wisdom is attained by studying the words written by the sages. The preface to Proverbs regards the sayings it introduces as a body of literature that should be studied. This passage views the comprehension of proverbs and enigmatic sayings as a goal in itself, a goal requiring effort to attain; it is a reward for studying the book. In contrast, elsewhere in Proverbs (particularly 1–9), comprehension of the father's words is not a means of attaining wisdom and its benefits. The pupil is supposed to attain wisdom by listening attentively to his father's words and holding fast to them, and these words are assumed to be clear and immediately understandable.

Elsewhere in Proverbs, mention of the speech of the wise refers either to the content and manner of their speech in daily life (12:18; 14:3; 15:2, 7), or to the message of their teachings (13:14; 16:23), rather than to specific proverbial utterances.

It appears, then, that the term *ḥăkamim* is applied to the authors of Wisdom in the latest stages of biblical Wisdom Literature. (The headings presumably belong to the stage when the collections were joined, as is implied by the words "these too" [are by the sages]" in 24:23.) This is not to say that *ḥăkamim* had become a designation restricted to authors of and only of Wisdom Literature. The creativity of the *ḥăkamim* may have extended far beyond what we call Wisdom Literature.

In fact, the above observations suggest just that. The meshalim of Wisdom (as distinct from those with other life-settings, such as oracular and popular meshalim) were not the only type of literature that *ḥăkamim* composed; if they were, the titles would be superfluous. It would be pointless to introduce a collection of proverbs within a book of proverbs by saying "these too are by proverb-writers" just as it would be pointless to introduce a group of psalms within a psalter by saying: "these too are by psalm-writers". In the titles in Proverbs, the term *ḥăkamim* seems to designate generally the "Schriftgelehrten", the scripturally learned, as it does occasionally in Sira (3:29; 8:8; 44:4b [n.b.: *ḥkmy syḥ bsprtm*]; cf. the description of the wisdom of the scribe in 38:24; 39:1-14) and in MH, where *ḥakam* usually means "scholar". If *ḥăkamim* does mean "Schriftgelehrten", the titles in Proverbs are meant to exalt the status of the ancient sayings, assuring us of their place in the national scriptural traditions. The introduction to *Avot* also serves this purpose.

* * *

§5.8 *The Book of Qohelet in Paraphrase*

1:1 THE TEACHINGS OF QOHELET THE DAVIDIDE, KING IN JERUSALEM

Qohelet's theme: life is absurd

(2) Qohelet used to say: Utterly absurd! Thoroughly absurd! Everything is absurd.

Since the world is changeless, all toil is futile.

(3) Man is not properly rewarded in life for all his toiling.

(4) Consider that when one generation dies off another takes its place, and yet for all this coming and going, humanity never changes. (5) Similarly, day by day the sun rises, then sets, then proceeds wearily under the world to the east, there but to rise once again. (6) Likewise the wind goes round and round, south to north, north to south, then it just goes around its rounds again. (7) And though all the rivers flow constantly into the sea, the sea never gets filled up once and for all. Yet the rivers continue to flow there.

(8) Words are all so inadequate that they do not allow one to really express himself. Nor can one satisfactorily see or fully hear.

(9) There are no events, present or future, that have not already occurred. In other words, nothing truly new ever happens in the world. (10) Now someone might imagine that this or that is new, but it has in fact already happened some time in the past. (11) And if people do imagine that something new has occurred, that is merely because they have forgotten the past. Likewise things yet to come will not be remembered by people who come thereafter.

Qohelet introduces himself and his inquiry.

(12) I am Qohelet. I have been king of Israel in Jerusalem.

(13) I set about to apply my intellect to the investigation and exploration of all that occurs in life. (Such an investigation is a miserable task, which God has imposed upon people to busy themselves with.) (14) As a result of this investigation, I concluded that all that happens in life is a vexatious absurdity—irremediably so, inasmuch as (15) nothing that goes awry can be righted, nor can things lacking be restored.

(16) I said to myself, "See, I have amassed more knowledge than anyone who ever ruled over Jerusalem before me. I have observed

much learning and knowledge". (17) But when I set about to deepen my understanding and to extend my knowledge, I came to realize that such knowledge too is vexatious, (18) because the more you know and understand, the more irritated and grieved you become.

He amassed wealth to provide pleasures, and he found them good but absurd.

(2:1) I said to myself, "Come, let's try out pleasure and enjoyment". But I soon came to realize that pleasure too is absurd, (2) and I deemed pleasure silly and amusement inane.

(3) But first I proceeded to drink my fill of wine (all the while keeping my wits about me, avoiding befuddlement), so that I might discover what is good for people to do in this world during the short time they live. (4) I did great things: I built myself houses, planted vineyards, (5) made gardens and orchards and planted fruit trees of all kinds in them. (6) I dug myself pools of water from which to irrigate a wood growing with trees. (7) I acquired slaves, male and female, and I had home-born servants as well. I also acquired for myself many herds of cattle and flocks, more than all who were before me in Jerusalem. (8) I amassed for myself silver and gold, the wealth of kings and nations. I acquired singers and songstresses and concubines—the 'pleasures of men'—quite a few of them. (9) Thus I grew far richer than anyone before me in Jerusalem, and all the while my powers of reason did not desert me. (10) I denied myself nothing my eyes desired; I refused myself no type of pleasure. Through this process I obtained pleasure by means of all my toil; thus all my toil led to pleasure. (11) But upon reflection I realized that all my toilsome efforts amounted to a vexatious absurdity, and that straining too hard in what one does in life does not bear commensurate rewards.

It is unjust that the wise die like the fools.

(12) Then I turned to reflect upon knowledge and ignorance (after all, my successor, who will control the fruits of my labors, may well turn out to be an ignoramus). (13) I recognized that knowledge is as superior to ignorance as light is to darkness, for (14) the knowledgeable man has insight, while the ignorant man is blind. But at the same time I realized that they both have the same fate, (15) and I thought, "That which happens to the ignoramus will happen to me too, so what's the point of my having become so learned?" And I recognized

that it was absurd for me to have grown so knowledgeable, (16) because the learned man, just like the ignorant one, is never remembered, but both are soon forgotten. Alas, death treats the learned man no better than the ignoramus! (17) So I became disgusted with life, being distressed at seeing what happens in the world, for everything is a vexatious absurdity.

It is unjust that toil does not always reap its rewards.

(18) Then I became disgusted with all the wealth that I had struggled to amass in my life, because I would be leaving it to someone who comes after me (19) (whether he will be capable or incompetent no one knows), and he will control all my wealth which I had labored for so capably in my life. This unjust allocation of benefits is absurd.

(20) So I turned to rid myself of all the illusions about my toil that I had harbored, (21) realizing that a man who toils with intelligence, knowledge, and skill may well end up turning his earnings over to someone who did not struggle for them. This lack of coordination between effort and gain is an absurdity and a great injustice. (22) For what does a man really get out of the toil and mental strain that fills his life?—(23) since his hustle and bustle just makes him distressed and rancorous during the day, and even at night he can't relax. That someone should work so hard for such miserable results is absurd.

(24) There is nothing better for a man than to eat and drink and provide himself with pleasure by his life's toil. But I realized that the opportunity to enjoy pleasure is also determined by God, (25) for God alone decides whether one will get to consume his goods or must spend his life fretting. (26) For God graces a man he favors with good sense and understanding, and pleasure too, while upon one he finds offensive he dumps the burden of gathering and amassing wealth only in order to turn it over to God's favorite. This unjust allocation of tasks and benefits is a vexatious absurdity.

A time awaits every deed and event, but man cannot know when it is.

(3:1) Every single thing that is done or happens in life has a time when it will occur:

(2) Being born will have its time, and dying will have its time. Planting will have its time, and uprooting plantings will have its time. (3) Killing will have its time, and healing will have its time. Tearing down will have its time, and building up will have its time.

(4) Weeping will have its time, and laughing will have its time. Mourning will have its time, and dancing will have its time.
(5) Throwing stones will have its time, and gathering stones will have its time. Embracing will have its time, and shunning embracing will have its time. (6) Seeking will have its time, and losing will have its time. Keeping will have its time, and throwing away will have its time. (7) Rending will have its time, and sewing will have its time. Keeping silent will have its time, and speaking will have its time.
(8) Loving will have its time, and hating will have its time. War will have its time, and peace will have its time.

(9) Since what will be will be, one is not repaid for straining too hard at whatever he may do.

(10) I observed the task that God has given man to busy himself with: (11) Having seen to it that everything occurs just when it should, God then goes and makes man weary himself in striving—with no chance whatsoever of success—to apprehend all that God brings about. (12) So I realized that the best thing man can do is to enjoy pleasures throughout his life. (13) Indeed, when any man eats and drinks and finds enjoyment as he toils away at life, this is the very gift of God.

(14) I also came to realize that whatever transpires is invariably what God has made happen. It is impossible to do other than what God determines, either more or less. Moreover, God has decreed things this way so that humans will live in fear of him. (15) Furthermore, both present and future merely repeat the past. Thus God keeps looking for what was sought before.

Death puts the seal on this life's inequity.

(16) I further observed that throughout the world wickedness is found in the courts, exactly where just judgment should reside. (17) I tried to take some comfort in reminding myself that because everything has a time when it will come to pass, everyone, righteous and wicked alike, will sooner or later face God's judgment. (18) But then I said to myself with regard to mankind, - - - and to show that they are only beasts. (19) For the very same fate comes upon man and beast: both die in the same way, because the same sort of breath keeps them alive. Therefore man is no better off than the beast, but both are absurd. (20) Both go to the same place. Both come from the dust, and both return there. (21) Furthermore, it is impossible to know if man's life-spirit goes upward at death while the beast's life-

spirit goes down to the ground. (22) So I concluded that the best thing to do is to get pleasure from all one does, because enjoyment of the present moment alone belongs to him, seeing that the future is inevitably hidden.

Observing life's oppressions is distressing.
(4:1) Considering next all the oppressions that take place in life, I saw that no one comforts the oppressed as they weep in misery. The oppressors have all the power, while the oppressed lack even a comforter. (2) So I reckoned the deceased, who have already died, more fortunate than the living, who are still alive. (3) But better off than either is someone who never comes into existence at all, for he never has to see the evil things that happen in this life.

Toil is absurd.
(4) I also observed what lies behind all toil and skill: mutual envy. That this is so is another vexatious absurdity. (5) It is true that to sit in idleness is self-destructive folly. (6) But it is also true that a little gotten without strain is better than twice as much gained through toil and vexation.

A lone man's toil is absurd.
(7) I observed another absurdity in this world: (8) the case of a man all alone, with no companion, with neither son nor brother, who nevertheless toils without pause. Neither is he himself sated by his wealth, no matter how much he earns. But then what am I myself doing in toiling and foregoing pleasure for no one's benefit? Such behavior is an absurdity and a bad business.

Having a companion is advantageous.
(9) Two companions are better off than a man alone, for they, at least, have something good in their life of toil. (10) For if they get into difficulty, they can help each other out, but woe to him who gets into difficulty and has no one to help him. (11) Also, when two lie down, they can keep each other warm, but what can the lone man do but lie there shivering? (12) And if someone attacks one of two, they can stand up to the attacker. And how much the stronger, then, are three together!

Even those wise in political maneuvering are soon forgotten.

(13) A poor youth who is shrewd is better off even than an old king, if that one is puerile and no longer has the sense to take precautions. (14) For it happened that one such youth, in spite of having been born in poverty in the old king's kingdom, went from prison to power. (15) Nevertheless, I could foresee that all the living, all who go about on earth, would join the following of whichever young man would take over next. (16) Limitless masses would follow the successor, and, what's more, even later generations would not appreciate that first shrewd youth. Surely this injustice is a vexatious absurdity.

Be cautious in making vows.

(17) Behave yourself when you go to the House of God, because obedience is more desirable to God than sacrifices offered by frivolous folk, for they do not know how to do wrong.

(5:1) Do not go shooting off your mouth or making careless vows to God, for he is too high and distant for casual converse. Therefore let your words be few. (2) For as a lot of hustle and bustle accompanies a dream, so does a lot of chatter accompany the voice of a scatterbrain. (3) When you make a vow to God do not delay in paying it, for he can't stand scatterbrains. What you vow—pay! (4) Indeed, it is better not to vow at all than to vow and renege. (5) Do not let your mouth bring punishment upon you by telling God that your vow was just a mistake. (If you do so, he may grow angry at what you have said and destroy everything you have earned; for too much talk is no better than a bunch of dreams and absurdities.) Better just to live in fear of God!

Bureaucratic "proteksia" leads to social injustice.

(7) If you see the poor being oppressed and justice and right being undermined in the state, do not be surprised, because every highly placed person has a higher-up covering for him, and there are higher ones covering for *them*. (8) More advantaged is a land if all its fields are tilled.

Get immediate satisfaction from whatever you have.

(9) One who has a love of money will never get enough of it to satisfy him, and one who loves wealth will never get enough income

for him. This fact too is an absurdity. (10) The only benefit the possessor of wealth gets from his property lies in its immediate enjoyment, for as wealth increases, so do those who are after it. (11) Sweet and untroubled is the sleep of the slave (regardless of how much he has eaten), whereas the rich man lies awake fretting about his money.

It is tragic when a toiler is denied enjoyment of his wealth.

(12) Here is a sick misfortune that I have observed in life: wealth being hoarded by its owner—harming him in the process—(13) and then being lost anyway in an unfortunate business, so should he beget a son he will have nothing for him. (14) That man must return to the earth as naked as he was born, taking none of his earnings with him. (15) This fact too—namely, that everyone loses his wealth at death—is a sick misfortune, for just as one comes into the world so shall he leave it. Thus he is no better off for having worked so hard, (16) eating in miserly darkness and intense rancor and sickness and wrath, when the gain is so paltry.

It is good when one is allowed to enjoy the product of his labor.

(17) Here is what I have seen to be good: to eat and drink and to have enjoyment in the toil one performs during the short time God gives one on earth, for that experience is man's portion. (18) It is a gift of God if, when he gives a man wealth and property, he also allows him to enjoy them and to take possession of his portion, thereby knowing pleasure in his toilsome life. (19) For such a person will not brood too much about the brevity of his life, because God is keeping him preoccupied with pleasures.

It is especially rankling when a man is deprived of his wealth and a stranger receives it.

(6:1) There is an evil I have observed in this world, and it is oppressive to think about it: (2) God may give a man as much wealth and prestige as he could desire and then prevent him from enjoying any of it. Instead, a stranger gets to enjoy it. This injustice is an absurdity and a sick misfortune. (3) Even a man who begets a hundred children and lives however so many years, if he does not receive satisfaction from his property and does not even have a proper burial—the stillborn child, I declare, is better off than he. (4) For that man is born into absurdity and returns to darkness at death, and in that darkness his name is forgotten. (5) A stillborn child, who never saw the light of day, has more repose than he. (6) And say a man were to live two thousand years and yet never know pleasure . . . Alas, what's the point? Everyone ends up dead anyway!

It is important to enjoy what you have.

(7) A man works and strains all his life for material gain, yet he never gets enough of it. (8) (So when it comes to satisfaction, the capable man—though he can make money—is no better off than the incompetent. And what's the point of knowing how to get along with people if you happen to be poor?)

(9) Better to enjoy what you see in front of you than to desire things you don't have. But even that enjoyment is a vexatious absurdity.

All is predetermined, but man cannot understand life.

(10) All that happens is predetermined and its nature is already known to God. So there is no point in arguing with God, who is more powerful than man. (11) For many words merely add to the world's absurdity, and they don't get a man any farther than silence does.

(12) Moreover, since no one can tell man just what will happen in the future, he cannot know in the first place what is really beneficial to do in the few days of his absurd, fleeting life.

Be mindful of death.

(7:1) Just as a good reputation is more beneficial than fragrant oil, so the day of death is better than the day of birth. (2) So too it is more beneficial to go to a house where people are mourning than to go to a house where they are feasting, inasmuch as all people will die, and the living should ponder that fact. (4) Indeed, the thoughtful man dwells on death, whereas the shallow-minded think only of having fun.

Attend to the wise man's rebuke.

(3) It is more beneficial to suffer the anger of a judicious man than to indulge in amusements, for by that man's mere scowl one can learn something. (5) Indeed, it is more beneficial to hear a sensible man rebuke you than to listen to the merry songs of the frivolous, (6) (for their merriment is as meaningless as the sound of burning thorns crackling under a pot). Nevertheless, even such a rebuke may

prove absurd, (7) for even a judicious man's reasoning may be corrupted by extorted wealth and bribes.

Be patient in adversity.

(8) It is better to wait to see how matters turn out than to get disturbed about them at the outset; indeed, patience is better than the presumptuousness of impatience. (9) So don't let yourself become irritated too quickly at what is happening to you, for nurturing resentment is senseless and self-destructive. (10) When the times turn against you, it is hardly wise to complain about the downturn of your fortunes.

(11) Good judgment is every bit as beneficial as a rich inheritance; in fact, it is even better. (12) For the protection good judgment provides is as great as that provided by silver; and in addition good judgment keeps its possessors alive. (19) Indeed, good sense benefits its possessor more than the wealth of all the rulers who are in a city.

Accept life as it comes.

(13) You should realize what God has ordained: no one can, by dint of effort, set right what God puts awry. (14) So when good fortune comes upon you, enjoy it, and when you find yourself in misfortune, accept it, recognizing that God makes things happen both ways in order to prevent man from knowing what the future will bring.

Avoid extremes in virtue and vice.

(15) In my absurd life I have seen cases both of a righteous man dying young, though he was righteous, and a wicked man living long, though he was wicked. (16) On the one hand, you should not become extremely righteous or perceptive, lest you see things that will shock you. (17) At the same time, you should not be downright wicked nor should you be an ignoramus, lest you die before your proper time. (18) It is best to follow both paths, letting yourself become neither extremely righteous and perceptive nor very wicked and ignorant. He who fears God will heed both these warnings.[66] (20) After all, no human being is so thoroughly righteous that he does only good and never sins. (21) For the same reason, you should not pay too much attention to everything people say, lest you overhear someone—

66. 7:19 placed after 7:12.

maybe even your very slave—speaking ill of you. (22) You know quite well that this might happen, for you undoubtedly have often spoken ill of others.

Qohelet's search reached a limit.

(23) And so it was that I applied my intellect to examine all these matters. I determined to understand them, but they proved to be far beyond my understanding. (24) Far beyond man's understanding are the events of this world, and much too deep for anyone to fathom.

He did, however, learn how difficult women can be.

(25) My thoughts next turned to explore and to seek out and attempt to grasp wisdom and solutions to problems, and also to understand wickedness, stupidity, folly, and inanity.

(26) What did I find? That woman is harder to take than death, for she is a trap, with snares for a heart and bonds for hands. God's favorite will escape her, but the one God dislikes will be caught by her.

(27) Here is what I have found (said Qohelet) as I put one and one together to come up with a solution. (28) Ceaselessly I sought a woman but could not find a good one. I did find one person in a thousand to be good, but among these I couldn't find a single good woman. (29) But I did come up with something, namely the realization that God makes people straight to start with, but they go and twist themselves in knots trying to find great solutions. (8:1a) Ah, who is smart enough to figure out what this all means?!

Be patient in the face of despotic authority.

(1b) It's just good sense to go around looking cheery, whereas brazenness makes for a surly mien. (2) So submit to the king's commands, but do not rush to swear oaths by God. (3) Better to leave the king's presence. Do not stick around when there's trouble, because he can do whatever he wishes; (4) for his word is law, and none dare call him to account for his behavior . (5) Whoever keeps the king's command will escape harm, and he can do so while reminding himself that a time of judgment will eventually come upon the despot (6) (since every matter, after all—judgment included—has its time). For, man's evil is oppressive to a man of insight, (7) because one cannot know just what the future will bring, being necessarily ignorant as to when events will occur.

(8) No man has authority over his life-spirit so as to keep it from escaping him. So authority evaporates in the day of death. Nor is there release in war, nor will wickedness allow an escape from death.

(9) All this is what I saw when I reflected on what happens when one man has authority to harm others.

Life is unjust, so soothe your pain with pleasures.

(10a) And then I saw the wicked brought to burial, and the cortege proceeded from the holy place itself, while people who had acted honestly when alive were left lying neglected in the city.

(10b) It is absurd, furthermore, (11) when the punishment of a wicked deed is not carried out quickly. And this delay encourages people to do evil, (12) for they see a sinner doing evil for many years yet living long. At the same time I am sure that it will go well with God-fearing people, because they are afraid of him, (13) whereas it will not go well with the wicked man, and his life will flit away like a shadow, because he is not afraid of God.

(14) So this, then, is an absurdity that occurs in life, namely that there are righteous people who receive what evildoers deserve, and there are evildoers who receive what the righteous deserve. I declared that such a state of affairs too is an absurdity.

(15) Seeing this, I once again praised pleasure, recognizing that nothing is better for man in this life than to eat, drink, and be merry, and this experience will be his companion as he toils away throughout the brief lifespan God has given him.

Qohelet's search taught him that life remains a mystery.

(16) When I decided to gain wisdom and to observe all that is done in the world (working at this without rest day or night), (17) I came to the realization that man cannot apprehend anything that God brings to pass—nothing of what happens on earth; indeed, however arduously one seeks, he will not gain the sought-for understanding. Even when it is a man of high intelligence who dedicates himself to attaining this understanding, it cannot be reached.

The universality of death strips life of meaning.

(9:1) Reflecting carefully on all these facts, I realized the following truth: although it is God himself who controls what happens to the righteous and the wise and all they do, no one can figure out whether God loves him or hates him. For everything in man's purview is (2) absurd, because everyone, whatever his moral quality, has the same fate—the righteous and the wicked, the good and the bad, the pure and the impure, he who sacrifices and he who does not offer sacrifice, the good person as well as the sinner, the oathtaker as well as the one who fears to swear oaths. (3) The worst thing on earth is the fact that all share the same fate of death, for which reason the hearts of people are full of evil and inanity throughout their lives, and afterwards—they join the dead!

For all that, life is better than nothing.

(4) Whoever is still alive at least has a bit of reliable knowledge (and in this regard a living dog is superior to a dead lion): (5) the living know that they will die, while the dead know nothing at all and no longer possess anything of value; even their memory is lost. (6) Everything they once possessed—down to their feelings of love, hatred, and jealousy—has already perished, and they no longer take part in anything that happens in the world of the living.

So enjoy life while you have it.

(7) So go ahead, eat your food and drink your wine in pleasure with a merry heart, because that is what God would have you do. (8) Wear fine white garments always, and keep your head anointed with oil. (9) Throughout the absurd days that God gives you here on earth, enjoy life with a woman you love, all your absurd days, for this experience is what you get out of life and your life's toil on earth. (10) All that you are able to do, go ahead and do it—but without straining yourself—for in Sheol, where you are headed, you will not be able to do or think or know or understand anything.

Human powers may be undone by happenstance.

(11) I next saw that in this world the fastest runner does not always win the race, nor the mightiest warrior always win the war, nor the talented always have food, nor the astute always have wealth, nor the knowing always gain favor, for all are subject to the vagaries of happenstance. (12) Nor does man know the time of his undoing. As fish are caught in an evil net and birds caught in a trap, so people are ensnared by a time of misfortune, when it snaps shut upon them suddenly.

Wisdom is powerful but folly may undo it.

(13) Here is another event I saw that bears upon the importance of intelligence, and I consider it significant. There was a small city with few people in it. And a great king came and encompassed it and built mighty siege works against it. (15) And in it he captured a man who was poor but smart, and that poor man saved the city by his wits. Yet he was soon forgotten. (16) I concluded: although in principle intelligence is superior to power, the mind of the poor man is held in contempt and his words may well be ignored.

(17) For all that, the intelligent man's words, spoken gently, still receive more attention than the shout of an official receives among fools. (18) What's more, intelligence is superior to weaponry. And yet, one ne'er-do-well can botch up much of value, (10:1) just as a fly may die and spoil an entire chalice of perfumer's ointment. Thus it is that a bit of folly can weigh heavier than intelligence.

(2) While the mind of the intelligent man is his blessing, the fool's is his bane. (3) The fool needs merely to walk along the road for his mind to betray him and make it evident to all that this man is a fool.

(4) If an official grows angry at you, hold your ground, for skill at soothing anger can make up for great mistakes.

(5) There is another evil I have seen in this world, an error caused by the ruler: (6) the promotion of an incompetent to a lofty position while rich men are left in low ranks. (7) I have even seen slaves riding horseback while princes walk on the ground like slaves.

Life is unpredictable, but wisdom can help you through it.

(8) One who digs a pit may fall into the very hole he dug, and one who takes down a wall may be bitten by a snake. (9) One who moves stones may be hurt by them, and one who splits logs may be endangered by flying chips.

(10) If the axe blade grows dull and the axeman does not sharpen the edge, then he must exert more force. But the skilled man, keeping his tools sharp, need not work so hard. (11) By the same token, the snake charmer's skills do not pay off if he fails to work his magic in time and so gets bitten.

The fool's blather hurts him.

(12) Whereas a judicious man's speech brings him favor, a fatuous man's talk brings him ruin. (13) For such a man may start out

speaking simple silliness, but he ends up uttering evil inanity. (14) And it is precisely the fatuous man who talks at length. For much speech is pointless, since man is ignorant of future events, and no one can inform him of them.

(15) In sum, all the fool's hard efforts merely exhaust him, for he hasn't the least idea where he's going.

Rulers should enjoy themselves in a proper manner.

(18) Sloth makes a roof sag, and slack hands make a house leak. (16) So woe to the land whose king is base and whose princes start feasting in the morning! (17) But fortunate is the land whose king is truly noble and whose princes feast at the proper time, in a manly, controlled fashion and not in drunkenness! (19) (Both sorts have the good fortune of being able to afford food and heart-cheering wine. Thus money keeps them all preoccupied.)

(20) (Incidentally, do not insult the king, even in your thoughts, and do not insult a rich man, even when you're in your bedroom, for your words will travel in the strangest ways—the very birds might tell!)

Prepare for the unexpected as best you can.

(11:1) Put your bread upon the water and let it float away; for sometime in the future your good deed will pay off. (2) In other words, help out seven or eight people in need, for if some misfortune occurs later, they will be there to help you.

(3) When the clouds are ready, they will pour out their rain on the earth; and wherever a tree may fall, in the south or in the north, in the place where it falls, there will it lie. (4) So realize: he who insists on waiting for just the right wind will never get around to sowing, and he who scrutinizes the clouds, fretting about rain, will never get around to reaping. (5) Just as you cannot grasp how a fetus receives life in the womb of a pregnant woman, so you are unable to understand the work of God, who makes everything happen. (6) So go ahead, sow your seed, doing your work both morning and evening, for you cannot know which of the two investments of work will prosper, the one or the other, or if they will be equally successful.

Enjoy your life while you have it—

(7) Sweet is life's light, and it is good to see the sun. (8) So no matter how many years a man may live, he should enjoy himself to

the very end, remembering that death's darkness will stretch on and on. All that follows is absurd.

—especially while you are young.

(9) Rejoice, young man, while you are still young, and let your heart give you cheer in the days of your prime. Follow your heart's inclination, and when you see something you like, pursue it. (But know that God will hold you responsible for all you do.) (10) And don't let yourself be vexed, and avoid things that cause you physical discomfort, for your prime years will flit away.

(12:1) And while you are still young, think of how you will die and return to your Creator. Do this before old age comes upon you with its misery, the time of life which will bring you no pleasure.

Enjoy life before the eternal night—

(2) Enjoy life while you can, before you die, and the light of life is extinguished, and the gloom becomes permanent; (3) when men in mourning writhe in grief—both house servants and men of power—and grinding-maids cease their work, having grown few in number, and gloom descends on the ladies of leisure, as they watch through the lattices, (4) and the doors facing the street are closed, as the mill grows silent. (And all the while plants are being reborn—the almond tree blossoming again, the squill again becoming full, the caperberry bush budding anew.) All this because a man is being borne to his eternal resting place, as mourners mill about in the street.

—when your life disintegrates into its components.

(6) So enjoy your life before it ends—as it disintegrates like a silver cord snapping, a golden bowl shattering, a jug breaking at the well, a jar crashing into the pit—before (7) your body returns to the earth, whence it came, and the life-spirit returns to God, its giver.

(8) Utterly absurd! (as the Qohelet used to say). Everything is absurd!

Qohelet was a sage who spoke fine and honest words.

(9) To this we may add that Qohelet was truly a sage—he constantly taught the people knowledge, and having heard and investigated others' wisdom he composed many sayings of his own.

(10) Qohelet sought to express his thoughts in pleasing words and wrote words that were completely true and honest.

But the words of sages have their perils and so should be read with caution.

(11) Yet the words of sages often sting us like goads, and the words of proverb-collectors may smart like the nails a shepherd uses to prod his sheep.

(12) So at the same time, my son, you should realize that the words of the sages should be treated with some caution. In fact, writing a great many books is pointless, and too much study just tires one out.

The main thing is to fear God and obey him.

(13) The last thing to be said, when all opinions have been heard, is this:

> "fear God and keep his commandments"

for *this* rule concerns everyone. (14) For God will bring every deed, even the hidden ones, into judgment, to determine whether it is good or evil.

BIBLIOGRAPHY

Throughout the book, commentaries are referred to by name of author only; other works by author + publication date.

Ahiqar

(Aramaic) text, translation, commentary: Lindenberger, 1983.

Albrecht, Karl

1896 'Das Geschlecht der hebräischen Hauptwörter'. *ZAW* 16:41-121.

Albright, William F.

1955 'Some Canaanite-Phoenician sources of Hebrew wisdom'. *VTSup* 3:1-15.

Allen, Thomas G.

1974 *The Book of the Dead*. Chicago.

Allgeier, A.

1925 *Das Buch des Predigers oder Koheleth*. HSAT VI, 2. Bonn.

Alster, B.

1975 *Studies in Sumerian Proverbs*. Copenhagen.

Alston, William P.

1967 'Pleasure'. *Encyclopedia of Philosophy*. New York. VI, 341-347.

Amenemhet

Pap. Millingen, Pap. Sallier I, II, *et al.* Text: Helck, 1969; Volten, 1945. 'The Instruction of King Amenemhet I for His Son Sesostris I', *AEL* I, 135-139.

Amenemopet

Pap. 8M 10474 *et al.* Text: Lange, 1925. 'The Instruction of Amenemope', *AEL* II, 146-163.

Anat, M.A.

1970 'The lament on the death of man in the scroll of Qoheleth' [Hebrew]. *Beth Mikra* 15:375-380.

Andersen, Francis I.

1974 *The Sentence in Biblical Hebrew*. Janua Linguarum 231. The Hague.

1976 *Job*. Tyndale OT Commentaries. London.

Anii

Pap. Boulaq 4, *et al.* Text: Suys, 1935; Volten, 1938. 'The Instruction of Any', *AEL* II, 135-146.

Astour, Michael C.

1968 'Two Ugaritic serpent charms'. *JNES* 27:13-36.

Ausejo, S. de

1948 'El género literario del Eclesiastés'. *Estudios Biblicos* 7:369-406.

Baer, Seligmann

1886 *Quinque Volumina*. Lipsiae.

Bailey, Lloyd R., Sr.

1979 *Biblical Perspectives on Death*. Philadelphia.

Barr, James
1961 *The Semantics of Biblical Language*. London.
1985 'Hebrew orthography and the Book of Job'. *JSS* 30:1-33.
Barthélemy, Dominique
1963 *Les Devanciers d'Aquila*. VTSup 10.
Barton, George A.
1908 *The Book of Ecclesiastes*. ICC (Repr. 1959). Edinburgh.
Barucq, André
1968 *Ecclésiaste*. Paris.
Baumgärtel, Fr.
1969 'Die Ochsenstachel und die Nägel in Koh 12,11'. *ZAW* 81:98.
Baumgartner, Walter
1933 *Israelitische und altorientalische Weisheit*. Tübingen.
Bendavid, Abba
1967 *Biblical Hebrew and Mishnaic Hebrew* [Hebrew]. Vol. 2. Jerusalem.
Bertram, Georg
1952 'Hebräischer und griechischer Qohelet'. *ZAW* 64:26-49.
Bickell, Gustav
1884 *Der Prediger über den Wert des Daseins*. Innsbruck.
Bickerman, Elias
1967 *Four Strange Books of the Bible*. New York.
Bidder, Roderich
1875 *Über Koheleths Stellung zum Unsterblichkeitsglauben*. Erlangen.
Birnbaum, Solomon A.
1971 *The Hebrew Scripts*. Leiden.
Blank, Sheldon H.
1962 'Ecclesiastes'. In *Interpreter's Dictionary of the Bible*, II, pp. 7-13. New York.
1970 Prolegomenon to Ginsburg, *Cohelet* (1970). New York.
Bonnet, Hans
1952 *Reallexikon der ägyptischen Religionsgeschichte*. Berlin.
Braun, Rainer
1973 *Kohelet und die frühhellenistische Popularphilosophie*. BZAW 130. Berlin.
Breton, Santiago
1973 'Qoheleth studies'. *Biblical Theology Bulletin* 3:22-50.
Brichto, Herbert C.
1963 *The Problem of 'Curse' in the Hebrew Bible*. Philadelphia.
Brin, Gershon
1960 'The roots 'ZR-'ZZ in the Bible' [Hebrew]. *Lešonenu* 24:8-14.
1975 *Studies in the Book of Ezekiel*. Tel Aviv.
Brockelmann, Carl
1956 *Hebräische Syntax*. Neukirchen.
Brown, Francis, Driver, S.R., Briggs, Charles A.
1907 *A Hebrew and English Lexicon of the Old Testament*. (Repr. 1966) Oxford.
Bronznik, Nahum
1980 "*aśot sĕparim harbeh 'eyn qeṣ* (Qoh 12:12)'. *Beth Mikra* 25:213-218.

Brunner, Hellmut
1957 *Altägyptische Erziehung*. Wiesbaden.
1963 'Der freie Wille Gottes in der ägyptischen Weisheit'. *SPOA*, pp. 103-117.
Bruns, J. Edgar
1965 'The imagery of Eccles 12,6a'. *JBL* 84:428-430.
Budde, Karl
1922 *Der Prediger*. In *Die Fünf Megillot*. KHAT XVII. Tübingen.
Buzy, Denis
1932 'Le Portrait de la vieillesse (Ecclésiaste, XII, 1-7)'. *RB* 41:329-340.
1934 'La Notion du bonheur dans l'Ecclésiaste'. *RB* 43:494-511.
1946 *L'Ecclésiaste*. Paris.
Camus, Albert
1951 *L'Homme révolté*. Paris.
1948 *Le Mythe de Sisyphe*. Paris: Gallimard. (ET Justin O'Brien, *The Myth of Sisyphus and other Essays*. New York: 1955).
Castellino, G.
1968 'Qohelet and his wisdom'. *CBQ* 30:15-28.
Claasen, W.T.
1983 'Speaker-oriented functions of *ki* in biblical Hebrew'. *JNSL* 11:29-46.
Coleridge, Samuel Taylor
1832 *The Stateman's Manual*. Burlington.
Coppens, J.
1979 'La structure de l'Ecclésiaste'. In *La Sagesse de l'Ancien Testament*; ed. M. Gilbert, pp. 288-292. Gembloux, Belgium.
Cosser, William
1953-54 'The meaning of "Life" in Prov., Job and Ecc.'. *Glasgow University Oriental Society Transactions* 15:48-53.
Crenshaw, James L.
1969 'Method in determining wisdom influence upon "historical" literature'. *JBL* 88:129-142. (Repr. Crenshaw, 1976:481-494).
1970 'Popular questioning of the justice of God in ancient Israel'. *ZAW* 82:380-95. (Repr. Crenshaw, *Studies*, 289-304).
1974 'The Eternal Gospel (Ecc. 3:11)'. In *Essays in Old Testament Ethics*. J.P. Hyatt Festschrift, ed. J.L. Crenshaw and John T. Willis; pp. 25-55. New York.
1975 'The problem of theodicy in Sirach: on human bondage'. *JBL* 94:47-64 (= Crenshaw, 1983b:119-140).
1976 *Studies in Ancient Israelite Wisdom* (selected, with a prolegomenon by James L. Crenshaw). New York.
1978 'The shadow of death in Qoheleth'. In *Israelite Wisdom: Samuel Terrien Festschrift*, pp. 205-216. Missoula.
1981a *Old Testament Wisdom*. Atlanta.
1981b 'Wisdom and authority: sapiential rhetoric and its warrants'. *VTSup* 32:10-29.
1983a 'Qoheleth in current research'. *HAR* 7:41-56.
1983b *Theodicy in the Old Testament* (edited with an introduction by J.L. Crenshaw). London.

1986a 'The expression *mî yôdēa'* in the Hebrew Bible'. *VT* 36:274-288.
1986b 'Youth and Old Age in Qoheleth'. *HAR* 10:1-13.
1987 *Ecclesiastes* (OTL). Philadelphia.

Cruickshank, John
1959 *Albert Camus*, London.

Crüsemann, Frank
1979 'Die unveränderbare Welt'. In *Der Gott der kleinen Leute*, ed. W. Schottroff and W. Stegemann. Vol. I, 80-104.

Dahood, Mitchell J.
1952 'Canaanite-Phoenician influence in Qoheleth'. *Bib* 33:30-52, 191-221.
1958 'Qoheleth and recent discoveries (Qumran)'. *Bib* 39:302-318.
1960 'Immortality in Prv 12,28'. *Bib* 41:176-181.
1962 'Qohelet and Northwest Semitic Philology'. *Bib* 43:349-365.
1965 'Canaanite words in Qoheleth 10,20'. *Bib* 46:210-212.
1966 'The Phoenician background of Qoheleth'. *Bib* 47:264-282.
1968 'The Phoenician contribution to biblical wisdom literature'. In *The Role of the Phoenicians in the Interaction of Mediterranean civilizations*, ed. W.A. Ward; pp. 123-148. Beirut.

Daube, David
1964 *The Sudden in the Scriptures*. Leiden.

Davidson, Donald
1980 *Essays in Actions and Events*. Oxford.

Delitzsch, Franz
1875 *Koheleth*. Leipzig.

Delitzsch, Friedrich
1920 *Die Lese- und Schreibfehler im AT*. Berlin/Leipzig.

Delsman, W.C.
1982 'Zur Sprache des Buches Koheleth'. In *Von Kanaan bis Kerala*, ed. W.C. Delsman *et al*. Neukirchen.

Dhorme, P.
1923 'L'Ecclésiaste ou Job?' *RB* 32:5-27.

Dieterlé, Christiane
1984 'A propos de la traduction de l'Ecclésiaste et de la Bible en français courant'. *Etudes théologiques et religieuses* 59:377-381.

Di Lella, Alexander
1966 *The Hebrew Text of Sirach*. The Hague.

Driver, G.R.
1954 'Problems and solutions'. *VT* 4:225-245.

Driver, Samuel R., and Gray, George B.
1921 *The Book of Job*. ICC. Edinburgh.

Duncker, Karl
1940 'On pleasure, emotion, and striving'. *Philosophy and Phenomenological Research*, 1:391-429.

Ehrlich, Arnold B.
1908-14 *Randglossen zur hebräischen Bibel*. Leipzig. (Repr. Hildesheim, 1968).

Eichrodt, Walther
1934 'Vorsehungsglaube und Theodizee im Alten Testament'. *Festschrift Otto Procksch*, pp. 45-70. Leipzig. (ET Crenshaw, 1983b:17-41).

Eliade, Mircia
1954 *The Myth of the Eternal Return*. New York.
Ellermeier, Friedrich
1963a 'Das Verbum ḤWŠ in Koh 2,25'. *ZAW* 75:197-217.
1963b 'Die Entmachung der Weisheit im Denken Qohelets'. *ZTK* 60:1-20.
1967 *Qohelet*. Teil I, Abschnitt 1. Herzberg.
Eloquent Peasant
Pap. Berlin 3023, 3025, 10499, Pap. BM 10274. 'The Eloquent Peasant', *AEL* I, 169-184.
Encyclopedia of Philosophy
7 vols. New York, 1967.
Eppenstein, Simon
1888 *Aus dem Kohelet-Kommentar des Tanchum Jerushalmi*. Berlin.
Euringer, Sebastian
1890 *Der Masorahtext des Koheleth kritisch untersucht*. Leipzig.
Fahlgren, K. Hj.
1932 *Ṣedāḳā, nahestehende und entgegengesetzte Begriffe im Alten Testament*. Uppsala.
Feldman, Emanuel
1977 *Biblical and Post-biblical Defilement and Mourning: Law as Theology*. New York.
Fichtner, Johannes
1933 *Die altorientalische Weisheit in ihrer israelitisch-jüdischen Ausprägung*. BZAW 62. Giessen.
1965 *Gottes Weisheit*. Stuttgart.
Fishbane, Michael
1985 *Biblical Interpretation in Ancient Israel*. Oxford.
Fletcher, Angus
1964 *Allegory*. Ithaca, NY.
Fohrer, Georg
1964 'Die Weisheit im Alten Testament'. In *Theologisches Wörterbuch zum Neuen Testament*, VII, pp. 476-496.
Forman, Charles C.
1958 'The pessimism of Ecclesiastes'. *JSS* 3:336-343.
1960 'Koheleth's use of Genesis'. *JSS* 5:256-263.
Fox, Michael V.
1968 'Aspects of the religion of the book of Proverbs'. *HUCA* 39:55-70.
1977a 'Frame-narrative and composition in the Book of Qohelet'. *HUCA* 48:83-106.
1977b 'A Study of Antef'. *Orientalia* 46:393-423.
1980a 'The identification of quotations in biblical literature'. *ZAW* 92:416-31.
1980b 'Two decades of research in Egyptian Wisdom Literature'. *ZÄS* 107:120-135.
1983 'The structure of Esther'. Isac Leo Seeligmann Volume, ed. A. Rofé; pp. 291-303. Jerusalem.
1985 *The Song of Songs and the Ancient Egyptian Love Songs*. Madison, WI.
1986 'The meaning of *hebel* for Qohelet'. *JBL* 105:409-27.
1988 'Aging and death in Qohelet 12'. *JSOT* 42:55-77.

Fox, Michael V., and Porten, Bezalel
1979 'Unsought Discoveries: Qohelet 7:23–8:1a', *HS* 19:26-38.
Frankfort, Henri
1961 *Ancient Egyptian Religion*. New York.
Freedman, David N.
1969 'Orthographic peculiarities in the Book of Job'. *EI* 9:36-44.
Fredericks, Daniel C.
1988 *Qoheleth's Language*. Lewiston, NY.
Frendo, Anthony
1981 'The "broken construct chain" in Qoh 10,10b'. *Bib* 62:544-545.
Galling, Kurt
1932 'Kohelet-Studien'. *ZAW* 50:276-299.
1934 'Stand und Aufgabe der Kohelet-Forschung'. *ThR* n.F. 6:355-373.
1950 'The scepter of wisdom. A note on the gold sheath of Zendjirli and Ecclesiastes 12,11'. *BASOR* 119:15-18.
1952 *Die Krise der Aufklärung in Israel*. Mainz.
1961 'Das Rätsel der Zeit im Urteil Kohelets (Koh 3, 1-15)'. *ZThK* 58:1-15.
1969 *Prediger Salomo*. HAT I, 18 (1st ed. 1940). Tübingen.
Gardiner, Alan H.
1909 *The Admonitions of an Egyptian Sage*. Leipzig (repr. Hildesheim, 1969).
Gemser, Berend
1937 *Sprüche Salomos*. HAT I, 16. Tübingen.
1960 'The instructions of 'Onchsheshonqy and biblical wisdom literature'. *VTSup* 7:102-128. (Repr. Crenshaw, *Studies*, 134-60).
1968 'The spiritual structure of biblical aphoristic wisdom'. In *Adhuc Loquitor*, pp. 138-149. (Repr. Crenshaw, *Studies*, 208-219). Leiden. (= *Homiletica in Bib* 21 [1962]:3-10).
Genung, John F.
1904 *Ecclesiastes, Words of Kohelet*. Boston.
Gerstenberger, Erhard
1965 *Wesen und Herkunft des 'Apodiktischen Rechts'*. WMANT 20. Neukirchen.
Gese, Hartmut
1958 *Lehre und Wirklichkeit in der alten Weisheit*. Tübingen.
1963 'Die Krisis der Weisheit bei Kohelet'. *SPOA*, pp. 139-151 (ET Crenshaw, 1983b:141ff.).
Gesenius, W.
1910 *Gesenius' Hebrew Grammar*. Ed. by E. Kautzsch, revised by A.E. Cowley. (Repr. 1963) Oxford.
Gibson, John C.L.
1982 *Textbook of Syrian Semitic Inscriptions*. Vol. III: *Phoenician Inscriptions*. Oxford.
Gilbert, Maurice
1981 'La description de la vieillesse en Qohelet XII 1-7 est-elle allégorique?' *VTSup* 32:96-109.
Ginsberg, H. Lewis
1937 (Ben Sira 50.25). *ZAW* 55:308-309.
1950 *Studies in Kohelet*. New York.

1952 'Supplementary studies in Kohelet'. *PAAJR*, pp. 35-62.
1955a 'The original language of Ben Sira 12:10-14'. *JBL* 74:93-95.
1955b 'The structure and contents of the Book of Koheleth'. *VTSup* 3:138-149.
1956 'Koheleth 12:4 in light of Ugaritic'. *Syria* 33:99-101.
1961 *Kohelet* [Hebrew]. Jerusalem.
1963 'The quintessence of Koheleth'. In *Biblical and Other Studies*, ed. A. Altmann, pp. 47-59. Cambridge.

Ginsburg, Christian D.
1861 *Coheleth* (reprint 1970). New York.

Gladson, Jerry A.
1978 *Retributive Paradoxes in Proverbs 10–29*. Ph.D. diss., Vanderbilt University, Nashville.

Glanville, Stephen R.K.
1955 *The Instructions of 'Onchsheshonqy. Catalogue of Demotic Papyri in the British Museum*, Vol. II. London.

Glasser, E.
1970 *Le Procès du bonheur par Qohelet*. Paris.

Goedicke, Hans
1977 *The Protocol of Neferyt*. Johns Hopkins Near Eastern Studies. Baltimore.

Good, Edwin M.
1965 *Irony in the Old Testament*. London.
1978 'The unfilled sea: style and meaning in Ecclesiastes 1:2-11'. In *Israelite Wisdom: Samuel Terrien Festschrift*, pp. 59-73. Missoula.

Gordis, Robert
1937 'Eccles. 1:17—its text and interpretation'. *JBL* 56:323-330.
1939/40 'Quotations in wisdom literature'. *JQR* 30:123-147.
1943 'The asseverative kaph in Ugaritic and Hebrew'. *JAOS* 63:176-178.
1943/44 'The social background of wisdom literature'. *HUCA* 18:77-118. (= *Poets, Prophets, and Sages*. Bloomington. 1971. pp. 160-197).
1946/47 'The original language of Qohelet'. *JQR* 37:67-84.
1949 'Quotations as a literary usage in biblical, oriental and rabbinic literature'. *HUCA* 22:157-219. (= *Poets, Prophets, and Sages*, pp. 104-159).
1949/50 'The translation-theory of Qohelet re-examined'. *JQR* 40:103-116.
1952 'Koheleth—Hebrew or Aramaic?' *JBL* 71:93-109.
1955a *Koheleth—the Man and His World*. (2nd ed. 1968) New York.
1955b 'Was Kohelet a Phoenician?' *JBL* 74:103-114.
1960 'Qohelet and Qumran—a study of style'. *Bib* 41:395-410.
1965 *The Book of God and Man*. Chicago.

Gordon, Cyrus H.
1955 'North Israelite influence on post-exilic Hebrew'. *IEJ* 5:85-88.
1965 *Ugaritic Textbook* (Analecta Orientalia). Rome.

Goshen-Gottstein, Moshe
1957 'The history of the Bible-text and comparative semitics'. *VT* 7:195-201.

Graetz, Heinrich
1871 *Kohelet*. Leipzig.
1872 'Die Integrität der Kapitel 27 und 28 im Hiob'. *Monatschrift für die Geschichte und Wissenschaft des Judenthums*. 21:241-250.

Greenberg, Moshe
1960 'NSH in Exodus 20:20 and the purpose of the Sinaitic theophany'. *JBL* 79:273-276.

Groot, J.J.M. de
1918 *Universismus*. Berlin.

Grossberg, Daniel
1979 'Nominalization in Biblical Hebrew'. *HS* 20:29-33.

Gruber, Mayer I.
1980 *Aspects of Nonverbal Communication in the Ancient Near East* Studia Pohl 12/I-II. Rome.

Hardjedef
'The Instruction of Prince Hardjedef', *AEL* I, 58-59.

Hasel, Gerhard F.
1969 Review of Ellermeier's *Qohelet*. *BO* 26:392-394.

Haupt, Paul
1905 *Koheleth oder Weltschmerz in der Bibel*. Leipzig.

Helck, Wolfgang
1969 *Der Text der 'Lehre Amenemhets I. für seinen Sohn'*. Wiesbaden.
1970 *Die Prophezeiung des Nfr.tj*. Wiesbaden.

Hengel, Martin
1974 *Judaism and Hellenism*. ET J. Bowden. Philadelphia.

Hermisson, Hans Jürgen
1968 *Studien zur israelitischen Spruchweisheit*. WMANT 28. Neukirchen.

Herrmann, W.
1953/54 'Zu Koheleth 3,14'. *WZMLU* 3:293.

Hertzberg, Hans Wilhelm
1959 'Palästinische Bezüge im Buche Kohelet'. In *Festschrift F. Baumgärtel*, pp. 63-73. Erlangen.
1963 *Der Prediger*. KAT N.F., XVII, 4. Gütersloh.

Hirschberg, H.H.
1961 'Some additional Arabic etymologies in Old Testament lexicography'. *VT* 11:372-385.

Hitzig, F., and Nowack, W.
1883 *Der Prediger Salomo's erklärt*. 2nd ed. KEHAT 7. Leipzig.

Höffken, Peter
1985 'Das Ego des Weisen'. *ThZ* 4:121-135.

Holladay, William
1958 *The Root šûbh in the Old Testament*. Leiden.
1962 'Style, irony, and authenticity in Jeremiah'. *JBL* 81:44-54.

Holm-Nielsen, Svend
1974 'On the interpretation of Qoheleth in early Christianity'. *VT* 24:168-177.

Holzclaw, Brooks
1971 *The Septuagint Book of Ecclesiastes*. Ph.D. dissertation, Hebrew Union College—Jewish Institute of Religion, Cincinnati, OH.

Horton, Ernest
1972 'Koheleth's concept of opposites'. *Numen* 19:1-21.

Hyvärinen, Kyösti
1977 *Die Übersetzung von Aquila*. Coniectanea Biblica, OT Ser. Lund: Gleerup.

Ipuwer
Papyrus Leyden 344 recto. 'The Admonitions of Ipuwer', *AEL* I, 149-163.

Irwin, William A.
1944 'Eccles. 4:13-16'. *JNES* 3:255-257.

Isaksson, Bo
1987 *Studies in the Language of Qoheleth*. Uppsala.

Iwry, Samuel
1966 '*whnmṣ*'—a striking variant reading in 1QIsa[a]'. *Textus* 5, 34-43.

James, Kenneth W.
1984 'Ecclesiastes: precurser of existentialists'. *The Bible Today* 22:85-90.

James, William
1902 *The Varieties of Religious Experience*. New York.

Japhet, Sara
1974/75 'The Commentary of R. Samuel Ben Meir to Qoheleth' [Hebrew]. *Tarbiz* 44:72-94.

Japhet, Sara, and Salters, Robert
1985 *The Commentary of R. Samuel ben Meir Rashbam on Qoheleth*. Jerusalem.

Jastrow, Marcus
1950 *A Dictionary of the Targumim, the Talmud Babli and Yerushalmi, and the Midrashic Literature*. New York.

Jenni, Ernst
1952 'Das Wort *'ōlām* im Alten Testament'. *ZAW* 64:197-248.
1953 'Das Wort *'ōlām* im Alten Testament'. *ZAW* 65:1-35.
1968 *Das hebräische Pi'el*. Zurich.

Johnston, Robert K.
1976 '"Confessions of a workaholic": A reappraisal of Qoheleth'. *CBQ* 38:14-28.

Joüon, Paul
1923 *Grammaire de l'Hébreu biblique*. Repr. 1965. Rome.
1930 'Notes philologiques sur le texte hébreu d'Ecclésiaste'. *Bib* 11:419-425.

Kagemeni
Papyrus Prisse 1-2. 'The Instruction Addressed to Kagemni', *AEL* I, 59-61.

Kamenetzky, Abraham S.
1904 'Die P'šita zu Koheleth'. *ZAW* 24:181-239.
1914 'Der Rätselname Koheleth'. *ZAW* 34:225-228.
1921 'Die ursprünglich beabsichtigte Aussprache der Pseudonyms QHLT'. *OLZ* 24:11-15.

Kennedy, James
1928 *An Aid to the Textual Amendment of the Old Testament*. Edinburgh.

Khakheperre-Sonb
(BM 5645) 'The Complaints of Khakheperre-Sonb', *AEL* I, 145-149.

Kleinert, Paul
1883 'Sind im Buche Koheleth ausserhebräische Einflüsse anzuerkennen?' *Theologische Studien und Kritiken* 56:761-782.

Klopfenstein, Martin A.
1972 'Die Skepsis des Qohelet'. *TZ* 28:97-109.
Knopf, Carl S.
1930 'The optimism of Koheleth'. *JBL* 49:195-199.
Koch, Klaus
1972 'Gibt es ein Vergeltungsdogma im Alten Testament?' in *Um das Prinzip der Vergeltung in Religion und Recht des Alten Testaments*, ed. K. Koch. Darmstadt. (= *ZTK* 52 [1955], 1-42) (ET Crenshaw 1983, 57-87).
König, Eduard
1897 *Lehrgebäude der hebräischen Sprache*. Vol. II, 2. Leipzig: J.C. Hinrichs.
Kopf, L.
1959 'Arabische Etymologien und Parallelen zum Bibelwörterbuch'. *VT* 9:247-287.
Kraeling, G.E.
1953 *The Brooklyn Museum Aramaic Papyri*. New Haven, CT.
Kroeber, Rudi
1963 *Der Prediger*. Berlin.
Kropak, Arno
1909 *Die Syntax des Autors der Chronik*. BZAW 16. Giessen.
Kuhn, Gottfried
1926 *Erklärung des Buches Koheleth*. BZAW 43. Giessen.
Kurz, Gerhard
1982 *Metapher, Allegorie, Symbol*. Göttingen.
Kutscher, Eduard Yechezkel
1974 *The Language and Linguistic Background of the Isaiah Scroll* (*1 Q Isa*[a]) (Studies on the Texts of the Desert of Judah, VI). Leiden.
Lambert, W.G.
1960 *Babylonian Wisdom Literature*. Oxford.
Lanczkowski, Günter
1960 'Ordnung'. *RGG* (3rd ed.) 4:1679.
Landsberger, Benno
1936 'Die babylonische Theodizee'. *ZA* 43:32-76.
Lane, D.J.
1979 'Peshiṭta Institute Communication XV: "Lilies that fester . . ."' *VT* 29:481-489.
Lang, Bernhard
1972 *Die weisheitliche Lehrrede*. Stuttgart.
Lange, H.O.
1925 *Das Weisheitsbuch des Amenemope*. Copenhagen.
Lauha, Aarre
1960 'Die Krise des religiösen Glaubens bei Kohelet'. *VTSup* 3:183-191.
1978 *Kohelet*. BKAT, 19. Neukirchen-Vluyn.
1983 'Omnia vanitas'. In *Glaube und Gerechtigkeit*, in mem. R. Gyllenberg; ed. J. Kiilunen et al. Helsinki.
Lazere, Donald
1973 *The Unique Creation of Albert Camus*. New Haven and London.
Leahy, Michael
1952 'The meaning of Ecclesiastes [12.2-5]' *IrTQ* 19:297-300.
Levin, Harry
1956 *Symbolism and Fiction*. Charlottesville, VA.

Levy, Ludwig
1912 *Das Buch Qoheleth. Ein Beitrag zur Geschichte des Sadduzäismus kritisch untersucht*. Leipzig.
Lichtheim, Miriam
1945 'The Song of the Harpers'. *JNES* 4:178-212.
1973-80 *Ancient Egyptian Literature*. Berkeley, CA. Vol. I: 1973; vol. II: 1976; vol. III: 1980.
1983 *Late Egyptian Wisdom Literature in the International Context*. OBO. Göttingen.
Lieberman, Saul
1962 *Hellenism in Jewish Palestine*. New York.
Lindblom, Johannes
1952 'Gibt es eine Eschatologie bei den alttestamentlichen Propheten?' *Studia Theologica* 6:79-114.
Lindenberger, James M.
1983 *The Aramaic Proverbs of Ahiqar*. Johns Hopkins Near Eastern Studies. Baltimore.
Loader, J.A.
1969 'Qohelet 3.2-8—a 'sonnet' in the Old Testament'. *ZAW* 81:240-242.
1979 *Polar Structures in the Book of Qohelet*. BZAW 152. Berlin.
Lohfink, Norbert
1979 'War Kohelet ein Frauenfeind?' *Bibliotheca Ephemeridum Theologicarum Lovaniensium* 51:259-287.
1981 '*Melek, šallîṭ* und *môšēl* bei Kohelet und die Abfassungszeit des Buchs'. *Bib* 62:535-543.
1983 'Warum ist der Tor unfähig, Böse zu handeln?' *ZDMG Sup* 5:113-120.
Loretz, Oswald
1963 'Zur Darbietungsform der "Ich-Erzählung" im Buche Qohelet'. *CBQ* 25:46-59.
1964 *Qohelet und der alte Orient*. Freiburg.
1965 'Gleiches Los trifft alle! Die Antwort des Buches Qohelet'. *Bibel und Kirche* 20:6-8.
1980 'Altorientalische und kanaanäische Topoi im Buche Kohelet'. *UF* 12:267-286.
Löw, I.
1924-34 (1967) *Die Flora der Juden*. Hildesheim.
Lyons, John
1977 *Semantics*. 2 vols. Cambridge.
Lys, Daniel
1977 *L'Ecclésiaste ou que vaut la vie?* Paris.
1979 'L'Etre et le Temps. Communication de Qohèlèth'. In *La Sagesse de l'Ancien Testament*, ed. M. Gilbert, pp. 249-258. Gembloux, Belgium.
MacDonald, Duncan Black
1899 (Eccl. iii 11). *JBL* 18:212f.
1936 *The Hebrew Philosophical Genius*. Princeton.
MacIntosh, A.A.
1969 'A consideration of Hebrew G'R'. *VT* 19:471-479.
McKane, William
1965 *Prophets and Wise Men*. London.
1970 *Proverbs: a New Approach*. London.

McNeile, Alan H.
1904 *An Introduction to Ecclesiastes*. Cambridge.
Margoliouth, D.S.
1911 'The prologue of Ecclesiastes'. *The Expositor* 8:463-470.
Matthes, H.
1928 'Die Verschleierung der Verfasserschaft bei englischen Dichtungen des 18. Jahrhunderts'. *Beiträge zur Erforschung der Sprache und Kultur Englands und Nordamerikas*, Bd. IV, (1928), pp. 33-113.
Merikare
Pap. Leningrad 116A, Pap. Moscow 4658, P. Carlsberg 6. Text: Volten, 1945. 'The Instruction Addressed to King Merikare', *AEL* I, 97-109.
Miller, Athanasius
1934 'Aufbau und Grundproblem des Predigers'. *Miscellanea Biblica* 2:104-122.
Miller, Patrick D., Jr.
1982 *Sin and Judgment in the Prophets*. SBL Monograph Series, 27. Chico, CA.
Mischel, Theodore
1952 'The meanings of "symbol" in literature'. *Arizona Quarterly* 8:69-79.
Mitchell, Hinckley G.
1913 '"Work" in Ecclesiastes'. *JBL* 32:123-138
Montgomery, James A.
1924 'Notes on Ecclesiastes'. *JBL* 43:241-44.
Morenz, Siegfried; with Müller, Dieter
1960 *Untersuchungen zur Rolle des Schicksals in der ägyptischen Religion. Abh. d. Sächsischen Ak. d. Wiss. zu Leipzig*, Phil.-hist. Kl., 52:1. Berlin.
Mowinckel, Sigmund
1960 'Psalms and wisdom'. *VTSup* 3:205-224.
Muilenburg, James
1954 'A Qoheleth scroll from Qumran'. *BASOR* 135:20-28.
Mulder, J.S.M.
1982 'Qoheleth's division and also its main point'. In *Von Kanaan bis Kerala*, ed. W.C. Delsman *et al.* Neukirchen.
Müller, Hans-Peter
1968 'Wie sprach Qohälät von Gott?' *VT* 18:507-521.
1986 'Theonome, Skepsis und Lebensfreude—zu Koh 1,12–3,15—'. *BZ* 30:1-19.
Muraoka, Takamitsu
1985 *Emphatic Words and Structures in Biblical Hebrew*. Jerusalem.
Murphy, Roland E.
1955 'The *Pensées* of Coheleth'. *CBQ* 17:304-314.
1962 'A consideration of the classification "wisdom psalms"'. *VTSup* 9:156-167. (Repr. Crenshaw, 1976:456-467).
1967 'Assumptions and problems in Old Testament wisdom research'. *CBQ* 29:407-418.
1969 'Form criticism and wisdom literature'. CBQ 31:475-483.
1979 'Qohelet's "quarrel" with the Fathers'. In *From Faith to Faith* (Donald G. Miller Festschrift), ed. D.Y. Hadidian, pp. 235-245, Pittsburgh.
1981 *Wisdom Literature*. In *Forms of OT Literature*, 13. Grand Rapids, MI.

1982 'Qohelet interpreted: the bearing of the past on the present'. *VT* 32:331-337.

1985 'Wisdom and creation'. *JBL* 104:3-11

Neferti

Papyrus Leningrad 1116B. Text: Helck, 1970. Text, translation, commentary: Goedicke, 1977. 'The Prophecies of Neferti', *AEL* I, 139-145.

Neher, André

1951 *Notes sur Qohelet*. Paris.

Nel, Philip Johannes

1982 *The Structure and Ethos of the Wisdom Admonitions in Proverbs*. BZAW 158. Berlin.

Nötscher, F.

1954 *Kohelet*. Würzburg.

1959 'Schicksal und Freiheit'. *Bib* 40:446-462

Ogden, Graham S.

1977 'The "Better"-Proverb (Ṭôb-Spruch), rhetorical criticism, and Qoheleth'. *JBL* 96:489-505.

1979 'Qoheleth's use of the "Nothing is Better"-Form'. *JBL* 98:339-350.

1980a 'Historical allusion in Qoheleth IV 13-16?' *VT* 30:309-315.

1980b 'Qoheleth IX 17- X 20'. *VT* 30:27-37.

1983 'Qoheleth XI 1-6'. *VT* 33:222-230.

1984a 'The mathematics of wisdom: Qoheleth IV 1-12'. *VT* 34:446-453.

1984b 'Qoheleth XI 7-XII 8: Qoheleth's summons to enjoyment and reflection'. *VT* 34:27-37.

1986 'The interpretation of *dor* in Ecclesiastes 1.4'. *JSOT* 34:91-92.

1988 *Qoheleth*. Sheffield.

Oldenberg, Hermann

1894 *Die Religion des Veda*. Berlin.

Onchsheshonqy

Pap. BM 10508. Glanville, 1955; Stricker, 1958; Lichtheim, 1983. 'The Instruction of Ankhsheshonq'. *AEL* III, 159-84.

Pardee, Dennis

1978 'The semitic root *mrr* and the etymology of Ugaritic *mr(r)//brk*'. *UF* 10:249-288.

Pedersen, Johannes

1930 'Scepticisme israélite'. *Revue d'Histoire et de Philosophie Religieuses* 10:317-370.

Pennacchini, Bruno

1977 'Qohelet ovvero il libro degli assurdi'. *Euntes Docete* 30:491-510.

Perles, Felix

1895 *Analekten zur Textkritik des Alten Testaments*. München.

1922 *Analekten zur Textkritik des Alten Testaments*. Neue Folge. Leipzig.

Pfeiffer, Egon

1965 'Die Gottesfurcht im Buche Kohelet'. In *Festschrift H.W. Hertzberg*, pp. 133-158. Göttingen.

Pfeiffer, Robert H.

1934 'The peculiar skepticism of Ecclesiastes'. *JBL* 53:100-109.

Phebhor

(= 'The Demotic Wisdom Book'); Pap. Insinger *et al.* Lichtheim, 1983; 'The Instruction of Papyrus Insinger', *AEL* III, 184-217.

Piotti, Franco
1977a 'Osservazioni su alcuni usi linguistici dell'Ecclesiaste'. *BeO* 19:49-56.
1977b 'Osservazioni su alcuni problemi esegetici nel libro dell'Ecclesiaste (Studio II): Il canto degli stolti (Qoh. 7,5)'. *BeO* 19:129-140.
1978 'Osservazioni su alcuni problemi esegetici nel libro dell'Ecclesiaste: Studio I'. *BeO* 20:169-181.

Plöger, Otto
1965 'Wahre die richtige Mitte; solch Mass ist in allem das Beste!' In *Festschrift H.W. Hertzberg*, pp. 159-173. Göttingen.

Plumptre, E.H.
1881 *Ecclesiastes*. Cambridge.

Podechard, E.
1912 *L'Ecclésiaste*. Paris.

Polzin, Robert
1980 *Moses and the Deuteronomist*. New York.

Preuss, Horst D.
1972 'Das Gottesbild der älteren Weisheit Israels'. *VTSup* 23:117-145.

Priest, John F.
1963 'Where is Wisdom to be placed?' *JBR* 31:275-282.

Ptahhotep
Pap. Prisse. Text, transl. Zába, 1956. 'The Instruction of Ptahhotep'. *AEL* I, 61-80.

Qimron, Elisha
1986 *The Hebrew of the Dead Sea Scrolls*. HSS 29. Atlanta, GA.

Rad, Gerhard von
1953 'Josephgeschichte und ältere Chokma'. *VTSup* 1:120-127.
1966 'Das Werk Jahwes'. In *Studia Biblia et Semitica*, Festschrift Th. Vriezen, 290-99. Wageningen.
1970 *Weisheit in Israel*. Neukirchen-Vluyn. (ET James D. Martin: *Wisdom in Israel*. London, 1972).

Rankin, Oliver S.
1936 *Israel's Wisdom Literature*. Edinburgh.
1956 "The Book of Ecclesiastes". *Interpreter's Bible*, V. Nashville.

Ranston, Harry
1923 'Koheleth and the early Greeks'. *JTS* 24:160-169.
1925 *Ecclesiastes and the Early Greek Wisdom Literature*. London.
1930 *The Old Testament Wisdom Books and Their Teaching*. London.

Rashbam (Samuel ben Meir). See Japhet and Salters.

Reif, Stefan C.
1981 (Review of C.F. Whitley's *Koheleth*). *VT* 31:120-126.

Reines, C.W.
1954a 'Koheleth on wisdom and wealth'. *JJS* 5:80-84.
1954b 'Koheleth VIII, 10'. *JJS* 5:86-87.

Renan, E.
1882 *L'Ecclésiaste traduit de l'hébreu avec une étude sur l'âge et le caractère du livre*. Paris.

Ricoeur, Paul
1976 *Interpretation Theory*. Forth Worth, TX.

Rofé, Alexander
1978 '"The Angel" in Qoh 5.5 in the light of a wisdom dialogue formula' [Hebrew]. *EI* 14:105-109.

Romberg, Bertil
1962 *Studies in the Narrative Technique of the First-Person Novel*. Lund.

Rousseau, François
1981 'Structure de Qohelet I 4-11 et Plan du Livre'. *VT* 31:200-217.

Rowley, H.H.
1963 *From Moses to Qumran*. New York.

Rudolph, Wilhelm
1959 *Vom Buch Kohelet*. Münster.

Rylaarsdam, J. Coert
1946 *Revelation in Jewish Wisdom Literature*. Chicago.

Sabourin, Leopold
1974 *The Psalms*. New York.

Salters, Robert B.
1977 'Text and exegesis in Koh 10,19'. *ZAW* 89:423-426.
1978 'Notes on the history of the interpretation of Koh 5,5'. *ZAW* 90:95-101.
1979 'Notes on the interpretation of Qoh 6,2'. *ZAW* 91:282-289.

Sawyer, John F.A.
1976 'The ruined house in Ecclesiastes 12: a reconstruction of the original parable'. *JBL* 94:519-531.

Schiffer, S.
1884 *Das Buch Kohelet, nach der Auffassung der Weisen des Talmud und Midrasch und der jüdischen Erklärer des Mittelalters I*. Frankfurt a.M.

Schmid, Hans Heinrich
1966 *Wesen und Geschichte der Weisheit*. BZAW 101. Berlin.
1968 *Gerechtigkeit als Weltordnung*. Beiträge zur historischen Theologie, 40. Tübingen.

Schmidt, J.
1936 *Studien zur Stilistik der alttestamentlichen Spruchliteratur*. Münster.

Schoors, A.
1981 'The particle *kî*'. *OTS* 21:240-76.
1982a 'Kethibh-Qere in Ecclesiastes'. In *Studia Paulo Naster Oblata*, II: Orientalia Antiqua, 215-222 (Orientalia Lovaniensia Analecta 13). Leuven.
1982b 'La structure littéraire de Qohéleth'. *OLP* 13:91-116.
1985a 'The Peshitta of Kohelet and its relation to the Septuagint'. *Orientalia Lovaniensia Analecta* 18:347-357.
1985b 'Koheleth: a perspective of life after death?' *ETL* 61:295-303.

Scott, R.B.Y.
1965 *Proverbs, Ecclesiastes*. *AB*, XVIII. New York.

Segal, Moshe T.
1958 *The Complete Book of Ben Sira* [Hebrew]. Jerusalem.

Serrano, J.J.
1954 'I saw the wicked buried (Ecc 8,10)'. *CBQ* 16:168-170.

Shaffer, Aaron
1967 'The Mesopotamian background of Qohelet 4:9-12' [Hebrew]. *EI* 8:246-250.

1969 'New information on the origin of the "three-fold cord"'. *EI* 9:159-160.

Sheppard, Gerald T.
1977 'The epilogue to Qoheleth as theological commentary'. *CBQ* 39:182-189.

Siegfried, K.
1898 *Prediger und Hoheslied*. HAT II, 3/2. Göttingen.

Simpson, William K., ed.
1972 *The Literature of Ancient Egypt*. New Haven & London.

Skehan, Patrick W.
1938 *The Literary Relationship between the Book of Wisdom and the Protocanonical Wisdom Books of the Old Testament*. Washington.
1967 'Wisdom's house'. *CBQ* 29:468-486.

Snaith, Norman H.
1963 'Time in the Old Testament'. In *Promise and Fulfillment, Essays Presented to S.H. Hooke*. Edinburgh.

Soden, Wolfram von
1965 'Die Frage nach der Gerechtigkeit Gottes im alten Orient'. *MDOG* 96:41-59.

Staerk, W.
1942-43 'Zur Exegese von Koh 10,20 und 11,1'. *ZAW* 59:216-218.

Stamm, J.J.
1946 *Das Leiden des Unschuldigen in Babylon und Israel*. Zürich.

Staples, W.E.
1943 'The "vanity" of Ecclesiastes'. *JNES* 2:95-104.
1945 '"Profit" in Ecclesiastes'. *JNES* 4:87-96.
1965 'The meaning of *ḥepeṣ* in Ecclesiastes'. *JNES* 24:110-112.

Steinmann, J.
1955 *Ainsi parlait Qohèlèt*. Paris.

Sternberg, Meir
1985 *The Poetics of Biblical Narrative*. Bloomington, IN.

Stricker, Bruno
1958 'De Wijsheid van Anchsjesjonq'. *Oudheidkundige Mededeelingen* 39:56-79.

Strobel, Albert
1967 *Das Buch Prediger (Kohelet)*. Düsseldorf.

Suys, Emile
1935 *La Sagesse d'Ani*. Analecta Orientalia. Rome.

Talmon, Shemaryahu
1981 'The ancient Hebrew alphabet and biblical text criticism'. *Mélanges Dominique Barthélemy*, ed. P. Casetti et al., pp. 497-530. Göttingen.

Tanchum Jerushalmi
See Eppenstein

Taylor, C.
1874 *The Dirge of Coheleth*. London.

Thilo, Martin
1923 *Der Prediger Salomo*. Bonn.

Torrey, Charles C.
1948-49 'The question of the original language of Qohelet'. *JQR* 39:151-160.
1952 'The problem of Ecclesiastes IV, 13-16'. *VT* 2:175-177.

Toy, Crawford H.
1899 *The Book of Proverbs*. ICC (Repr. 1959). Edinburgh.
Tur-Sinai, Naphtali H.
1962ff. *Pešuṭo šel Miqra'*. [Qohelet in vol. IVb.] Jerusalem.
Tyler, Thomas
1899 *Ecclesiastes*. London.
Vawter, Bruce
1972 'Intimations of immortality in the Old Testament'. *JBL* 91:158-171.
Vergote, Jozef
1963 'La notion de Dieu dans les livres de sagesse égyptiens'. *SPOA*, pp. 159-190.
Volten, Aksel
1937 *Studien zum Weisheitsbuch des Anii*. Copenhagen.
1945 *Zwei altägyptische politische Schriften*. Analecta Aegyptiaca IV. Copenhagen.
1955 'Zwei ägyptische Wörter'. *Ägyptologische Studien*. Ed. O. Firchow, pp. 362-65. Berlin.
Volz, Paul
1911 'Koheleth'. In *Hiob und Weisheit*. Göttingen.
Waard, Jan de
1979 'The translator and textual criticism (with particular reference to Eccl 2,25)'. *Bib* 60:509-529.
1982 'The structure of Qoheleth'. *Proc. 8th World Congress of Jewish Studies*, pp. 57-63. Jerusalem.
Waldman, Nahum M.
1979 'The *dābār ra'* of Eccl 8.3'. *JBL* 98:407-408
Weinfeld, Moshe
1972 *Deuteronomy and the Deuteronomic School*. Oxford.
1985 *Justice and Righteousness in Israel and the Nations* [Hebrew]. Jerusalem.
Westermann, Claus
1977 *Der Aufbau des Buches Hiob*. Calwer Theologische Monographien, A.6. Stuttgart.
Whitley, Charles F.
1979 *Koheleth, His Language and Thought*. BZAW 148. Berlin.
Whybray, R.N.
1965 *Wisdom in Proverbs*. London.
1974 *The Intellectual Tradition in the Old Testament*. BZAW 135. Berlin.
1978 'Qoheleth the immoralist? (Qoh 7:16-17)'. In *Israelite Wisdom: Samuel Terrien Festschrift*, pp. 191-204. Missoula.
1981 'The identification and use of quotations in Ecclesiastes'. *VTSup* 32:435-451.
1982 'Qoheleth, Preacher of Joy'. *JSOT* 23:87-98.
Wilch, John R.
1969 *Time and Event*. Leiden.
Wildeboer, Gerrit
1898 *Der Prediger*. In: Budde *et al.*, *Die Fünf Megillot*. Freiburg.
Williams, James G.
1971 'What does it profit a man?: The wisdom of Koheleth'. *Judaism* 20:179-193. (Repr. Crenshaw, 1976:375-389).
1981 *Those Who Ponder Proverbs*. Sheffield.

1987 'Proverbs and Ecclesiastes'. In *The Literary Guide to the Bible*, ed. R. Alter and F. Kermode, pp. 263-282. Cambridge, MA.

Williams, Ronald J.
1976 *Hebrew Syntax*. 2nd ed. Toronto.

Wilson, Gerald R.
1984 '"The words of the wise": the intent and significance of Qoheleth 12:9-14.' *JBL* 103:175-192.
1987 Review of J.A. Loader, *Ecclesiastes*. HS 28; 187f.

Winston, David
1979 *The Wisdom of Solomon*. AB 43. Garden City, New York.

Wittgenstein, Ludwig
1958 *Philosophical Investigations*. Trans. G. Anscombe. Oxford.

Witzenrath, Hagia
1979 *Süss ist das Licht*. St. Ottilien.

Wölfel, Eberhard
1958 *Luther und die Skepsis*. Munich.

Wolff, Hans W.
1937 *Das Zitat im Prophetenspruch*. Beiheft zu Evangelische Theologie, 4. Munich.

Wright, Addison G.
1968 'The riddle of the sphinx: the structure of the Book of Qoheleth'. *CBQ* 30:313-334.
1980 'The riddle of the sphinx revisited: numerical patterns in the Book of Qoheleth'. *CBQ* 42:38-51.
1983 'Additional numerical patterns in Qohelet'. *CBQ* 45:32-43.

Yaḥyah = Yosef ben David ibn Yaḥyah
1539 *Peruš Ḥameš Hamm^e^gillot* [Hebrew]. Bologna.

Žaba, Zbynek
1956 *Les Maximes de Ptahhotep*. Prague.

Zapletal, Vincenz
1911 *Das Buch Kohelet kritisch und metrisch untersucht*. Freiburg.

Zer-Kavod, Mordecai
1973 *Qohelet* [Hebrew]. Jerusalem.

Zimmerli, Walther
1933 'Zur Struktur der alttestamentlichen Weisheit'. *ZAW* 51:177-204. (ET in Crenshaw, 1976:175-207).
1962 *Das Buch des Predigers Salomo*. ATD XVI, 1. Göttingen.
1963 'Ort und Grenze der Weisheit im Rahmen der alttestamentlichen Theologie'. *SPOA*, pp. 121-138. (ET in Crenshaw, 1976:314-326).
1974 'Das Buch Kohelet—Traktat oder Sentenzensammlung?' *VT* 24:221-230.

Zimmermann, Frank
1945-46 'The Aramaic provenance of Qohelet'. *JQR* 36:17-45.
1949-50 'The question of Hebrew in Qohelet'. *JQR* 40:79-102.
1958 *The Book of Tobit*. New York.
1973 *The Inner World of Qohelet*. New York.

Zirkel, G.
1792 *Untersuchungen über den Prediger mit philosophischen und kritischen Bemerkungen*. Würzburg.

INDEXES

INDEX OF BIBLICAL REFERENCES

POST-BIBLICAL JEWISH TEXTS, QUMRAN, APOCRYPHA, NT, RABBINIC TEXTS
(in alphabetical order)

ANCIENT NEAR EASTERN AND CLASSICAL GREEK TEXTS

INDEX OF AUTHORS

INDEX OF SUBJECTS

INDEX OF HEBREW WORDS (DISCUSSED OUTSIDE OF COMMENTARY, *q.v. ad loc.*)